BOOKS B

The Seven Storey Mountain

The Sign of Jonas

New Seeds of Contemplation

Conjectures of a Guilty Bystander

Zen and the Birds of Appetite

The Collected Poems of Thomas Merton

The Literary Essays of Thomas Merton

Mystics and Zen Masters

The Hidden Ground of Love (Letters I)

The Road to Joy (Letters II)

The School of Charity (Letters III)

The Courage for Truth (Letters IV)

Witness to Freedom (Letters V)

Love and Living

The Monastic Journey

The Asian Journal

Run to the Mountain (Journals I)

Entering the Silence (Journals II)

A Search for Solitude (Journals III)

Turning Toward the World (Journals IV)

Dancing in the Water of Life (Journals V)

Learning to Love (Journals VI)

The Other Side of the Mountain

THE JOURNALS OF THOMAS MERTON / Volume 7: 1967–1968 / Patrick Hart, O.C.S.O., General Editor

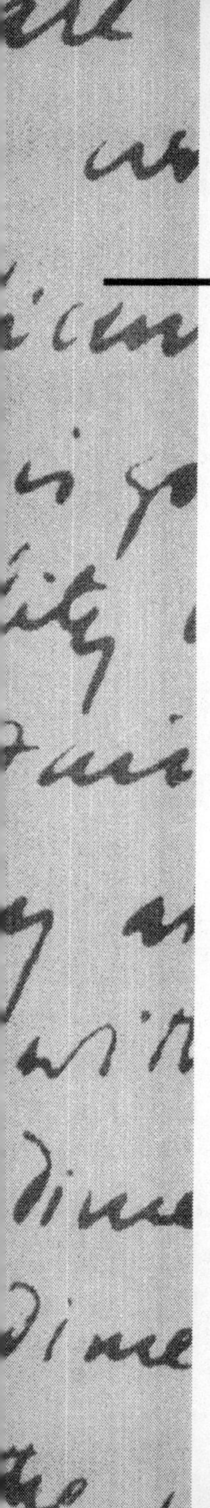

Thomas Merton

The Other Side of the Mountain

The End of the Journey

EDITED BY PATRICK HART, O.C.S.O.

HarperOne
An Imprint of HarperCollins*Publishers*

HarperOne

Grateful acknowledgment is made to the following for permission to reprint previously published material:

For journal material by Thomas Merton in *Woods, Shore, Desert*, used by permission of The Museum of New Mexico Press. For material by Thomas Merton from *The Asian Journals of Thomas Merton*, copyright © 1975 by The Trustees of the Merton Legacy Trust, and from *Thomas Merton in Alaska*, copyright © 1989 by The Merton Legacy Trust. Reprinted by permission of New Directions Publishing Corp. For lines from *In Praise of Krishna* by Edward C. Dimock and Denise Levertov. Copyright © 1967 by The Asia Society, Inc. Used by permission of Doubleday, a division of Bantam Doubleday Dell Publishing Group, Inc. For lines from *Selected Poems* by Robinson Jeffers. Copyright © 1925 and renewed 1953 by Robinson Jeffers. Reprinted by permission of Random House, Inc. For lines from "Virgin Youth," from *The Complete Poems of D. H. Lawrence* by D. H. Lawrence, edited by V. de Sola Pinto and F. W. Roberts. Copyright © 1964, 1971 by Angelo Ravagli and C. M. Weekley, Executors of the Estate of Frieda Lawrence Ravagli. Used by permission of Viking Penguin, a division of Penguin Books USA Inc., Laurence Pollinger Limited, and the Estate of Frieda Lawrence Ravagli.

Book design by David Bullen

Library of Congress Cataloging-in-Publication Data

Merton, Thomas, 1915–1968.
The other side of the mountain : the end of the journey / Thomas Merton : edited by Patrick Hart.
p. cm. — (The journals of Thomas Merton : v. 7)
Includes index.
ISBN 978-0-06-065487-0
1. Merton, Thomas. 1915—1968—Diaries. 2. Trappists—United States—Biography. I. Hart, Patrick. II. Title. III. Series: Merton, Thomas, 1915–1968. Journals of Thomas Merton : v. 7.
BX4705.M542A3 1998
271'.12502—dc21 98-12655

10 11 RRDH 10

There is another side of Kanchenjunga and of every mountain—the side that has never been photographed and turned into postcards. That is the only side worth seeing.

November 19, 1968

Contents

Acknowledgments *xi*

Introduction *xiii*

PART I: The Election of a New Abbot *1*
October 1967–May 1968

PART II: Woods, Shore, Desert *89*
A Notebook, May 1968

PART III: Preparing for Asia *115*
May 1968–September 1968

PART IV: New Mexico, Alaska, California *169*
September 1968–October 1968

PART V: The Far East: The Last Days *203*
October 1968–December 1968

A Glossary of Asian Terms *331*

Index *337*

Acknowledgments

This is the seventh and final volume of Thomas Merton's personal journals, a project that began in 1990 when the trustees of the Merton Legacy Trust entered into a contract with HarperSanFrancisco Publishers. Shortly after I was appointed general editor of the series, plans were made to seek out various Merton scholars who would be willing to be editors for a portion of the journals. We were very fortunate to find these editors, who have all greatly excelled at cooperation, hard work, and meeting deadlines! I owe an enormous debt of gratitude to each of them: Christine M. Bochen, Lawrence S. Cunningham, Robert E. Daggy, Victor A. Kramer, and Jonathan Montaldo.

There were countless other persons who assisted in this long-range project, and once again I want to express my deep gratitude to Abbot Timothy Kelly and the community of Gethsemani for allowing me the time and space to undertake and complete this work.

The trustees of the Merton Legacy Trust (currently Robert Giroux, James Laughlin, and Tommie O'Callaghan) have been cooperative in supporting the project, and Anne McCormick, secretary for the Merton Legacy Trust, has expedited matters with HarperSanFrancisco over the years. James Laughlin in particular must be singled out for a word of special thanks, since he did the lion's share of the research and negotiations on the original manuscript of *The Asian Journal*, which he edited in conjunction with Naomi Burton Stone and myself, with the invaluable assistance of Amiya Chakravarty. It was Mr. Laughlin who contacted the various persons mentioned in this last journal to verify words and phrases sometimes quite unfamiliar to the other editors and at times indecipherable. I also want to thank him and New Directions for allowing us to use the published version of the Alaskan and Asian journals. We have included neither the various appendixes, nor the section on Merton's supplementary readings, nor the many photographs he took during his Asian pilgrimage, but only what was, strictly speaking, *journal*. We want to recommend that readers desiring a more complete account of Merton's journey to the Far East consult the New Directions editions of *Thomas Merton in Alaska* and *The Asian Journal of Thomas Merton*.

I am grateful to the Museum of New Mexico Press for permission to use material from *Woods, Shore, Desert*, Merton's May 1968 notebook, published in 1982. Joel Weishaus provided an introduction and notes to this volume, although Merton himself had made the selections for this small journal from his ongoing journal. He had dictated it onto a tape, which he sent to Mary Ann Schmidt of Waldorf, Maryland, who transcribed it and returned the typescript for his final correction. We are indebted to Mary Ann Schmidt and Joel Weishaus for their help in this first publishing venture with the Museum of New Mexico Press.

In preparing the last volume of the journals, I was greatly assisted by Robert E. Daggy, director of the Merton Center at Bellarmine College, Erlinda Paguio, and Phil Sager, reference librarian at the University of Louisville Library. Tim Fullerton of Ann Arbor, Michigan, an acknowledged authority on the Far East and its various monastic traditions, checked the manuscript for spelling and also prepared the glossary of Asian terms found in the back of the book as an appendix. For all these services I am deeply grateful.

There are many others who have contributed in one way or another to this project, including Brothers Elias Dietz, Paul Quenon, Anton Rusnak, Malachy Samanns, and Columban (a.k.a. Richard) Weber of Gethsemani Abbey, Patrick O'Connell of Gannon University, Erie, Pennsylvania, Ron Seitz of Fountain Hills, Arizona, Robert Urekew of St. Catherine's College, Springfield, Kentucky, and Ron Whitehead of *Literary Renaissance* for his insights into the poetry of Robinson Jeffers. Finally my heartfelt thanks to John Loudon, Karen Levine, Terri Leonard, and the entire staff at HarperSanFrancisco for their untiring cooperation and patience demonstrated on numerous occasions during the years of collaboration on this monumental undertaking.

Introduction

In many ways "the mountain" has come to be identified with Thomas Merton, following *The Seven Storey Mountain*, his autobiography, which appeared fifty years ago. In none of Merton's writings have there been so many references to mountains as in this last volume of the journals, which we are calling *The Other Side of the Mountain*. Merton reflects on their extraordinary beauty and symbolism when in Alaska, but his most sustained writing on the subject occurs about a week after his meetings with the Dalai Lama, while making a retreat at the Mim Tea Plantation near Dharamsala. He recounts a dream he had on November 19, 1968: "Last night I had a curious dream about Kanchenjunga. I was looking at the mountain and it was pure white, absolutely pure, especially the peaks that lie to the west. And I saw the pure beauty of their shape and outline, all in white. And I heard a voice saying—or got the idea of: 'There is another side to the mountain.'" Merton continues to reflect on this phenomenon in the same journal entry, realizing that he is seeing the mountain from the other side. He then takes more photographs of the mountain in the afternoon and concludes his thoughts with these memorable lines: "The full beauty of the mountain is not seen until you too consent to the impossible paradox: it is and is not. When nothing more needs to be said, the smoke of ideas clears, the mountain is SEEN."

The seventh volume of Thomas Merton's journals has at least this much in common with the first volume, which I also edited—both were written from a variety of locations. Merton was traveling in his premonastic days (1939–1941), from New York to Cuba and back again to New York, then to St. Bonaventure's at Olean, New York, with brief visits to the Trappist monasteries of Gethsemani and the Our Lady of the Valley in Rhode Island. During the period covered by this last volume, Merton had received permission to do some traveling. The five other volumes were written for the most part at Gethsemani and the journal was kept in a single ledger. When traveling, Merton used several notebooks and ledgers in keeping his journal. These in turn had to be checked against one another and the entries arranged in chronological order.

The first section, which we have titled "The Election of a New Abbot," prepares the stage for what follows. During the last months of 1967 and the early weeks of 1968, Father Louis, as Merton was known in the monastery, was deeply concerned about the prospect of a new abbot after the resignation of Abbot James Fox. He feared the worst, and lest some should vote for him, he wrote a statement declaring his incompetence for the job and reminding the community that he had taken a private vow never to accept the abbatial office. He made it clear to all who consulted him that he was supporting Father Flavian Burns, who he felt would be sympathetic to his eremitical desires. Perhaps he also hoped that, as abbot, Father Flavian might be more open to some traveling, in contrast to the former abbot, who insisted that monks, and above all hermits, should not travel. Merton does not conceal his jubilation with the election of Abbot Flavian Burns.

It becomes apparent rather soon after the election of the new abbot that Merton is seriously thinking of some travel. Following a number of invitations, permission was given to visit two monasteries in May. He kept a special notebook for his journal entries during the few weeks he spent at these two monasteries, the first a rather primitive Benedictine monastery, the Monastery of Christ in the Desert in Abiquiu, New Mexico, not far from the studio of Georgia O'Keeffe, and the second a newly founded Cistercian (Trappistine) monastery, Our Lady of the Redwoods, in northern California. Merton later transcribed parts of this journal and had it typed up with the idea of publishing a small book on the experience. Although this was not published until after his death, it did appear under the title he had chosen: *Woods, Shore, Desert.*

Even before his time away from Gethsemani visiting New Mexico and California in May 1968, he had received a pressing invitation to attend a meeting of monastic superiors of the Far East in Bangkok, Thailand, in December. He presented the invitation to the abbot, who spent some time in consultation and discernment before responding. After several months of waiting and additional letters from people like Dom Jean Leclercq urging Merton to come, the abbot finally gave Father Louis permission to spend six months in the Far East, not only attending the meeting in Bangkok, but giving retreats at a couple of Cistercian monasteries in Indonesia and Hong Kong. Above all Merton was very interested in making contact with various Buddhist monasteries in India, especially the Tibetan Buddhists in exile at

Dharamsala. He felt this would be an ideal time to learn from the wisdom of the East by actually meeting the monks in their own monasteries.

Not having any recent experience in preparing for travel, Merton had much to learn about obtaining a passport, securing visas, getting vaccinations, and shopping for proper clothing for travel. He especially wanted a jacket with many pockets for his notebooks, address books, and film for his camera. He found it all challenging, and it seemed to revive his youthful spirits. He was like a child going to the circus. During his time of preparation for the trip to the Far East, he sought out contacts from various persons he knew. Dom Aelred Graham, for example, put Merton in touch with Harold Talbott, who in turn arranged for some meetings with the Dalai Lama. His friend Amiya Chakravarty introduced him to some of his lama friends in India and was actually present in India during Merton's pilgrimage.

Several weeks before his departure for Asia, he made a brief trip to Washington to meet with the people at the Indonesian embassy, where they discussed Java, mysticism, and what awaited him in the Far East. After Ron and Sally Seitz met his plane on the return flight, there was another dinner, this time at the Embassy Club; Merton then returned with Fr. John Loftus to St. Bonaventure Hall at Bellarmine College, where he spent the night with the Franciscan friars.

His entry of August 26 about that evening is classic in his enthusiasm for one American ritual—football. The Packers beat the Dallas Cowboys and, as Merton comments, it was "damn good football." Merton then waxes exuberant: "Football is one of the really valid and deep American rituals. It has a religious seriousness which American religion can never achieve. A comic, contemplative dynamism, a gratuity, a movement from play to play, a definitiveness that responds to some deep need, a religious need, a sense of meaning that is at once final and provisional: a substratum of dependable regularity, continuity, and an ever renewed variety, openness to new possibilities, new chances. It happens. It is done." I was completely surprised by Merton's eloquence on America's favorite sport.

As the days drew closer to the time of his departure, he was busy cleaning his hermitage, discarding old letters and papers, and sending books and manuscripts to the Merton Center at Bellarmine College for safekeeping. Fr. Daniel Walsh, who taught philosophy at both Gethsemani and Bellarmine, was usually the one who delivered the books to the Merton Center. Before leaving he also gave Fr. Walsh a copy of an unpublished manuscript he had been revising, "The Inner Experience"; it was eventually published in *Cistercian Studies* serially over a period of two years (1983–1984). He asked Fr. Walsh to read the manuscript while he was in the Far East and report back to him on his return as to the feasibility of its publication. In 1967 he had made it clear in his Trust document that it should not be published *as a book*, but could be shown to scholars. Although the manuscript was never published as a book, it is available in offprints from *Cistercian Studies*.

September 9, Merton's last full day at Gethsemani, began with the Eucharist in his hermitage chapel, with a couple of us monks and Philip Stark, who had helped out with the typing and layout of Merton's poetry magazine, *Monks Pond*. He invited us to celebrate the Mass with him and join him in breakfast afterwards. It was a truly memorable occasion, made more so by the fact that he got his camera from the hermitage and began taking photographs of us in the woods in front of the hermitage. He was going to the East with great expectations, open to whatever he could learn as he visited the various monasteries.

Before actually departing for Asia, however, he had some stops to make both in the States and in Alaska. He wanted to visit the Monastery of Christ in the Desert in New Mexico again, and after a short visit to the Poor Clares in Chicago, he was on a flight to Alaska, where he had agreed to give a retreat to the priests and religious sisters in the Anchorage area. This was partly to help defray expenses of his trip, a factor he was always conscious of throughout his Asian trip. He wanted to act responsibly as a monk with a vow of poverty.

As the journal moves back to the California coast following his time in Alaska, one senses his impatience to get moving to Asia, the real point of his journey. In his October 15 entry, Merton comments with poetic imagination as the plane lifts off the ground in San Francisco: "The moment of take-off was ecstatic. The dewy wing was suddenly covered with rivers of cold sweat running backward. The window wept jagged shining courses of tears. Joy. We left the ground—I with Christian mantras and a great sense of destiny, of being at last on my true way . . ." He then adds seriously: "May I not come back without having settled the great affair. And found also the great compassion . . ." And finally: "I am going home, to the home where I have never been in this body, where I have never been in this washable suit . . ." These passages poignantly show the intense excitement and sense of destiny that Merton experienced at this so-longed-for moment.

After a brief stop in Honolulu, Merton was off for Bangkok, Thailand, finishing Hesse's *Siddhartha*. October 17 and 18 were spent in Bangkok;

October 19 he departed for a week in Calcutta. The monk from America found Calcutta shocking in its poverty, its beggars heart-rending, yet its people so beautiful. He met his friend Amiya Chakravarty on October 21 and together they visited the painter Jamini Roy. Merton was full of appreciation for the artist and his work. However, he was not totally without criticism of what he saw elsewhere; after witnessing a swami who reminded him of Groucho Marx's manifest contempt for his competitors, Merton comments, not without irony: "Even his Kleenex is saffron!"

The next stop for Merton was New Delhi (October 28–31), where he read Tucci and met Harold Talbott, who knew the Dalai Lama, made contacts for Merton, and was very helpful in preparing the American monk for what would be the high point of his time in Asia, his three audiences with His Holiness, the Dalai Lama. Harold Talbott accompanied Merton to Dharamsala, where he met more Tibetan Buddhists, especially Sonam Kazi and his wife and daughter. On November 4, Merton had his first audience with the Dalai Lama, which was a great experience for both of them. Merton returned on November 6 for a second audience, and on November 8 a third, which Merton says was in many ways the best. By then, Merton felt they knew one another better and were able to speak from the heart as friends. The Dalai Lama felt the same way.

Madras was next on Merton's itinerary (November 26–28); then Ceylon from November 29 to December 6, and finally Bangkok again on December 7. He spent that night in a hotel, but the next day went out to Red Cross headquarters on Silom Road, where the conference would be held for religious superiors of the Far East. There he met Dom Jean Leclercq, an old friend, who had been instrumental in arranging the invitation for Merton. Other Benedictines and Cistercians were already there awaiting the opening of the conference.

On the day of his last entry in this journal, December 8, only two days before his death in a small cottage room on the outskirts of Bangkok, Merton wrote me what was his last letter, which concludes: "I think of you all on this Feast Day and with Christmas approaching I feel homesick for Gethsemani. But I hope to be at least in a monastery—Rawa Seneng (in Indonesia). Also I look forward to being at our monastery at Hong Kong, and may be seeing our three volunteers there (or is it two?). No more for the moment. Best love to all. Louie."

He wrote these lines in his room at the Oriental Hotel in Bangkok, just a few minutes before leaving for Red Cross headquarters on the outskirts of the city. By Christmas he was, after all, back at Gethsemani, lying buried alongside the abbey church overlooking the woodland knobs that had become so familiar to him during his twenty-seven years of monastic life at Gethsemani.

At about ten o'clock on the morning of December 10, we received an incredible cable from the American embassy in Bangkok. It said little more than that Thomas Merton had died. But how? And where? These agonizing questions remained unanswered for some hours. The abbot called me into his office at once, where I stayed for the next two hours, which seemed to us an eternity. Two hours of waiting and consoling one another and hoping against hope that it was all a terrible mistake. While we desperately tried to telephone the American embassy in Bangkok and the State Department in Washington for further clarification, the American embassy in Bangkok was trying to reach us by phone. About noon the call finally got through to us, and the tragic news was confirmed.

We learned that death was caused by accidental electrocution at about two in the afternoon (Bangkok time) on December 10. He had delivered a paper entitled "Marxism and Monastic Perspectives" at ten o'clock that morning. It was received with considerable enthusiasm by the members of the conference, and all of them were looking forward to a discussion of the paper, with questions and answers, in the late afternoon. A group of the participants had lunch with Merton, after which they went to their respective rooms. He had told one of his companions that he felt rather tired and was looking forward to the siesta.

Having read the medical and police reports as well as several eyewitness accounts that were sent to us from Bangkok, I have attempted to reconstruct the scenario of his death as follows: Merton returned to his cottage about one-thirty and proceeded to take a shower before retiring for a rest. While barefoot on the terrazzo floor, he apparently had reached for the large standing fan (to either turn it on or pull it closer to the bed) when he received the full 220 volts of direct current. (This is normal voltage for Bangkok.) He collapsed, and the large fan tumbled over on top of him. When he was discovered about an hour later by two of the monks who shared his cottage, the fan, still running, lay across his body. They could not get into the room at first because the door was bolted from the inside. One of them ran for help, and two of the abbots came immediately. They broke through the upper panel of the door, opened it, and entered. One of the abbots tried to remove the fan at once from the body, but though he wore shoes, he also received a slight electrical shock. Fortunately, someone rushed over to the outlet and pulled the cord from the socket. Later examination revealed defective wiring in the fan. A Korean prioress who was a distinguished medical doctor came to the scene. After examining the body, she pronounced him dead by electric shock.

Almost a week later, after an attempt to have an autopsy performed that proved unsuccessful due to international red tape, his body was flown back to California (ironically, by a U.S. Air Force jet from Vietnam). From there it was transferred to a commercial plane in Oakland and flown to Louisville, where it was met by the abbot and a group of monks with the local undertaker. The casket was opened at the funeral parlor in New Haven, where several of the monks identified the body. The casket was then sealed, never to be opened again.

The body arrived at the abbey early on the afternoon of December 17. Services in the church began almost immediately with the chanting of the funeral liturgy by the monks and the many friends who came to pay their last respects to our Father Louis and the world's Thomas Merton. At dusk under a light snowfall, his body was laid to rest in the monastic cemetery beneath a solitary cedar tree. A simple white cross marks his grave, no different from those of the rest of the monks who have been buried there during the past 150 years. May his ever searching spirit now rest in God's peace.

PART I

The Election of a New Abbot

October 1967–May 1968

October 18, 1967

There was an eclipse of the moon about 4 to 5 this morning. The clouds cleared a little and I was able to see it begin. Then after I said Mass I went out and the eclipse was closer to full, the clouds had almost completely gone. The moon was beautiful, dimly red, like a globe of almost transparent amber, with a shapeless foetus of darkness curled in the midst of it. It hung there between two tall pines, silent, unexplained, small, with a modest suggestion of bloodiness, an omen without fierceness and without comment, pure.

There was a great deal of rain yesterday, and I talked with J[ohn] Ford, a Louisville attorney, about the estate, the Trust, etc. I hope finally something will get done. We have been at it for three years and nothing has happened. This is a new one—I hope he will act. I should have got a Kentucky lawyer long ago, I guess.

Last evening at supper (wild rice, barbecued beans, knocked out my stomach) I read some of Leonard Woolf's Autobiography—the 4th volume *(Downhill All the Way)*. What a job they did with that Hogarth Press! And what their list brings back to me—the days when I bought second-hand novels and poetry in London Bookshops—Eliot, Graves, Lawrence—and Roger Fry whom they published also. Bloomsbury and their friends—and the Royal Hotel which L.W. sued. All this was a world where I was once a citizen.

Curious contest with the record of Janis Ian sent by a nun at Regina Laudis [monastery, Bethlehem, Connecticut]. Articulate, sensitive, vulnerable, disconcerting: a 15-year-old girl.

October 23, 1967

Blazing bright days, cool nights, my face still hot from burn as we sat yesterday at top of the long new farm cornfield—Gene Meatyard, Jonathan Williams, Guy Davenport, Bonnie and I—in noon sun and drank some beer. Hills glimmering with heat and color. Sky deep blue. All distances sharp. White dead corn leaves blowing about in the hot dust of the field, fully ravaged, fully harvested.

Gene brought some of his photos—including ones taken around the beatup house down the road in June (the house now repaired and occupied, with a pickup standing outside under the locust tree).

Jonathan had an exciting and beautiful new book of concrete poetry.

Guy picked up the avocado seed Bob Shepherd [from Lexington] threw away there the other day when it was much colder.

Telegram from Doris Dana[1] sent October 20, reached me (the note of the phone message) yesterday, 22nd. Not bad for here! The other day Rosemary Haughton came out (between lectures in Minneapolis and Chicago). It was curious to meet a theologian who is six months pregnant. In a long black cloak with hair blowing in the wind she sat on the concrete dam of Dom Frederic's Lake. I hope my picture of that is good.[2] She is quiet, intelligent, not the obstreperous kind of activist progressive, concerned about a real contemplative life continuing, etc.

Saturday, with some satisfaction, finished "The Sacred City" essay (or rather Sunday morning when I added a final half page) on Monte Alban. I enjoyed writing this and it came easy.[3]

J. W. Hackett has sent a volume of his English Haiku. I am not convinced Haiku can or should be written in English. His are, it seems to me, somewhat weakened by too many present participles and adverbs. I don't see how you can make a Haiku out of "-ing" and "-ly." Dismantle and rewrite as concrete poetry! Then he might have something!

Last evening after supper—an intruder barged in here, frankly boasting that he had easily figured out the combination of the padlock on the highway gate. Car full of suits on hangers strung across the back seat left halfway

1 Doris Dana was a friend of Jacques and Raïssa Maritain and was part of the literary and artistic circle, including John Howard Griffin, who spent time at Kolbsheim, the chateau of the Gruneliuses near Strasbourg.

2 The photograph of Rosemary Haughton by Thomas Merton did indeed turn out well; in fact, it has been used on the jacket of one of Haughton's books, *The Theology of Experience* (New York: Newman Press, 1972).

3 "The Sacred City" was later included in a volume of essays by Merton on Native Americans titled *Ishi Means Man* with an introduction by Dorothy Day, which was published by Unicorn Press (Greensboro, NC) in 1976.

up the hill. Had no real reason for being here except curiosity, wanted to get his nose into everything. Why this? Why that? Why do you live in such a place? Young, boasted about his exploits as a "private investigator"—trailing women to Holiday Inns. Maybe he was investigating me. I thought about it, pacing up and down in the dark, after I had got rid of him. Certainly he has now cased the place, knows how to get in and steal things if he wants to. I don't think he was malicious or systematic, just nosey and disorganized—a budding operator. He gave his name as Ken Hill and said he came from Chicago. Maybe! I asked where he was going. Vague. Could be Memphis, perhaps. A red car: I'm too dumb to know what kind and I forgot to take a look at the plates.

October 25, 1967

I do not have much news of what happened in Washington Saturday—an enormous peace mobilization at which there was evidently some violence. An ex-novice whom I happened to meet outside the gate Saturday said that troops had been called to "protect the Pentagon" and in his opinion this made sense "because of all those juvenile delinquents"! Roger Barnard—who has good judgment—surmises in *Peace News* that Johnson will sooner or later stop bombing Vietnam and call a Peace Conference knowing that North Vietnam wants something more than that. Then, having "failed" in his "honest" efforts for peace he will flatten North Vietnam. Or try to. An invasion, etc. The stupidity and blindness of American power, which, in its own terms is perfectly "logical"—and yet its terms are fantastically arbitrary and respond only to the "reality" of a thinking that goes on within an artificial and closed system. To defend your own reality and then impose it forcefully on the outside world is paranoia.

October 27, 1967

Troops of small lavender clouds in an obedient procession, go off east before a warm wind. The night has been rainy but the morning star shines clear in the gaps of cloud and the troops are ending raggedly. Maybe it will be a nice day to talk to Doris Dana who arrived (or was supposed to) last evening.

Ted Colteran was in the Washington Peace Mobilization—said it was much less violent and turbulent than the news made it to be, but people were beaten and the troops were scared, edgy, mean. A former monk from here (a name I can't place) was with him. Mailer was arrested.

Was in town again Wednesday—lunch with [Dr. James] Wygal and saw Tommie O'Callaghan to talk about the Trust. I want to get this finally set up but maybe I am getting too involved in it. Anyway John Ford seems willing to work on it fast. And since I have started on it I'm going on with it. Useless to leave this hanging in the air. Jim persuaded me to stay in late, and said he would drive me out. I foolishly did. Wish I had come back in the afternoon with George in the truck. Got home tired at 10 after sitting around drinking bourbon I didn't want in dull places—and finally on the way out in the car spent most of the time arguing with him and the priest whose name I didn't get about whether I should accept an abbatial election. I am determined *not* to take it if I am voted for and they had all the obvious reasons why "I ought" to, but they seemed to me foolish. "With your reputation you can do so much good!" Bull shit. It is all part of the same stupid line Jim takes when he says I ought to write a movie or something that would make a big splash and get back in the center of attention. It is childish. And it is against everything I have ever lived for. To become a personage!!

I keep repeating that there is *nothing* I can do here to make things any better or to prevent this place from going to seed, and I have no real reason for doing it if I *could*. Is this institution worth preserving? Maybe—but let someone do it who knows how and is interested. Not me!

The small clouds have not cleared. They have given place to big ones, and there will be rain.

October 28, 1967

It did not rain yesterday. Coldish, windy. Walking in empty cornfield with Doris Dana talking about Jacques Maritain, Kolbsheim, John [Howard] Griffin, Spain, Gabriela Mistral, Pomaire (my Spanish publisher who also does the Gabriela paperbacks), my problem with Tadié,[4] etc. Had some fun with a Japanese movie camera she had borrowed and brought down—a beautiful thing!

Am absorbed and excited by Nelson Reed's book on *The Caste War in Yucatan*. It clicks perfectly with what I have been reading of Cargo Cults and with the Black Power movement in U.S. I want to write about this!

4 Marie Tadié was Merton's French translator and agent.

October 29, 1967

Yesterday, drove with Doris to Lexington and we went out with Carolyn Hammer past Athens *(Aythens)* to John Jacob Niles' farm for lunch—and to hear his setting of three of my poems. It was really a moving experience for me.

First of all the house was a complete—and delightful—surprise. I don't know what I expected, but this was an entrancing place. We dipped down into a wooded hollow, and suddenly, after a church, and turning a corner, trees and stone walls, I saw this interesting house and realized that we were going to turn in. It is fascinating. Doors carved with statements. Stone walls and steps up and down, brick fireplaces, rambling halls, and the dining room with a big picture window looking into the close hollow, over a lower roof, at a wall of wooded hill, and in front of the window a bare sycamore and a tulip poplar with a few golden leaves left. A fascinating place.

Before dinner we drank some of their own cider, which was good, and John played some ballads on a lute.

As we were finishing dinner the singer and pianist arrived and had coffee. Then the songs. John has set Messenger, Carol, Responsory (1948) and is working on Evening. I thought the settings very effective and satisfactory. In fact was very moved by them. But above all by this lovely girl, Jackie Roberts, who put her whole heart into singing them. What was most beautiful was that! I do think John Niles has brought out a lot of what I wanted to say and made me value my own poems more. It was to me a very intense experience, and to Doris also I think. Carolyn apparently does not like the settings, but she has her blind spots.

Jackie Roberts in her green dress was unforgettable, and the pianist was a sweet dark girl too. I was so grateful to them for their own response to the music and the poems.

John Niles is a character and I like him. Carolyn commented on his cockiness, but who cares? He has a good weather-beaten, self-willed face, is a bit of a madman and writes good songs. He said Joan Baez was a whore (about which I put up an argument), and some nut stole his manuscripts. And he can carve messages on doors, besides play the lute and sing a toothy song in a metallic voice.

It was an afternoon I enjoyed, and I burst into tears at Jackie's singing. And John said he didn't like Robert Frost, but that my poetry moved him to tears. So we were all ready to weep and in fact weeping.

The thing that struck me most—the wonderful pale fall light of Kentucky on the stones and the quiet of the Kentucky hollow.

November 1, 1967

Rainy night. Quiet.

Fr. Chrysogonus [Waddell, of Gethsemani], yesterday, spoke of the Abbots' meeting, where he had been. Said it was "charismatic." I hope so. Nothing definite yet about Dom James [Fox]'s resignation. C. said he thought that was discussed in a "session de vie" session at the end. Meanwhile Dan Walsh[5] says that Brother Kevin [Shine, of Gethsemani] picked up some news on a phone call from the Abbot, who said the meeting had resolved to ask that the abbatial term of office be limited to three or six years. (Dan said three, but admitted six as possible. I hardly think they would say three. Not practical!) Certainly not for life anyway. I am not sure whether this makes perfect sense in every way, but considering the situation it is probably the best thing.

Dan is evidently very much taken up with those who say Pope Paul is hopeless, etc. as if this meant anything particular! The whole institutional structure is questionable: why blame everything on the poor man who can't help being what he is—a curial official trained under Pius XII, with a few lively ideas on Catholic Action acquired in the '20's and '30's. One almost feels that now the test of true Christian spirit is the willingness to say anathema to Paul! One ought rather to be sorry for him—and for those who think it is relevant to curse him.

This is not for me. I can't be part of any of it, for or against. It all strikes me as a bit childish. Meanwhile, the Message of Contemplatives—dutifully printed in the *Osservatore*, with the usual picture of a monk with his hood up and his back to the camera—has been totally and utterly forgotten—dropped into a well of silence as if it had never been which is proper and right. The whole idea was silly.

Of course it will be once again dutifully reprinted in the *Collectanea [Cisterciensia]*, etc.

This morning I read an article of [Gregorio] Penco on the "Return to Paradise" in the Camaldolese magazine *Vita Monastica*. The usual, neat, competent rehash of a few texts—from Mabillon's Benedictine Saints, from

5 Rev. Daniel C. Walsh (1907–75) was Merton's teacher and friend at Columbia University. When he retired from Columbia and Manhattanville, he came to Kentucky, where he taught philosophy at Gethsemani as well as at Bellarmine College and St. Mary's Seminary.

Eucherius, Jerome, Peter of Celles, Aelred, etc.—and the usual anonymous sermons dug up from somewhere by Dom [Jean] Leclercq. Practically everything was familiar. The texts are beautiful in the same way that romanesque architecture is—filled with sap and life and sense of symbol and order. They have a rich unexpressed content that one gets from between the lines if one is a "knower" and it is all very satisfying. And yet . . .

It has occurred to me to question the value of such an exercise. Certainly it is valuable. But only within a very limited sphere of its own. It has become entirely esoteric, or almost. It belongs entirely to that Latin-Medieval-Christendom which was the basis of European civilization and all that: and no doubt it may be closer to the new African monasticism than, say, the latest in secular Christianity. Certainly it is good to be able to understand and enjoy it. But just as certainly it has to be seen in a much wider context—if at all.

Certainly, too, I don't feel impelled to "do anything about it." I'll read it from time to time—and appreciate my hermitage in the light of topic sentences from the 9th–12th centuries. Perhaps even regret that my own vocation is not all that simple. But surely I can't live as if that were all! Or as if the Bible were all, either. (Same applies of course to Eckhart and the Rhinish mystics and John of the Cross—though they can be a bridge to other religious traditions.)

It rained steadily all day and slowed down in the evening with a fine, full rainbow in the east. I did some work on the Caste War article. Seem to have some arthritis in my right hand. Makes writing painful. J[ames] Laughlin sent a clipping—a letter of Brother Antoninus [William Everson] and the *[New York] Times Book Review* about "Women" and "Woman" and about how his love poems were after all the sign he had been a "bad monk" etc. Extremely silly. It seemed to me to be unreal and sentimental. Fuss about "Woman" with a capital "W." But obviously when one is in love there is no telling what will come out of it. Though I certainly disagree with his thesis that what matters is "Woman" and not "Women." He seems to be rather hung up in the "Woman" business. I certainly hope I have had all my share of it and won't get involved in any more. I look back in the pages of this journal and read the inanities of last year!! Grief!

November 2, 1967

I think I have a good title for these Journals—i.e. for what is to be published (what I hope to put on tape and have typed): *The Vow of Conversation*.

Material for anti-haikus on day of the dead
. . . Food thunders dimly in the angered gut
. . . Back and forth to outhouse in dark rain-mist,
Splash of *blanc* gelusil from overflowing spoon.

November 7, 1967

Steel grey morning, but not quite freezing. The other day it was very cold—down in the twenties (cold for November). Yesterday there were a few large flakes of snow but nothing like last year: the big fall that broke the trees!

I have been working on the Ghost Dance canto of *Lograire*. Goes like a charm! Everything there in Cora DuBois, a mimeograph report from Berkeley. Beautiful, haunting, sad stuff. All you have to do is quote the Indians' own words!

Joost Meerloo here this weekend. I was happy to finally meet him, a really alert and creative mind—full of ideas, not bogged down in his profession (psychoanalysis). Tells of the sterility of conferences—academic rituals where no one listens. I am less and less inclined about all that myself. If the rules relax and it comes to *me* to decide whether or not to accept invitations, I think I shall refuse them. It would be stupid to accept. Nothing to gain, much to lose. The people I need to meet I can meet *here* (or I can go out to meet them somewhere privately).

Still, two things—I regret I can't go to this thing organized by the Blackstone Rangers (Negro gang) on Race, in Chicago (really fantastic!) and regret I had to say "no" to the sweet little girl at Washington University who wanted me there for three days as Ginsberg and Nemerov (?) had been.

November 12, 1967. Sunday

Cool clear evening—7 p.m. Formalhaut out bright in the South under my sign, Aquarius, and above me many friends, Swan, Eagle, Perseus and Andromeda, Cassiopeia. There were some new faces in the conference this afternoon—cantors from other monasteries here for a meeting. Still talking on Sufism—was tempted to talk on Cargo Cults, but I have put that on tape. The Burridge book *(Mambu)* is excellent.

Naomi [Burton Stone] is coming (is in fact here, or should be) and I hope now we can finally wind up all this Trust business, which turned out to be much more elaborate than I anticipated. As usual, I begin to have doubts about it when it is too late. But I think I have done right, though this recourse to law is neither "monastic" nor "anarchic." Still, I think it would be silly to leave the pile of paper that I have covered with ink merely to rot or get lost in the monastic library. What is left over after my death (and there is bound to be plenty!) might as well get published. I have no guarantee of living many more years. Perhaps five, perhaps ten.

Walked today again down by St. Bernard's Lake in the dry brown grass of the pasture, thinking about some ideas of [indecipherable] on contemplation—and about so many other things, too. [John] Slate's death. The lawyers. The Trust. The dead tree standing in the water. Sr. Thérèse [Lentfoehr, the poet] (here Tuesday, briefly). Tommie O'Callaghan, who called today to say they are all going to Amsterdam for three years—she is one of my trustees!

Yesterday I hurried down in the rain for an afternoon concelebration and Brother Richard [Schmidlin]'s profession. At the end we all recessed singing "The Church's One Foundation" which reminded me of dreary evening chapel at Oakham 35 years ago. Renewal? For me that's a return to a really dead past. Victorian England.

The other day I called M. from Bardstown—first time in months—since the end of June I believe. It was a sad sort of call and in the end she was crying. She is moving to Miami. I felt we really weren't communicating: she was trying to tell me I ought to leave and "reach out for happiness." No way of explaining to her that life in some city would be for me utterly meaningless. And also that I could not live happily with a woman—and that with her it would be a disaster for both of us. Yet I wish I could have a decent talk with her. But what would be the use?

November 14, 1967

Today I went in to Louisville with Naomi B. and at Tommie O'Callaghan's we signed the Trust agreement—and I am glad that is done. It had to be done, and now it is a weight off my mind. Whether or not everything is perfectly taken care of, at least I have done what was necessary. And I think the agreement is about as practical as anything could be. John Ford was very efficient and cooperative about it.

Yesterday I had a quiet afternoon talking to Naomi and we went over to St. Rose's Priory—she wanted to say a prayer for some Dominican election—and I liked seeing that church—first time I have ever been in it (passed it at night once a few years ago). It rather fascinates me, up on its hill, with its own kind of Kentucky Gothic, and it has a lot of character. And a sort of austere loneliness that I know from the old Gethsemani and from Loretto too. Something that has become very much part of my own experience in twenty-five years here.

Moonlight night. Whump whump of guns at [Fort] Knox shake my windows.

A letter from Br. F[rederic Collins] in Chile asked: if they elected me Prior, would I accept. I said no. But I wouldn't object to helping out in Chile.

Having put all my writings in the hands of this Trust I am much less concerned about getting anything "done"—still less about getting it published, obviously! I feel much freer and readier to forget all that, and make more out of solitude.

November 18, 1967

Another bright cool fall day. I have a cold—or an allergy attack or something—and the dust in the hermitage doesn't help it: so I went out in the sun and took a few pictures. Today a letter came from AFSC (The Friends) in Philadelphia asking me to form part of an unofficial peace team that is to meet and talk with representatives of the NLF (Viet Cong) and try to get up some concrete proposals for Washington. A most unusual invitation, so unusual that if I were left to myself I'd have no alternative but to accept—and in my case I could not take it upon myself to refuse. I can't, in conscience, refuse. So I decided to turn it over to the Abbot. Was not able to talk to him, he was busy. Gave him the letter and I know very well what he will do! I don't think there is a chance in a million of his seeing the importance and significance of it and he won't think for 10 seconds of letting me go. And I'll probably have to put up with one of his unreasoned sermons. All of which poses a problem. It really raises the question of my staying here. It seems so absurd to go on year after year putting up with such utter nonsense. And yet frankly, I see no alternative that is any less nonsensical for me. That certainly does not justify anything—it is a sign of confusion that I perhaps don't know how to get out of. I am certainly committed to the solitary life and to "contemplation" and the way I can have these most effectively is here. Or is it? In any case, being here, I have forfeited all freedom to do things that perhaps I *should* do—and this is a real problem. All I can do is trust blindly that there is some solution which I don't yet see or know and that it will come by surprise at the right time, just as the hermitage itself did. But I certainly can't feel complacent or secure about leaving this entirely in the hands of someone who *can't* comprehend it and has all kinds of psychological reasons for not letting himself even try. It is a sick situation.

The cantors from our U.S. monasteries were up at the hermitage yesterday—end of a meeting they've had here! A naive sort of bunch, earnest, well-meaning, caught up in the usual binds and preoccupations. Still, I liked them, and they were, for better or worse, clearly *Cistercians*—i.e. not only in black and white, but also—simple, earnest, wanting something intangible and expecting to get it, and not too well endowed with ideas. But nice guys, and I was glad to see Fr. Paul from Vina [New Clairvaux Abbey, California]. He had been a novice of mine here and somehow we'd had a hard time getting on when he left. But I realized now that I really like him and he is a good sort. Also had a short talk with Fr. Methodius from Conyers [Holy Spirit Monastery, Georgia]—who talks so fast he can say plenty in a short talk. About June Yungblut, to whom I must write, and so on. (She wants to come here again and I'd enjoy seeing her and talking about her thesis on Beckett.)

November 21, 1967

Presentation—a Feast that has all but disappeared. Enjoyed the Mass alone in the hermitage in spite of my bad cold. I wonder if Smith's allergy shots are helping or making things worse. Yesterday I had to go to Lexington to the dentist. First time in the Medical Center at the Dental School. Esoteric new dentistry—everything different. Instead of the old spittoon with its private whirlpool, a tube that sucks your spit voraciously into the wall—and maybe your teeth too if you are not careful. It is more fun with a girl holding a tube in your mouth while the drill destroys your teeth, vaporizes them or something. After all the leveling I found five teeth had been reduced to little points on which presently were edified new temporary teeth, smooth and clear, that do not tear pieces out of my tongue. Gold caps are said to be coming next week. All this happened while I lay on a kind of dental divan covered with white leather. Or probably some good imitation. I was on this for two and a half hours and glad to get off. John Loughlin, the dentist, very efficient and solicitous, took me to lunch in the doctor's cafeteria later. After which I went to the University, could not find Carolyn Hammer in the Library, ended up reading about Sitting Bull and the Wounded Knee massacre (dreadful!).

After that, returned to the Medical Center to wait for Brother Clement to come down with five stitches in his jaw, and while waiting met and spoke to Governor Breathitt (whose wife was having her teeth fixed too). A nice quiet guy. We spoke a little about conservation, strip mining and all that.

Then it turned out Fr. Abbot was upstairs in the hospital waiting for an operation that is minor—or perhaps not so minor. We went up to see him. By that time it was late. We drove home in the dark.

I learned today his resignation had been accepted in Rome.

Obviously no chance of my going to Cambodia! (A long note about that was in my mail when I got home.)

November 22, 1967

Rain and mist all day for St. Cecilia [Feast day]. Hugo Rahner on the sacred dance in refectory. His book on *Man at Play* is very good. Other day when Rahner was talking of *homo ludens* [man playing], the witty Brother Isidore (in refectory near me) whipped out a box of cough drops and pointed to the name *Ludens*. Monastic humor.

My cold is better. Rest of the allergy not so. For some reason I have a sore tongue.

Today I did a little work on the article promised a long time ago to *The Journal of Ecumenical Studies*—Monasticism and Ecumenism. Got off to a slow, difficult start, but it was good to get some real work done at the typewriter for a change, instead of just writing letters, or trying to. Some people keep *insisting* that I reply to them when it is obvious that I am not going to. There are others whose letters I don't even read. Yet still others are very honest and human and touching, like the college girl who complained of her boyfriend deserting her at parties. And then how she wouldn't say "I love you" when he came back. I felt very sorry for her (and of course will write!).

In two weeks the nuns will be here. I started making notes of things to talk about.

Pasternak's Georgian letters are good. Real love for his friends, and contagious enthusiasm about Tiflis, etc. There is a great newness and freshness about P.—his own bright and living world. A paradise man, full of wonder, and even the Stalinists never stamped it all out of him. Never silenced him really.

November 25, 1967

All day it has been deceptively like spring. Not only because of light and cool-warm air (warm with a slightly biting March-like wind), but because I fasted and it felt like Lent. Then in the evening (I had my meal about 4 instead of supper at 5) it was suddenly much lighter, as though it were March.

At noon, when I was not eating, I was out by St. Bernard's lake (which is surprisingly low) and the sky, hills, trees kept taking on an air of clarity and freshness that took me back to springs twenty years ago when Lents were hard and I was new in the monastery.

Strange feeling! Recapturing the freshness of those days when my whole monastic life was still ahead of me, when all was still open: but now it is all behind me, and the years have closed in upon their silly, unsatisfactory history, one by one. But the air is like spring and fresh as ever. And I was amazed at it. Had to stop to gaze and wonder: loblolly pines we planted ten or fifteen years ago are twenty feet high. The fire tower shines in the sun like new—though it was put up ten years ago (with what hopes, on my part!). Flashing water of the lake. A bluejay flying down as bright as metal. I went over to the wood where the Jonathan Daniel sculptures are now, and read some selections from Origen. And again stood amazed at the quiet, the bright sun, the spring-like light. The sharp outline of the pasture. Knolls, the brightness of bare trees in the hopeful sun. And yet it is *not* spring. We are on the threshold of a hard winter.

With my meal I was reading Lévi-Strauss's *Tristes Tropiques*. The most "literary" and readable of his books. He is an intelligent and fluent writer, sensitive to real problems, ironic, objective, alert, humane. I like the book.

November 26, 1967. Last Sunday after Pentecost

6 a.m. (really 5 or earlier by true sun time) still completely dark. The stars are those of a March evening sky—with the moon in Virgo. Arcturus, Spica. Overhead Leo, the Twins. The Charioteer going down in the NW. Corvus in the South. Friends! (Last year's poem "The Lion" was written earlier in November—but I feel a lot better now! Yesterday was a fruitful day.)

Seabury Press sent proofs of a devotional book by Alan Paton. It is good—in touch with authentic realities of Christian life and traditional, a good Franciscan sense of things. Yet the kind of book I myself will no longer (I think) attempt to write. I feel strange about writing a blurb for it. To do so is to harm—again—the integrity of all that kind of literature. The integrity which the book business has made so tawdry and thin. Nothing against Seabury, I like them. But the whole business of *selling* this kind of thing. Devotional literature should circulate free in mimeograph. Or should be printed, smuggled around underground, like the sex books. But soon everyone would see that this too is only a further bit of craftiness, a slyer business gambit! Oh well. I'd like to encourage Paton and this is a serious Christian book: innocent looking yet dangerous, for it will induce some seminarian to throw his life away in some tragic struggle—that will never be recognized by anyone except God. For today there is no obscurity, no nonentity to compare with that of the Christian saint!

I keep thinking about Joe Carroll, who left and didn't come back. (This is the second time.) Probably this time he is through. In a way I'll miss him: he was part of the peculiar monastic world here and part of my own world this summer. I'll remember our attempt to find St. Matthews by driving through Cherokee Park, and getting lost in the labyrinth of winding roads, coming again and again to the same bridges and then again and again to the University of Louisville School of Music and the Presbyterian Seminary. But it was a lovely summer morning and nobody cared!

November 28, 1967

Sunday afternoon as I was starting out for a walk to the usual place—(this year to what was to be known as Charlie O'Bryan's Pasture, beyond cow-barns—St. Bernard's field and lake), a jeep came out of the gate with a bunch of monks obviously heading for Edelin's[6] to see the Abbot's hermitage. So I got in with them and off we went past the distillery and over the creek and into the hills with dogs after us. The way in is up the back road. Then through the woods on a bumpy track rutted already by the heavy cement trucks. He is out on a rocky spur, high over the valley, the place where I climbed up on the feast of St. Joseph in 1965—I remember it well! It will be a beautiful little house, very interesting design (Brother Clement's memoir to Frank Lloyd Wright, whom he worked for at one time) and a lot of care is going into it. High, isolated, quiet, with a big view (screened by trees, however) and the strange sunny quiet of those high ridges with the trees on the other ridges, just the same height. Only the foundation is finished, but it will be a real pretty place. The only thing is I have trouble imagining him in it. I guess he will make himself think he likes it—but is that what he wants? I wonder. But you don't really know people here. The fact that he was able to choose such a place and get the whole thing going is a very sobering thought! It is one of the only things I have ever found in the man to admire. He has my respect at least for this: he has got himself one very fine hermitage going! And I remember too that it is because from the first time I mentioned Edelin's to him, he got completely hung up on the place, and it was because of this that the rest of us got permission to be hermits. So there is something to the mystery!

I must admit that in a way I envy the place he has. My own hermitage has lots of advantages and is in many ways much better (for instance it is surrounded by very pleasant woods with a big variety of places to walk, to sit, to meditate, to say office, etc.). But his place has the exciting and romantic character of a kind of hawk's nest perched *on top* of all those woods, in that strange lonely area so different from our valley over here. It is remote, lonely, strange, wild. For a moment I thought again about the hollow I like so much over there, and want to see it again. Very quiet, very pleasant, unchanged. I could visualize a little place something like Niles's house there! (Obviously not that big. But that kind of use of a hillside in a hollow!)

6 "Edelin's" (or "Edelin's place") was named after Everett Edelin, who gave some wooded property close to Gethsemani for the purpose of establishing a "laura," or a cluster of hermitages at some distance from one another. It eventually became the site of a hermitage for Dom James Fox, the previous abbot.

Yesterday afternoon I walked over to see Fr. Hilarion in his trailer. It was quiet and sunny. He is very happy and relaxed there, very much changed (as far as his mood goes—no more strain and tension) and seems completely satisfied. I was happy to see that he had settled down so well. Materially he has the least desirable set-up. His camp was thrown together for him at the last minute. But the trailer, though dull, is compact and clean. Less dirty than my place!

Yesterday too Glenn Hinson was going to come out but had to change his plans.

Today my usual routine was turned upside down—lately I have been intellectually overfed and in the mornings I read less and less. Today I read almost nothing at all in the early morning, a bit of Dorothy Emmett's book, which is good, and a couple of pages of the Castelli volume—the symposium on hermeneutics. Like it, but I have to stop. I can't cover much ground. The piece by G. Fessard, S.J., seems to me absolutely insane. What kind of a joker is this? A lot of other stuff is good, though: H. Mt. [Mount Athos], Ricoeur, etc.

Not having read in the morning (ended up with some projects for work—and publication—sent suggestion to New Directions, etc.) I went out this afternoon, read some of the stuff on meditation in one of Winston King's books—on Burmese Buddhism. Good. Then came back and began a new Penguin containing Basho's travel notes. Completely shattered by them. One of the most beautiful books I have ever read in my life. It gives me a whole new (old) view of my own life. The whole thing is pitched right on my tone. Deeply moving in every kind of way. Seldom have I found a book to which I responded so totally.

December 2, 1967

Strong wind and long storm of rain all day long, sometimes blowing up violently out of the south, bending the black pines and flooding my porch, sometimes dying off while rays of low cloud fly north under the iron ceiling. I went down to the monastery just long enough to pick up my mail and my laundry, and hurried back to change and hang my wet clothes in front of a fire (though most of my firewood on the porch is wet). I fasted, but ate my one meal a little early (about 2:30). Cleaned up my front room. I have a new vacuum cleaner, which is a help. Dust allergy finally made it necessary to get one: the broom doesn't do the job.

The other day I got some rather touching fan mail. Two letters, one from a man, one from a woman, both teaching at Keele University (one of the new English universities) and both thanking me for my "Notes on Love" (in *Frontier*) and saying how much they agreed, how right I was, what an unusual viewpoint, etc. Well, if these notes helped two people to love each other better and with more trust in love's truth, then all that happened between me and M. was worthwhile. I feel sad about M.—she has gone to work in M———. What a hole! I haven't heard from her there—don't know her phone number. I wrote her a note the other day, but I have run out of things to say: the situation is somewhat artificial and strained because evidently she thinks I should leave here and can't understand why I don't, as if my staying here were somehow a betrayal. But that is no longer reasonable.

Some of the pictures I took the other day when I was miserable with cold and allergy, turned out very well. Contact sheets from Greg Griffin came today.

Touching picture of little Raphael Smith, Carleton Smith's son, my Godchild, from this summer just as their marriage broke up. Ghastly mess. The baby looks pathetic. I think of the seemingly terrible, cruel remark of Basho on the abandoned child! This poor little baby is not abandoned, but he will grow up in a hard world. And how can I be a Godfather to him in my situation? Everywhere you turn in the "religious life" you run into absurdities and contradictions. But that is also true everywhere. The whole of society is absurd, and we all contribute to it without knowing. I am unable to help C. Smith—except by rather cruel letters, trying to force him to use his own resources instead of striving to get others to solve things for him. But I understand his desperation—it is his own fault, but how understandable. I can imagine myself in the same position.

A good day to begin saying the Advent Office, dark, rainy, windy, desolate.

December 7, 1967

The last four or five days have been quite fantastic: among the most unusual in my life. I hardly know how to write about them. There should be a whole new key—and a kind of joy unusual in this journal—where I am usually diffident and sad.

I have to change the superficial ideas and judgments I have made about the contemplative religious life, the contemplative orders. They were silly and arbitrary, and without faith.

The retreat, or meeting, or whatever you want to call it, with the fifteen contemplative nuns who were here from Sunday evening (December 3rd) on has been a wonderful thing. Much more than I expected.[7]

First of all—their obvious *quality*. All of them—or almost all—real contemplatives, and were really human (all of them certainly that)—completely simple, honest, authentic people. I have never before had such a sense of community with any group—including when Sr. Luke[8] and Sr. Jane Marie came over from Loretto—and two of our own monks, Br. Maurice and Br. Wilfrid up here this morning for Mass. Mass at the hermitage today was unutterably good, something I simply can't articulate. People who *should* have been undisposed finding themselves completely united—for instance as we ended up singing "We Shall Overcome" with a sense that our own revolution was well under way! Sounds silly enough. But it was very real.

Sitting together in silence after Communion, with the rising sun shining into the cottage, was indescribably beautiful. Everyone so obviously happy! I was tired only on the first day. After that it was all easy.

I'd like to write about them all—but perhaps shouldn't try. But I do feel very close to all of them—with each in some special way. A sense of awe and privilege at being able to come together with such people.

7 This first of two retreats given at Gethsemani by Thomas Merton in 1967 and 1968 was organized by Sr. Elaine Bane, a Franciscan from Allegany, and included a group of Carmelite prioresses, a few Poor Clares, and several other contemplative religious women. The conferences were taped, later transcribed and edited by Sr. Jane Marie Richardson, a Sister of Loretto, and published as *The Springs of Contemplation* by Farrar, Straus & Giroux in 1992. It was reissued in paperback edition in 1997 by Ave Maria Press (Notre Dame, IN).

8 Sr. Mary Luke Tobin, a Sister of Loretto, Nerinx, Kentucky, was the only American woman observer at Vatican II. Between sessions she returned from Rome to Kentucky and usually conferred with Merton and several other monks of Gethsemani who were interested in this momentous council of the church.

First of all Sr. Elaine Michael [Bane] from the OSF at Allegany. Intelligence, earnestness, response—someone you enjoy working with (we organized this together).

The two Passionists from Scranton—Sr. Elizabeth, Sr. Louise, both beautiful people (especially in their black habits), ardent, deep, articulate, contemplative, alive! Mother Jane from Jackson (Mississippi) Carmel—a very special person. All of them! Very impressed with Mother Francis Clare, of the New Orleans Poor Clares, also intelligent, witty, sharp, and a real mystic (though obese—as if that had anything to do with it!). Mother Agnes, the old, silent, little bent-over Abbess of the Poor Clares in Newport News, taking everything in bright-eyed. It all sounds silly, but they are all better than the best you find anywhere. Immensely encouraging, because they are what they are not just *in spite of* the communities to which they are committed, but because of them. I am completely confident in the contemplative orders once again. There is a lot that needs changing, but our life is fundamentally one of the soundest and most healthy things in the Church, and I am sure has all kinds of promise. It was a great help to me to see and experience this.

At Mass today: I opened with a prayer of Lancelot Andrewes instead of the *Confiteor* [I confess]. Sr. Elizabeth read the Epistle. We had a dialogue homily (first time for me!). Everyone joined in with petitions in the prayer of the people, mementoes, etc. Afterwards—another prayer of Lancelot Andrewes and a prayer from the Old Syrian Liturgy for hermits. Then we sat and had coffee and had a wonderful time. The hermitage is blessed with the memory of it.

These four days have been very moving and I feel completely renewed by them: the best retreat I ever made in my life.

December 9, 1967

Yesterday, Immaculate Conception [Feast], I was pretty tired. Went down to Concelebration, came back and lay down for an hour (sort of drugged sleep), then got up and went for a quiet walk and some meditation by the lake beyond St. Bernard's field. Springlike sun. No one around. I needed the silence. Coming back—the small footprints of my nuns still in the mud of the road by the sheep barn. I remembered their happiness, especially when they were at Mass in the hermitage.

———

Today: grey morning. I tried to get some letters written. The "Cross Fighters" article came back from *Harper's* and I sent it to Teo Savory.[9] A letter from Dame Hildelith at Stanbrook. Lovely Shaker slides (Sabbathday Lake) sent by Bob Rambusch. The Carthusians are building a two-million-dollar charterhouse in Vermont (Jim Forest sent a clipping with sardonic comments).

Merrill Jackson arrived for dinner in a Louisville taxi. We talked a bit in the hermitage (he knew Malcolm X) and later went to Bardstown to get some cans of soup and replenish my supply. The taxi driver, very awed at having a famous passenger, had got six or seven copies of *Seeds of Contemplation*, which he had been reading while he waited. Found some potato soup with difficulty in the supermarket and when I opened it the can was labeled wrong. It turned out to be some kind of beef soup which I did not like.

I remember the Sisters leaving on Thursday—one car after the other and finally the green station wagon from New Orleans roaring off with Sister Kathleen at the wheel. Last I saw of her she was barreling down the middle of the highway.

I remember Mother Elizabeth and her black cape, Mother Louise and her black sweater: the firmness of our handshakes, the solemn promise of prayers. Sister Elaine Michael—my first sight of her sitting obscurely at the corner of the long table.

Really, it was wonderful to have them here, and to have such a perfect mutual understanding, such an atmosphere of unity and sense of realistic purpose: for once possibilities were not only hopeful but even realized, to some extent!

December 10, 1967. Second Sunday of Advent

Rainy. Denise Levertov was here with Wendell Berry and Tanya and the Meatyards. They came up to the hermitage and spent the afternoon. I like Denise very much. A good warm person. She left a good poem ("Tenebrae") and we talked a little about Sister Norbert in San Francisco who is in trouble about protesting against the war. Rather heartbreaking. Denise has had trouble with Eshleman too. We agreed about him.

9 Teo Savory was a poet and editor of Unicorn Press, first in Santa Barbara and later Greensboro, North Carolina. "The Cross Fighters" was later included in the collection *Ishi Means Man*.

I am hoping this next week will be quiet—a time of fasting and retreat. Too many people here lately. Also I need to get some work done.

December 12, 1967

After two days of wind and rain, a quiet, moonlit night. Fine clouds yesterday evening, piling up black out of the SW, and riding off in a line northward without coming over the monastery. High sweep of pink curves overhead. Then the black descended on us with dark and there was rain.

Today I got considerable work done—additions to *Faith and Violence*[10] (Finally getting off the ground with this. Hope nothing else goes wrong after Notre Dame Press fell asleep on it.)

Doris Dana sent the Stephens book on *Travels in Yucatan* and I began it. A fine work! Great reading.

This afternoon I went to return the tray that Mrs. Gannon sent over full of doughnuts the day I had Mass with the nuns in the hermitage. No one there but Brother Pachomius. He said Leo [Gannon] had suddenly lost the sight of his left eye and was in Louisville seeing an eye specialist.

As I sat in the jakes after dinner with the door open as usual, I saw one, then two golden crowned kinglets playing and feeding in the saplings outside, flipping and hanging upside down and almost somersaulting in the air. Both males, with pretty bright crowns. Very dapper.

A handsome card, irises, from Masao Abe in Japan. The usual pre-Christmas mail—and a copy of *Floating Bear*, Diane di Prima's little mimeographed magazine which is always good. Maybe I'll send her something. This issue had something by Kerouac: I had forgotten his existence. And G. Snyder. And some Japanese. And even one by a computer at MIT which was not bad at all!!

I am sick of responding to requests for articles for this or that collection that someone is editing. Several times lately I have written such and heard nothing more about them. Wesley First and some Columbia collection.

10 *Faith and Violence* was a paperback volume published by the University of Notre Dame Press in 1968 while Merton was still committed to Farrar, Straus & Giroux for prose works. Only through Naomi Burton's timely intervention was the situation rectified.

Msgr. Robert Fox and his East Harlem picture book. Ned O'Gorman. Even Ed Rice's thing on monasticism. I must write him about it. [Bob] Lax is back at Olean.

December 14, 1967

On November 20 the population of the U.S. reached 200,000,000. Eerie business of watching this rise of the flood of people in the world! Only three countries have larger populations: China, India, USSR. The population of the U.S. has exactly doubled in my lifetime. It was 100 million in 1915. Expected to reach 300 million in 33 years—if *present* rate of increase continues. But it may accelerate.

In spite of left-wing enthusiasm for Che Guevara ("martyr") and Regis Debray ("confessor") the Bolivian guerrillas have clearly failed. The CIA, etc. too strong and too smart for them. Victory at once for Bolivian dictatorship, Washington Power and Official Russian and Maoist doctrines. The Bolivian Communists were not with Che and Regis—they are heretics. Nevertheless, in all this mess, they stand out as human beings one admires and appreciates (though not all Che did is exactly lovely perhaps). Hence I don't take back my poem on Che (sent to London some weeks ago).

Yesterday—after confession a short conversation with Fr. Matthew [Kelty] about the coming abbatial election. Later, after dinner, Brother Job [Maurer] walked up with me to the hermitage to talk about his departure (soon), and while we drank some of his oversweet blackberry wine this conversation turned to the abbatial election too.

The following things seem to be crystallizing out:

1. Fr. Baldwin seems most likely to get it.

2. Even those who will probably vote him in (which I won't) are not entirely happy about him. He is simply the one most likely to be tolerated by a majority. But tolerated grudgingly by many of them. Many would prefer Fr. Flavian [Burns], who knows more about what real monasticism is. Others are actively campaigning for Dom Augustine (of Conyers) but these are largely the people who want TV and summer vacations, baseball, swimming, etc. (which they may easily get out of Baldwin, in fact!)

3. Fr. Baldwin is Dom James's candidate, and will perhaps let himself be dictated to by Dom J., at least on some things. Will most likely continue Dom J.'s policies in my regard! (Keep me quiet and immobile and

out of monastic discussions as far as possible. Try to shut me up on war, race, etc.)

4. More important—Fr. Baldwin is the favorite of an immature, confused, feminine element among the younger (and not so young) members of the community. This is what I don't like. It portends a kind of wishy-washy, indeterminate, superficial "togetherness"—a kind of monastic aimlessness and flaccidity, in which the place will rapidly lose whatever seriousness it still has left. In other words—with the hard-headed and single-minded obsessiveness of Dom James out of the way, the basic frivolity and unseriousness of so many of *his* monastic policies will come out fully in the open to be exploited by his little favorites under Fr. Baldwin. A rather sick and distressing prospect!

Is there any chance of Fr. Flavian getting it? Too many resent his "leaving the community." His ideas are respected, and those who want a real monastic life will be readier to vote for him. Fr. Matthew has some good ideas, but is too volatile. He hasn't a chance. Neither has Fr. Callistus, whom I respect: I am surprised that there is so little esteem for him. The other "strict" candidate is Fr. Anastasius. But he is so rigid, so emotional, and has so little imagination that he would probably be hopeless, and I think most people sense that.

The candidates I could in conscience vote for are Frs. Flavian, Callistus, Eudes [Bamberger], Timothy (at Rome), Hilarion (hermit)—but of all these and others like them, only Fr. Flavian has any chance whatever.

The prospects for this monastery are not good: weakening, confusion, decadence, irrelevance. We are already well on the way, and even a strong, very definite and clear-sighted administration would have a hard time turning us back. Fr. Baldwin will never provide it.

December 15, 1967

Cold night. Full moon. Fasting has been good this week—though I have not gone very far with it I feel hungry (one solid meal a day—and small one: some soup in the evening). Book from Solesmes on Barsanuphius and John came to review. Began it, then walked out under the moon, impressed with it. And with the laxity of my own life this last year—and worse still in 1966! Perhaps things are slightly better, but I hope next year I can cut down on the visits and contacts. Some things are necessary (like the retreat of the contemplative nuns). Others are not—mere picnics, etc. Glad I cut off going to Willetts. That was really out of place.

I have begun, finally, to write the introduction to the *Time-Life* Bible. It is due in two weeks, and I'll never get it in by then. Great reluctance in getting down to it, but I am surprised to find that once I start it goes ahead pretty smoothly and I seem to enjoy it.

December 18, 1967

Rain yesterday and last night. I did not go down to concelebration and did not get out for a decent walk in the afternoon—but stayed close to the monastery, walked up and down by the woodshed, as when I was Master of Novices. So as to be near to give the conference.

At my conference I thought I owed it to the community to make a clear statement of my position on the abbatial election: and said I would *not* accept, in conscience, under *any* circumstances. I did not elaborate. There are probably a few people around who would vote for me—and more might if I were not a hermit. But I am enough of a maverick and an outsider to be safe. And most of them know how I feel without any need of announcements. But I thought it was best to be definite.

To tell the truth—I think the abbotship, at least as it is understood by the majority of Superiors in the Order, especially those of Dom James's generation, is simply *obsolete*. It is ridiculous to carry on such a pointless charade. Dom James has emptied the whole thing of meaning, not because he was a "bad abbot" but precisely because, in the official mind, he was a "good" one. But even a "good" one does more harm than good: he hurts people and saves the institution. He can't help *using* people—and Dom J. has certainly done that, without being altogether aware of it perhaps.

I refuse absolutely to go through this nonsense of being the "Master" and "Abbas" and "Dom" and running other people's lives—or pretending to—and fighting their resistance, whether sane or neurotic. The worst of it is the constant struggle with those whose submission has to take the form of pseudo-protest: an exhausting battle of self-defeating complexes. That is about all the present set-up seems to be good for. Maybe Dom J. has got me so prejudiced I see it wrongly.

Incidentally, however, Fr. Baldwin is *not* J.'s candidate. I think Dom James would like Fr. Eudes to get it. Eudes is a better man than Baldwin—smarter. But he would *rule*. And that is bad. Baldwin will be less direct—a manipulator and wheedler. But in the long run perhaps the one most acceptable to the majority, easiest for them to bear with. In that case . . . OK!

December 19, 1967

Yesterday—went in to Louisville in rain and mist on the truck with George [Reiter] for a meeting at John Ford's office, about policy for the M[erton] collection at Bellarmine (and the other collections). Paul Birkel, Betty Delius, Pat Oliver, Martha Schumann. It was pleasant in the office on the 9th floor of the Kentucky Home Life Building, looking out north over the river in the fog. I think we got quite a lot done, and all piled back into the elevator with a sense of achievement. We drove up the new river road and then to Bauer's on Brownsboro Road—I had lunch with Pat and Martha, got some food at the supermarket, then over to Bellarmine and did a little work in the M[erton] Room, organizing and identifying material. Finally the sun came out. Marie Charron came (she had a tough time with the stencils of *Journal of My Escape [from the Nazis])* and Tommie O'Callaghan with Colleen. Sat in the sun on the hillside waiting for George to come in the truck, and drove home, reading a xerox of the Colman McCarthy piece (heavily slanted) in *N[ational] C[atholic] R[eporter]*. This is not the right perspective either! Same schizoid active-contemplative split with emphasis on the active side.

When I got back, a pile of mail was waiting, with a Christmas card from one of the Shaker eldresses at Canterbury, N.H. and a nice message. Also a very favorable review of *Mystics and Zen [Masters]* from Hermes. Masui sent it in proof.

Reading Basho again. Deeply moved by the purity and beauty of his travel notes and Haiku.

"All who have achieved real excellence in any art, possess one thing in common, that is, a mind to obey nature, to be one with nature throughout the four seasons of the year. Whatever such a mind sees is flower, and whatever such a mind dreams of is moon. It is only a barbarous mind that sees other than the flower, merely an animal mind that dreams of other than the moon. The first lesson for the artist is, therefore, to learn how to overcome such barbarism and animality, to follow nature, to be one with nature."

(Penguin—p. 72)

I suspect that the Western language and vocabulary could be most misleading here. V.S. "one with nature" as a kind of foggy pantheism. The point: *not seeing something etc.* than what *is*. Seeing it in its *isness*—and not interpreting it or dressing it up with "mind."

In town—George picked up another blank book like this—and some ball-point refills.

December 22, 1967

After a couple of warm, spring-like days (rainy though) it is cold and looks like snow. Real Advent weather. Christmas is very close. In the avalanche of cards, etc., a couple of fat envelopes have arrived with some poems for the magazine I thought of starting: it would be only four issues. *Monk's Pond* (maybe as title). Some good poems from Margaret Randall (sad—sad—about her breakup with Sergio). Others from Keith Wilson, whom I'm going to like, I think. There's also an old unpublished piece on Tibetan mysticism by [Walter Yeeling] Evans-Wentz I might use.

I finished the *Time-Life* Bible Introduction—very glad to get it off my back too! Relieved. I hope I don't get into anything else like that. Yesterday afternoon as I was walking along thinking about it on the road by the Sheepbarn, I consoled myself with the thought I was getting ten dollars a page and then with a shock realized I was getting a *hundred* dollars a page. That didn't make me feel better. On the contrary: that's the trouble! I feel more at home—and write better—when I am doing something for the *Catholic Worker* for nothing.

Idiot monastery business. Sunday I announced tersely at my conference that under no circumstances would I accept the job of abbot. Later, perhaps facetiously, I mimeographed a statement, giving various reasons. I thought the touch was light enough, but today I got an irate note from the Prior blowing off steam about it, saying I had insulted the community, was wildly uncharitable, and comparing me to Bernard Shaw (as a satanic monster of pride). Apparently what troubled people most was the sentence where I said I did not want to spend the rest of my life "arguing about trifles with 125 confused and anxiety-ridden monks." This evidently threw a lot of people into tailspins, thereby proving that I was right.

But in a thing like this it is not enough to be "right." The fact is that the community is full of half-sick people, immensely vulnerable, wasting their lives in petty, neurotic machinations—and one simply does not needle such people. It does no good, and encourages their sickness. Also it is perhaps more the fault of the system than their own. I should not have hurt them. Actually, living apart from the "community," I forget what a hornet's nest it really can be. And all these people suffer intensely and make each other suffer. I have no business stirring it all up and making it worse. The frantic indignation of the Prior was really rather pitiful. Here is a mature and presumably experienced man: and he is so hypersensitive and unbalanced! Furthermore, some people are seriously thinking of him as abbot. God help us if *he* (Anastasius) is elected! It will be even more of a looney bin than it is already.

Actually, it is saddening. And I feel so foolish and helpless. Foolish for having stayed here so long: helpless to do anything to improve matters—not feeling that I should really leave . . . At least I should keep my mouth shut, be more considerate, and also stay out of their way.

It is always uncomfortable to know that you have to live with other people's delusions about you, of one kind or another. No point in overstimulating their imaginations and their resentments!

The only man I think capable of handling the job of abbot adequately—if anyone—is Fr. Flavian. I don't see anyone else to vote for. The saner part of the community seems to be for him. The absentee votes might swing it against him, for Baldwin.

December 23, 1967

It is going to be a cold night. Bright stars, cold woods, silence. A card from M. today: thought of her suddenly the other day, almost saw her it was so vivid. That was the day the card was mailed. From C———, not M———. Certainly I feel less real, somehow, without our constant communication, our sense of being in communion (so intense last year). The drab, futile silences of this artificial life, with all its tensions and its pretenses: but I know it would be worse somewhere else. And marriage, for me, would be terrible! Anyway, that's all over. In a month I'll be 53, and no one in his right mind would get married for the first time at such an age.

Yet this afternoon I wondered if I'd really missed the point of life after all. A dreadful thought!

I gave the hermitage a good cleaning. Burned a lot of Christmas cards and wrappings. Repaired the stile that rotted and broke under me a few weeks ago. Ready for Christmas. Today I went down early for an ordination Mass. Brother Jerome from Vina, subdeacon. Thought of my own subdiaconate nineteen years ago. Things look very different now.

Some good poems came today from Lorine Niedecker. Superb poems in fact! Like her very much. Same kind of fascination as Louis Zukofsky (to whom I owe a letter).

December 24, 1967. Sunday and Christmas Eve

With my breakfast I read an appalling article in Italian on "The Monk in the Church." The Church is a big sacramental machine. In it the monastery has its place as a "center of edification" because of the "exercises of the contemplative life." But aha! There is a problem! If the Bishop is Father of the Diocese and Abbot is Father of the monastery, *Saperisti* ["those in the know"]! Two Fathers! Aha! Another answer. The Bishop is Father of sacraments, the Abbot is Father of asceticism. Valid Sacrament, come from Papa Bishop. Valid obedience and humiliations from Papa Abbot: Viva!

All this is based on Vatican II, which makes me wonder what is so new about *Perfectae caritatis* [Decree on the Appropriate Renewal of the Religious Life]. The whole thing is sickening. The mechanical, cause-and-effect, official machinery of Catholicism. Dreadfully dead, putrid. And yet people are committed to this insane validism, this unchristian obsession: obviously someone like our poor Prior knows nothing else but this moronic one-two-three system of compulsions. And how can you tell them anything else? It is the old hang-up on magic: following the instructions on the bottle to get the infallible effect. A monastery is a place where, though there are more detailed instructions on the bottle, we follow them all meticulously, and the whole Church turns on with our magic tonic. Is LSD more honest? We do this because we think it makes us respectable: we are fully justified by Tierce, Sext, None, Vespers and Compline and by blind obedience to the ascetic Dad, no matter how absurd.

The Church is a great treadmill, and when you turn it, it churns out an ineffable substance called grace, and he who gets his pail full is thereafter untouchable, impervious to everything, neither man nor God can tell him *anything*. He is justified. He is *right*. He has a right to bash your head in if you even think of questioning it.

December 26, 1967

Christmas night—was good. Dom James' last sermon—simple and quite moving. The Mass was uncomplicated and everyone seemed much more awake and alive than last year, apparently because they had had an English

Vigil they enjoyed. Then there was the new church. When I got back I had several hours of curious, light, dream-filled sleep. I could not remember any of the dreams.

Frs. Flavian and Hilarion came up after dinner for a General Chapter of hermits and the three of us drank up all my Mass wine. General subject of conversation: Flavian *must* be abbot and what to do about this place.

Later I went over to Gannons' and then their dog followed me back and I couldn't get rid of it all night. Wouldn't let it in or feed it. Finally when I got up it was so cold I let the dog in—by that time it was starved, ran in triumphantly and jumped on my bed with enormous tail wagging and saying "I love you—*feed* me!" I finally took the dog back about 8:30—everybody worried and Mom G. out looking for it all over the place.

More good poems came in today. I had to write a few letters and finally got out for a short walk.

December 30, 1967

Very cold. Down around zero. Snow. Bright stars. Strange crackings in the big water buckets under the gutters—I forgot to empty them and the bottoms will break out under the pressure of ice!

The other day I had a talk with Fr. Anastasius making (I hope) peace, but he still seems tense and suspicious. I don't think it is really possible to get along completely with him, but with an effort we'll manage, though if he is abbot it would take some doing! I might have to go to Chile (John Harris consulted the *I Ching* for me in Cornwall and turned up the same hexagram I did years ago when thinking of South America.

Fear not
Departure toward the South
Brings good fortune!)

Well. "One must see the great man!" Br. Frederic and Fr. Callistus will be here from Chile for the election and I will talk with them. Also Dom Colomban [abbot of Gethsemani's founding abbey in France].

How great can the man get? Letter from Cardinal Antoniutti reproving our Abbots for their reforming desires has not even been read here, not even the Prior has seen it. Dom James certainly has his own way of handling unpleasant orders from above. Ignoring them. I have learned that from him! I saw a copy of the letter sent by Fr. Anselm Atkins, from Ga. [Conyers] brought by John and June Yungblut who are here now, leaving today.

I have [James] Mooney's wonderful *Ghost Dance* book finally and am reading the new George Steiner book *[Language and Silence]* which critics have to a great extent ignored or treated coldly. Very good.

January 3, 1968. Wednesday

The year struggles with its own blackness.

Dark, wet mush of snow under frozen rain for two days. Everything is curtained in purple greyness and ice. Fog gets in the throat. A desolation of wetness and waste, turning to mud.

Only New Year's Day was bright. Very cold. Everything hard and sparkling, trees heavy with snow. I went for a walk up the side of Vineyard Knob, on the road to the fire tower, in secret hope of "raising the sparks" (as the Hassidim say) and they rose a little. It was quiet, but too bright, as if this celebration belonged not to the new year or to any year.

More germane to this new year is darkness, wetness, ice and cold, the scent of illness.

But maybe that is good. Who can tell?

In a couple of weeks we will have the abbatial election.

In a few days Dom Colomban is coming from Melleray to preside. With him, from Chimay [Belgian monastery], editor of the *Collectanea*.

Fr. Flavian seems to be our best hope for abbot. Dom James told him not to accept the election! Incredible! Fr. Flavian does not intend to follow any such advice if they vote for him!

Yesterday I asked a local sage and oracle—Fr. Roger [Reno]—who was likely to get it. He said it was between Frs. Baldwin and Flavian and Dom Augustine of Georgia. He ought also I think take account of Fr. Anastasius the Prior and the conservatives' candidate. Of these four I believe Fr. Anastasius is the one Dom James would settle for because then in effect he could continue to dominate the course of things in the monastery.

January 4, 1967

You shall not die in the bluegrass land of A. . . .
rather the gods intend you for Elysion
with golden Rhadamanthos at the world's end.

(Fitzgerald's Homer)

The question of Chile is bound to come up when Fr. Callistus and Br. Frederic are here for the election. I have no intention of accepting superiorship there if I can help it (again—I can always refuse an election), nor do I have any intention of volunteering to go there (unless the situation here under a new abbot becomes impossible.)

The morning was dark, with a harder bluer darkness than yesterday. The hills stood out stark and black, the pines were black over thin pale sheets of snow. A more interesting and tougher murkiness. Snowflakes began to blow when I went down to the monastery from the hermitage, but by 10:30 the sun was fairly out and it was rapidly getting colder.

By afternoon it looked like a New Year—with fresh, cold light and a biting wind burnishing the frozen snow. A wind out of the NW from the Great Lakes.

After cleaning up the cabinet where I keep writing materials (and finding two reams of paper I didn't know I had) I went out for a walk in the wind.

I am getting down to work on *Nat Turner* for *Katallagete* [Southern magazine]—a clever but false book I think.

Evening—new moon—snow hard crackling and squealing under my rubber boots. The dark pines over the hermitage. The graceful black fans and branches of the tall oaks between my field and the monastery. I said Compline and looked at the cold valley and tasted its peace. Who is entitled to such peace? I don't know. But I would be foolish to leave it for no reason.

Incredible barbarity of the Viet Nam War—the weapons used, the ways of killing utterly defenseless people. It is appalling. Surely the moral sense of this country is eroded—except that there are protests and how few really know even a little of the facts! Certainly this can't go on: the country is under judgment.

January 5, 1967

It is turning into the most brilliant of winters.

At 6:45—stepped out into the zero cold for a breath of air. Dark. Brilliance of Venus hanging as it were on one of the dim horns of Scorpio. Frozen snow. Deep wide blue-brown tracks of the tractor that came to get my gas tank that other day when everything was mucky. Bright hermitage settled quietly under black pines. I came in from saying the Little Hours [Office during the day] and the Rosary in the snow with nose in pain and sinuses aching. Ears burn now in the silent sunlit room. Whisper of the gas fire. Blue shadows where feet have left frozen prints out there in the snow. I drank a glass of dry sherry and am warm! Lovely morning! How lovely life can be!

Nat Turner is nothing but Styron's own complex loneliness as a Southern writer. A well-fashioned book, but little or nothing to do with the real Turner—I have no sense that this fastidious and analytical mind is that of a prophet.

George Steiner's book *Language and Silence* is an important one and I can't read more than half a page without having to get up and walk up and down and let all the ideas sink in a little. Very much on my wavelength. Interesting criticism of F. R. Leavis—both criticism and appreciation—failure of the peculiar kind of integrity Leavis represents because it closes in on itself, refuses the future, refuses most of the present, and then becomes mere snobbery. I am now in the article on Lévi-Strauss. The section on the Jews is harrowing, lucid, deep, everyone should know this!

January 6, 1967. Epiphany

Damp, leaden darkness. Falling snow (small wet flakes). Accidents. Yesterday in the frozen brightness I fell and badly bruised my knee—for a moment the pain gripped my guts with nausea and I thought I would pass out or vomit. Reeled—nowhere to sit. I think I may have broken the camera—the Rollerflex—i.e. bashed it so that the back may be letting in light. Will see what happens to this film in Gregory Griffin's tank.

Also another accident: yesterday morning woke up at the sound of a frozen gallon jug of water bursting—and the unfrozen water running out all over the floor. And this morning dropped an egg as I was getting it out of the icebox. My hands don't feel and grip properly (awful clumsiness trying to load the camera).

Last night curious dreams, perhaps about death. I am caught suddenly in a flood which has risen and cut off my way of escape—not *all* escape, but my way to where I want to go. Can go back to some unfamiliar place over there—where? Fields, snow, upriver, a road, a possible bridge left over from some other dream.

(Sudden recollection and as it were a voice: "*It is not a bridge*"—i.e. no bridge necessary!)

Yesterday—I went into the Guesthouse to see Dom Colomban and P. Charles Dumont who arrived Friday night—tales of their journey by air from Paris, and especially the wild ride from Kennedy to LaGuardia to make their connection.

P. Charles speaks very softly with a Belgian accent and I can hardly distinguish what he is saying. Dom Colomban heartily approves my desire *not* to be Abbot. Lamentations on the abbatial condition (he is perfectly right).

January 8, 1967

Bitter cold. Zero. Clear. Frozen snow. At eight the red sun rose over the snowy woods with an old bit of con-trail bent over it in the sky like a circumflex accent.

I finished (Saturday and with additions yesterday) the short piece on Pasternak's Georgian Letters which Helen Wolff asked me to write. Am sending off today final tape of *Vow of Conversation* for typing. Working on *Nat Turner.* An ambiguous book, brilliant in parts, uncertain and tedious in others.

George Steiner on Marxist critics, etc. Still interesting, but not the best part of the book. Useful however.

Yesterday Dom Colomban got me before Mass in the Sacristy and asked me to come to dinner with him, Dom James and Fr. Charles in that Guest House Room. Drank white New York wine and talked French and had a long conversation with him afterwards—about the election etc. And about an invitation which has come from Dom Leclercq for me to attend a monastic-ecumenical meeting in Bangkok! Dom C. approves on principle but of course it is up to the next Abbot. The meeting is in December—but by that time probably the whole of SE Asia will be at war. (Though the Presidential election may make a difference. I doubt it however!)

People are tense over the abbatial election. Br. Clement ruptured his ulcer. Fr. Anastasius down with a heavy cold, Fr. Baldwin looking anxious, drawn and thin. Fr. Flavian looks best of the candidates—happy and confident—and the community is full of wild indefinite ideas of dark horses and strange possibilities—all the obvious choices having become half credible at best: from too much speculation.

I tried to correct this by a word or two in my Sunday conference—the last unless the new abbot reappoint me for it.

Meanwhile there has been a last-minute political flurry to make sure the community votes for an English choral office before someone cool to the idea becomes abbot (I don't think any of the candidates would be against it really). But just to make *sure*. And Cardinal Antoniutti's letter remains of course unheard of here. Amusing.

I wonder if Dom James will be capable of settling down in his hermitage and keeping his fingers entirely out of community politics. I doubt it. I think he will make things a bit uncomfortable for the new abbot. Certainly I wouldn't want the job with him hovering around in the background and with his little clique still active in the business end of the monastery. I am sure people will be running to him and using him against this new abbot.

The huge icicle on the SW corner of my porch is a good five feet long—it reaches almost ½ way to the ground!

Evening.

Cold all day—never stopped freezing, even in the sun. That long icicle seems to be several inches longer. Tonight the cold is bitter. Last night the thermometer at the monastery said 8 below and at Gannons' 15 below. I can't tell by my sheltered thermometer on the porch. It was probably well below zero here. Felt like it.

Down at the monastery it seems, surprisingly, as if there were quite a few people going to vote for Fr. Anastasius. Certainly not the smartest people in the community. Many of the former brothers—who were reputed to be against him—turn out to be *for* him. They might end up by swinging it for him, which would really be a disaster for the monastery. At least it would mean the end of any real hope of openness and development (except such development as he would be talked into by the liturgy people, because he might listen to them). He is a closed, unimaginative, opinionated, emotional man, and moreover has a temper. God preserve us!

January 10, 1968

Days of gloomy and sunless cold. In the dusk of evening, walking out on the edge of my hill, with all the hard outlines of this world lost in white snow, it is like walking in space. Woods hang like clouds over the invisible fields and bottoms.

Yesterday I would have gone to town but it snowed, the roads were bad. I came back up and finished *Nat Turner* and wrote my article—after lunch with Fr. Charles, ill and alone (the two abbots out to the Little Sisters of the Poor and to a hospital where two of our professed are—to get them to renounce their votes).

Bonhoeffer says, "It is only when one sees the anger and wrath of God hanging like grim realities over the heads of one's enemies that one can know something of what it means to love and forgive them."

This is the key to the dishonesty of Styron's treatment of Nat Turner. Styron "enjoys" wrath as an indulgence which is not seen as having anything serious to do with religion whatever. Religion suddenly appears on the last page as a suggested preposterous reconciliation (in purely sentimental terms). To treat a prophet of wrath while having no idea of the meaning of wrath, and reduce that wrath to the same level as masturbation fantasies! The whole thing is an affront to the Negro—though it is well-meant, even "sympathetic."

It reduced me finally to desperation!

How can white people do anything but cheat and delude the Negro, when that is only part of their own crass self-delusion and bad faith!

January 11, 1968

The abbatial election is the day after tomorrow.

Yesterday I went down to the monastery on an errand to Fr. Charles and Dom Colomban in the Guest House, and in the corridor ran into Fr. Callistus and Br. Frederic, who had just arrived by plane from Chile, sunburned by the Chilean summer. Fr. Anastasius was talking to them. He looks tired and worn.

It really does seem, incredibly, that he has a very good chance of being elected, and of course I see why now. He is first of all a conservative, and then he is the candidate of all those inarticulate, unimaginative people who have passively accepted the new changes without really wanting them and who in their hearts want only security and no more change—or only slow change. For these people, monastic life means chiefly a secure routine. They *like law.* They want obedience and rule, because it simplifies their existence. It *reassures* them. It makes life safe and predictable. It guarantees that they will not be confronted with more than they can cope with. They have bent their wills to that. They want it confirmed.

Fr. Anastasius is the one man who will do that: he represents the status quo more than anyone else. And suddenly I realize that *this is what most of the community probably want*—just a secure routine, dignified by a certain continuity with the past and a general atmosphere of worship and obedient endurance (up to a very safe point!). Also it can be made to look like courage. He is a virile, aggressive, hard-working character, and I admit this is good. The cenobitic types who vote for him will represent a genuine reaction against the femininity of Fr. Baldwin, his flexibility, his openness, his unpredictability.

The election will be decided on what way they go who vote first for Dom Augustine and Fr. Baldwin (assuming Fr. B. does not get it and I much doubt he will though he is still favorite). If they swing to Fr. Flavian—who represents a high and genuinely monastic ideal (but openness too) then he'll get it. If they fear Fr. Flavian as too lofty and incomprehensible and as a "hermit," they will swing to Fr. Anastasius. For too many Fr. Flavian is a "threat" because they don't understand him and don't know what to expect of him.

If it turns out to be between Fr. Flavian and Fr. Baldwin, then I think it is hard to predict how the voters for Fr. A. will divide between them.

My own position: obviously for me Fr. Anastasius would be a very difficult superior—harder even than Dom James. He would be very obstructive and negative in everything that regards my writing, correspondence, other contacts. At best he would tolerate my present situation insofar as it has been passed on by Dom James. But he would also be looking for trouble and glad when he could find it. Though he is strongly anti-hermit, he might prefer to have me *out* of the community and in the hermitage and just do his best to isolate me here completely—as Dom James wanted to. If in doubt about any of my affairs he will consult Dom James and Dom J. will give out a harder line for me *through another* than he would dare to do directly. But it will certainly guarantee my solitude.

However, the real issue is not how easy or how hard it may be to get on with the next abbot—but the honesty and faith of my own commitment. Hence the need to concentrate on the *main thing.*

This still needs clarifying.

It is not simply a matter of saying I have vows here and that's that. Certainly I mean to keep my vows and stay within the Order—also to live up as far as possible to my hermit commitment.

How far my writing and my contacts imply a further commitment is another question.

For instance if I am completely silenced here, and if the Chile foundation wants me very badly, should I pull up stakes and go there? Of course if I am *sent*—no problem!

Should I regard my situation as that of Pasternak under Zhdanor and Co. and go on working as best I can with a certain vital protest *inside* of my silence? There is no doubt that it was right and best for Pasternak to *stay* in Russia, even and especially after the Nobel Prize affair.

Bonhoeffer:

"Who stands his ground? Only the man for whom the ultimate criterion is not his reason, his principles, his conscience, his freedom, his virtue, but who is ready to sacrifice all these things when he is called to obedient and responsible action in faith and exclusive allegiance to God—the responsible man seeks to make his whole life a response to the question and call of God. Where are these responsible men?"

January 13, 1968

The day of the election. In a few minutes I start down to early concelebration. It is still night (4:30). When I got up snow was falling and now it turns to rain.

Yesterday it took a long time just to vote for the scrutators, and what will it be today? I don't expect it to become much before evening. However—yesterday we also voted on whether any legislation of the General Chapter, making the abbatial term *temporary*, should be retroactive. In other words if this new man's term should automatically be limited if that becomes law—(otherwise he would be for life anyway).

A surprisingly large majority voted *against* a life-abbot—and for a temporary abbotship. In the circumstances that was a very good sign: everyone was relieved by it because it is a sign that the community is sick of the kind of authority represented by Dom James (though well disposed to him personally). They don't want a power-type who wants to be on for life and have a completely free hand.

Obviously a temporary abbotship has other disadvantages. But the reaction against power-establishment is hopeful. I feel more optimistic about today's election.

I happened to glance through some old notes of mine—novitiate conferences on the vows—dating back ten years. Incredible and quite embarrassing. I was astonished to find them so legalistic, so rigid, so narrow. Yet in those days I thought myself quite broad and many regarded me as a dangerous radical. I was only doing what I thought I had to do—teaching what all the authorities held! That it now seems completely unrealistic and false is a sign that there has really been something of a revolution. Felt the same about the Bishops' Pastoral.[11] It is in some sense an advance, but it seems to lack a real inner sense of the Church: they are still talking of a Church of *Law*, and they are in a bind they can't really get out of.

Bonhoeffer is right—people "in the world" who may seem to be "criminal types—small people with small aims" etc. turn out sometimes to be "much more under grace than under wrath, but the Christian *world in particular stands much more under wrath than under grace.*" I think of my notes on the vows in this light! And I pray that today in our election it may be grace and not wrath we stand under.

January 15, 1967. St. Paul the Hermit

Two momentous days, heavy with snow and heavier with happenings. Fr. Flavian was elected abbot by a large majority and surprisingly fast (third ballot). Fr. Anastasius was nowhere—I got as many votes as he did, although I had made it doubly and triply clear that I could never accept. Everyone is very pleased and everyone also is quite clear about what the election means: a definite option for the *new* and an expression of final dissatisfaction with all represented by Dom James, since Fr. Flavian is first of all clearly a man with a mind and ideas of his own, and one who definitely stood up *against* Dom James's ideas. His going to the hermitage was largely

11 Merton is here referring to a Pastoral Letter published by the United States Bishops in November 1967 titled, "The Church in Our Day."

a protest against the futile job of running a foundation under Dom J., and Dom J. has not really forgiven this.

So therefore it is clear that this was one of the candidates who would be completely independent of Dom J. and of his policies.

Result—a real sense of liberation. Almost a shock to realize that the secrecy, the suppression and the manipulation exercised by Dom James no longer dominate us. That we have a man we can talk to, work with frankly, exchange ideas with, propose real experiments to (not just tinkering with the liturgy!).

The election was peaceful, even happy. Of course with all the preliminaries it took time to get moving and we were in there forty-five minutes before starting to vote on the first ballot. Then after that it was about an hour before the result was announced. Fr. Flavian was already an obvious winner with over thirty votes and he doubled them in the next two ballots. Dom Augustine of Georgia got a few votes, Fr. Baldwin was second in the running throughout, the only other significant competitor.

Between ballots, the cloister full of people reading, I read long chunks of David Jones's *Anathemata*, somehow very moving and sonorous in that charged silence, and one felt a blessing over it all even before having any idea how it would turn out.

It was all over by about 9:30.

By that time it was snowing again.

I stayed at the monastery most of the day, as I had a talk with Dom Augustine and Dom Eusebius [Wagner, of New Clairvaux, California]. Then after dinner an interview in the gatehouse with an ex-nun—rather an unusual little person, going through a period of trial and rejection but I think quite holy and with perhaps a real call to sanctity (though she is thought by some to be crazy). A very simple, innocent little being with great aspirations, who seems to get around in an extraordinary way. (Was at the Council, i.e., on the fringes of it and met a lot of people.)

Sunday—yesterday—the confirmation had still not come through from the Abbot General at La Oliva in Spain. I helped Dom Colomban put through a phone call to this monastery lost in the hills of Navarre. Some talk with the operator in Madrid. The cable sent the day before about the election had not yet reached the General. The election was confirmed and after None and a great fuss of a community photograph in the Chapter Room, Dom Flavian was installed and I made my promise of obedience with a great sense of meaning—i.e. a sense of authentic *human* possibilities in a context of real friendship among all those who are F.'s generation and who will collaborate with him now.

A real sense of community with all the other men who will really do most of the work—choir and brothers. Dom James's policy was to keep everyone separated and play them all against each other, trying to keep them uninformed or only partially informed.

This morning—a special concelebration and a proper Mass composed by Fr. Chrysogonus. Very free one too. As a "farewell" to Dom James. However, Dom J. has not even moved out of his office. Dom Flavian has a room in the guesthouse and it does not look as if Dom J. will be out of there for a couple of weeks yet.

At Communion, as I approached the altar, I suddenly realized that the bond of understanding that really does exist among the men here now, among themselves and with Dom Flavian, is really strong enough to do something—and to do much—with the institutional structure, or in spite of it. That if Dom F. himself is for change, the blocks set up by an authoritarian system cannot be completely decisive—though they can still be a nuisance.

I realize how seriously I misjudged the community the other day—saying they were all conservatives and wanted security above all. They voted with courage and imagination and their option was for openness, growth, greater freedom, real progress. Also, as I realized at my conference yesterday afternoon, they have summed up the situation pretty well and can *express* what their real hopes are—a man who is open, whom you can talk to, who will admit his mistakes and not push them off on to someone else (one of the brothers said this!), who will listen to new ideas, who has definite principles but is willing to tolerate different ideas, etc.

The result of this election has been a real sense of a *bond* between us all, and already at this morning's Mass Dom J. seemed suddenly remote from all this, a stranger to it, and the farewell really meant *farewell.* Certainly he is honored and remembered for the good he has done, but also the isolation in which he has always really lived now appears for what it is. He has lived in the midst of the community deeply isolated from it, yet manipulating its inmost heart, alienating it, and at the same time soothing it with clichés and with a dramatic "presence" and influence. Certainly he has sacrificed himself very much, but one feels it was for the institution rather than for the people in it and he expected them to let him sacrifice *them* in the same way. To some extent they did, some more, some less. But now they are done with that: they want to build a real community, not a corporation.

January 19, 1968

I have been sick with flu for several days—and badly.

It began Tuesday (I caught it of course in the community where it has been going around. The election was a good way to catch it!). After dinner I went for a walk in the woods and could hardly drag myself back to the hermitage. Went to bed early. The next day I probably would have pulled out of it quickly if I could have stayed in bed, but I had to go down to the monastery—once again I would hardly get back to the hermitage, and went straight to bed. Thursday I had to go down again (to take my laundry bag and to tell Fr. Charles Dumont that I would not be able to spend the afternoon with him) and that really fixed me. So I fell into bed without dinner and lay there for sixteen hours or more hot under the blankets, aching, smashed in stupid sleep, with my head like a music box playing over and over and over "The Shadow of Your Smile" (version of Ives Montgomery). I am up with a dry cough, gut in a shambles, high fever, nauseated by everything, unable to say Office or do anything whatever except occasionally get up to make tea and take a pill.

Yesterday afternoon was pretty horrible. I haven't felt so sick in a long time.

Today, after a deep, sweaty sleep, I felt much better, said Lauds and Mass and had a light breakfast, went back to bed, but the sun was up bright and I felt alive again. Only problem—I couldn't move around without sweating profusely.

Had some soup and eggs at noon and began to feel myself again. Went back to lie down, and everything began to be seen more sharply and clearly experienced: sound of a truck on the road ¼ mile away. Sense of where I am, where the road is, of the woods around, sense of having a world to be part of, not just to be a hump of matter.

Curious what thoughts came to me with deep conviction—"Must not go back to the Willetts'" etc.

Went down again to the monastery in mid-afternoon.

They are on retreat and someone told me the retreat-master had started out by saying Buddhists were life-denying and Christians life-affirming! I couldn't care less about such platitudes. What does he mean by *life?*

An experience like this sickness is purifying and renewing because it reminds you not to be too attached to the narrow view of what you think life is—the immediate task, the business of getting done what you think is important, of enjoying what you want right now, etc. Sickness pulls the rug from under all of it. Haven't been able to do anything, think anything. Yet in the evening—the bare trees against the metallic blue of the evening were incredibly beautiful: as suspended in a kind of Buddhist emptiness. Does it occur to anyone that Sunyata is the very ground of life?

January 21, 1968. III Sunday after Epiphany

Another grey day. Snow still fairly thick on the ground, and now black with coal dust around the monastery.

I did not concelebrate, but ate dinner at the monastery.

In the afternoon went out for the first decent walk in almost a week—out to the Pond by St. Bernard's field with its green ice and its dead trees and silences.

When I was making supper someone came banging on the door. It was Brother Thomas from the monastery with a message that Sy Freedgood was dead. I went down to call his wife Anne, and found out that his house in Bridgehampton had burned down last night and he was not able to get out. Suffering with bursitis he had been taking a lot of pills and drinking too and was probably too groggy to escape—a very tragic thing—yet somehow last spring everything about him pointed to death—a kind of dysfunction. (His accident on the way here was sign enough!) I could not talk to Anne, who was on the way from Bridgehampton to New York, but spoke to one of her friends in the N.Y. apartment. Poor Sy! I wired Lax, who is now in Olean.

Before I heard the news I was playing some Mozart Quintets on the record player and enjoying them. I no longer feel like listening to anything, Mozart or anything else.

Sy's grandiose plans in the spring—for getting me out "like Faulkner" once a year, etc. etc. We did have a pretty good day in Lexington!

It is already a hard year, and I don't know what else is coming, but I have a feeling it is going to be hard all the way and for everybody.

January 23, 1968

Poor Sy! Mass for him yesterday (Library Chapel) and today (hermitage). I remember so many things: Sy and Rice at my baptism; the time we rented the house in Woodstock for the summer and then didn't go—a good thing—(I sublet my apartment to him). Bramachari. Sy's place in Long Beach, the brothers and uncles. That crazy paper we started.

Sy trying to teach me Judo on a sandbar in the lagoon behind Long Beach. I don't remember if he was at Olean—maybe.

Last year he was here looking terrible in his fur hat and bandaged face and I knew he was finished. Yet he was full of ideas and plans. We made a voluble, profane tape. Talked of his analysis. And his analyst on whom he greatly depended. And death, which he had very much on his mind. It must have been tough on Anne to cope with all his drive and all his despair. (In Bardstown—he wasted time and money sending an insulting telegram to some superior at *Fortune*, about some job he (Sy) was really not doing.)

A dark, wet night. Yesterday much of the snow melted and when I woke rain was falling. It may be drizzling still.

I have got most of the material together for the first issue of *Monks Pond* and am happy with it—especially the selections from Keith Wilson, Al Hamilton—most especially the selections from Shen Hui[12] which are extraordinary.

I am reading Reza Arasteh's fine book *Final Integration* and I think it brings a whole lot of threads together and makes much sense—as opposed to so much of the fragmentary and short-sighted views of sociology and psychology in America. This really has something new to say—and yet it is in line with the wisdom of the millennia. And very germane to monasticism.

January 24, 1968

Brighter weather—quite cold. Bitter cold morning with blue clouds and sun trying to get through. Later it was fully bright. The last two days I have participated in dialog with a group together with Fr. Vincent Martin the retreat-master. Quite good. He is an unusual person—was a Benedictine in

12 The Shen Hui article did appear in the first volume of *Monks Pond*, a small journal edited by Merton in 1968, four issues in all. "Selections from the Dialogues of the Zen Master Shen Hui (8th century A.D.)," with an introduction by Wei-wu-wei. The four issues of *Monks Pond* were reissued in a facsimile edition in one volume by the University of Kentucky Press, Lexington, in 1989.

China, then a Lt. Col. in the Chinese Army in World War II, then imprisoned in the same camp with Fr. David [Murphy, of Gethsemani] and the Chinese Trappists. Then studied at Harvard under Gordon Allport. He is a monk of Vallyermo but after a year at Weston has been a couple of years at Dormition Abbey in Jerusalem. A very likeable and intelligent person with good ideas. He seems to be giving a good retreat. Anyway the dialog discussions were fruitful. This afternoon he went up to the hermitage with Fr. Eudes and Fr. Matthew and I got to know him better.

January 26, 1968

Two nights ago—early morning, before dawn: the old moon—dying crescent—hung in the South with Antares (of Scorpius) almost caught in the crescent. And as if the moon were holding up Scorpius in a balancing act. A forbidding sign. Venus nearby.

Dom James has still not moved out to the woods—is still in fact in his office. Dom Flavian waits in the Guesthouse for him to move. Some of my mail still comes to me with a mark of Dom J. on it: for instance a telegram from Bob Giroux about Sy's death.

Last evening Bro. Victor came up with a can of water—Fr. Hilarion with him—and told me an American spy ship had been captured by North Koreans. A weird story, with ominous repercussions. Johnson rattling the sabre, calling up reserves, etc. etc. It didn't sound like something seriously believable—though I don't doubt the ship is where it is: captured. It sounded like some sort of a contrived "incident," too phony to amount to anything, so phony it's just embarrassing . . .

But today again I heard Washington is making a big thing out of it, and on my way back from dinner I stopped to talk to Andy Boone who was picking up the ashcans from the furnace room. He said, "What do you think about the war?" I said, "Is war really declared?" He said, "It will be by two o'clock tonight."

Well, one always takes Andy Boone with a grain of salt.

But Bro. Clement gave some details. The whole thing sounds incredibly fishy, absurdly so: a completely contrived "incident"—not even the simplest appear to be convinced of it. Even Andy Boone said, "What was that boat doing in there anyway?" And why no signals?

Maybe Johnson has finally got his big war, but he still hasn't got the country with him. Never was anyone such an unconvincing fraud! On the other hand, if he is determined to have a world war in Asia, there will be a pile of trouble here at home. I don't relish the prospect! (Even Andy Boone is talking of "Civil War.")

Got some letters written in the morning, though this is harder and harder to do. So much of the mail seems completely pointless. And in fact a great deal of it is simply a matter of someone trying to get your name for something, to line you up for some cause or other, or to engage you in a chain of pseudo-events and pseudo-decisions: or more simply to get some money out of you: or to use you in some way.

This afternoon—a quiet walk in the sun: again down by St. Bernard's pond. Gannons' dog tagged along—that pretty collie bitch with a feathery tail—running busily into everything, immense interest in all kinds of smells, mysteries, secrets in the bushes and in the grass. She ran on the melting ice, rolled in the manure spread over the pasture (rolled twice!), came out of the brush with her tail full of dead leaves and in a final paroxysm of energy chased a cat into the cowbarn. A completely successful afternoon for *her* anyway!!

I had Buber's *Ten Rungs* in my pocket and couldn't read a line of it, only looked at the sun, the dead grass, the green soft ice, the blue sky, and felt utterly blank. Will there never be any peace on earth in our lifetime? Will they never do anything but kill, and then kill some more? Apparently they are caught in that impasse: the system is completely violent and involved in violence, and there is no way out but violence: and that leads only to more violence. Really—what is ahead but the apocalypse?

January 31, 1968

Clear, thin new moon appearing and disappearing between slow slate blue clouds—and the living black skeletons of the trees against the evening sky. More artillery than usual whumping at Knox. It is my fifty-third birthday.

We do not have a war—only "the Pueblo crisis," with senators shouting like complete morons about "wiping those yellow bastards off the map" or words to that effect. Complete inanity.

But the guns at Knox nevertheless shake all my windows.

A warm, clear, quiet afternoon. I did not work but went for a walk down to the pond. All the water is clear of ice except in one shady corner. There were some wild ducks down at the end. They rose and circled and then headed south into a strong wind that broke up their formation. What are they doing going south now? Maybe the winter is far from over, though this was a springlike afternoon.

The other day I was in town. It embarrasses me. Of course, I had to see the proctologist and that is always embarrassing—with your head down and your asshole up in the air, trying to talk about Mexican Indians. I had more money than usual, so bought some records—and then felt guilty. But the new Dylan record (John Wesley Hardin) is his best. Very encouraging. He'd had a bad accident and everyone thought he was finished.

Also got Coltrane's *Ascension* which is shattering. A fantastic and prophetic piece of music.

I keep getting more and more good stuff for *Monks Pond.* Today some fragments of Paul Klee translated by Anselm Hollo. Very welcome. I think it will be a good magazine.

In town I visited Tommie O'Callaghan, recovering from an operation. She is at home now. Lovely photographs of the children taken by Gene Meatyard. First time I have been to Dan [Walsh]'s apartment in Lenahan Hall. George picked us up there to drive home.

Dennis Goulet [University of Indiana, Bloomington] came Saturday and brought Richard Chi, who is a very interesting person. I wish I could find out more about the Zen Master he studied under. Hope to see more of him. He brought a lovely and mysterious painting of a 17th-century Zen monk, Tao Chi. Fascinating—very direct and arresting picture! A landscape with a gripping subliminal quality. Goulet said "like Van Gogh"—and yet it isn't really. Not the Van Gogh swirl and flame form, a different kind of structure, more mysterious, more dreamlike, more detached than Van Gogh.

February 4, 1968. Fifth Sunday after Ephiphany

In the east, blue and purple clouds laid on lightly as if with a dry brush—and clear blue sky above them. The field is heavy with frost. Gas is getting low in the tank—repeated promises on the part of Brother A. that he will refill it, but he doesn't. I still have enough for a few days maybe, if I ration it.

Haven't done much work in the last week or so—too many interruptions. For instance, Friday afternoon just as I was getting ready to type some of the *Geography of Lograire*, the Chaplain from Nazareth showed up with Fr. Malcolm Boyd and I was glad to meet him, yet felt I talked too much and too wildly—or anyway too irresponsibly, perhaps overcompensating for the fact that I'd rather *not* have been visited.

Yesterday, Carolyn Hammer, John Jacob Niles and Rena with Bob Shepherd and Hanna came over. This was a pleasant visit in the field and warm sun by the Pond, and I enjoyed it. Salad and wine! And good talk, and not too long. After they left I had time to clean up my place a bit and burn some of the paper and boxes and bags that have piled up since Christmas.

Nevertheless I have to face the fact that there are too many people coming around, and a lot of them are simply busting in uninvited and are a nuisance. And going to town is a bigger nuisance. True, I have to see the doctor, and there are still things to do, but more and more I have a sense of untruth and ambiguity in all my "social" existence, from my conferences in the monastery to visits with people from outside.

A few rare exceptions. Richard Chi for instance is probably one I can talk with on a level of real communication (Buddhism). I enjoy the Niles, Carolyn, etc. but with Carolyn there is a kind of estrangement—she is closing in on a kind of defensive conservatism all round. I guess she is lonely and afraid, if the truth be told. She distrusts my radicalism on some points, and feels I fail her somehow. Yet I myself see no real value in "radical action" for my own part. There is nothing really effective I can do and apart from saying what I think (as in the book *Faith and Violence*) there is nothing to contribute. Besides, things are so fluid and so uncertain that an opinion loses its significance in three weeks. I cannot get involved in the surface of activity that concerns itself only with immediate gestures and demonstrations, and perhaps the best thing for me to do is simply to shut up—until something really new happens.

At this point I am getting more and more letters from people wondering if with a new Abbot, I am "coming out" to join in all kinds of things, to speak here, to lecture there, to give retreats, to meet students, to join in marches. Not only is Dom Flavian just as opposed to all that as Dom James was, but the Order itself would not countenance it—and I myself feel that it would be futile and irrelevant for me—not what I am called to be doing.

February 6, 1968

"The Pueblo incident" has not turned into anything. Johnson obviously can't afford a second war. And the whole thing simply shows up the folly of the U.S. trying to police the whole world with spying engineers of one kind or another—and with fuzz-armies.

Somehow the conflict seems much clearer: it is really racial, and the racism of the U.S., though armed with everything under the sun, is up a blind alley. It has no future—except perhaps a kind of fat, fascist desperation.

A sunny day, more like spring—after the usual cold night and freezing morning. I am not writing letters, though I have many that require answers. So much of the mail is utterly pointless. Except for some that come from kids, high school or college, really suffering from the stupidity and inhumanity of their elders. Some of these people must be real bastards!

I got some of the *Geography of Lograire* on paper—so much work needs to be done on it, but typing is a step. Then I can correct, revise, add. But this is not something you just sit down to every day.

Bob Giroux sent some [Cesare] Pavese. I may write on him, though it is foolish to branch out more. Yet I really do like him.

I need quiet. I need to get down to more reading and meditation. The problem of people is of my own making—as problem and as ambiguity.

February 8, 1968

Yesterday—Feast of St. Romuald incidentally—finally got a mimeo copy of *Journal of My Escape from the Nazis.* Naomi has written repeatedly about it. Work on the new liturgy books has held up everything else here. I forget when I sent the ms to Marie Charron to type—maybe September of last year. I wanted the stencils for November. Got them finally in December, and have been waiting ever since for them to be run off. Yesterday, when I looked at the first and only copy so far, I found to my dismay that some of the chapters (unnumbered in the original) were in the wrong place—the dog cemetery, for example, comes before I met B. And so B. is alluded to and she has not yet been introduced. And so on. Marie C. must have dropped the ms. and got it back together wrong. Yet I thought I carefully numbered the pages in pencil. Maybe not. I send the text today.

Whatever the mess—this is a book I am pleased with—this *Journal of Escape*. I have always thought of it as one of my best. Not that it holds together perfectly as a book, but there is good writing and it comes from the center where I have really experienced myself and my life. It represents a very vital and crucial—and fruitful—moment of my existence. Perhaps now I am returning to some such moment of breakthrough. I hope I am. I won't have many more chances! *Geography of Lograire* may in parts have some of the same sardonic vitality, but with much more involvement and complexity.

World Revolution. Strangely enough, the obsessive efforts of the U.S. to *contain* by violence all revolutionary activity anywhere in the world only precipitate revolution. And guarantee that it has to be violent.

1. Soviet policy of "peaceful coexistence" has finally been made to appear ludicrous by VN war. North VN *forced* into the fight, forced to drop the cautious Soviet line and go over to the uncompromising line of MAD.
2. Non-violence in Civil Rights—has been completely discredited by white racist violence which is entirely insensitive to meaning of non-violence. Which is dominated by its own obsessions and myths, and creates violence. Self-fulfilling prophecy.
3. The draft is necessary not to defend the country but to maintain an army big enough to police the world and put down revolution the way the Alabama State Troopers put down Negro demonstrations: of course the help of national armies is also required.
4. This policy justifies the Chinese one of starting guerrilla war everywhere possible so as to involve and scatter U.S. forces.
5. This in turn encourages the desperation of resisters and race revolutionists at home.
6. The present policies of the U.S. make clear that a semblance of world peace and order depends on *a revolution in the U.S.* which will align this country *with* Third World revolutionaries, not *against* them.
7. But such a revolution cannot possibly succeed. At least not with the present line-up, Black Power—Hippies—Peace Movement—Acid-heads and Poets against the U.S. army, government, police.
8. Johnson will attempt some sort of compromise gesture that may effectively lull the awakening suspicions and questions of "good ordinary folks" and draw the sting out of much of the resistance. Then when he is re-elected—step up police repression and control by force, subtle and

overt, perhaps withdrawing to some extent from vast foreign involvements—a more fascist idolatrous idea.

9. A lot depends on what happens to American money. If there is an economic collapse . . .

No pronouncements. No statements. No fuss. No "action." Sit quiet and use your eyes and ears and your head. Try to understand the meaning of events in these next months. This is a critical year for the U.S. and for the world. Everything is crystallizing out much more clearly and uncompromisingly than at any time since World War II. We'll see what happens! Meanwhile, let no one imagine Johnson is merely an uncouth idiot. He has both the clearsightedness and the fatal blindness of the operator who manipulates for immediate pragmatic ends and cannot *see* the ultimate human consequences of his manipulation. And he controls more power at the moment than any human being in the history of the world—though he can't make that power do what he really wants. It is the power of a Saul and of a Goliath. Vulnerable to some black David, maybe. But that one is not yet on the scene as far as I know.

That demented woman, Marie Tadié, is threatening to sue the monastery for $15,000, because I finally persuaded Dom James to drop her as agent before he retired—rather than pass her on to the next abbot. Who could be expected to handle such a porcupine? Her megalomania, autism and greed are unlimited. I was very imprudent to let her start selling books for me in France. When? Perhaps in 1960 or 61. She then began putting herself forward as my "exclusive agent and translator." Trouble began seriously in 1963 or 64 when she sold the *Black Revolution* separately in France and then in Italy, then in Barcelona (Catalan!). I began, too late, trying to control her, and to prevent her from taking over everything I had. I did manage to keep her hands off the German rights. In 1965 when I moved to the hermitage I wanted to break off all business with her and let the publishers handle everything. Dom James would not do this. Instead he started to deal with her himself and got into untold difficulties, complicating matters still further. I had trouble persuading him to drop her even when he planned to retire. When Naomi came in November it was finally decided to put the whole thing in the hands of Kraemer-Rains in Paris and that is where it now is. (He is a good lawyer and a friend of Maritain's, recommended by Doris Dana.)

February 10, 1968

Bitter cold again—below 32 all day and now rapidly getting down toward 20. It will be another cold night. In late afternoon, after finishing some mail, I walked out to say Office. The moon was up (it will be full in three or four days) and two deer were standing motionless out in the middle of the field, watching me, their big ears spread out, their grey winter coats almost green against the field. The farmers meanwhile are farming with fire, burning the alfalfa fields to kill weevil. Roaring of the flame throwers in St. Teresa's field circled my place, and acrid blue smoke floating through the pines.

I just learned a day or two ago about the big drive of the Vietcong in Vietnam—they almost took a lot of cities at once by guerrilla action, and gave a great show of revolutionary strength, so that although they did not hold on to much of anything they completely changed the picture. It is the beginning of the end in Vietnam because there is just nothing left for the Americans to "support" except themselves. Morally the country belongs to the NLF, because of the stupidity and inefficacy of the technical ideas of Americans—strategic hamlets, crop-burning, etc. It is a great failure of *power*, and a victory, whether you like it or not, for human spirit, even if that spirit is ruthless, totalist, etc. It is a victory of people and of authentic human concern over a technological and military machine. But the war is not over yet. Is there going to be another Dien Ben Phu, this time for America? I am not so sure. But the war *cannot* be won by the U.S. now. Or the military objectives of the U.S. *cannot* be attained.

J. Laughlin came Thursday. In two days we got a lot of work done on the Trust, copyrights, permissions, etc. Friday—were in Louisville all day—first at Bellarmine, then John Ford's office. John Ford, J., Tommie and Fr. John Loftus and I had lunch at *The Old House*—a good one, too. That is a place I like (Cunningham's has been sold and things are happening to it). Then back to John Ford's. Maybe all the rules for permissions, etc., may complicate my life but in the end I hope they will prevent some legal snarl that would frustrate publication or use of my stuff. Libraries and publishers like rules as much as monks do, in fact more. J. is full of stories about people pirating Ezra Pound, etc. By 3 p.m. I was exhausted. But Tommie wanted us to stay for dinner and I had got permission (as J. did not want to return—so I needed someone else to drive me back). Then began a long drag between

4 and 10:30. First—lying down, trying to rest in the guestroom at O'C.'s. Traffic noise. Dog barking. Kids playing. Not unpleasant. Then trying to get some news on TV—only local at that time. Then a rush down to the Pendennis Club—a big idiot place, dinner in a large, green, classical kind of a dining room with absurd music (the kind of stuff they played for the dansant [dancing] on the Cunard Line). The food was OK, but I did not feel like eating. The place was just ludicrous and all I could think of was getting out of it. The tedious, oppressive world of the wealthy.

What I really wanted, and finally got—was to go down to the new place that has opened in a warehouse building on Washington Street. Very good jazz there. Clark Terry, a trumpeter who was with Ellington, is there for four days. It was very satisfying. The only problem—Tommie had invited a lot of people who were not really interested in jazz and who sat around garrulously talking when I wanted to listen. One man kept asking me to *justify* it, explain what could possibly be good about it, instead of listening to it. Still, it was good. The players were stacked up on a high stage in the middle of everyone but facing a wall, practically. It is a long high narrow cellar. Power and seriousness of the jazz. As if they were playing for their own sake and for the sound's sake and had no relationship to the people around them. And yet for the most part everyone seemed to like it. Without understanding that here was one place in Louisville where something was definitely being done and said. Ron Seitz came with Sally, and Pat Huntington was with me so we formed an enclave of appreciation—maybe. Anyway, that was one place where I felt at home, if only I weren't in a crowd of uninvolved people. It would have been better at a table, two or three with nothing to say.

When we got out it was very cold. I didn't get back to the woods until nearly two, fell into bed and slept five hours. Then got up for Office and Mass, etc. The quiet of the hermitage is good. The sound of the jazz was good. In between—a vast morass of nonsense, babble, riding, talking, pretending, etc. For a moment I thought: nice if I had my own car, could simply drive out of here about seven and come back when I felt like it and not depend on people who want to entertain you by the hour.

Actually, of course, this is an exception. Once was enough. And it was exhausting.

February 12, 1968

Zero yesterday and below 20 tonight. Spica, Vega, Arcturus; brilliant. Frost shines on the ground in the light of the setting moon. Very cold, very silent, when I was out during meditation—only a distant train—to have only one far noise is now equivalent to silence.

I finished [Ronald] Segal's badly written but perceptive survey *The Race War* [New York: Viking, 1967]. It really clarifies the situation—shows how serious and how irrational it is. These are elementary truths—and people like Johnson evidently can't see them. To think that a society as complex and sophisticated as the U.S. seems to be, should bog down, finally, is something as trivial, as stupid, and as self-defeating.

One conclusion: the real importance of resistance *within* the U.S. Not only for ourselves but for everyone else—for the human race. Yet the hang-ups are now so inexorable . . .

Thinking too of the meeting in Bangkok—the AIM Meeting of Asian Superiors in December to which I may or may not eventually go. What sense can monastic renewal and "implantation" in Asia have if the (Christian) monasteries are implicitly identified with Western power? Dom Leclercq sees this of course. Utility of the meeting could be in clarification of this problem first of all.

Yesterday before Concelebration Dom Flavian handed me a blue envelope from the BBC—invitation to an interview with Malcolm Muggeridge for TV. Obviously turned down. I am suggesting to Fr. Flavian that Muggeridge should nevertheless stop by here for an informal visit.

February 13, 1968

Bright morning—freezing, but less cold than before—and with a hint of the smell of spring-earth in the cold air. A beautiful sunrise, the woods all peaceful and silent, the dried old fruits on the yellow poplar shining like precious artifacts. I have a new level in my (elementary) star-consciousness. I can now tell where constellations may be in the daytime when they are invisible. Not many, of course! But for example: the sun is rising in Aquarius and so I know that in the blue sky overhead the beautiful swan, invisible, spreads its wide wings over me. A lovely thought, for some reason.

I am really turned on by social anthropology and cargo cults. Jarvic's book *The Revolution in Anthropology* is, I think, important, though I distrust Popperites. But he very smartly shows how Cargo has found anthropologists in an impasse and thrown them into a crisis—and their response has been a ritual methodological celebration which has, itself, the qualities of a Cargo cult. This is useful and instructive and leads somewhere! Where? I hope to discover.

Yesterday—finished a first draft on the question of Monastic Discipline. More to be done!

Since Hayden Carruth's reprimand I have had more esteem for the crows around here and I find, in fact, that we seem to get on much more peacefully. Two sat high in an oak beyond my gate as I walked on the brow of the hill at sunrise saying the Little Hours. They listened without protest to my singing of the antiphons. We are part of a menage, a liturgy, a fellowship of sorts.

February 20, 1968

Still bitter cold.

Yesterday in rain and sleet Parrish's workmen poured the foundation for an addition on to the hermitage: a lavatory and a room for a chapel. Right now I am eager and anxious for the chapel to be finished, to have the Blessed Sacrament reserved, and to go into a kind of Lenten retreat with much more quiet prayer and less of a log jam of conflicting activities.

Monday, Tommie O'C. came out unexpectedly with some relatives, so the whole afternoon was gone and then I foolishly decided to go in to Washington St., which meant the night gone, too. Only value—talking to Melvin Jackson, the bass player, a really dedicated artist. And the combo turned on and really *played* in an all but empty place. Power and unity and drive. It was very fine, very real. But again, exhausting to get back here, sleep four hours, and try to salvage something from the next day. All I did accomplish finally (and that wasn't much) was to talk to Joseph Mulloy (formerly accused of "sedition" in Pike County), who is resisting draft induction this Friday. I gave him a letter of support—on moral rather than political (resistance) grounds.

February 22, 1968

Zero again. Heavy frost. Very cold night. I had a dream that President Johnson was assassinated in Louisville. It seemed like a rather trite event and few paid much serious attention, though of course the police and military went about finding the assassin. He was found almost immediately. This fact was heralded by a long, bizarre, sadistic bugle call. I asked a passing soldier who it was (three soldiers, dark silhouettes on a sloping lawn) and he said "some British Pastor in Israel."

After that I lay awake and listened to the hard ice cracking and hardening some more in the rain-barrel outside.

There is very little real news of Vietnam—guesses, opinions, surmises. There is evidently hard fighting in Hue but we're not told, and the Vietcong are massed around Khe Sanh. Yet at the same time Khe Sanh does not seem to have any special meaning (strategically) for *either* side. It is another symbolic position. And both sides are looking for a big propaganda victory by killing as many of the other side as they can—if possible by simply exterminating the others. Not to gain any significant objective, just to clobber the enemy. Just simply to kill.

I still haven't been able to really straighten out the messed-up text of the *Journal of My Escape*. Impossible to get stencils run off. Bro. Martin and the novices are all tied up in liturgical texts that are being turned out in hundreds. I can see where I can just about forget further mimeographing or offset duplication for my own stuff here. If I can get out my four issues of *Monks Pond* that ought to be enough, and that will be a problem in itself.

I hope that in Lent I'll be able to go into retreat and keep visitors out—or at least away from the hermitage. One or two engagements: I hope to see [James] Baker, the Ph.D. candidate from Florida, Ash Wednesday, Winston King later in March, and Donald Allchin before Easter. Also have a date to see Jim Wygal in March and should see Dr. Ryan March 11. Hope I can keep it down to *that!* If Tim Hogan gets in the habit of coming over from Nazareth it will be a real nuisance. Might as well let him know clearly. (He and Jim Gorman brought Joseph Mulloy here Tuesday.)

February 24, 1968

A magazine in English—in Burma or somewhere (India?)—has an article by a Buddhist lay-woman on her practice of meditation—emphasizing *mindfulness* of suffering in its existential reality, not escaping into ecstasy, etc. On one of the pages with this article—the following advertisement.

If you use Balm
use only the *strongest* Balm
de Songa's Dali Brand
  BURMA BALM (picture of jar—radiating light)
So powerful yet only K1 a jar
Relieves all pain—and quickly!
  From de Songa's, of course.

Bitter cold all the time. Waning moon, almost at its end, we probably won't see any more of it tomorrow. Year of the Monkey is what this is, I learned the other day from some news article on Vietnam.

Yesterday: I went to a Council Meeting, as I am now back on the Council. Quiet, reasonable, a very good atmosphere of peace, charity, sense. Fr. Flavian is impressive as Abbot, quiet, simple, definite, completely honest, not extending himself beyond his limits but functioning within them in a dedicated way. I think he will be sane and good. Of course the tough times have not yet begun. Under Dom James my struggles and exasperation led me to do wrong and unwise things without clearly seeing what I was doing—and thinking myself justified. Under Dom Flavian I am interested in being more honest and more serious—and a better hermit. It will be a struggle, because I have let things get potentially out of hand by thoughtlessness and carelessness with people, visitors, drinking, etc. Just to aim at moderation does not really work. Well, I should do that, but more than that. In the end, something more absolute is required—and a more real solitude. I really think that the idea of "helping others" and "being open" has led me into a real illusion.

February 25, 1968. Quinquagesima

From a letter of Hans Magnus Engenberger resigning a job at Wesleyan University and leaving the U.S. for Cuba in protest against the war and the whole situation:

I believe the class which rules the U.S. of America and the government which implements its policies to be the most dangerous body of men on earth . . . a threat to everyone who is not part of it. It is waging an undeclared war against more than a billion people.

Its aim is to establish its political, economic and military predominance over every other power in the world. Its mortal enemy is revolutionary change.

This letter was written on my birthday.

Yesterday I wrote a short piece on Wilderness (the Nash book) in the afternoon. Importance of the "ecological conscience." (Same war as above!!)

Though it is still cold (with a bitterly biting wind) there were a few moments this afternoon when the coming of spring might almost be credible—perhaps because I so desire it after this cold winter. Out in St. Bernard's field, just as the clock was striking two, the sound of the bells came clear in a lull of the wind, and with the wind down the sun was suddenly warm. Fern-like walnut trees in the hollow stood as if ready for summer, and I looked at the distant valley and at the slight haze in the sky. Perhaps warm weather will once again be possible.

Then in the evening—the bare trees had a certain way of beating themselves up against the blue late sky, as if they knew for sure the promise of sap in them. I sang the *Te Lucis* and realized it is a lovely hymn.

As I was ending my conference Bro. Kevin gave me a telegram from Jim Forest saying he was not coming. But I had not even heard he was coming. It was from Atlanta. Maybe he was intending to bring [Thich] Nhat Hanh here. There may be a letter about it tomorrow.

February 26, 1968

In spite of the bright, bitter cold (below 20) the whistling of the cardinals gives some hint of spring. It, too, is confident.

The more I read of Cargo cults the more I am excited by the material: it seems to be tremendously important and significant for our time. It opens new perspectives in *everything*.

"Most important . . . to eliminate states of relaxation or inner emptiness, when inner resources are insufficient. . . .

"The tendency to disperse oneself, to chatter, to make conquests (or I would add simply to make an impression) marks the degeneration of the creative tendency to reflect reality in one's own soul."

These are good observations in Malinowski's diary (p. 112).[13]

I laugh at him, but he was really working things through in his own life and this shows it.

But I use him nevertheless, perhaps a little ruthlessly, in *Lograire*.

Nothing against him: it is a certain kind of mentality, pre-war European, etc. in confrontation with Cargo (in my poem).

"To get up, to walk around, to look for what is hidden around the

13 Bronislaw Kasper Malinowski (1884–1942), the Polish anthropologist, was born in Kraków and taught in Poland, England, and the United States. He lectured at Yale University from 1939 until the time of his death in 1942.

corner—all this is merely to run away from oneself, to exchange one person for another" (p. 115). Good!

February 29, 1968

Bleak leap-year extra day. Black, with a few snowflakes, like yesterday (Ash Wednesday) when no snow stayed on the ground but there was sleet and the rain-buckets nearly filled. All the grass is white with, not snow, death.

Tried some books. Carlos Fuentes' *Change of Skin*, new, from Farrar, Straus & Giroux—starts out lovely, fuzzy, but doesn't hold me. I guess it is a good job but it doesn't hold me. What do I care about those people?

Very good, though, the new Robert Duncan, *Bending the Bow*, from New Directions, with a fine terse, complex introduction, putting it all in a setting—and also a great poem on Christ in the Garden—like Rilke.

Also, the new Gary Snyder—strong, clear, definite poetry, a man of solid experience. No faking.

David Ignatow—a good poet but describing a person that stands between himself and life—and on which sometimes are projected ritual murders. He screams. The screams are unreal (*Rescue the Dead*). I notice in the poems of Vassar girls a hell of a lot of death wish.

Maybe I am losing all my friends by failure to answer about *Monks Pond.* Have I written to Russell Edson? He sent fine stuff. I must tell him so finally. Good things yesterday from Anselm Hollo, translations of Klee and a poem of his own. Must write Jonathan Greene, Wendell Berry, etc. etc. Will try to get the second number lined up today. First is stalled in Cassian's printshop. Liturgy choking every press.

Wrote "The Study of Zen" Tuesday and yesterday for the N[ew] D[irections] Zen book which I think is now finished.[14]

Snowflakes meet on the pages of the Breviary. Empty belly ". . . *et flagella tuae iracundiae, quae pro peccatis nostris meremur, averte* [. . . and turn away the scourges of your anger, which we deserve for our sins]" (Prayer of the day). Ezechias. Centurion. Down in the monastery they now have English vigils. I cling to the Latin. I need the continuity!

14 *Zen and the Birds of Appetite*, published in 1968.

March 4, 1968

Still unusually cold—about 20 (7 a.m.) but the days have been bright (not completely warm) with the unmistakable brightness of spring.

Friday (March 1st) I went down to help get together the pages of the first issue of *Monks Pond.*

Then a disturbing and curious incident. I met Bro. Benedict who was on his way up to get me. Some woman had come unannounced from California claiming she *had* to see me. Against my better judgment I consented to do so. An attractive, poised person, in some way intriguing, with guarded statements about time cycles, the apocalypse, or coming crisis, a mission. All that. Well, I have no difficulty believing in a coming crisis! Things are very ominous indeed. And in many ways seemingly desperate. (Refusal of Johnson to consider anything but continuing to kill uselessly in Vietnam.)

Much of what she said was incredible; some of it may have had a basis of truth, but in general she adds up to a problem. She intends to stay here (not at the monastery, the Abbot refused her) in the neighborhood and continue "her work" in which I am supposed to have some mysterious part. It could turn into a trying and absurd situation. The Abbot thinks she is insane. I think she is at best deluded; and yet she seems to have something (perhaps I find her appealing). But I am afraid of the whole business—a great mess of false mysticism involving me, the Abbey, etc. It could be very tedious. How to deal with it? I'm trying to keep out of her way and she has not (as far as I know) tried to see me since Friday.

Finished Peter Lawrence on Cargo (chiefly *Yali*), and realize I have to try to get some of this on paper soon.

The other day (Saturday) I sent off the final ms. of *Zen and the Birds of Appetite* to New Directions after writing "The Study of Zen" previously.

Parrish's men have done no work here for two weeks.

March 7, 1968

Sagittarius rising. I said the Mass of St. Thomas Aquinas. Then made coffee and read a couple of privately circulated papers from the meeting in Chicago last November. Kathleen Aberle, James Boggs. Terribly clear! They seem to be among the few that know I can't avoid this same kind of conclusion—but don't know what to do.

Yesterday my crocuses finally began to appear. There has been a long dry spell now. Still no work on my new addition—and it would have been in good time for the big truck to get up here with cement.

Tuesday I had to go to Dr. Mitchell about bad knees. In the infirmary going to change clothes, I ran into Fr. Raymond [Flanagan] who started a furious argument with me. Apparently in *U.S. Catholic*, which I have not seen, there is not only my letter about the draft but a reprint of the *Motive* interview. Raymond (who is radical right) was livid about both. He started his usual rapid-fire series of accusations and misrepresentations. I told him he always twisted and distorted everything. He said he was going to write against me and "cut me to pieces." I said this would make *him* look cheap. He said it would make him a hero (*sic!*). I replied that I supposed that was what he wanted, etc. That kind of stupid blather.

When I, in a calmer moment, told him I thought he *should* express his opinions, he flew into a bigger rage. "What do you mean, *opinions?* It is not a matter of *opinions* but of *truth.*" I guess he has the charism of infallibility. Among other things he said he was going to prove I was an atheist. I guess in his theology anyone who doesn't agree with him or accept his ideas without question is a godless communist.

Finally he left and I got into my black suit.

And then Bro. Camillus got into it, not arguing, just expressing his way of seeing things. (1) We ought to fight China. (2) We ought to have clobbered Russia at the time of the Hungarian revolution in '56. (3) But we failed because we were afraid of the H. bomb: "We did not want to make the necessary sacrifice" (*sic*). So it was purely an ascetic question—a matter of generosity with the lives of a few million people. And we failed!

This sick distortion of Christianity is deep in all the thinking of the warmakers. A perverse, death-loving, self-destructive theology of hate. And yet Camillus is a mild, rather dumb, harmless little guy! Probably the real trouble is that these people live in an entirely imaginary world. Raymond, however, has always been a bit paranoid. The man is pathetic. He is ultra conservative; no one will listen to him in the monastery. Even Bruce won't accept his latest book. And he falls back on his secular friends and on the Prior, Anastasius, pouring out his woes to them. He has always detested me as an arrant-heretic. I feel sorry for him.

In Louisville: lunch with Fr. Ephrem Compte and an Anglican friend who was at Boquen [abbey] last summer. Then saw Fr. John Loftus in St. Anthony's Hospital and Jim Wygal in the Baptist Hospital. Both have had heart attacks. "The Woman" has left and gone either to Louisville or Dayton. I have not seen her since Friday and am relieved she is away from the monastery.

March 8, 1968

Yesterday and today were two fine bright spring days and I took both afternoons off to meditate in the woods, Thursday—back by the waterhole in the woods where you used to go through to Hanekamps'; today in a place I had never been to before, a rocky, scrubby hollow across monks creek next to the old Linton place, near Fr. Flavian's hermitage. I found a good rocky point with a strange view of the knobs and sat there in the sun, said Vespers, read a little Eckhart. It was great, and I am amazed I have not been doing more of it. What else, really, is there? I suppose for one thing I have been too anxious to answer letters and for another I have tried to keep up with articles, etc. I am asked to write—or get myself into writing. Mostly the afternoons are pretty occupied with mail, and that is a waste.

I really enjoyed being in the wild, silent spot where no one as yet goes. It is very much out of the way—and I am aware I will need an out-of-the-way place like that to hide in if too many people start coming to the hermitage on summer afternoons.

And really I am ready to let the writing go to the dogs if necessary, and to prefer this: which is what I really want and what I am here for.

This evening, Mother Francis Clare, Abbess of the Poor Clares in New Orleans, stopped by on her way to Boston. Problems of contemplative renewal in cloistered orders. Most of them are frantically clinging to the *status quo*—reformers are suspect. Yet she is looking for the right thing. The real contemplative life cannot be saved by clinging to baroque observances, grilles, veils, etc. I have no answers, for I have no experience of the problems of these nuns: but from what I hear, the problems are appalling. She is to speak at the meeting of Vicars for Religious and wants help. We are supposed to have another consultation before the meeting.

March 9, 1968

Back to Blake—after thirty years. I remember the profound overturning of the roots that took place in my study of him. And the same—even much more profound, is required.

And the Mills of Satan were separated into a moony Space
Among the rocks of Albions Temples, and Satans Druid sons
Offer the Human Victims throughout all the Earth, and Albions
Dread Tomb immortal on his Rock, overshadowed the whole Earth:
Where Satan making to himself Laws from his own identity,
Compell'd others to serve him in mortal gratitude & submission
Being call'd God: setting himself above all that is called God.
And all the Spectres of the Dead calling themselves Sons of God
In his Synagogues worship Satan under the Unutterable Name.

The thing that is terrifying about this is that it is *true.* The fiendish, divided, fanaticism which issues in bloodthirsty moral indignation *everywhere*—in the religious and irreligious, the priest and anti-priest, the war hawk and the pacifist. At times one gets horrible flashes of it—here in the monastery as well, in the twistedness, the forbidding, tense rigorism or the drive to "produce" something. And it is also in myself. This is the real "original sin" and its traces are in us together with grace. How to be entirely open to grace? Not with this idolatry.

And it was enquir'd: Why in a Great Solemn Assembly
The Innocent should be condem'd for the Guilty?

(*Milton I*)

And Leutha's plea for Satan—how deep!

I think Blake would be my desert-island book now. I must get into it—and be on my desert-island alone with the mercy.

March 11, 1968

It is gray and cold again, but there have been warm spring days and spring is now irreversible. The crocuses are bunched together in the cold wet grass. I saw my Towhee in the bushes the other day—silent—but today I heard him, and his discreet, questioning chirp, in the rose hedge. There is a solitary mocking bird, apparently with no mate, that patrols the whole length of the rose hedge and tries to keep every other bird from resting there.

Saturday there was rain at last—after a month or so—and at night, with the rain softly falling, a frog began singing in the waterhole behind the hermitage. Now it sounds as if there are half a dozen of them there, singing their interminable spring celebration.

Attacks on me in the correspondence column of *The Record* for supporting Mulloy in his conscientious objection. Apparently he is thought to be a real red. I very much doubt it. But the country is very tense now. The war is going badly. The Viet Cong are getting into the cities. Khe Sanh is a big threat. Many more people are being drafted. We are on the way to general mobilization. Johnson says he isn't going to be the first President to lose a war. So a few more thousands of people have to die to save face for him.

I took a couple of notebooks out to the woods and went through my notes on *L'Étranger* [*The Stranger*]. Then on the way back, ran into two brothers with a truck and got them to transport three little beech trees I transplanted. Was late having supper, and tired. Will be late going to bed.

March 12, 1968

I wrote the first draft of an article on *The Stranger* this morning. In the afternoon I transplanted a few small pine trees, but it started raining again and I came in to write some letters. Dan Walsh says that in the Senate, Sen. Morse produced evidence that the "Pueblo affair" was something inspired by Washington itself. More and more, Johnson appears to be a completely unscrupulous and untrustworthy operator. Dan says he is not likely to be re-elected but I am not so sure. Rockefeller may get the Republican nomination, in which case there will be at least a choice—though not much of one. I don't know what will be happening in December when the AIM meeting is supposed to be in Bangkok. Maybe all SE Asia will be in a war—or maybe it will be everywhere!

This evening I had some Rice-a-roni for supper and read a very lively interview with Stravinsky in *New York Review* which, for some reason, cheered me up considerably. Just the encouragement of having a civilized man around—still! And it was very witty. Then I turned to the *Catholic Worker* and read some of the letters and a story about two girls trying to help a drunk. When I looked up, out the window, it was snowing again.

March 14, 1968

Cold again. The nights are freezing—down in the twenties. Hard frost in the mornings, buckets solid ice. But the cold is different. The sun comes up bright, and the other morning there was spring birdsong even in the snow.

I must admit the frogs are silenced until the noon sun melts the ice. Then they sing in the afternoon.

My solitude is radically changing. I no longer take it for granted that the afternoon is for writing—just because that was the way it had to be in community. Why not early morning? Then in the afternoon I am free to go out to the woods—and it gets me away from the hermitage at a time when people might be tempted just to "drop in" (as Fr. Tim Hogan did with Malcolm Boyd, and others have from time to time).

Yesterday afternoon again, in bright sun and cold wind, I took off for the East Farm (Linton's) and discovered a pond I had never seen. It was in the hollow over on the SE corner of the farm where the low cedars are—and I had not been there for well over 10 years. Maybe 12 years, even. Anyway, this was a warm, quiet, out-of-the-way corner, lots of rocks, a steep dip, a small artificial pond half full of bullrushes—probably the one Fr. John of the Cross used to go swimming in when it was more clear. I stayed quiet in the sun there for a long time. Small clouds high above the bare trees. Sun on the pale green water. Warmth. Peace. A most fruitful afternoon. And I came back out into the cold wind on the high fields wondering why I wasted my afternoons writing letters. Of course, I have to—and I have to write some now. They will continue to be letters of refusal. Every week now I refuse two or three invitations to meetings and conferences—important ones—but I do not think I can get mixed up in them or that there is any point in so doing. Fr. Flavian would probably let me go if I insisted—but I am not going to insist. Still question about Bangkok. This I *should* go to—Dom Leclercq is a good judge of such things. Fr. Flavian is still not definite about it. But will Bangkok be a place one can get to, this December? Or will the whole place be up in flames?

Ever increasing frenzy, tension, explosiveness of this country. You feel it in the monastery with people like Raymond. In the priesthood with so many upset, one way or another, and so many leaving. So many just cracking up, falling apart. People in Detroit buying guns. Groups of vigilantes being formed to shoot Negroes. Louisville is a violent place, too. Letters in *U.S. Catholic* about the war article—some of the shrillest came from Louisville. This is a really mad country, and an explosion of the madness is inevitable. The only question—can it somehow be *less bad* than one anticipates? Total chaos is quite possible, though I don't anticipate that. But the fears, frustrations, hatreds, irrationalities, hysterias, are all there and all powerful enough to blow everything wide open. One feels that they *want* violence. It is preferable to the uncertainty of "waiting."

March 15, 1968

"Parents! Don't let your teenagers waste their time and energies in worthless and dangerous pleasures. . . . Give them a stimulating interest in life, . . . give them an opportunity to make a million dollars in the Stock Market. . . . *The Teenagers' Guide to the Stockmarket*—$3.45. . . . Other Library of Wall Street Books: *How to Read the Wall Street Journal for Pleasure and Profit* . . . etc."

Even better—a newspaper clipping on an undertaker in Atlanta: he has "adapted the drive-in-window for busy persons to drive by and view a deceased friend without leaving their car.

". . . having five windows in a row built as an extension to his Funeral Home. Each window is six feet long and will contain a body in its coffin. . . ."

"So many people want to come by and see the remains of a relative or friend . . . but they just don't have time. This way they can drive by and just keep on going."

"The deceased will be lying in a lighted window, sort of tilted to the front, so they can conveniently be seen," he added.

"It's purely imagination," he said. "I dreamed it one night."

"Another thing," he noted, "people won't have to dress up to view the remains."

Curiosity seekers?

"We expect these, but we think they will eventually tire."

Each window will contain a name plaque and each will have wall-to-wall carpeting and drapes.

Ah! The wisdom of dreams!

More attacks in *The Record*. A devout Catholic is burning my books. I must be godless, as I wish to save lives rather than kill Commies for Christ.

Saw Fr. [indecipherable] from Minnesota yesterday. He distributed a pamphlet to 800 high-school seniors in his town, telling them to resist the draft. A very honest, simple guy. He "wonders about his future."

Went out again to my small west pond and did some Zen. It was right. When I came back, I saw two cars waiting by my gate. I hid in the cedars until three priests appeared, disappointed. They drove off, and I returned to the hermitage.

March 16, 1968

Warmer. Rain in the night. Frogs again. At first the waterhole—(four feet long at most) had one frog or two. Now they are a small nation, loud in the night. The innocent nation, chanting blissfully in praise of the spring rain. Last evening I pruned a few little trees—including the beeches I had planted.

Today I have to go down to see Fr. Vernon Robertson, who evidently wants to get me involved in something—and I will try not to. He has been pestering me to come to Louisville to give a talk at Bellarmine. And this is confirming me in my resolution to keep *out* of all that.

Almost every day I have to write a letter to someone refusing an invitation to attend a conference, or a workshop, or to give talks on the contemplative life, or poetry, etc. I can see more and more clearly how for me this would be a sheer waste, a Pascalian diversion, participation in a common delusion. (For others, no: they have the grace and mission to go around talking.) For me what matters is silence, meditation—and writing: but writing is secondary. To willingly and deliberately abandon this to go out and talk would be stupidity—for me. And for others, retirement into my kind of solitude would be equally stupid. They could not do it—and I could not do what they do.

March 20, 1968

In the last couple of days Parrish's men have been back, raised the walls of the chapel wing, which is very small but adds a lot to the hermitage both inside and out—gives it a more interesting shape outside—more of a "line." And, inside, gives it a whole new feeling—a new dimension of space with the SW window of the kitchen transformed into a door going somewhere. And I realized that this was what the house has been needing.

The floor has not been poured yet because the plumbers had not put the pipe in yet. (Yesterday Br. Martin and Bob M. began with that.) Today it may rain and the concrete mixer might not be able to get here.

Abbots are beginning to arrive for Dom Flavian's blessing which is tomorrow. Yesterday I had a talk with Dom Edward of Berryville, former Superior of the Spencer foundation in Chile. A nice fellow—is from South Africa. Fairly progressive. We walked down the back road and out into the bottoms and returned. Nothing really new was said. The usual questions: new liturgy, communication, community, friendships, trouble with Rome, Antoniutti, new Delegate, etc. These are things in which Abbots and monks are all very much involved and yet I can't see much in them that is of decisive importance or even real newness. Mostly a matter of catching up with things that needed to be done years ago—but couldn't.

The same applies to the contemplative communities of nuns. Three Superiors were here Monday. Mother Francis of the New Orleans Poor Clares, Mother Philomena of the Chicago Poor Clares and Mother Jane of the Carmel in Jackson, Mississippi.

I am not sure it was a good idea to make those tapes last year—the "thinking out loud" ones for the various groups of sisters. Well—not a bad idea either. Perhaps they were some use. But seeing the transcripts I have been sobered and jolted. The result is an appalling, semi-articulate mish-mash of sentences that don't end, or vanish in mid air, of clichés, idiot colloquialisms, vague suppositions, intuitions that don't get anywhere, feeble humor, etc. It is good to see how bad this kind of thing can get. How sloppy, how untrue to my real thinking in many ways. Mere disorganized spontaneity is not enough. At one point I found myself sounding like Timothy Leary!

Incredible things in the news. New laws (in New York) permitting police to shoot to kill if they even *suspect* someone might be carrying a weapon, or if they resist arrest! Rumors of prison camps being prepared for the summer rioters (probably with some basis of truth). Utter corruption and hopelessness of South Vietnam, where the Americans are really being *beaten*—but where they may resort to tactical nuclear weapons. A sudden (late) awakening of Congress to the gravity of the situation, the lies they have believed (Tonkin Gulf incident, Pueblo incident), the mistakes they have made. Even the general public is perhaps beginning to get some idea of the enormity of the wrong that has been done by the Johnson administration. The country itself is almost on the verge of an economic crisis. One gets the sense that suddenly everyone—including business (*Wall Street Journal*, etc.)—is waking up and trying to prevent a disaster before it is too late.

I have never had such a feeling of the strange madness that possesses this country. And yet there is still some hope—based not on reason but on a basic good will and a luck that might still hold. Or *is* there a basic good will? Has it all been mortgaged to a police state? Are we already *there?* We may be!

The red sun came up under a shaggy horn of blood and purple cloud and has now disappeared.

March 21, 1968. St. Benedict

Rain for two days. The carpenters got some of the frame for the roof on yesterday, but were much interrupted by rain. At night I awoke with the rain beating down heavily and wondered if the foundation were flooded, and if it would overflow into the kitchen. There was no way of seeing, without going out into the downpour. But it worried me and I lay awake awhile, listening to the frogs.

Today—the Abbatial Blessing. Dom Flavian looked happy, and there were many abbots around. I got out fast so as not to get involved with them. Dom James preached—the same sermon he preached for twenty years here—against "activism"—only with much more emotional intensity. He was all worked up. Probably because of that recent *NCR* article which I haven't seen.

Before the Mass I spoke to Archbishop McDonough, who was very cordial, as usual, and gave me permission to have the Blessed Sacrament reserved when my chapel is finished. But Bishop Maloney looked at me as if he thought I was going to toss a Molotov cocktail into the Cathedral.

This afternoon, because of the rain, no workmen came, and I took advantage of the quiet to write my review of the Arasteh book, *Final Integration*, which I found excellent. A very warm and good letter came from Walter Weisskopf, about my reply to his article in *ICIS*. I was moved by his letter. He worries much as I do, and is *not* an optimist à la [Herbert] Marcuse. Neither am I.

March 22, 1968

More than twelve hours of snow. A real blizzard, sometimes blinding to be out in. One of the heaviest snows I have ever seen here—though it was wet and a lot of it melted. Otherwise it would have been much deeper. But when I went out after supper it was almost up to my knees—deeper in places. During supper two tall pines out in front of the hermitage crashed down due to the weight of icy snow on them, and the dark woods rang from time to time with ominous cracks and crashes. I have hesitated to go to bed—and am sitting up waiting for the storm to let up. I think it is calming down now—or the snow is turning to fine, small rain.

A fantastic fact. China has 750 million people *half of whom* are under thirty. Can we begin to grasp something of what that means? That this is not necessarily *our* world? But for some Americans this simple fact may prove an irresistible temptation to genocide. The horror of it!

March 23, 1968

A strange and difficult night. Snow continued to fall most of the night and I could hear the big pines hanging over the house and cracking with their load. I slept with all my clothes on, coat and shoes, in case my bedroom should suddenly be filled with snowy branches and pieces of the roof.

Got up frequently and went out on to the porch, into the clouds of cold, blowing snow. Then back to bed and to strange dreams.

This morning there are a few clouds left, but it is clear, freezing, and the old moon rides up there in the clear. A flight of excited starlings passes in front of the moon.

> And Anitharmon named the Female, Jerusalem the holy
> Wond'ring she saw the Lamb of God within Jerusalem's Veil
> The divine Vision seen within the inmost recess
> Of fair Jerusalem's bosom in a gently beaming fire
>
> Blake, *Four Zoas ["Night the Eighth"]*

March 26, 1968

Sun bright and warm on Sunday and Monday has nevertheless not melted all the snow. The woods are a shambles. Fallen and uprooted pines everywhere. But anyway, two good afternoons of sun—one over on Linton's, in the desolate brushy area that looks toward Boone's, the other at the hidden pond: standing in rubber boots in the water of the spillway with the current tugging gently at my feet.

Mother Philomena of the Chicago Poor Clares, and six of the nuns, were here yesterday. I had a brief visit with them. They go to their new convent April 1.

This morning I tried to read some Karl Rahner. Heavy, plodding, uninteresting stuff. Probably there's a point in it somewhere later, something important. But he is trying to convince theologians and bishops, and I am neither. Why bother reading him? (Though I have in the past liked some of his stuff, viz. "The Dynamic Element in the Church.")

And then Hugo Rahner. I have read bits of a new book (*Theology of Proclamation*). But I come to this:

"Through the historical visibility of the Papacy our faith must experience the divinity of the Church and seek it with anxious love. . . . Loving faith will discover there hidden divinity . . . surrendered to the human element. Only in this most bitter visibility does the invisible become comprehensible."[15]

Quite apart from the Church doctrine on the Papacy—the tone of the statement, the manner, the resonances, make me impatient and suspicious. Most of the time I don't bother about the Papacy one way or another. I accept it and hope for the best. This kind of writing tempts me to active questioning and to doubt. So anyone who does not *experience* the invisible divinity by looking at Pope Paul is a "gnostic"? Especially if he claims to experience the presence of God somewhere else—in his own heart for example? How can I believe this does not reflect in Rahner an unconscious bad faith, bred of his Jesuit hangups? A willful effort to convince *himself*? And to use me to help him do it!

The kenoticism of Altizer seems to me more open and more honest. (The Blake book.)[16]

But is this whole kenotic thing too much of a mannerism?

I obey Church authority because I trust God to bring good out of their errors as well as out of their good will. Because we are all sinners anyway, all subject to error, and because if we deal charitably and humbly with one another, the Spirit will take care of the rest. But there is such a thing as an idolatry of office, and I don't yet believe the Pope is another incarnation!

15 See *The Theology of Proclamation* by Hugo Rahner, S.J., translated from the German, *Eine Theologie der Verkundigung*, by Richard Dimmler, S.J., William Dych, S.J., Joseph Halpin, S.J., and Clement Petrick, S.J. (New York: Herder & Herder, 1968).

16 Thomas J. J. Altizer's *The New Apocalypse: The Radical Christian Vision of William Blake* was published by Michigan State University Press (Ann Arbor) in 1967. Merton wrote a review article that appeared in the *Sewanee Review* 76 (Autumn 1968) and was later included in *The Literary Essays of Thomas Merton*, edited by Patrick Hart (New York: New Directions, 1982).

March 28, 1968

Sr. Luke, back from the meeting of Vicars for Religious in Detroit, and soon off to Rome to fight the Curia for American nuns (in the storm over the IHMs [Immaculate Heart of Mary Sisters] and Cardinal McIntyre) came over today. We (she and I and another Sister) went for a walk up the road toward the firetower, got a ride in the forester's truck, climbed the tower, and had a good afternoon. She said Mother Jane and Mother Francis did well at the Vicars' meeting. (Re: meetings of contemplative Superiors.)

A stupid problem has arisen with Robert Williams, the Negro singer, about the Freedom Songs I wrote at his request and gave him two or three years ago. He never got anywhere with them. He showed them to [Alexander] Peloquin, and Peloquin wanted to compose and produce them with someone else. And I guess that has been the source of the trouble. I have not been too clear about what has happened—whether Williams transferred the rights to Peloquin or not. Peloquin wants to produce them at this year's Liturgical Conference, asked if I objected. I said "no" as long as it was all right with Williams. Williams seemed to have no objection at first, then a day later came through with a virulent letter calling me an un-Christian traitor, etc. Now the atmosphere is heavy with threats and accusations. Probably the real trouble is with Peloquin, but Williams has been too confused and unrealistic about it too. And very masochistic. I suppose that's easy to say!

Then on top of all that, today a curious letter came from "The Woman of the Apocalypse." Quite imaginative and colorful and "apocalyptic": how not? It seems part of her mission includes "marriage"—and I am not sure how intimately this is supposed to concern me. She accuses me of being afraid. Yes, I am. How much of this wild stuff am I going to have to contend with? When you add up the people who send in bizarre prophetic or "metaphysical" books—letters, accusations, petitions, suggestions . . . Most of which I no longer even read. That includes a multitude of good and even excellent "causes." Being a writer has its hazards.

Worked a little with the new Canon FX John Griffin[17] had lent me—a marvelous apparatus. I think it is going to be very good.

---

17 John Howard Griffin's loaned camera was taken by Thomas Merton on his Asian journey and was returned to Gethsemani with his personal effects.

Yesterday I killed three spiders, two in the hermitage, and one in the jakes, because all looked like the poisonous kind (Brown recluses). I am pretty sure they were, and am taking no chances.

A very good talk for a couple of hours with Winston King yesterday. He is a good person to know—well up on his Buddhism and I think deeply interested in meditation. He spoke of Shibuyama Roshi (whom I would like to meet), and others. Lent me some copies of *Psycholofia* with good stuff in them—I enjoyed a couple of articles on Monta therapy this morning.

The concrete mixer has still not got up my hill. The wing is roofed but has no floor, and consequently nothing has been done on the inside.

The mockingbird who has policed the rose-fence all winter now has a mate (who came out of nowhere). He sings so sweetly, and does not chase the cardinals. They are nesting in the rose-bushes of the fence.

Two wild ducks went by fast in the evening when I was saying Compline. Only *two!* The sky should have been dark with them!

March 30, 1968

Dogs barking in the dark woods. The east sky streaked with blue and orange, pale dawn.

I have given up on Hugo Rahner's *Theology of Proclamation* and on Skinner's *Walden Two*—I see the "importance" of the latter but it bores me. I forget the dozen other books I have given up on lately. But last evening I was reading *The Essential Lenny Bruce* and almost blew my mind. Completely gone in laughter, the kind that doubles you up and almost makes you roll on the floor. Surely that is some indication of the healthiness, and sanity of this satire which so many people regarded as "obscene." In reality, it is much more *pure* than the sinister doubletalk of the "moral" murderers and cops. Lenny Bruce was one of the few who were really *clean*.

Yesterday, hot spring afternoon, the plumbers fixed up the pipes in the new addition so the floor could finally be poured. I cut down some of the (hundreds of) small pines that were bent down to the ground in the blizzard and can't recover. Freddy Hicks is to cut up the big ones and take away saw-logs from them. He was here saying he would vote for Bobby Kennedy. A lot of people would, I think, if he got the nomination. It might be harder for him to get nominated than elected. The power of the Johnson machine. In spite of the noise of the war hawks I think the majority of people in this country are utterly sick of Johnson and recognize his falsity.

Five books on (one *by*) Joyce arrived for review, for the *Sewanee [Review]*. Plenty of time. They don't need it until November.

Dom Flavian was talking yesterday about perhaps taking me to the General Chapter as translator—after which I might go to Tilburg in Holland, where I have been invited, etc. But the prospect does not appeal to me in the least. Still, I told him that though I didn't particularly *want* to go I would do so if he thought fit.

April 6, 1968

I have a week to write about, and one of the more turbulent ones in my quiet life. Passion Week of 1968—including the Saturday before it. That was a beautiful day, peaceful in the morning. Then I went down and had lunch with Maurice Lavanoux and William Schickel . . . and some of the monks. Peaceful enough. M. Lavanoux had come to see the Church, and liked it. A pleasant lunch and good conversation.

After that I went out to the Gatehouse where four college girls from St. Louis were waiting for me. We were supposed to do a tape interview for a magazine at Washington University. But their tape recorder broke down, and wouldn't work in the Gatehouse. So I took them up to the hermitage to record on mine.

It turned out Freddy Hicks was outside with a couple of shaggy boys cutting up and removing the pine trees that came down in the storm the other day. So chainsaws were on the tape, too, but not too loud I think. As we made the tape we drank beer. Sue S., the girl who was promoting most of it, was very intense, asked a lot of leading questions on fashionable topics—pre-marital sex, etc. And we finished the tape in good style and decided to go over to Bardstown to Hawk's place [Hawk Rogers's restaurant] for steaks, and I got a bottle of bourbon and we made a night of it. In the end I took them over to Thompson Willett's and we drank some more whiskey. By the time we were going home Sue was drunk and lit into me hysterically for agreeing (politely—in order not to argue) with T.W.'s conservative opinions.

Then, after a haunted sort of night in which I barely slept, went down to the monastery in the rain—brief conversation with John Ford who was on a weekend retreat, then off in the rain to Bardstown with the girls to say Mass in the house of Beatrice Rogers since I had promised her to do so the evening before.

That part of it was good. The Rogers are a Negro family and Beatrice works at Willetts' as well as at Hawk's—and I am fond of her and her husband. The mass was fine and so was the breakfast after—a true ecclesial experience, much peace, everyone getting along, the girls, the Willetts' etc. It was a real grace, though I had no permission . . . Still, in post-conciliar liberty I thought "OK—this is what I do."

Then the girls drove off to St. Louis in the rain and I came back to the hermitage, prepared a conference for the novices on Cassian and went down to give it.

But I remained upset about Sue, her attack, her neurosis, her mini-skirt, buxomness, etc., etc. Obviously the two of us could get in a lot of trouble and make each other thoroughly miserable. I must take care.

Later in the week she called Fr. Jim Gannon, a former monk and student of mine who was in her home parish in Akron and gave him a glowing account of her visit to me. He wrote me a troubled letter saying I was preaching heresy, etc., etc. So that is the way the whole thing is: crazy, neurotic, absurd. The other girls were quieter, sweeter, all good kids: but I felt it was perhaps a mistake to get involved with them. Except for that Mass at Beatrice's: and that was good. I'll never forget it. That was Passion Sunday.

Morning—news came through about Johnson's announcement that he would not run for President—that the country was dangerously divided by dissensions. That he felt he must sacrifice himself to settle the Vietnam War. And he stopped the bombing in North Vietnam. The feeling of relief was tremendous. But the next day Dan Walsh, who has a lot of inside knowledge of the Democratic Party, told me it was all a ruse, that the plan is for Johnson eventually to be "drafted" again at the convention and this is a way of circumventing Bobby Kennedy. That was depressing.

Monday I wrote my preface to Richard Chi's book on Shen Hui—the first draft. Went over it Tuesday and gave it to Fr. Hilarion for typing. And I began reading the Joyce books I have to review. It was exciting to get back in touch with Joyce after all these years.

Tuesday—quiet. I went for a walk on the old Linton farm, in the orchard over there. Some wild cherry trees in bloom in the woods on the edge of it.

Looked down through the thicket at Fr. Flavian's hermitage. Wished my hermitage were over on *that* part of the property which is more inaccessible. Women can't get to it as the only road there goes through the enclosure. But I suppose if I were there I'd have them drive around to the Tobacco barn and then walk through the fields! Why do I always end up with women? (Friday, when I spoke to the Abbot—Fr. Flavian—he was saying: "Maybe you ought to change your hermitage to a different place." I wish I could. But would it really help? And would it be right or reasonable to build a new one? The only alternative would be to move into his, and I don't particularly like it. Maybe he'd like mine, as being more convenient!)

Fr. Flavian told me that Dom James in *his* hermitage is writing many voluminous letters, including a seven-page Easter circular. This made me laugh like crazy since Dom James was always preaching so furiously against letter-writing. And *his* letters have to be dictated on a dictaphone and typed by (his former) secretaries.

Wednesday—also quiet. Read a bit on Joyce, with some letters. (I have never preached against letter-writing, and my correspondence is a pain in the ass.)

Wednesday evening Donald Allchin arrived (late) with a seminarian from General Theological Seminary, N.Y. Thursday we had planned to drive to Shakertown and did in fact do so. But when I got up Thursday it was raining in torrents and the rain continued all day. Apparently it was the end of a tornado that had hit Arkansas and Tennessee. We started out nevertheless, and got to Pleasant Hill, walked from building to building in pelting rain. The restaurant wasn't open and we went to the Imperial House in Lexington. Then when the seminarian went off to the U.K. to hunt up a long lost cousin, Donald and I sat in Gene Meatyard's shop. After that we stopped briefly at Carolyn Hammer's and went to a place called Lum's for supper. By then it was evening.

Lum's was a curious sort of goldfish-bowl glass place out in a flat suburb near a railway viaduct. Serves all kinds of beer—we drank Carlson's (Danish). The TV was on for the news. Some tanks plowed around in Vietnam, then Martin Luther King appeared—talking the previous night in Memphis. I was impressed by his tenseness and strength. A sort of vague visual, auditory impression. At almost that very moment he was being killed. We left, and right away on the car radio came the news that he had been shot and had been taken to the hospital in a "critical condition." Later, long before we were in Bardstown, it was announced he was dead.

So then we decided to go to Hawk's, and there we sat for two or three hours talking to Hawk in an empty section of the place (a party was going on in the other section). It was a moving and sad experience. Got home late again (about 11:30) and again slept little—barely two hours.

Lum's in Lexington. Red gloves, Japanese lights. Beer list. Bottles slipped over counter. Red waistcoats of Kentucky boy waiters. Girl at cashier desk the kind of thin, waiflike blonde I get attracted to. Long talk with her getting directions on how to get to Bluegrass Parkway. While we were eating a long, long freight train went by, cars on high embankment silhouetted against a sort of ragged, vapor sunset. A livid light between clouds. And over there a TV with now (after the excitement of M. L. King) the jovial man in South Africa who just had the first successful heart transplant. He said he had been down to the beach to "get a little ozone." Didn't sound English, didn't sound anything. His smile looked fixed, wax. But he was real. He had an African Negro's heart in him, beating along. They asked him if he felt any different towards his wife and I really fell off my chair laughing. No one else could figure out what was funny.

When I was in Lum's I was dutifully thinking, "Here is the world." Red gloves, beer, freight trains. The man and child. The girls at the next table, defensive, vague, aloof. One felt the place was full of more or less miserable people. Yet think of it: all the best beers in the world were at their disposal and the place was a *good idea.* And the freight train was going by, going by, silhouetted against an ambiguous sunset.

So the murder of M. L. King—it lay on the top of the traveling car like an animal, a beast of the apocalypse. And it finally confirmed all the apprehensions—the feeling that 1968 is a beast of a year. That the things are finally, inexorably, spelling themselves out. Why? Are things happening because people in desperation *want* them to happen? Or do they *have to happen?* Is the human race self-destructive? Is the Christian message of love a pitiful delusion? Or must one just "love" in an impossible situation? And what sense can possibly be made by an authoritarian Church that comes out 100 years late with its official pronouncements?

Rainy night. Big, columned Baptist churches. Highway with huge lights and wrong turns. Radio. Nashville. Louisville. Indianapolis. Jazz, news, ads.

M. L. King gradually coming clear through all the rock 'n' roll as definitively *dead.* And southerners probably celebrating, and Negroes getting ready to tear everything apart.

Hawk with his arm around me saying "This is my *boy,* this is my *friend.*" Beatrice asking me to do the Rogers coat-of-arms for her hallway. I could cry.

"Did you get all those girls straightened out?" said Hawk!

Today was peaceful. The sun finally came out after dinner. I went out to the woods, read some René Char in view of the translation I am to do for Unicorn Press. Was by the remote little pond deep in the knobs. Silence. Aloneness. Sun. Feet on crumbling shale. I took my shirt off and got the sun on my shoulders—together with a fairly cold breeze. Bro. Benedict made me a sign that Negroes were rioting in fifteen cities.

Yesterday I wrote a letter to Mrs. King and sent it via June Yungblut. June had written a letter Wednesday from Atlanta—a curiously sensitive and prophetic letter: (she and John had been urging M. L. King to make a retreat here).

"Martin is going to Memphis today. . . . He won't be back until the weekend so John won't see him (i.e. about the retreat) until next week. I hope both he and Nhat Hanh will soon go to Gethsemani. . . . If Martin had taken a period there he might have had the wisdom in repose to stay out of Memphis in the first place, and it was a mistake to go there. He had done no preparation and came in cold to a hot situation where the young militants had him just where they wanted him. . . . If there is violence today Memphis will be to King what Cuba was to Kennedy. . . . If Memphis is to be Martin's Jerusalem instead of Washington, how ironical that it is primarily a nightclub for Mississippi which is dry wherein the crucifixion may take place and that the Sanhedrin will be composed of Negro militants."

And after that, maybe, the deluge.

April 9, 1968. Tuesday in Holy Week

More rain yesterday. This morning, a fresh, marvelous spring morning, clear pre-dawn, mist hanging low in the next field, coming right up to the rose-hedge. Trees beyond the field stand clear over the mist, against the red streaks of the East. The air and wet woods ringing with a din of birds, mad song of a mockingbird in the nest, cardinals, wrens, and the solemn drums of a big woodpecker.

Palm Sunday was rainy. Talked with three young men from the Hough (ghetto) area in Cleveland where they are "living like monks," one white, two Negro—the latter seeming very solid and alive and interested in meditation. They said Hough was peaceful. But there were very serious riots in Chicago, Washington, elsewhere. The funeral of M. L. King is today. June wrote again, about the calm and heroism of Coretta King. John Howard Griffin—a shocked note from a Motel in Utica "when will they also shoot the rest of us?"

Yesterday—in Louisville—Alex Peloquin came down from Boston and played his setting he has done of my Four Freedom Songs—this was at O'Callaghans'. The songs were good, tough, would make a good TV show (Belafonte, possibly??) They were to have been first presented at the Liturgical Conference at which M. L. King was to have been present.

Still no more work on the wing of my building. Maybe today?

April 14, 1968. Easter Sunday

The last three days of Holy Week were beautiful, brilliant days. The finest of all the spring. My redbuds are in bloom and the apple trees are in full bloom down by the monastery beehives. It was wonderful today walking under their great dim clouds full of booming bees.

Parrish's men poured the floor of my chapel Holy Thursday and put tar on the roof Good Friday. Now the inner wall needs to be finished and the room has to be painted.

Holy Thursday afternoon I rode over to see Dom James's hermitage which is nearly finished. It is a curious place, and there are many things I would not like about it. But they have taken a lot of trouble with it—and it has built-in air-conditioning . . .

As I was coming back to the hermitage from the monastery after dinner, a deer, a big doe, flew down the field in the bottoms head up, white-flag of tail erect, passing in front of me barely fifty yards away.

Last week I finished my review of Altizer's book on Blake for *The Sewanee Review*. The second issue of *Monks Pond* is in the works. I keep getting good letters about the first one. Must now write my essay on "War and the Crisis of Meaning" which I have been preparing for a long time.

It is a delight to be in the Easter Office again—almost unbelievable, the first day or two, each year. It is *Easter!* The Alleluias are back, the short lesson from Hosea, etc.

April 16, 1968. Easter Tuesday

Easter Day, grey and stuffy, ended in thunderstorms while I was having supper (and reading the *Confessions of Zeno*). Yesterday was cool and clear, and today too, the same bright, sharp, cool dawn full of birdsong. Everything is breaking into leaf, the dogwoods are coming out, the flowers still greenish white (the one in the monastery yard is the first one to be fully white). Yesterday I went for a walk over to the distant little hidden pond on Linton's farm and stood there a while in the sun. Came back to give a conference. Met Andy Boone, who stopped to give me his view on world affairs: "The Bible says the last shall be first" and so, he contends the colored people of the world will take over. Closer to home and of more immediate concern: "When the Niggers get through busting up the cities they'll come out in the country and there's plenty of white trash around that'll join 'em." Thus for Andy it's a class war, not a race war, and he has identified himself with those the revolution is *against.* He advised me to get a radio—indeed even TV—so I'd know "when they was comin'."

He assured me that a fire in Louisville was somehow connected with these apocalyptic events. "A big building—a big six-story building." (It turned out to be a bar on Broadway.) Nothing to do with rioting. However, the riots after M. L. King's death were widespread and a lot of information about them was withheld (in many cities no information about casualties, arrests, etc. was available).

April 18, 1968. Easter Thursday

There was a violent thunderstorm about midnight and it went on a long time. Big downpour. This morning, before dawn, misty moon, mist hanging low over the wet fields and bottoms, and a towhee waking in the hedge. Black wet trees against the clouds.

The workmen came yesterday again (after another interval), put up a bit of partition. I hope they will soon be finished. I planted a lot of bulbs that the novices dug up out of their garden and were going to throw away: a bad time to transplant them! I hope a few will survive. The work hurt my back, and for some reason I felt extremely tired, unable to do anything. Lately I have noticed this tendency to fatigue, with pains in the chest: I wonder vaguely if I am building up to a heart attack. But examinations generally show my heart is in perfect condition, and I have no intention of worrying about it. Maybe I'll get a check-up later this year when there's more time.

Last evening at supper I finished Lenny Bruce. Sometimes he is really inspired—sometimes just dull. And, though he is in some sense a kind of "martyr" for honesty, yet I think his gospel of excess was delusive and self-destroying. That is the problem! Also read the last half of Freud's *Civilization and Its Discontents*—a truly prophetic book! A bit of Ibn Battuta, whose travels are sometimes marvelous. But I don't read much these days.

Reading a good book by Nasr on Islam. And this afternoon, in the sun, out on the quiet bottom by the creek, began the *Ashtavakra Gita*—very much what I have been needing. This morning, in the mail, a mysterious telegram, probably not phoned in, asking me to meet someone tomorrow "where we were before." At first could not identify the sender. It was from a suburb of St. Louis and I thought it might be one of the college girls, here a few weeks ago. Then it occurred to me that it must be the woman from California with the apocalyptic mission. Very embarrassing! A sort of clandestine meeting is suggested. I'll leave a note for her at the Gatehouse, I think, explaining why this is entirely impossible.

All of which brings up the problem of real solitude: I don't have it here. I am not really living as a hermit. I see too many people, have too much active work to do, the place is too noisy, too accessible. People are always coming up here, and I have been too slack about granting visits, interviews, etc., going to town too often, socializing, drinking, and all that. All I have is a certain privacy, but real solitude is less and less possible here. Everyone now knows where the hermitage is and in May I am going to the convent of the Redwoods in California. Once I start traveling around, what hope will there be?

In this morning's mail was a letter from [Ernesto] Cardenal, asking me once again to come to Solentiname, assuring me the solitude is real there (and I certainly believe it is—there could hardly be a more hidden, more inaccessible place—an island on a tropical lake in Central America). I have to seriously think about this. At any rate, I ought to be able to spend a few weeks there some time (perhaps on the way to Chile, if I can get sent down there to "help out" temporarily). I really wish something could be worked out. My situation here is not really satisfactory. And moving to another part of the property is no real solution. At least I want to *see* what's there on the island. It is certainly isolated. Only problem is I am getting old, might have a hard time adjusting to a tropical climate, diet, etc., and am very susceptible to dysentery.

But I honestly feel I may have to move somewhere else. Or make some pretty firm rearrangements here. As it is, I have a lot of people to see. Dom Damasus Winzen is supposed to be coming tomorrow. [W. H.] "Ping" Ferry next week. Carolyn [Hammer] was here today with Jonathan Greene, but her visits are brief, not too distracting and I think they fit my life all right. Ping, too. Wherever I go, *some* visits will be unavoidable. But here I have far too many, too much mail, etc., etc. Of course, things are so much better and quieter than when I was in the monastery, it is an immense improvement. But much more is needed and more discipline on my own part.

April 23, 1968

Sunday I went down late and did not concelebrate. Left a note for "the Woman" at the Gatehouse saying I could absolutely not see her, and went off to the other end of the farm—bright sun, green fields, dogwoods, black birds, quail—I felt a little guilty for being so negative but it was the only thing to do. In the evening—at my conference, talked about some poems of J. D. de Dadelsen whom I have just discovered. Good for this purpose. After supper, went over to the Guesthouse to see Dom Damasus Winzen and Br. David Steindl-Rast from Mt. Saviour. Br. David is the one who is at Columbia and studying Zen at the N.Y. Zendo. Spoke of Panikkar, of his idea of a Study Center for various religious (Hindu-Buddhist-Christian). The magazine *Monastic Studies* will probably expand to include articles by Buddhists, etc.

Yesterday (Monday) afternoon I had a long and good talk with Dom Damasus. Mostly about changes in the Church, the unsettled state of "the young ones," the "loss of center" and of depth, etc. It was good to get his viewpoint: he is one of the few with a real monastic sense in this country. He does not seem at all optimistic about American monasticism and says Fr. Aelred, the Superior of Christ in the Desert, is almost in despair over it. Yet Christ in the Desert is one of the "best" places in the country. (I hope to see something of it on the way back from California.) Main point: the lack of any real *depth* in the monks—they are either immature or unsettled (and will leave) or they have "adjusted" by narrowing themselves down to some petty limits and restrictions they think they can "handle" so that in effect they live peacefully in little worlds of their own. I agreed with this. It is sad.

Yesterday one of the men came and put a coat of paint on the inside of the new wing. Today, nobody; nothing. They have been on this since February. It has taken them longer to build this wing than the whole rest of the house! The fault is probably that of the plumbers, who almost never show up at all. A small wing, 14 x 20, with two rooms in it—one a shower-toilet.

Friday, early, I wrote a response to an article by [Michael] Novak on "The Secular Saint" to be in the magazine of the Center at Santa Barbara. I had some doubts about writing it. More and more doubts about getting involved in this sort of opinion-mongering which is so fruitless.

While I was thinking up my response to Novak, full of strong breakfast coffee, there was a heavy thunderstorm and downpour of rain—before dawn. The day remained hot and stuffy. I find this kind of weather makes me more and more weary, and I seem to have trouble breathing. I called T. J. Smith, the allergist, about it and am supposed to see him Monday. All afternoon it was hot. Thunderheads piled up in the South, sun hid from time to time. About suppertime a storm passed by in the South but we only got a little of the edge of it. Now (7 p.m.) it is clear and cool. The last of the parade of distant thunderheads East over Tennessee an hour ago.

April 25, 1968

A beautiful spring day—one of those than which no more beautiful is possible. Everything green and cool (a light frost in the early morning). Bright sun, clear sky, almost everything now fully in leaf except that some of the oaks are still silver rather than green.

But I went down to the mail box and got terrible news. A rolled-up newspaper from New Zealand (I don't know who sent it) tells of a shipwreck, a "giant ferry" sunk in the entrance to Wellington Harbor. All the pictures and headlines and then, on the last page, in the list of the dead: Agnes Gertrude Merton, 79, Christchurch.

Poor Aunt Kit! It happened April 10, two weeks ago, Wednesday in Holy Week. And no one had told me about it. I said Mass for her—the Mass of the Holy Cross.

Off and on, kept wondering if it were really true. Perhaps there was some mistake.

In the afternoon, the workmen were here. They finished painting, putting in doors. I did a minimum of necessary work and went out to mourn quietly, walking in the bottoms. The need to lament, to express and offer up sorrow and loss. Finally, after the workmen had gone, I sat down and read everything in the paper—a supplement of the Sunday *Dominion-Times* or whatever it is. It was awful. All kinds of doubletalk, covering complete mystery and confusion. No one really knows what happened. This ship was caught in a storm and though it had "the latest" in all equipment, nothing worked, much of the life-saving equipment was inadequate, the people were constantly reassured there was "no danger." Then suddenly they had to abandon ship, life rafts capsized or were dashed against the rocks, etc. A frightful mess. And in the middle of it all, poor, sweet Aunt Kit, old and without strength to fight a cold, wild sea! I look at the sweater she knitted me to protect me against "the cold" and the whole thing is unbearable.

What can be said about such things? Nothing will do. Absurdity won't. An awful sense that somehow it had to be this way because it was, and no one can say why, really. And yet "what did she ever do to deserve it?" Such a question does not make sense, and the God I believe in is not one who can be "blamed," for it is he who suffers this incomprehensibility in me more than I do myself. But there is a stark absence of all relatedness between the quiet, gentle, unselfish courage of Aunt Kit's life and this dreadful, violent death. What have these waves and currents to do with her?

In the end—one gets poetic and wonders if somehow they became "worthy" of her, but there is still no proportion—none whatever.

And, I suppose, that is what death really is for everyone. But it is usually made so comfortable—so faked. When it is naked and terrible we remember what death really is.

Perhaps that is it: no faked death for Aunt Kit—the real thing, with face unveiled. But still it is not easy for love to bear it! Or even possible. May God grant her peace, light and rest in Christ. My poor dear.

And now winter comes to her little garden on Repton Street, and that is the end of it. It does not have another spring.

I had hoped, if I went to Bangkok, to visit her in December. I don't know if I'll go to visit the others—or even if I will go to Bangkok at all.

Meanwhile "the woman (??)" sent me one of her scrolls, in excellent Chinese characters—perhaps in her own blood—and cryptic messages translated. They add up to the information that I am not done with her (or was this someone else??).

The rest of the mail was good. Good letter from Anselm Hollo. I can use his [Pentti] Saarikoski translations in *Monks Pond*; better still from Richard Chi who likes my piece on Shen Hui. Yesterday I talked briefly to a Maryknoll missionary who knows Dumoulin and Enomiye [Lasalle] in Japan.

April 30, 1968. (Tuesday)

Another bright, sunny morning. My chapel was finished Friday (Feast of Our Lady of Good Counsel). Worked late cleaning out, putting up the ikons, etc. and said Mass there Saturday morning, Sunday (II after Easter—Good Shepherd [Gospel]), etc. John H. Griffin was here Friday, briefly, talking of the wicked situation in the cities, has a theory of white extremists provoking violence, and it is certainly true that the people killed in riots are mostly black. We went to take pictures of the distillery and then he left with a fever (he is not supposed to walk around much).

My chapel is plain, bright, white-walled, bright warm red of ikons, simplicity, light, peace.

Makes a great difference having a chapel, a place for prayer *only* (*oratorium hoc sit quod dictus* [let the oratory be what its name implies]).[18] The altar next to the fireplace and bookcase in the front room was never satisfactory—and gas heater popping and banging two feet away. So I am glad of the chapel, say most of the hours of the Office there, and this is good.

Sunday I said Mass here and did not go down to concelebration. Tried also to get caught up on letters. A fine, quiet, sunny morning. Spent several hours with Ping Ferry who came through Saturday having been in Berea. Had some sandwiches in the hermitage and then drove around taking pictures.

May 4, 1968. (Derby Day)

A lovely day—just like Derby Day two years ago. And another picnic—this time with John and Rena Niles and Bob and Hanna Shepherd. We ate

18 Quoted from *The Rule of Saint Benedict*, with an introduction, a new translation of the Rule, and a commentary, all reviewed in the light of earlier monasticism by Reverend Basilius Steidle, a Benedictine monk of the Archabbey of Beuron (Canon City, CO: Holy Cross Abbey, 1967). See chap. 52.1.

our salads by the monuments (alias the Watts Towers), the old spires off the Church Steeple, set up in the woods. A very pleasant place. John filled the woods with shouts of Ber-tha-a-a! And I hoped no monks were around to hear him. He has set ten poems, from *Emblems [of a Season of Fury]*, to music. Not all mine—some are my translations of Cortes and Cuadra. I'd like to hear them, and may perhaps some time in June.

Today the plumbers finished installing bathroom fixtures, but they don't work yet—no septic tank. The white irises are beginning to bloom. The grass is deep and green.

Had a discussion yesterday with Fr. Flavian, who just returned from Chile, about the invitation to go to the meeting of the Superior Generals of Active Congregations of Nuns that are thinking of having "Houses of Prayer" (or communities where people can go for more or less long retreats). I don't especially want to go, but they keep pressing, got a couple of bishops to support them. Even then, he doesn't see it. To him it is only a nuisance and a distraction. He does not see it as something one might be concerned about. If I thought very strongly I ought to go, I guess I could: but I don't want to override his own preference. I don't know for sure if I could do any good. But it is strange, this almost complete *insensitivity*, on his part, to their real need.

However, I am supposed to leave Monday for California—the convent at Whitethorn—for a series of conferences and seminars or what have you—discussions. As the French say "with broken batons." I am on the whole glad to be going and look forward to it. Even if they don't get anything out of it, I probably will. One thing to talk about will be the curious question of the "contemplative mystique"—and its relation with the cloistered feminine mystique, the pure victim souls shut away from the world and praying for it. There is so much hokum in this idea! And yet we do have to be serious about solitude, discipline, prayer.

Got a new vaccine from the allergist. Don't know if it will help. Some splendid poems of Anselm Hollo came in the mail.

This afternoon I cleaned up a bit, burned a big pile of brush and trash behind the hermitage—the cartons that the bathroom fixtures came in and a lot of other junk with pine branches brought down in the blizzard at the end of Lent. Tomorrow is already the III Sunday after Easter. "A little while and you shall see me, yet a little while and you shall not see me—because I go to the Father" [John 16:17]. Which reminds me that I got a lovely card from Nhat Hanh the other day—he must leave the country June 15 when his visa expires. Meanwhile the war goes on and Johnson's peace gesture was obviously another phoney.

PART II

Woods, Shore, Desert

A Notebook, May 1968

Prelude

"I have written out of my own book which was opened in me."

(Boehme)

". . . And Palmers for to seke strange strondes."

(Chaucer)

"Where are we really going? Always home."

(Novalis)

"For our goal was not only the East or rather the East was not only a country and something geographical but it was the home and youth of the soul."

(H. Hesse)

"Whether he lives a life of action or withdraws from the world, the ignorant man does not find spiritual peace."

(Astavakra Gita)[1]

Points for "Monastic Vocation."

"The wise man who has known the truth of the self plays the game of life and there is no similarity between his way of living and the deluded who live in the world as mere beasts of burden."

(Astavakra Gita)

"Where there is I, there is bondage. Where there is no I, there is release. Neither reject nor accept anything."

(Astavakra Gita)

"Orthodoxy is the principle of absolute freedom. . . ."

(Yelchaninov)[2]

---

1 The *Astavakra Gita,* or *Samhita,* is a dialogue between Astavakra, the Hindu sage to whom the text is ascribed, and his disciple, Janaka.

2 Alexander Yelchaninov (1881–1934) was a Russian priest and teacher.

The fear of placing rules, thoughts, and words above the fact or outside the fact, this fear is important in Orthodoxy, is the basis of the freedom of the Orthodox.

Aversion to propaganda, to indoctrination and to undue restraints: Orthodoxy, says Yelchaninov, means "putting our whole faith in the actual presence of religious life and all the rest will come of itself."

Three dreams of Descartes are central in his philosophy. They have a religious importance. The God of Descartes is absolute reality, timeless, simple, instantaneous action, breaking through into the conscious like a thunder clap.[3]

Port Royal.

Return to sources.

Vernacular use of Bible and the Fathers. Emphasis on redemption and grace. Emphasis on liberty or a more flexible idea of authority. They were ruined by the authoritarians.

The Jansenism of the end of the 17th century was something different. It was merely anti-Jesuit. Yes, they were pessimistic. Yes, they were combative. This is an example of a debate which made everybody wrong.

The priest, Monsieur de Sainte Martre, he went sneaking out from Paris by night, along the wall of Port Royal to a tree which he climbed and from which he gave conference to the nuns inside. Of this Sainte-Beuve says: "Voilà presque du scabreux, ce me semble; voilà les balcons nocturnes de Port Royal!" ["There, nearly scabrous, it seems to me; there the nocturnal balconies of Port Royal"].[4]

The serenades!

The nocturnal balconies of California.

---

3 Merton's reference to Descartes comes from Georges Poulet, *Studies in Human Time* (Baltimore: Johns Hopkins Press, 1956), 50–72.

4 Charles Augustin Sainte-Beuve (1804–69) was a French essayist, poet, critic, journalist, professor, senator, and novelist. See his *Port Royal* (Paris: Gallimard, 1961).

Brother rather than father. Partnership in seeking to understand our monastic vocation.

A happening.

Presence and witness but also speaking of the unfamiliar . . . speaking of something new to which you might not yet have access.

An experiment in openness.

Problems.

Too much conformity to roles. Is it just a matter of brushing up the roles and adjusting the roles? A role is not necessarily a vocation. One can be alienated by role filling.

Background.

Nazareth, Beguines, mystics of the Rhineland, beginning of the modern consciousness.

Problems.

Contemplative mystique. Feminine mystique. Theology of vows. Monastic life as an eschatalogical sign. Risk and hope. The promise of God to the poor or the promises of the beast to the rich. Judgment of power. Ecclesiastical power. Power prevents renewal. Power prevents real change. Garments of skins in the Greek Fathers. Hindu Kosas, then modern consciousness. Montaigne, Descartes, Pascal, Sufis, and Zen.

Astavakra Gita.

Christ consciousness in the New Testament.

Pascal said, "It is the joy of having found God which is the source of the sorrow of having offended Him."

Pascal said, "He is not found except by the ways taught by the Gospel. He is not preserved except by the ways taught in the Gospel."

"Thou wouldst not seek Me if thou hadst not already found Me." (cf. St. Bernard, Pascal)

Of Pascal, Poulet says, "Lived time is for Pascal as it had been for St. Augustine. The present of an immediate consciousness in which appear and combine themselves with it retrospective and prospective movements which give to that present an amplitude and *a boundless temporal density.*"[5]

---

5 Blaise Pascal (1623–62) was a child prodigy in mathematics and physics. From 1654 on, residing within the cloister of Port Royal, he concentrated on spiritual pursuits. His most famous literary works are the *Pensées* and *Provincial Letters.* The quotes here are from Poulet, *Studies in Human Time*, 74–95.

Words of Martin Luther King, recently shot, copied on the plane.

He said: "So I say to you, seek God and discover Him and make Him a power in your life. Without Him all our efforts turn to ashes and our sunrises to darkest nights."

May 6, 1968

O'Hare, big fish with tail fins elevated in light smog.

One leaves earth.

"Not seeing, he appears to see."

(Astavakra Gita)

Snow-covered mountains. Thirty-nine thousand feet over Idaho. Frozen lakes. Not a house, not a road. Gulfs. No announcement. Hidden again.

We are all secrets. But now, where there are suggested gaps, one can divine rocks and snow. "Be a mountain diviner!"

Whorled dark profile of a river in snow. A cliff in the fog. And now a dark road straight through a long fresh snow field. Snaggy reaches of snow pattern. Claws of mountain and valley. Light shadow or breaking cloud on snow. Swing and reach of long, gaunt, black, white forks.

The new consciousness.

Reading the calligraphy of snow and rock from the air.

A sign of snow on a mountainside as if my own ancestors were hailing me.

We bump. We burst into secrets.

Blue-shadowed mountains and woods under the cloud, then tiny shinings, tin-roofed houses at a crossroad. An olive-green valley floor. A low ridge thinly picked out at the very top in blown snow. The rest, deep green. One of the most lovely calligraphies I have ever seen. Distant inscaped mountains and near flat lowland. A scrawl of long fire. Smoke a mile or two long. Then a brown rich-veined river. A four-lane super highway with nothing on it.

Utah? It's dry.

Far down, a bright-nosed armed jet goes by very fast.

Six thousand dead sheep.[6]

6 On March 21, 1968, the *New York Times* reported that "about 5,000 sheep have been struck down by some mysterious killing agent. . . . Suspicion was pointed tonight at nerve gas being tested at the Army's Dugway Proving Ground [Utah]." The Army refused to comment on the incident. Two days later Dr. D. A. Osguthorpe, head of a special investigating team, said, "We are as positive as medical science can ever be" that nerve gas from tests conducted by the Army had killed 6,400 sheep in western Utah's Skull Valley.

Utah. Something I saw shining alone in a valley a moment ago could have been our monastery.

"New secret poison gas harms no one but the enemy."

Six thousand dead sheep.

Over the Nevada desert, nothing.

A long compacted serpent of cloud running north-south dominates, presides over the other looser clouds floating below relaxed, flaccid, and abandoned, flying slowly from west to east.

Six thousand dead sheep.

Real desert, not snow.

Salt.

A copper mine:

Red involved shamanic sign inscribed on the flat waste.

A sign of a stream ending in nothing. Pure dead, unsigned flats. Nada!

San Francisco. Two daiquiris in the airport bar. Impression of relaxation. Even only in the airport, a sense of recovering something of myself that has been long lost.

On the little plane to Eureka, the same sense of ease, of openness. Sense of relaxation while waiting because this is a different land, a different country, a more South American or Central American city. Significant?

A. Stern says of Sartre, "Each philosopher can only give the truth of his own existence. That is to say, philosophy is not a universal or impersonal science. Each individual perspective requires the others as its complements. The existentialist world view is determined by his actions and his means of action."[7]

Unamuno said, "Philosophy is a product of each philosopher and each philosopher is a man of flesh and blood who addresses himself to other men of flesh and blood like himself, and whatever he may do, he does not philosophize with his reason alone but with his will, his feeling, his flesh and

7 Alfred Stern, *Sartre, His Philosophy and Existential Psychoanalysis* (New York: Dell, 1967). Merton's opening sentence is an exact quote: "Each philosopher can only give the truth of his existence." The rest of the quote is either Merton's own journal writing or from another, unknown source.

blood, with his whole soul and his whole body. It is the man who philosophizes in us."[8]

Contrast Hegel, who said, "The teaching of philosophy is precisely what frees man from the endless crowd of finite aims and intentions by making him so indifferent to them that their existence or nonexistence is to him a matter of no moment."

Consistency.

Is the pseudomonastic experience an attempt to convince ourselves that we are somehow necessary? . . . Justification by monastic works or by a metaphysical consciousness?

Sartre said of the *Salauds*, "They tried to overcome their contingency by inventing a necessary being."

Monastic discipline: Learning to exist as a subject without a world? Primacy of the conscious subject, creating a certain consciousness to justify our existence instead of appreciating the primacy of existence as concrete, subjective, given, not to be acquired!

Fatal emphasis (in a monastic life) on acquiring something. What about this imperative? Does it make sense? "Convince yourself that you exist!" Baloney!

May 7, 1968

It was quiet flying to Eureka yesterday afternoon in a half-empty plane. One jet flight a day to this forgotten lumber town. Distant presences of Lassen peak and Mount Shasta, especially Shasta . . . like great silent Mexican gods, white and solemn. Massively suspended alone, over haze and over thousands of lower ridges.

The redwood lands appear. Even from the air you can see that the trees are huge. And from the air, too, you can see where the hillsides have been slashed into, ravaged, sacked, stripped, eroded with no hope of regrowth of these marvelous trees.

We land in Eureka, a windy, vacant field by the ocean. Vast sea, like lead, with a cold steady, humid wind blowing off it . . . almost as if there were no town at all; a few low wooden buildings, and a palm tree, and rhododendron

8 The Unamuno quotation is from Stern's *Sartre*. Merton inserted the words "whole" and "in" in the last sentence. Stern lists both the Spanish original of Miguel de Unamuno's *Del Sentimiento tragico de la Vida* (Madrid, 1913; New York, 1959) and the American edition, *The Tragic Sense of Life* (New York: Dover Publications, 1954) as his sources.

in bloom. I see Sister Leslie and Father Roger at the gate. Sister compliments me on wearing a beret.

Eureka, a curious low town of wooden buildings—strange leaden light. It is a fine day for Eureka. You can see the sun. Most of the time it is hidden in fog.

Signs.

A baroque yellow and black Victorian mansion which I five times photographed.

The place strangely reminds me of Little Neck, Long Island, or maybe Alaska, or maybe Siberia . . . God knows. The strange desolate windy low-slung non-town, yet with stores. We get a couple of cans of beer.

Driving down through the redwoods was indescribably beautiful along Eel River. There is one long stretch where the big trees have been protected and saved—like a completely primeval forest. Everything from the big ferns at the base of the trees, the dense undergrowth, the long enormous shafts towering endlessly in shadow penetrated here and there by light. A most moving place—like a cathedral. I kept thinking of the notes of Francis Ponge on the fir forest of Central France. But what could one say about *these*?

May 13, 1968

I am on the Pacific Shore—perhaps fifty miles south of Cape Mendocino. Wide open, deserted hillside frequently only by sheep and swallows, sun and wind. No people for miles either way. Breakers on the black sand. Crying gulls fly down and land neatly on their own shadows.

I am half way between Needle Rock, where there is an abandoned house and Bear Harbor, where there is another abandoned house—three miles between them. No human habitation in sight on all the miles of shore line either way, though there is a small sheep ranch hidden beyond Needle Rock.

North, toward Shelter Cove, a manufactory of clouds where the wind piles up smoky moisture along the steep flanks of the mountains. Their tops are completely hidden.

Back inland, in the Mattole Valley at the convent, it is probably raining.

South, bare twin pyramids. And down at the shore, a point of rock on which there is a silent immobile convocation of seabirds, perhaps pelicans.

Far out at sea, a long low coastal vessel seems to get nowhere. It hangs in an isolated patch of light like something in eternity.

And yet, someone has been here before me with a small box of sun-kissed seedless raisins and I too have one of these. So this other may have been a nun from the Redwoods.

A huge shark lolls in the swells making his way southward, close in shore, showing his dorsal fin.

Faint cry of a lamb on the mountain side muffled by sea wind.

When I came four or five days ago to Needle Rock, I told the rancher I would be out on this mountainside for a few days. He had just finished shearing. All the sheep were still penned in at the ranch. Now they are all over the mountain again.

This morning I sheltered under a low thick pine while sheep stood bare and mute in the pelting shower.

Song sparrows everywhere in the twisted trees—"neither accept nor reject anything."

(Astavakra Gita)

Low tide. Long rollers trail white sleeves of foam behind them, reaching for the sand, like hands for the keyboard of an instrument.

May 14, 1968

Sister Katryn danced barefoot in the choir Sunday after Mass. Beauty of these Flemish nuns and of the American nuns too. More beautiful in their simple blue and gray dresses without veils than in the affected and voluminous Cistercian habit—the cowl and choker. But they wear light cowls in choir and can wear such veils as they please. Some, like the chantress, a dignified mantilla. Others, a headband, others, nothing.

I told them I wanted to ask my Abbot's permission to spend Lent in the abandoned house at Needle Rock. Sister Dominique said they would all fight one another for the chance to bring me supplies.

Yesterday afternoon, late, waiting by the small barn with gray, well-weathered redwood shingles. The calm ocean with high cumulus clouds reflected in it and swallows circling the barn in the sunny air.

Not to run from one thought to the next, says Theophane the Recluse, but to give each one time to settle in the heart.

Attention. Concentration of the spirit in the heart.

Vigilance. Concentration of the will in the heart.

Sobriety. Concentration of feeling in the heart.

Bear Harbor is in many ways better than Needle Rock—more isolated, more sheltered. A newer house in better repair, with a generator. You reach it finally after barns, and the tall eucalyptus grove.

Flowers at Bear Harbor. Besides wild irises three or four feet high, there are calla lilies growing wild among the ferns and the strange bank . . . and a profusion of roses and a lot of flowering shrubs that I cannot name.

Bear Harbor—rocky cove piled up with driftwood logs, some of which have been half burned. Much of it could serve for firewood.

When Father Roger drove me out here this morning, it was low tide. Four cars or trucks were parked by the old dead tree at Needle Rock and people were fishing for abalone. Two other cars met us on the road as we went down. That's too many.

There were even two cars at Bear Harbor and two pair of young men . . . one of them a teacher interested in Zen.

About a mile from Bear Harbor, there is a hollow in which I am now sitting, where one could comfortably put a small trailer. A small loud stream, many quail.

The calm ocean . . . very blue through the trees. Calla lilies growing wild. A very active flycatcher. The sun shines through his wings as through a Japanese fan. It is the feast of St. Pachomius. Many ferns. A large unfamiliar hawktype bird flew over a little while ago, perhaps a young eagle.

I called Ping Ferry in Santa Barbara last evening. He spoke of birds, of the shore, of Robinson Jeffers and told me the name of the big jay bird all dark-blue with a black crest which I saw yesterday. It is called Steller's Jay. Does the jay know whose bird he is? I doubt it. A marvelous blue!

My piece on the "Wild Places" is to be printed in *Center Magazine.*[9]

Two ailing lombardy poplars, an ancient picket fence among the thistles: there must have been a house here once. Behind me a high wall of wooded mountain, green firs with many solitary, burned masts standing out above them. Wild fox gloves by the stream just where it sings loudest.

Yesterday, when Father Roger came to pick me up, he brought the mail. Most of it useless. There was a letter from Naomi Burton who said that the

9 "The Wild Places," *Center Magazine* (Santa Barbara, CA: Fund for the Republic) (July 1968): 40–44.

Journal of My Escape from the Nazis passes from hand to hand at Doubleday and nobody knows what to make of it. She likes it but the rest are idiots.

Lecture édifiante [edifying reading]. The Russian priest Sylvester wrote a famous book called the *Domostroy.* This Sylvester was the advisor of Ivan the Terrible but before he became terrible, so says the author I am reading. *Domostroy* seems to be the Russian equivalent of *Good Housekeeping.* Good Housekeeping for a Tzar whose housekeeping is not yet terrible.

Eugene Popov, honorary member of the Ecclesiastical Academy of St. Petersburg, taught that it was "a sin to make the sign of the cross with gloves on."

I wonder about the definition of Orthodoxy as hostility to rules worked out by Yelchaninov and quoted at the beginning. I wonder.

Eight crows wheel in the sky. An interesting evolution of shadows on the bare hillside beneath them. Sometimes the crows fly low and their dance mingles with the dance of their own shadows on the almost perpendicular olive wall of the mountain pasture. Below, the sighs of the ocean.

"How many incarnations hast thou devoted to the actions of body, mind and speech? They have brought thee nothing but pain. Why not cease from them?"

(Astavakra Gita)

Reincarnation or not, I am as tired of talking and writing as if I had done it for centuries. Now it is time to listen at length to this Asian ocean. Over there, Asia.

Yesterday, in this place, looking southwest, I thought of New Zealand and the *Wahine* and my Aunt Kit getting into the last lifeboat. It capsized.

I was sitting in the shade near the spot where the jay cried out on the branch over my head yesterday and awakened me as I was dozing in the sun. A red pick-up truck came up the dirt road. The owner of the land was in it with his wife and said he would be willing to rent me his house at Bear Harbor if plans work out for him in September, but he can't commit himself until then.

Frank Jones, Box 81, West Port, California.

May 16, 1968

I am flying over snowy mountains towards Las Vegas and Albuquerque and I read Han Yu's versatilities about mountains in the book of late T'ang poems I got yesterday at City Lights.

The snow suddenly gives place to a copper-colored desert.

We drove down together this time yesterday from Thorn. Mother Myriam is going reluctantly to the Chapter of Abbesses at Cîteaux. Sister Katryn drove. Al Groth, the neighbor, with the Heineken's beer rode in the back seat. I cashed Dan Walsh's check at Garberville together with another small royalty on the Bellarmine book, the symposium about the Council.

Eel River Valley. Redwoods. Redwood tourist traps, but also real groves. After lunch at Ukiah we went among fruit-growing towns, old brown wineries, conservative Cloverdale with a few oranges still in the trees and signs saying, "Impeach Earl Warren" and "Don't sell anything to the Reds."

Below, now, Death Valley.

At Santa Rosa, four gamblers were yelling in a cool Hofbrau. Draft Löwenbraü! Then we went to a place for prescriptions by the hospital. Then off on the bright freeway to the city.

The fine wide ranches, low white houses, eucalyptus, pepper wood pine, fruit trees. We crossed the Golden Gate Bridge in bright sunlight, the whole city clear.

A man, chased in vain by a painter who wanted to prevent him, had jumped off the bridge about an hour before.

Downtown San Francisco. I walked about a bit while the sisters went to find Portia, their postulant with whom they were to stay. Portia was getting off work at Penney's.

I called [Lawrence] Ferlinghetti. I went first to City Lights but he was not there. I got the T'ang poets, Heilo, something on Zen, William Carlos Williams, "Kora in Hell." We had supper at an Italian restaurant, Polo's. Ferlinghetti came after we had finished the bottle of Chianti. I went off with him to an Espresso place on Grant Avenue, the Trieste, where a young musician told of some visions he had had. Good visions, and not on drugs either.

Below, completely arid rocks, valley floor streaked with salt, bone dry. Twenty minutes from Las Vegas.

Turbulence at lower altitudes, we hear.

And some, like champions, Fen or Yü.

When the stakes are down, eager for the prize ahead,
The foremost and strongest rearing high above . . .
The losers looking foolish and speechless with rage.

In the little Italian restaurant in the North Beach area where I had an early breakfast today, a Chinese man, looking as though bewildered with drugs or something, ate repeated orders of macaroni with bottles of beer. It was seven o'clock in the morning. Much comment in Italian by the staff and the patrons. One of the hatted Italians whirled his finger next to the temple and pointed to the man, "you're crazy."

"I fear that heaven, just like man can lose its sight by lusting after beauty."

(Lu T'ung)

We bump down into Las Vegas over burned red and ocher canyons. Interesting rock peaks—like Sinai. Turbulence.

I stayed overnight last night at City Lights publications offices. A bedroom with a mattress on the floor, a guitar and a tape recorder and a window opening on a fire escape—a block from Telegraph Hill. Noise of cars roaring up the steep streets all night. Finally it got quiet about 1:30. I think I slept from 2 to 5 and also an hour somewhere around midnight.

Morning. Lovely little Chinese girls going in all directions to school, one with a violin.

A wide meteorite crater in the Arizona desert, like a brown and red morning glory.

I am the utter poverty of God. I am His emptiness, littleness, nothingness, lostness. When this is understood, my life in His freedom, the self-emptying of God in me is the fullness of grace. A love for God that knows no reason because He is the fullness of grace. A love for God that knows no reason because He is God; a love without measure, a love for God as personal. The Ishvara appears as personal in order to inspire this love. Love for all, hatred of none is the fruit and manifestation of love for God—peace and satisfaction. Forgetfulness of worldly pleasure, selfishness and so on in the love for God, channeling all passion and emotion into the love for God.

Technology as Karma.

What can be done has to be done. The burden of possibility that has to be fulfilled, possibilities which demand so imperatively to be fulfilled that everything else is sacrificed for their fulfillment.

Computer Karma in American civilization.

Distinguish work as narcotic (that is being an operator and all that goes with it) from healthy and free work. But also consider the wrong need for non-action. The *Astavakra Gita* says: "Do not let the fruit of action be your motive and do not be attached to non-action." In other words, do not let your left hand know what your right hand is doing. Work to please God alone.

Krishna says in the *Bhagavad Gita*, "By devotion in work He knows me, knows what in truth I am and who I am. Then having known me in truth, He enters into me."

The states of life. *Brahmacharya.* The life of the student in chastity under his Guru. *Grhastha.* The life of the householder begetting children, practicing Karma Yoga. *Vanaprastha.* The forest life. My present life. A life of privacy and of quasiretirement. Is there one more stage? Yes. *Sanyasa.* Total renunciation. Homelessness, begging. The Sanyasin lives only on food given to him. He is freed from all ritual obligations. The sacred fire is kindled only within. No household shrine. No temple. He is entirely turned to deliverance, renouncing all activity and attachment, all fear, all greed, all care, without home, without roof, without place, without name, without office, without function, without reputation, without care for reputation, without being known.

May 17, 1968

I am at the Monastery of Christ in the Desert, Abiquiu, New Mexico. I was bombarded by impressions getting here yesterday. The vast sweep of the Rio Grande Valley.

Sangre de Cristo Mountains, blue and snowy.

But after Santa Fe, marvelous long line of snowless, arid mountains, clean long shapes stretching for miles under pure light. Mesas, full rivers, cotton woods, sage brush, high red cliffs, piñon pines. Most impressed of all by the miles of emptiness.

This monastery is thirteen miles by dirt road from the nearest highway. In that distance, only one other house is passed—Skull Ranch. Around the monastery, nothing. Perfect silence. Bright stars at night dimly light the guest room. The only noise, the puttering of the pilot light in the gas heater. The adobe building is full of beautiful Santos [images of saints in sculpture or painting], old ones and new ones, serious as painted desert birds.

New Mexican workman on the lovely chapel whose roof recently fell in. It has to be redone.

Nakashima's placing of the chapel: working its lines into the setting of cliffs, is great. Inexhaustible interest of the building from all angles and in all lights. It is the best monastic building in the country.

There are only two monks here now: Dom Aelred, the founder, and Father Gregory. Both from the founding group at Mount Saviour. They were previously at Portsmouth Priory. There is also a hermit, Father Denis [Hines], a Cistercian from Snowmass in Colorado whom I have not yet seen.

Yesterday I said good-bye to Mother Myriam and Sister Katryn at the airport in San Francisco. Her plane left two hours after mine for New York and Brussels and for the General Chapter of Abbesses at Cîteaux which she expects to find hopelessly frustrating. Our Abbot General is trying to keep her at any price from going and talking to anybody in Rome. In fact, he is trying to prevent her and all the others from going anywhere, making contacts, getting experience, exchanging ideas.

"All blue is precious," said a friend of Gertrude Stein. There is very much of it here. A fortune in clear sky and the air . . . so good it almost knocked me down when I got off the plane in Albuquerque.

Father Roger, at the Redwoods, could not pronounce Albuquerque.

Alone, amid red rocks, small pine and cedar, facing the high wall on the other side of the Chama canyon. But east, the view opens out on distant mountains beyond the wider valley where the monastery is.

Light and shadow on the wind erosion patterns of the rocks. Silence except for the gull-like, questioning cries of jays.

Distant sound of muddy rushing water in the Chama River below me. I could use up rolls of film on nothing but these rocks. The whole canyon replete with emptiness.

"When the mind is stirred and perceives things before it as objects of thought, it will find in itself something lacking."

(Astavakra Gita)

To find this "something lacking" is already a beginning of wisdom.

Ignorance seeks to make good the "lacking" with better and more complete or more mysterious objects. The lack itself will be complete as void.

Not to deny subject and object but to realize them as void.

The alleluia antiphon for Terce at the Redwoods Monastery, composed by Sister Dominique, stays with me and is associated with the monastery.

The young redwoods clustered outside the big window of the chapel and then the ocean, Needle Rock and Bear Harbor.

The sun on the vast water, the sound of the waves. Yet the sound of the wind in the piñon pines here is very much the same.

The liturgy at the Redwoods was excellent. I enjoyed the daily concelebration with Father Roger, with the nuns coming up to stand around close to the altar at the end of the offertory and one of them extinguishing the candles as they retired after communion.

I have not yet concelebrated here at Christ in the Desert. That is to be this evening when I go back from the canyon to the monastery. In spite of the cedars and piñon pines, this is real desert in which one could well get lost among boulders, except that the end of the canyon is well in sight.

Just as in California around Thorn, I could see hollows and valleys like those of Kentucky, so here the view out at the end of the canyon is something like that from my own hermitage . . . a straight line of dark green hills with hollows and open patches. Only here, there is also a red wall of cliff and it is all much higher and the air is much clearer.

For the first time since I have been away, I now have the feeling that I might be glad to get back to Kentucky, but not to mail and visitors and invitations that I will have to refuse and other things that I will not be able to avoid.

A gang of gray jays flies down into the canyon with plaintive cat-like cries over my head. Some stop to question my presence. They reply to one another all over the canyon. They would rob me if they thought I had anything worthwhile. Gray Jay, "Whiskey Jack," a camp robber, inquisitive, versatile (says the bird book).

May 18, 1968

When I got in from my day in the canyon yesterday, after passing the goat barn and reaching the adobe building of the monastery guest house, I saw Father Gregory with some people and he introduced me to Don Devereux and his wife—Ping Ferry's friends from Santa Fe. There was much talk of Indians at supper.

Today in Don's old truck, we went to Abiquiu. I mailed six rolls of film to John Griffin to develop and we drove around the plaza—saw the adobe walls of Georgia O'Keeffe's house, the garden full of vegetation. Then, down the road, the site of the old pueblo that Don knew about, and two shrines. The site was superb, high over the valley, and one could imagine something of the way it was in the ancient civilization. The east opening of the shrine toward distant snow-covered mountains where obviously the sun rises at the June equinox. I came away with pockets full of pottery fragments and a tiny, almost entire obsidian arrowhead, like black glass.

I have run out of black and white film and had to get color film in Abiquiu. I took pictures of a lot of odd volcanic rocks lying around on Ghost Ranch. Vast sprinklers were watering the alfalfa and the lawns, neat houses of the Presbyterians, conference rooms and so forth of this religious center.

Don was telling me about the Alianza and Tijerina, an attack on a courthouse and a murder. Tijerina fled to the mountains and was interviewed secretly in his mountain hideout by Peter Nabokov, the young newspaper man whose book on the Indians I reviewed.

Simmering unrest in all this area. People set fire secretly to the government forest. There is much resentment about the land being taken from them—land which was granted to their ancestors by the Spanish crown.

Mexicans are working on the damaged church at Christ in the Desert and there is a water problem there.

I got up in the middle of the night with stomach cramps and ran barefoot down the cold pebble path to the hut with the toilet in it not knowing whether the toilet would flush. Fortunately, it did.

Arsenio, the Indian cook, makes fine breakfast for the workmen.

Father Aelred bought some beer the other day and Arsenio drank up a whole case of it in one night.

This morning I began looking at the copy of [René] Daumal's *Mount Analogue*, which Ferlinghetti just published and which he gave me in San Francisco.

Up the canyon from where I now sit, a couple of miles below the monastery, there is the heavy, domed architecture of a fat mountain ringed with pillared red cliffs, ponderous as the great Babylonian movie palaces of the 1920s, but far bigger.

Fresh wind, song of an ordinary robin in the low gnarled cedars.

May 19, 1968. Fifth Sunday after Easter

From *Mount Analogue*: "How it was proved that a hitherto unknown continent really existed with mountains much higher than the Himalaya . . . how it happened that no one detected it before . . . how we reached it, what creatures we met there—how another expedition pursuing quite different goals barely missed destruction."

Last night at dusk, the three tame white ducks went running very fast through the green alfalfa to the river, plunging into the swift waters, swimming to the other side, standing up in the shallows, flapping their white wings. Then the fourth discovered their absence and followed them through another corner of the alfalfa field.

The calls of the crows here in New Mexico as in California, are more muted, more melodious, briefer, less insistent than in the east. The crows seem to be flying at a greater psychic altitude, in a different realm. Yes, of course, a realm of high rocks and stunted piñon pine.

The curvature of space around Mount Analogue makes it possible for people to live as though Mount Analogue did not exist. Hence, everyone comes from an unknown country and almost everyone from a too well known country.

Georgia O'Keeffe did not come to the monastery to lunch today since she had to wait at her house at Abiquiu for a framer. Others came. Peter Nabokov, and so forth. We ate a large salad in the hot sun. I went quickly to rest afterwards to escape conversation.

This morning I had a long and rather funny talk with Father Denis at his field-stone hermitage by the river. He has a nice red cat. We talked of the Cistercian Order and of the monasteries and people in it—a discouraging topic.

May 20, 1968

Evening. Sun setting over Memphis Airport. I have come in a slow prop plane over flooded Arkansas country from Dallas. Between Albuquerque and Dallas, I finished *Mount Analogue*, a very fine book. It ends at a strange moment, a sign for the eschatological conscience—or it does not end, for the climb has only begun.

Peter Nabokov came to the monastery in the afternoon yesterday. I was glad to meet him and talk to him. There was much to say about the Poor People's March, for he had been at a demonstration in Albuquerque the day before. He said Albuquerque was very sweet—sweet, he meant, to the poor people.

May 22, 1968

All the time in the Chama canyon, I was looking out for rattle snakes. It is full of sidewinders. I went gingerly among the rocks and looked everywhere before sitting down. I thought they would like best the heat of the day and the burning rocks, but Denis said they preferred dusk, evening, and the night, yet the nights are cold. In the end, I saw no rattlers except at the zoo in Ghost Ranch Museum. There, a huge ugly monster of a diamondback and three indescribably beautiful others, whose name I forgot—long, lithe, silvery, sandy snakes with neat rattles, lifting up their heads gracefully with swollen sacks of poison. They were too beautiful, too alive, too much themselves to be labeled, still less to have an emotion, fear, admiration, or surprise projected on them. You would meet one in the rocks and hardly see it, for it would be so much like the silver, dead, weathered cedar branches lying everywhere and exactly the color of sand or a desert vegetation. I understand the Indians' respect for the snake—so different from the attitude ingrained in us since Genesis—our hatred and contempt.

In the desert one does not fight snakes, one simply lives with them and keeps out of their way.

The buildings of San Francisco, the two-spired church in North Beach, the apartments and streets of Telegraph Hill in warm, pale, South American or desert colors—snake colors, but charming and restful. Pretty as Havana and less noisy, though there was plenty of motor noise at night with cars climbing those steep hills.

Poulet says, "The starting point of the comic art of Molière is situated in the occasion in which a being is comprehended only through his actions." A demeanor, proper to an occasion, a basis of judgment, for instance: "This is a flying doctor." How do you know? He has a stethoscope. He flies. He is non-conformist.

Picture of South African heart-transplant patient passing a ball to international rugby players, who grin. When will we know if his heart now beats differently for his old wife! It is a Negro heart! Comedy: demeanor and *mis*demeanor!

A demeanor is therefore a misdemeanor. A misdemeanor in another is a cause of satisfaction to one whose own demeanor is not missing. We are not accustomed to seeing gentlemen act like this: which proves that we ourselves are gentlemen. (Not flying doctors or heart transplants with Negro hearts.) Until such time as the very fact of being a gentleman itself becomes ridiculous.

He is no menace to existence, clinging to a vanished order! Only the menace is to be taken seriously.

The gentleman is funny! And long-haired students sit in the office of Grayson Kirk at Columbia smoking his cigars as if they liked cigars. But then, you see, the gentleman can also eventually call the police, thereby reestablishing some claim to reality, and it is the long-hairs who are now funny (in jail?).

Thus says Poulet, "The comic is the perception of an ephemeral and local fracture in the middle of a durable and normal world." Well, that remains to be seen.

"Let the painter come to terms with his impatience." Words of Molière on The Painter of Frescoes and the comic playwright. Nominalism of Molière. Repeated hammering on one point until the character is depersonalized, generalized: "*miser! miser! miser!*" This is also the art of torture in the police state. To repeat an accusation until it sticks and the accused is both generalized and objectivized by pain.

To "make an example of."

"Now the soul is pleased when it *makes an example* of somebody else." Words of Poulet. "It will renew in itself the idea of the very lively pleasure it tasted that first time." Comedy is indeed close to torture!

And the French are now perhaps succeeding in making an example of de Gaulle, who first of all, made an example of himself.

"*Par exemple* [for example]!" the two meanings—*qui peut servir de modèle* [which can serve as a model] or *châtiment qui peut servir de leçon* [punishment that can teach a lesson].

But de Gaulle was always the pure exclamation, the *par exemple!* with the kepi on his head, who the other day exclaimed (as I saw in the San Francisco paper): "*La réforme, oui; le chienlit, non* [Reform, yes; vulgarity, no]!"

Somewhere, when I was in some plane or in some canyon, Dan and Phil Berrigan and some others took A-1 draft files from a draft center in a Baltimore suburb and burned them in a parking lot. Somewhere I heard they were arrested but I've seen no paper and don't know anything, but an envelope came from Dan with a text of a preface to his new book, evidently on the Hanoi trip, saying he was going to do this. It was mailed from Baltimore, May 17th, and had scrawled on it, "Wish us luck."

John Griffin sent one of my pictures of Needle Rock, which he developed and enlarged. I also have the contact. The Agfa film brought out the great *Yang-Yin* of sea rock mist, diffused light and half hidden mountain—an interior landscape, yet there. In other words, what is written within me is there, "Thou art that."

I dream every night of the west.

May 30, 1968

The country which is nowhere is the real home; only it seems that the Pacific Shore at Needle Rock is more nowhere than this, and Bear Harbor is more nowhere still. (I was tempted to cross that out but in these notes, I am leaving everything, permitting everything.)

And are you there, my dears? Still under the big trees, going about your ways and your tasks, up the steep slope to the roomy wooden place where the chasubles are woven—Sister Gerarda on a bicycle to the guest quarters, Sister William to bake hosts, big warm Sister Veronica in the kitchen, Sister Katryn to be an obscure descendent of Eckhart's Sister Katrei. Sister Katryn and Sister Christofora were the ones who seemed to respond the most knowingly whenever Eckhart was mentioned.

Sister Dominique, the impulsive, the blue-dressed, the full of melodies, who drove me in the car to the store to buy Levis; big gentle Sister Leslie from Vassar and blue-eyed Sister Diane from Arizona interested in Ashrams and Sister Shalom and Sister Cecilia, who came later to the party—and Mother Myriam, the Abbess, was responsible for this wonderful place. Which ones have I forgotten besides the two postulants, small dark Carole with the Volkswagen and big Portia from San Francisco?

Near the monastery, the tall silent redwoods, the house of the Looks and another house, neighbors by the Mattole River. The county line: here Mendocino, there Humboldt. My desolate shore is Mendocino. I must return.

The convicts came in an olive drab bus to cut brush along the roadside by the guest house. Smoking remains of green bonfires all along the limits of Al Groth's place. I did not see the convicts working—I was at the empty shore that day. I returned only after they were gone.

As we approached Sausalito, on the highway to San Francisco, someone pointed out San Quentin as the place where the convicts came from. A sinister white building on the bay.

Again I remember the Hofbrau outside Santa Rosa—the German Hofbrau in a wide Mexican valley by the American super highway. We took the wrong turn, got in the wrong parking lot, then out again into the right parking lot. The nuns waited in the car.

All around the hospital in Santa Rosa, the low offices of the gynecologists.

When I came, the convicts were cutting brush five miles northeast of Thorn. When I left, they were working and leaving bonfires near the monastery. Father Roger said: "They will not cross the stream."

I remember the desk smelling of oranges and my money in the top left-hand drawer in the old Bond Street wallet my guardian gave me on my 18th birthday before I started for the Riviera and Italy.

The narrow shower and the waste can full of orange peels, squeezed grapefruit, the sponge on the wash basin, bed heavy with dreams, the window curtain that pulled the wrong way, the dish of fruit on the bedroom table, the broken vase of roses replaced by field flowers, mail to go in a cardboard box in the utility room of unit one, mail read and thrown in the waste baskets smelling of oranges. Instant coffee at 4:30 a.m. with the Japanese coil—Do not touch for a few seconds after.

In the earthenware mug—"mug." I tell Father Roger, "not a cup, a *mug*."

Yogi [Fr. Roger's dog] and the cats. He fought them over his meat. He let them have his milk. Yogi used to belong to Diane. She asked about Ashrams, Diane!

Yogi romping over from unit one across the grass in the mist. I am going to the end of Lauds and to the whole-wheat bread and coffee and breakfast.

The long low monastery—its significance in the mist—chimneys—ventilators, like gray signs—the tops of the redwoods lost in the mist.

Chickens in the evening roosting in a line on a branch over the drinking fountain. No use.

Water in the drums of gasoline. Loggers explain to Father Roger as they siphon rust out of his engine—We do not go driving into the hills, drops of rust on the rusty ground.

I told them Sidi Abdesalam (the Sufi from Morocco) had asked me about my dreams, about my Abbot, and had said, "Within a year, there will be some change." And indeed, there was a change—for the better.

Then I arrived back here in Kentucky in all this rain. The small hardwoods are full of green leaves, but are they real trees?

The worshipful cold spring light on the sandbanks of Eel River, the immense silent redwoods. Who can see such trees and bear to be away from them? I must go back. It is not right that I should die under lesser trees.

While I was coming back, the students at Columbia were flying the Viet Cong flag over each building and each building had its own commune.

Leslie knew the name of every flower between Eureka and the monastery.

Cold spring light on the sandbanks of Eel River. Communes, gasoline drums, burned stumps of the redwood trees big enough for houses. I told them in the store I came from Kentucky and they were pleased. Not so, in the airport bar. There is no point in living ten miles from Jim Beam. Who needs Kentucky?

Rain. Work. Talk. Meetings. And a curfew on rioting Louisville.

End of Terce. I walk into the sacristy listening for the lovely Alleluias of Dominique. I leave the door half open. The nuns' voices, the tall trees outside the big window. The mysterious sky above the frosted sky-light. I pick up the amice to begin to vest for concelebration.

Putting it all back after Mass. The folded [altar] cloths in the drawer, the table. Diane walking outside the enormous window, looked up into the sunlight and seemed happy.

Climbing to the top of the high ridge before the sea: tall firs reaching into the sun above smokes, mists. Then down into the ferns!

I drove back with Gracie. We met the logger at a crossing in his white helmet in his pickup. Therefore Father Roger's truck broke down Thursday because this was the day after.

Looking down from the steep height, I saw Gracie, very small, very far, carrying her blanket from the dead tree to the car.

Winifred, her spring painting, a larva or fetus inspiring white reeds.

As we climbed the steep road, Winifred's hair was wet and stringy as if she had been swimming. And I opened letters.

Gracie told me about her son and his school. One of the little white bastards wrote "nigger" in the toilet. Others told her son they were sorry such a thing could happen in San Rafael.

The towhee in the wet Kentucky wood. Void. Nightfall. My meetings are temporarily over.

Hisamatsu: natural, rational and Zen spontaneity. "This is true self," he says, "going beneath spontaneity."

Hisamatsu also says, "There is a big difference between the ultimate self and the self discussed in psychology. When one reaches ultimate self, spontaneity is changed into ultimate spontaneity. Zen spontaneity comes from ultimate self . . . formless self which is never occupied with any form." And he adds, "In western music, great silence is not found."

In our monasteries, we have been content to find our way to a kind of peace, a simple undisturbed thoughtful life. And this is certainly good, but is it good enough?

I, for one, realize that now I need more. Not simply to be quiet, somewhat productive, to pray, to read, to cultivate leisure—*otium sanctum* [holy leisure]! There is a need of effort, deepening, change and transformation. Not that I must undertake a special project of self-transformation or that I must "work on myself." In that regard, it would be better to forget it. Just to go for walks, live in peace, let change come quietly and invisibly on the inside.

But I do have a past to break with, an accumulation of inertia, waste, wrong, foolishness, rot, junk, a great need of clarification of mindfulness, or rather of no mind—a return to genuine practice, right effort, need to push on to the great doubt. Need for the Spirit.

Hang on to the clear light!

PART III

Preparing for Asia

May 1968–September 1968

May 21, 1968. [Gethsemani]

This morning I got back to the hermitage from California and New Mexico. I arrived in Louisville on a slow propeller plane from Dallas, with long stops at Memphis and Nashville, at about 11 last night. Slept at the O'Callaghans' and drove out with Ron Seitz this morning—also Ed Ford with his hair like Bob Dylan's and his paintings, drawings, poems and fairy stories in the back seat. Actually a very good surrealist type of poet.

On the flight from Dallas—Northern Texas and Arkansas—(Red River, Arkansas River)—there were floods everywhere, calligraphies of birds and oxbows and lakes and flooded fields. Later—the lovely patterns of lighted towns. Everything greener and greener, and today, with all the grass knee deep and the young trees having grown a foot in two weeks, I scarcely recognized Kentucky. The Bardstown Road was almost unfamiliar, and I had a hard time adjusting to it. This evening—it is a wonder to see the cumulus clouds over the green hills in the south, and to live again in a forest of hardwoods, of oaks, elms, maples and hickories.

Northern California was unforgettable. I want very much to go back. Especially to Bear Harbor, the isolated cove on the Pacific shore where the Jones house is and which, I think, can be rented: the barrier, the reef, the eucalyptus trees, the steep slopes crowned by fir, the cove full of drift-redwood logs—black sand, black stones, and restless sea—the whole show, those deserted pyramids, the hollow full of wild iris, the steep road overhanging the sea, Needle Rock. I seem to remember every vale of that shore where I spent four days—and on the last day met Jones the owner and his wife in their red pickup and talked about perhaps renting their guesthouse. (The idea: that the convent of Redwoods would rent it as a place of solitary retreat, and I would perhaps go for Lent or for a month or two sometime in the year.)

In the other, small notebook I have notes I made on the spot, in California and New Mexico. Now I just put down what occurs to me this evening, now that I am home again: to try to establish the shape of an experience, a pilgrimage, memories of which keep coming back in recurrent flashes and impressions.

Such as the landing at Eureka, after looking down on the slashed redwood lands from the plane (after the first impression of San Francisco as a city I was immediately in love with as I was with Havana). Eureka: the feel of the desolate, calming Pacific winds. The emptiness of an incredible little town, with a Japanese freighter landing redwood to take to Asia. Sister Leslie in her grey habit and black stockings and glasses and her gentleness, driving the station wagon. Fr. Roger glad that I wore a beret (since he is Belgian). Sister Leslie admitting she once went to Vassar and wanting a certain root beer (instead of which we bought Olympia beer). Then the barns. Stories of the big flood in the Eel River Valley two (or three) years ago. And then the Redwoods. It was evening, and a cold wind blew in their immense shadows. We got out of the car and walked toward the river, and slid in a deep bank of sand down toward the water. The vast silence of the trees. Nothing. Immense girth and trunks going up forever. I have never seen anything so exciting as a big grove of them: but there are too few big groves left.

Then as we got nearer the monastery the deprived valleys and hollows looked something like Kentucky. Place where the convicts were clearing along the road to slow down forest fires. Then, behind big trees, the monastery itself, like a long, low, Japanese building. The big window of the chapel looking out at your redwoods, and the chickens perching on a low branch over the drinking fountain. (This made Fr. Roger furious and it was funny to see him chase them off. They made a lot of noise.)

Late dusk, and I had an immense supper of vegetables and bits of fish. Then I went to bed in the room that was to smell of oranges for ten days. And instant coffee, made with the Japanese bent coil in an earthenware mug of water. Reading first part of a book on Sartre which I abandoned, and then bits of [André] Ravier *La Mystique et les mystiques*, some of which not bad, much of which useless.

First day I went over the ridge into the valley which turned out to be "inside the enclosure." Some giant firs and redwoods, but only a few. And a small orchard with a high fence around it (15 feet) to keep out the deer. I wonder how the photos will turn out that I took of old logs with strange abstract patterns on them.

Fr. Roger's dog Yogi, which belonged to Sr. Diane before she entered. Yogi liking to go for walks, running from the guest house, expressing delight, chasing the cats away from his food.

I gave talks on "the veils," on Karma Yoga, Bhakti Yoga, the "contemplative mystique," the "feminine mystique" (a curse), and then on Sufism. In the room with big windows looking on a tiny yard with a sort of Zen garden in it. And the big blinds that the Sisters found hard to manage. A lot of good discussion. Mother Myriam especially very smart. All the community excellent. And I remember their liturgy. I would come in at the side and see the end of the choir only, perhaps Sr. Leslie, perhaps Diane, perhaps another, as they changed around. Some with veils, some not, and Sr. Veronica the big lovely Flemish cook who made me good meals and said ritually "enjoy your dinner" and gave me picnic lunches to take to the shore of the ocean.

I had the days to myself mostly, and all the work was in the evenings: Vespers at 3:30, then from 4 to 6 a conference, or "workshop" or whatever—then more after supper, the late session being more informal.

Couple of times went across the road and drank a bottle of Heineken's at Al Groth's house.

Concelebration every morning with Fr. Roger, sometimes preaching a homily. The voices and chants of the nuns very good. I cannot forget the Alleluia for Tierce, composed by Sr. Dominique. A lovely melody all involved in my memories of the Pacific, as I went out there after Mass. I went out first the second day (Wednesday 8th) driven by the postulant Carole, in her Volkswagen. The mist, the immense drop of the slope down to the invisible sea. Then, as the road wound down, the sea appeared. The bare pines where the slope had burnt. More turns. Sheep. The ranch, far below, by the surf, and finally the abandoned house, the barn, the dead tree at Needle Rock. The steep path down to the black sand. The piled driftlogs. The court of logs with arbitrary, ceremonious buildings. The tripod rocks with gulls and pelicans sitting on it. I walked barefoot in the sand until after three hours I discovered the sand was all volcanic glass and my feet were cut to pieces. Huge undertow of the Pacific. In any case, the gray waters could be seen to be very cold, and as I walked in the surf a sudden big wave soaked me up to the thighs and I did not dry all afternoon. After that walked on the high pasture over the sea and did not, on any of the other days I was there, go to the beach again. Friday I drove out with Gracie Jones (many stories of Vina) and this time climbed high up on the slope. It was a bright day and the sea was calm, and I looked out over the glittering blue water, realizing more and more that this was where I really belonged. I shall never forget it. I need the sound of those waves, that desolation, that emptiness.

I finished the talks on Sunday 12th (after Fr. Roger and I drove to Ettersburg—the Indian woman in the house, and the goats). On the 13th and 14th I was out all day at the shore—13th near the Pyramids, and the 14th I found Bear Harbor.

The 40 acres—stripped of redwood and fir, which the convent bought. But I am not concerned with a place near the convent. I must stay by the ocean—at least for a couple of months. I need the silence and the emptying. Radical change in my ideas out there. I must give up a lot of the useless activity I am engaged in—especially correspondence.

On Wednesday 16th Mother Myriam and Sr. (the dancer) Katryn and I drove down from the convent to San Francisco—through Garberville, the Eel River Valley, then Willits, Ukiah, "Conservative Cloverdale" with its oranges, Santa Rosa, etc., to San Francisco. They went to Penney's where Portia, that big sweet postulant, works. I meanwhile went for a walk and had some beers in a hotel bar where a Filipino fairy talked about his days in the Coast Guard and the barkeep was full of witticisms. I called Ferlinghetti who came and joined us all in an Italian restaurant and then took me to North Beach to an espresso place and eventually let me sleep in the City Lights Publication office, half way up Telegraph Hill. Pictures in the stairway of René Daumal's *Mount Analogue* cover. A good collection of H. M. Engensbuyer's verse in the office, which I read in the morning waiting for the nuns to return.

I could go on all night with this but I must go to bed. Fresh smell of the woods around the hermitage. A loud whippoorwill.

Andrew Lytle writes from the *Sewanee*, "That's awfully good on Blake and the New Theology."

May 24, 1968

A week ago today I spent the day up among the red rocks of the Chama canyon, watching out for snakes, watched by a gang of gray jays, staring at the high red wall of cliff on the other side, hiding from hot sun under a small piñon pine—ragged but adequate shade.

Christ of the Desert—with its elegant flop-eared Nubian goats, cared for by a Cistercian hermit from Snowmass. We had a long conversation in his hermitage, which he built of field stone, by the river. That was Sunday morning. The Church there is beautiful, but has had to be partially rebuilt since the roof started letting in rain and snow and even the walls began to be ruined this winter. Mass in the Chapter Room of the little transformed adobe farm house, which is a pleasant place. Everywhere in the monastery are good *santos and bultos* [images of saints] speckled like birds. New Mexico is an impressive place and I await from there the black and white and yellow Navajo rug Dom Aelred bought for my chapel (with two very small rugs I was able to afford for myself).

Don and Eileen Devereux came up from Santa Fe Friday and stayed the weekend. Saturday Don and I and a boy who hitchhiked in from Iowa went to the site of an old pueblo on the mountain above Abiquiu. Then to Ghost Ranch. There I spent the rest of the day in the rock and scrub this time SE of the monastery. And walked back along the road in the evening toward the big bulking cliffs under which the church is half hidden. Sunday—Peter Nabokov (whose book *Two Leggings* I reviewed) showed up with a Puerto Rican priest and a Christian Brother (Bro. Godfrey—quite a personality), all of whom were involved in the Poor People's March.

Left Christ of the Desert Monday morning in the monastery jeep. Drove with Dom Aelred and Fr. Gregory to Santa Fe. They were most hospitable to me and I have an idea they would be delighted to have me join them there—which I can't very well do, I guess. But even as a hermit, they'd be glad to have me, and said so. It is a good place, yet rather precarious at the moment (only three there, including Fr. Denis). They live on hope. But such a good site! I wonder they don't have dozens of postulants. Can they survive on goats milk cheese and on retreats? I don't know. But it is a great place for a monastery.

At Santa Fe airport the plane that was to take me to Albuquerque was late and I drove there (to A.) with two women who were stranded in the airport—both full of conservative and Republican talk. In the tree-shaded suburbs of Albuquerque, talking of "Mr. Nixon" and averring that "Rockefeller and his wife" would not "make a good President," I had lunch in the Kachina room at the airport, looking at all the ruddy, blond, WASP types and wondering how many right wing organizations they belonged to. Then off to Dallas on a Continental flight, an hour and a half in the big crowded airport, served in the Luau Room by a Baptist grandma in a Hawaiian nightgown, and then finally back to Louisville on a slow prop-flight that stayed a ½ hour in Memphis and another 1/2 hour at Nashville. Tommie and Frank O'Callaghan met me at the airport about 11 p.m. and I sat up late with them, talking, and finally slept.

Lonely for the Pacific and the Redwoods. A sense that somehow when I was there I was unutterably happy—and maybe I was. Certainly, every minute I was there, especially by the sea, I felt I was at home—as if I had come a very long way to where I really belonged. Maybe it's absurd, I don't know. But that is the way it feels. I seem to be alienated and exiled here. As if there were really no reason whatever—except a few tenaciously fictitious ones—for being here. As if I were utterly cheating myself by staying where I am only a stranger—and will never be anything else. I know how easy it is to be deluded by such things and so I try not to pay attention. In the end, I think I came to the best decision when I was out there: to try to get permission to spend Lent at least at Bear Harbor, but to maintain my "stability" here. This evening, the whole thing seems futile—as if it were not really an honest solution at all, only a compromise, and a very unreal one. As if I ought frankly to ditch the place and go where I will have real solitude, and won't be caught in this artificial *pretense* that keeps me here.

Or perhaps even Nicaragua . . .

Of course the problem arises from the fact that I felt very related to these bright and open nuns, mostly Europeans (and two bright Americans), much more in rapport with them than with people at Gethsemani (with many of whom I am nevertheless on very good terms—after all most of them were my students or novices at one time or other. Yet we have so little in common!).

I must not kid myself about this. But it would certainly be very good to live alone in the cove at Bear Harbor and come in once a week to give the nuns a talk and pick up supplies. This is at least for Lent. I think Fr. Flavian would allow it—but he has not committed himself. (He left today for the Abbots' meeting.)

May 28, 1968

Sunday, after three violent thunderstorms in the night, it rained hard all day. After dinner I went to Loretto for a conversation with some contemplative nun Superiors and Bishop Breitenbeck. The nuns, including Mother Angela of Savannah Carmel, Sr. Elaine Michael from Allegany, Mother Jane from Jackson Carmel, Mother Francis of the New Orleans Poor Clares, Sr. Elizabeth of the Carmel of Roxbury—are here for conferences.

Once again, realization of the paralyzing problems of these contemplative convents and of their need. Bishop Breitenbeck wants to help them—few can. We talked of some possibilities, and I said I would try to reach the Pope through Fr. F[iliberto Guala] in Frattocchie. Many of the convents were afraid of any change, don't know what to do, preserve silly or inhuman regulations and customs, are under attack from all sides, and see hope only in utter conservatism—which means purely and simply their extinction. Others want to develop and are prevented from doing so.

Although it does not seem to be my "line" to think in institutional terms, still there are *people* involved who badly need help. And those who are concerned enough to come here are really alert and well informed and want to do something. I have given them two talks based on Marcuse, others on the "Feminine Mystique" (as in California), and on Zen, etc.

Sr. Anita (Fr. John of the Cross's sister) came from Cleveland (Carmel) and I was delighted to see her so alive, unspoiled, spontaneous—a great nun. I was the one who advised her to go to Cleveland Carmel. Her Prioress seems like a good sort too.

I haven't had time for anything else but these conferences. The other day, before the nuns came, I got the second issue of *Monks Pond* assembled and sent a few copies out.

Last night there was a big race riot in Louisville. Shops wrecked on 4th Street and all the rest. Curfew. National Guard. It is probably still going on to some extent. There is going to be more and more of this everywhere. Obviously there is no hope of the Poor People's March achieving anything.

Phil Berrigan has been sentenced to 6 years in prison for pouring blood in the draft files in Baltimore and will also be tried with Dan for burning other draft files. *Six years!* It is a bit of a shock to find one's friends so concretely and tangibly on the outs with society. In a way, both Phil and Dan are saying openly and plainly what all of us know in our hearts: that this is a totalitarian society in which freedom is pure illusion. Their way of saying it is a bit blunt, and a lot of people are so dazed by the statement that they don't grasp it at all. Those of us who do grasp it are, to say the least, sobered. If in fact I basically agree with them, then how long will I myself be out of jail? I suppose I can say "as long as I don't make a special effort to get in"—which is what they did. All I can say is that I haven't deliberately broken any laws. But one of these days I may find myself in a position where I will have to.

June 4, 1968

Storms, rains and floods over Pentecost.

The nuns' meeting was tiring for me—two sessions daily lasting about 3 hours each at which naturally I had to do most of the talking. Too much. And while I only planned on 3 days there were two extra ½ days, with Sunday and Monday. I do not have the art of doing this well—I put too much into it. And am evidently driven by illusions I am unaware of. Probably the old narcissism. Anyway the result of it all is a feeling that psychologically I don't *need* this anymore. I can do the work if they need it, but it is certainly not necessary for me. Hence I'll be more free about it and expect a certain residue of ambivalence in myself. Certainly the complex business of being a "personality" and of exorcising the public demon it involves—all this is too much. And it perpetuates itself in the doing. Conclusion: there are probably others around who could do this job for the nuns better and more comfortably than I. Though there is a tendency to tell me that I have a sort of charism for it. I take that with a grain of salt. But certainly I can and must help them.

Fr. Eudes came back from the Abbots' meeting with an invitation to me to become "Editor-in-chief" of a new publication project, translations of the Cistercian Fathers. Obviously I can't take on such a job, even as a figure head—another phoney role. But I suppose I will have to be at least nominally a member of the board.

Still not able to use the washroom and toilet though the fixtures are there. No septic tank yet. The job was begun over four months ago. I don't complain and don't especially care. But it would not do to make repeated demands. People are getting a little critical of hermits, especially as Dom James, five miles away, requires a certain amount of attention. The people who do his chores for him are getting very critical of the situation (e.g. Bro. Nicholas on Sunday when Hilarion and I had to be driven out there). This reflects on the rest of us. I'll keep my trap shut, and I do try to ask for as little as possible (and do as much as I possibly can for myself).

Yesterday Fr. Baldwin asked me to give an afternoon session to the Novice Masters' meeting (next week)—this, of course, in the hermitage. OK. But it is another ambiguous situation. Visiting the famous hermit, satisfying one's curiosity as to what he is up to, noticing if there are empty beer cans in the kitchen, etc. And then the inevitable conference, dialogue, maybe a jazz record, to introduce them to Coltrane. That is what my life is becoming here. I cannot be completely adjusted to it. But what can I do about it? It would be just as false to say "no" to everybody and just keep to myself as if I possibly could make my own world and live in it without interference by anybody else. That would be even more unrealistic.

What I hope to do is to go into retreat for July and August—or for part of them anyhow. Even that won't be complete. Phil Stark (S.J.) is coming to help out with typing then.

Useless nostalgia for Needle Rock, Bear Harbor, the Redwoods!

June 5, 1968. Ember Wednesday (Pentecost)

Yesterday a letter came from Aunt Ka in New Zealand, about Aunt Kit's death in the *Wahine* disaster. Ka has had an enormous amount of mail to answer on account of it, of course—it being world news. They have had more trouble there, storms, earthquakes, etc. She is shaken by all these things.

This morning is cool, clear. The woods heavy with the scent of honeysuckle, and never so lush (with all the rain). I am about finished with Marcuse's *One Dimensional Man*—a good and important book. It was sent by the Asphodel Bookshop in exchange for some copies of *Monks Pond.* I agree with most of it except for the idea of a future in which science absorbs all metaphysics and final causes and means become ends in themselves. It seems to be a vicious circle.

Lax is supposed to be coming from Colorado and may arrive today. I was glad to have a quiet, more or less free day yesterday (apart from writing letters).

8:45 a.m. A few minutes ago Fr. Hilarion and John Willett came up in the truck with a 5 gallon can of water and told me Robert Kennedy had been shot in Los Angeles, after winning the California primary. A young 25-year-old man shot him almost at point blank range "to save my country"—a right-wing fanatic? Kennedy was still alive and being operated on. I hope he survives! Above all for the sake of his family.

8:15 p.m. I said Mass for Robert Kennedy when I went down today. News kept coming through: bullet removed from his brain, he is alive but will remain in critical condition for 36 hours. About the assassin—all kinds of rumors.

—"The police won't reveal anything about him."

—According to Br. Wilfrid, the man "couldn't speak a word of English and nobody could understand him—probably a Communist."

—According to someone else he had worked all evening side by side with Kennedy in the campaign Headquarters—probably a "Democrat"!

—Tonight it is said he came originally from Jordan. Though he is an American citizen his statement that he shot K. "because I love my country" is to be interpreted as pro-Arab and anti-Israel. It remains to be seen if this is really the story. It sounds a bit fishy to me, so far.

After writing another couple of letters I had a quiet afternoon—it was hot—over on Linton Farm. We are getting real June weather now. Hot, bright, with big cumulus clouds all over the sky and some wind in the right places. Dan Walsh is not here and no one knows where he is (nothing especially new about that). A card from Lax says he will be here later than he expected. Maybe next week?

June 6, 1968

More sorrow. I went down to the monastery with my laundry—saw the flag at half-mast and asked someone if R. Kennedy were dead. Of course, he was! The news was very depressing: there seemed to have been so much hope he would survive. I sent a telegram to Ethel. I wonder where Dan is.

A murder is bad enough in itself—but a political assassination of one whose brother has already been the victim of one, and when R.K. was in a good position to get the Presidential Nomination and even the presidency: it is shattering. He was liberal enough—though not by any means an ideal candidate: but he had possibilities and the country as a whole liked him: would have accepted him.

The most disturbing thing about it is something hard to formulate: but it seems to be another step toward degradation and totalism on part of the whole country. It will be used as an excuse for tightening up police control—"law and order"—and then in fact not to stop murderers but to silence protest, and jail non-conformists. And to prevent the kind of change Kennedy might have wanted to effect politically. The situation seems to me very grave.

I don't expect McCarthy to be nominated. Johnson's machine is too powerful. If it is a choice between Humphrey and Nixon, Tweedledee and Tweedledum—in fact, two nonentities—I can't vote at all. Still less for a goof like Reagan. And how vote for Rockefeller? He may be fairly capable but, like all these others, he will push the Vietnam War to its limit.

If McCarthy is not nominated I don't see my way to voting for anybody.

I wonder what effect this will have on the country—the people, or does it matter? They will be perhaps more docile about accepting another step toward a police state.

Meanwhile, of course, there will be more murders. They will become more and more part of political life. The definitive way of making one's point—i.e. for right wingers and fanatics of any kind.

I did some work on *Lograire*, morning and afternoon. It is hot. Drinking too much sweetened tea. Some of *Lograire* depresses me, but the O'Hare canto seemed good today. Perhaps because I can think of nothing I'd like better than to fly back to California. Maybe that's pure delusion. Perhaps I need to go much further: for instance the letter from Margaret Gardiner about the Orkneys made a lot of sense to me. The islands are gradually getting deserted. No one would bother anybody *there!!*

June 7, 1968

When I was having supper, Bro. Richard called to ask if I knew where Dan was. Nobody seems to know. A telegram came from the Kennedys asking him to the funeral. He can't be found.

Bro. Victor's theory of the assassination: "The Mafia? Same for Martin Luther King. And the guy who shot King has been ground up into mincemeat. They'll never find *him*." Why the *Mafia* should have wanted to kill M. L. King is not explained.

An intercom phone was finally put in the hermitage two weeks ago. It is useful. Most people don't yet know about it. Three calls in two weeks, and I made one call: all to do with guests: the nuns, Bishop Breitenbeck, Dan, and Bob Lax. Now a telegram from Kansas City says Bob arrives tomorrow evening. I have to go to Lexington (during the day) to hear John Niles' setting of several songs (mine and translations of Cuadra, Cortes, etc.).

I had a good talk with Fr. Flavian. He seems open to the idea of my spending some time in solitude by the Pacific, and even perhaps going to Asia to see some Buddhist centers.

Meanwhile, whether I ever get to Asia or not, I see the importance of real seriousness about meditative discipline—not just quiet and privacy (which I don't always have anyway), and deepening. Have really reached the point in my life where one thing only is important: call it "liberation" or whatever you like. Though I may write or not, I no longer *need* to and will more and more refuse to write so many prefaces and articles. (But really the ones I do write I am interested in. Even then I am losing interest.)

I know I have been through all this before, but now it does seem to be more decisive. Now I do think it is *final*.

June 13, 1968. Corpus Christi

After several days of clammy Kentucky heat, a bright day, bright and clear as September. The plumbers finally came, put in the septic tank, connected the water pipes—and I have a working bathroom at last. After shoveling some dirt that had been left, I took a shower, and drank shandygaff (for by chance I had a can of English ginger beer, very expensive, left by Jonathan Greene). The hills were particularly beautiful and green.

Bob Lax came Saturday night, when I was getting home from a day at Niles's in Lexington, listening to his setting for poems of mine and for translations of Cuadra, Cortes, Carrera A. Again, I enjoyed being in that house and seeing Bob Shepherd's place on Pebblebrook Farm, but nevertheless it was a tiring day. Good visit with Lax—but several picnics I also found exhausting in the very hot weather. The O'Callaghans with their children, Tuesday, for example. Better yesterday when it was cooler and only Jonathan Greene came over. We took some photos in the woods, at the station, at the distillery, which I hoped would be good.

This morning I did a little more work on *Lograire*. Lax left after dinner. I don't know if he should return to Greece. Kalymnos seems to be the only place he really likes anywhere. I don't blame him. But also I don't trust a police state sustained by C.I.A.

The other night when it was too hot to go to bed, I was sitting up with nothing on but a pair of underpants when a couple of admirers suddenly appeared in front of the cottage. I told them to get the hell out, thereby once again ruining my image. But one of them wrote a very nice note of apology nevertheless. And today I met a couple of others standing looking in awe at the "No Trespassing" sign. Brief conversation by the stile. One is to do an MIT thesis on my early poems. Meanwhile I was a bit depressed by a longish dissertation on my work (James Baker's—the first formal one, I guess). It was all right, he had done a lot of work, read an enormous amount of my writing (certainly not all of it!) and was highly sympathetic to my ideas. That was all fine. Yet the whole thing showed me clearly so many limitations in my work. So much that has been provisional, inconclusive, half-baked. I have always said too much, too soon. And then had to revise my opinions. My own work is to me extremely dissatisfying. It seems trivial. I hardly have the heart to continue with it—certainly not with the old stuff. But is the new any better?

Would I do better creative work alone out by the Pacific? I have a feeling I probably would. Gracie Jones sent some pictures of the Redwoods and of the shore at Needle Rock. I remember those extraordinary days.

June 14, 1968

Another fine day.

I had a good talk with Fr. Flavian. He had received a letter from the Prior of our monastery in Indonesia. The latter, assuming I was going to the regional meeting of Asian Abbots at Bangkok, asked if I could preach a retreat at Rawa Seneng [Trappist monastery in Indonesia]. Fr. Flavian said I could do this if I wanted to—and I want to. It is an opportunity to get to Asia and to get some badly needed experience. However—it is a long way off. Five months at least.

It will mean not taking on any more writing jobs for next winter, as I hope to go to Japan too, see some Zen places, and perhaps go from there to San Francisco and the northern coast.

Needle Rock is, I guess, within sight of Cape Mendocino and hence is one of the points south of Canada that are nearest to Asia. Spanish ships from the Philippines used to steer for Krig Peak, which is behind the cape. Then go south along the coast to San Francisco.

June 15, 1968. Saturday

Finally got back to my routine of Saturday fasting. Went out in the sun to Linton's farm and got a good burn on my shoulders, reading a little about Islam mystics and feeling once again something like myself. The visits have been a drag, no matter how much I like Lax, Jonathan Greene, Ron Seitz, Dick Sisto, etc. I just need to have long periods of no talking and no special thinking and immediate contact with the sun, the grass, the dirt, the leaves. Undistracted by statements, jokes, opinions, news. And undistracted by my own ideas, my own writing.

I got home and shaved on the porch and had my one meal about 3:30 p.m. Then fell on the bed in a stupor, slept an hour, got up and said Office, read a few Zen texts in Spanish in *Cona Franca* and finally some René Char (which Jonathan Greene left with me) which I very much enjoyed again. Fascination of his language and line:

Buses, milans, martres, ratiers,
Et les funèbres farandoles,
Se tiennent aux endroits sauvages.
[Buzzards, kites, martens, ratters,
and funereal farandoles
keep to primeval places.]

It takes me back to the summer of 1966 when I was so much under his spell (along with all the other spells of that time!).

I am a bit annoyed at the fussy, importunate efforts of Fr. Basil (of Spencer) to involve me in his editorial project and in a symposium which is connected with it. I half consented to go to this, and then the next step was to try to involve me in a debate with Louis Lekai on "Cîteaux and

Eremitism." Nuts! I wrote and said I only intended to go insofar as it might be necessary for the publication project and not as a member of a debating society. As I see it now I won't go at all. The decision is apparently up to me. So I feel much more peaceful about it. I have no need whatever to please or accommodate these people. The whole thing seems to me useless and silly. Others who want an excuse to get out and talk can go. I have no interest whatever in any of it.

It is impossible to go near the monastery without having to stop and talk to five or ten people. Idiotic. Without being brusque, I try to cut it short and get away as fast as I can.

June 17, 1968

The novice masters of the American monasteries are having a meeting here, and since I am an item, a tourist attraction on the grand tour of Gethsemani, I am to give them a paper in the hermitage tomorrow. And of course the following day they go onto Dom James. Reports are of enormous rattlesnakes ("Bigger than your arm") being shot around Dom J's hermitage by monastery vigilantes. And also of brothers being tired of driving Dom J back and forth on that rough road. I am very glad I had the sense not to get involved in the Laura project [colony of hermits] that was at first (1964) considered for Bell Hollow and the rest of Edelin's place.

On the contrary—Ping Ferry speaks of getting land at Big Sur and intimates that there could be a place for me on it. But Big Sur sounds too popular. Not only are the hippies moving there, not only are the Camaldolese there, but also several ex-Gethsemani Trappists are priests in that vicinity.

I finished an article on silence ("Creative Silence") which against my better judgment I undertook to write for a Baptist Student magazine. The decision was made in the guest room at the Redwoods—perhaps after returning from the beach. When I had finished it I was content enough, but I had trouble getting started!

June 23, 1968

Very hot. Steamy, heavy, soggy. It will be a dreary night—especially if [Andy] Boone lets his dogs out again to chase foxes in the hollow behind my place! (Which he did the other night.) But it doesn't matter. I am fortunate indeed to be in the woods.

This afternoon I found a tolerable breeze in the woods near the cottage, on the SW, on the hill before you get to the sheepbarn. Walked there content in the afternoon before conference. Suddenly a big deer started up very nearby (did not hear it come). When you are used to only rabbits, squirrels and woodchucks, a deer at 50 ft. seems enormous. Big as a house!

The flycatchers nesting on my waterpipe (from the roof gutter) are charming and keep busy with the flies that are so annoying.

John Wu's son came with his wife Teresa—on their honeymoon—the other day. I said Mass for them in the hermitage chapel on the Feast of the Sacred Heart and they are two very charming young people—but I have had so many visits I am mortally tired of them. The last two free days have been a blessing. So too was the sunny afternoon of the feast when I went off to the far end of a beanfield on Linton's and took my shirt off and meditated in the sun—(on the *Yoga Vasishta*—excellent). Realize more and more that what really matters to me is meditation—and whatever creative work really springs from it.

Though there is very little enthusiasm at Doubleday over *Journal of My Escape [from the Nazis]*, Naomi has been authorized to make me an offer and I am accepting it. Maybe I'm wrong. I think Doubleday is a bunch of nitwits. But Naomi likes the book and has fought hard for it—will continue to—and New Directions has several other jobs on hand. *Geography of Lograire*—tentative first draft (with more to come, I hope) has gone to be typed.

Election in France today. A critical situation!

It looks as though Fr. Flavian will approve my going to Bangkok, as well as Indonesia, if Thailand doesn't get into complete war—as I am afraid it will. In any case I am planning on Indonesia (and scarcely believe it possible!) hoping also for Japan and some Zen monastery. If I get to the Asian Abbots' meeting I will probably be involved in several retreats, or conferences, in Asian monasteries. What I really want is, however, to meet Buddhists. But what I want most of all is to spend a couple of months entirely alone somewhere on the shore of the Pacific.

June 24, 1968

I decided I had better take this occasion to go to town before going into a (relative) period of retreat for part of July-August. Did not go to any doctor—everything more or less OK in that regard—but spent the day in the U. of Louisville Library—trying to find something useful on structuralism. Nothing. No Lévi-Strauss, no Barthes, Lacan, etc. I raked through several bound volumes of the *NRF* and found a good article by Foucault.[1]

However, with the help of one of the reference librarians I did find some practical information on visas, shots, vaccinations, etc. for travel in SE Asia and Indonesia. Marco Pallis[2] has sent one good address in Japan and Amiya Chakravarty[3] does not exclude the possibility of getting into *Burma* even!! That could be exciting (great xenophobia there—understandable—you can only stay 24 hours).

Before leaving I had a long wait at the steel building and watched two of the Farm establishment (Bro. Christopher and Bro. Alban) play a fast game of handball against the wall of the horsebarn. The new look in monasticism! Bro. Irenaeus drove me in and took Bro. Chrysostom to the airport—he is going to a cantors' workshop at Spencer.

I have sent the whole first draft of *Lograire* to Paula Hocks for typing (minus a few pages of Ghost Dance yet to be done). And also I have accepted an offer from Doubleday for *Journal of My Escape from the Nazis*, though they are very cool towards it for the most part. Yet Naomi is for it and so is one other senior editor. I think I'd better leave it to them rather than give it to New Directions, which will normally have *Lograire*.

June 26, 1968

Don Devereux wants me to come to New Mexico to see some of the Indian festivals! I wish I could go!

1 *NRF* refers to *La Nouvelle Revue Française*, a French journal Merton researched at the University of Louisville library. Vol. 12 contained two articles by Michel Foucault, the French psychologist, "La metanior prose et le labyrinthe" (1963) and "La prose d'Actaeon" (1964).

2 Marco Pallis was born in Liverpool, England, in 1895, of Greek parents and was educated at Harrow and Liverpool University. He is best known for his 1939 book about his experiences in Tibet, *Peaks and Lamas*, which made an enormous impression on Merton. He visited Merton while touring the United States with the English Consort of Viols.

3 Amiya Chakravarty was for many years a philosophy professor at State University College, New Paltz, New York. He was a long-time friend, correspondent, and adviser for Merton's reading in Asian religions; Merton dedicated his book *Zen and the Birds of Appetite* to him.

An invitation came today to preach a retreat (next January) at Our Lady of the Genesee. Of course, I'll refuse.

Another invitation to go all over the country speaking—all expenses paid and $6,000 beyond that. Nuts. This sort of thing would be useless and absurd for me. The fact that one might do *some* good etc., is no argument. No matter what you do, you might do *some* good.

Anselm Atkins was here (from Conyers) briefly yesterday. We had a short talk on the library balcony.

I once again went over the mimeo of *Journal of My Escape*, rearranged the chapters (still mixed up after Marie Charron got the whole thing in confusion) and think I finally have it in good enough shape for the editors at Doubleday.

Translated a couple of poems of René Char and put them on tape along with the notes I made about the May Journey to the West (the stuff in the small notebook, not this one).

June 29, 1968. Saturday. SS Peter and Paul

More invitations. Yesterday the Esalen Institute—to conduct a seminar at Big Sur—and to speak in San Francisco. This is more attractive than most but I can't accept it either. Bishop Breitenbeck who is going around trying to help nuns get organized wants me to join in that. But Fr. Flavian isn't having any. Etc. But I do look at maps of the Pacific, study flights: San Francisco-Manila-Singapore, Jakarta—I do think it is best to give my efforts to the most "abandoned"—and remote—and those in Asia and Africa from whom there is also so much to *learn*.

I am reading [Frantz] Fanon's *Black Skins, White Masks*—a really extraordinary book. From every point of view—as a piece of existentialist philosophizing, an analysis of the race question, as a work of literature (got it from Jim Lowell at the Asphodel Bookshop in exchange for *Monks Pond*).

Also reading Vance Packard's *Naked Society*—timely enough! The new crime bill now permits all kinds of bugging, wire-tapping, evidence so obtained can be used in court, etc. A big step towards a Police State. Not *towards:* we are in many respects already there. All these new things (bugging equipment, gasses, armored cars, etc.) will be used more and more against forces of change and dissent. And less against criminals than against dissenters.

I am spending the afternoon reading Santi Deva in the woods near the hermitage—the oak grove to the SW. A cool, breezy spot on a hot afternoon. (I changed my mind about going across the road and out to the small pond in the knobs—or—on the way there yesterday I ran into too many people.) Quiet—except for someone firing a gun at the pond across the road: typical!

Thinking deeply of Santi Deva and my own need of discipline. What a fool I have been, in the literal and biblical sense of the word: thoughtless, impulsive, lazy, self-interested, yet alien to myself, untrue to myself, following the most stupid fantasies, guided by the most idiotic emotions and needs. Yes, I know, it is partly unavoidable. But I know too that in spite of all contradictions there is a center and a strength to which I *always* can have access if I really desire it. And the grace to desire it is surely there.

It would do no good to anyone if I just went around talking—no matter how articulately—in this condition. There is still so much to learn, so much deepening to be done, so much to surrender. My real business is something far different from simply giving out words and ideas and "doing things"—even to help others. The best thing I can give to others is to liberate myself from the common delusions and be, for myself and for them, free. Then grace can work in and through me for everyone.

What impresses me most at this reading of Santi Deva is not only the emphasis on solitude but the idea of solitude as part of the clarification which includes living for others: dissolution of the self in "belonging to everyone" and regarding everyone's suffering as one's own. This is really incomprehensible unless one shares something of the deep existential Buddhist concept of suffering as bound up with the arbitrary formation of an illusory ego-self. To be "homeless" is to abandon one's attachment to a particular ego—and yet to care for one's own life (in the highest sense) in the service of others. A deep and beautiful idea.

"Be thou jealous of thine own self when thou seest that it is at ease and thy fellow in distress, that it is in high estate and he is brought low, that it is at rest and he is at labour. Make thine own self lose its pleasures and bear the sorrow of its fellows . . . etc."

Reference to be given to helping others to enlightenment, therefore helping those who are *closest* to it.

July 1, 1968

Very hot. One of the hottest days I can remember here. Clammy and stuffy—but with a breeze—even though hot—in the woods. I spent part of the afternoon there, beginning Heiler's book on *Prayer,* which I find very moving and true. This is a good time to read it, as I hope to make July at least relatively a time of retreat, silence and prayer. I do have one or two appointments (I need to see John Ford to keep straight on contracts for these TV performances of *Freedom Songs,* etc.—all of which belong to Robert Williams). A call came today from Richard Walsh of NCCM [National Conference of Catholic Men] (about these songs and this silly show).

This afternoon I finally got down to the job of editing *Monks Pond III,* sweating all over the manuscripts and my letters of acceptance (or rejection).

Now—night falling—it is still very close, but thunder is heard in the distance and maybe it will rain and cool off during the night. Meanwhile, a loud racket of many birds in the stifling dusk (cardinals, jays, larks). And guns at the lake across the B[ardstown] road.

July 3, 1968

"Intellectual alienation is a creation of middle-class society. What I call middle-class society is any society that becomes rigidified in pre-determined forms forbidding all evolution, all gains, all progress, all discovery. I call middle class a closed society in which life has no taste, in which the air is tainted, in which ideas and men are corrupt. And I think that a man who takes a stand against this death is in a sense a revolutionary." *—Fanon*

Yesterday I finished Fanon's intelligent, well-written, eminently true book *Black Skins, White Masks.* Written earlier than the *Wretched,* it is more incisive, dispassionate, less angry. He still thought he could communicate with white men.

Today I begin Kierkegaard's *Attack upon Christendom.* A fascinating and deeply disturbing book. All very well to smile at Bishop Mynster "living out his days to be buried with full music," but what priest is *not* a Bishop Mynster? The very idea is that we will fulfill an *office,* in other words be respected members of an establishment and carry out our job. And the implication is that *in so doing* we automatically witness to the truth—become links in a chain of witnesses. What could be more false?

Yesterday (Visitation) a violent storm during dinner. I never saw such a black sky at noon or so much wind out in the front garden of the monastery.

(Yesterday) In the afternoon I finished selecting stuff for *Monks Pond III*, and feel happy about it. So much fine poetry: [Pentti] Saarikoski, [Ted] Enslin's Journal, Marvin Cohen, Bes[milr] Brigham's Mexican Tigers, I hope 3 or 4 of [Anselm] Hollo on Bears. Little Chris Meatyard's lovely "Inner Light" poem (he is what? 12, 13?) Another fine poem by a 12 year old I am saving for IV.

(evening)

In the morning I went out early and finished cutting down and trimming the young pines still bent over since last winter's big blizzards. The bush boundary of my yard, toward the woods, is now clear—relatively (some sumac coming up along the fence line, however!). This work made my back sore again—so I have to be careful. In the afternoon I went to the farthest end of the soybean field on Linton's and took off my shirt to get the sun on my neck and shoulders while I meditated (Hatha and Yoga Vasishta). A quiet and profitable afternoon and God knows I need much more of this! How much precious time and energy I have wasted in the last three years, doing things that have nothing whatever to do with my real purposes and which only frustrate and confuse me. It is a wonder I haven't lost my vocation to solitude by trifling and evasion.

One thing is very clear: all that passes for *aggiornamento* is not necessarily good or healthy. One has to remain pretty critical and independent about *all* ideas. And come to one's own conclusions on a basis of one's own frank experience. Both the conservatives and the progressives seem to me to be full of the same kind of intolerance, arrogance, empty-headedness, and to be dominated by different kinds of conformism: in either case the dread of being left out of their reference group. I have to go my own way in terms of needs that to me are fundamental: need to live a life of prayer, need to liberate myself from my own "cares" and "unique" need for an authentic monastic solitude (not mere privacy), and need for a real understanding and use of Asian insights in religion.

I naturally think a lot about Indonesia, but haven't read much yet—have only leafed through a couple of volumes of the *National Geographic*—Borobudur, Bali dancers, an amphibious jeep about to cross to Bai Strait, 25 varieties of poisonous snakes, active volcanoes, etc. The traditional religious art and architecture strike me as dull. The people—beautiful. I plan dutifully to read the article on Java in the (1911) *Encyclopedia Britannica* in our monastic library.

New Directions sent me Bro. Antoninus's book on Jeffers. I began reading it immediately, on account of the coast. (I never paid much attention to Jeffers before. But Ping was talking about him when I was at the Redwoods and called him in Santa Barbara, enthusiastic about the sunny day at the shore—May 13—and Steller's Jay.)

This evening I went back and read over the parts of this Journal about California and New Mexico. May and June. And coming back here. Once again—I am uneasy about staying here. Should I go to New Mexico? That sounds foolish. (But transfer to California is legally questionable—by Church Law—as I don't want to go to Vina.) All this had to be decided not on the basis of the old legal concepts but of something much more fundamental. I guess I am not clear just where this basis is to be sought so the time is not yet come. (If ever it will.) Meanwhile, Dom Eusebius has resigned and there is to be an election at Vina.

July 5, 1968

Attack upon Christendom. How can one laugh and shudder at the same time? The book is so incontrovertibly *true.* And to find myself a priest. And to find my own life so utterly false and trivial—in the light of the New Testament. And to look around me everywhere and find people desperately—or complacently—going through certain motions to prove that they are Christians. (And far more people not giving a damn and not even paying attention, so that "proving one is a Christian" comes to mean begging for *just a little attention* from the world—some grudging admission that a Christian can be an honest man.)

At least this: I have enough self-respect left to refuse to be abbot and to refuse to go around to meetings and lectures and functions. And I have felt a little compunction about continuing to proclaim a "message" just because that is what people expect of me. It is not easy to talk of prayer in a world where a President claims he prays for light in his decisions and then decides on genocidal attacks upon a small nation. And where a Catholic Bishop praises this as a "work of love."

Paralyzing incomprehension—what does one do when he realizes he is part of an organization whose members systematically try to "make a fool of God"? I suppose I begin by recognizing that I have done it as much as the best of them.

But then a "God is dead" Church is no better, nor are the "God is dead" Christians an improvement over the others. Just the same established flippancy and triviality. And even more successful. They make a good living out of God's death.

(Evening)

What a difference between Fr. Flavian, as abbot, and Dom James. And what a difference in our relationship. I get a real sense of openness, of possibilities, of going somewhere—and at times it is almost incredible. I seem to be dreaming.

He is *very* interested in perhaps starting something out on the Coast. And today, in so many words, he asked me if I were willing to start it: i.e. to go out there and get some sort of small hermit colony going. I said I certainly would do that any time. When he goes out for the Vina election he will go over to Redwoods and look at the various places: Bear Harbor, Needle Rock, Ettersburg. . . . It is fantastic. I don't know if he intends to buy Bear Harbor—or if Jones will sell it. But the mere fact that he goes ahead and *thinks of it!* One slowly comes back to life, with the realization that all things are possible.

I don't know where this will end up—on the coast, in New Mexico, or where. But I am certainly ready for anything in that line. It would mean going out and occupying the place and living there, preparing for the time when he himself might retire and come there. The proposition seems to be a small laura for four or five hermits, not a separate institution, not with new rules, canonical statutes, etc., but a place to live in solitude, perhaps within the framework of the Order. For that side of it—I leave it to him. He is a canonist and has good sense.

I told him frankly that I thought we had gone as far as we can go here. The real solitude is not possible here, at least for me. The area is getting very crowded. I am too near the road. Today again a couple of retreatants showed up on my porch—just wanting to "see" me, etc.

July 9, 1967

Strange thing, this morning: after Mass (St. Albert—hermit) [Feast Day], and coffee and light breakfast and article on Panama Canal in *Bulletin [of the] A[tomic] Scientist*, tried to work on Gordon Leff and the Franciscan poverty business (*Heretics in Late M[iddle] A[ges]*) and couldn't keep my eyes open. Fell asleep on it. Went and lay down dopey for ½ hour, then got up and looked for something new. So Darcy O'Brien on *The Conscience of Joyce*. Not a marvelous book itself (a bit obvious—and limited perspectives), but Joyce himself woke me up again and now I am very involved in it. Dedalus's aesthetics. The essentially *contemplative* vocation of Joyce. His revolt is that of the contemplative and creative man called to self-transcendence and "held down" by the prosaic, legalistic, provincial Catholicism of the Irish middle class—the bourgeois Catholicism of the 19th century—which continues in another form in the 20th—liberal, pragmatic, pedestrian, "practical," exalting matter and science, etc. and still putting down contemplation as "gnostic," "unchristian," enemies of the imagination, but not really earthy either. O'Brien tends to give Joyce this same stereotyped business: "rejection of the faith" (the girl standing in the water), "hatred of life." (How can he say such a thing? Surely he'll take that back.)

Perhaps the power of my response is due in part to the fact that I had to read and comment on two indifferent, typical, contemporary stories about sexual overkill—including the Ranière one in *Latitudes*. Opposite pole to Joyce—matter above all of ethical *taste*, of standpoint and implicit judgment. Joyce is [indecipherable], reasonable, Christian, free; the others reflect an attitude that is to me sick, barbarian, irrational, in effect swinish. *America is a swinish culture*. And yet it isn't. All this is broadcast everywhere and yet people remain "nice" and halfway decent. Or do they? How deep does the decency go? A curious thing. And I can't judge. But "officially" in literature, etc., there are no more bounds—not that the most outspoken and far-out are the most degraded. They are perhaps more healthy (the underground paper bunch) than the ones who are ½ way reputable. It's the *Playboy* mentality that seems to me sickest.

I'm frankly on Joyce's side (and he was once thought to be the ultimate in "filth")—and [François] Rabelais's. True priestly mentalities—"monks" in the old Celtic style—free from the littleness and nastiness of the moralizers without imagination and without real morality.

A lot of dreams last night I can't remember.

July 12, 1968

Hot again. Man and boys in the field in the bottoms, surveying for the sewage disposal plant. I passed them, sweating heavily, at the end of my walk this afternoon. And it is the first chance I have had for a walk this week.

Phil Stark, Jesuit scholastic, is here. He offered to help with typing and I took him up on it, in order to get the next two issues of *Monks Pond* done. But now the electric typewriter has broken down.

Steps are now being taken to get my passport and visas for Japan, Thailand, Singapore, Indonesia, New Zealand (I decided I'd better see my family there on the way home). Maybe also Taiwan, where John Wu will be. I am waiting for some addresses, particularly of Zen temples, from Amiya Chakravarty. I may possibly have a meeting with some Non-Superiors at Redwoods on the way out. A good letter came from Mother Myriam the other day. I hope to fly to Japan around November 1.

The Darcy O'Brien book on Joyce is simply pathetic. The man seems to have no conception of what Joyce is all about. Identifies him completely with the romantic idealism of Stephen D. in portrait. Says he was a dualist, a manichaean, etc. Found a sexy letter to J.'s wife and gloated over it, etc. O'Brien is the kind of person who feels himself threatened by the kind of idealism that was *part* of Joyce's youthful character. This kind of book is simply stupid—probably a Ph.D. dissertation that got into print because of that horny letter or something. No—it's Princeton Press—someone must have taken it seriously as "scholarship"!!

I am also disappointed in Heiler on *Prayer* with his black-and-white division of mysticism (bad—quietistic—world-renouncing—life-denying) and prophecy (good—dynamic—world-affirming—life-loving). This is a mere cliché. Has nothing to do with the reality of either mysticism or prophecy—except I would say both are "life-affirming" in a very strong sense—but it depends [on] what you mean by "life."

Was in Louisville Wednesday to see John Ford on legal business. Had lunch in the cellar of the Normandy Inn which I liked. Saw Tommie—three of her big-eyed kids with wide brimmed straw hats in the train station going off somewhere with Grandma. Colleen, with a lovely smile, "How did you know we were here?"

July 19, 1968

Stifling hot weather. Airless nights. Had a lot of trouble getting to sleep last night.

During the day—when free I have been walking in the same place in the woods over the hill SW of the hermitage where it is shady and breezy. A good place for meditation. And I am glad that I am spending more afternoons meditating rather than writing. In fact since returning from California I haven't written much of anything—a few random short pieces—such as the bit on "Peace and Revolution" for Eileen Egan which I did Sunday (14th). A comment on the Cyclops epistle in Ulysses!

Letter from Ping who wants to take a week or so with me to explore the coast in California—in October—before I go to the Orient. More than anything I want to find a really quiet, isolated place—

—where no one knows I am (I want to disappear).

—where I can get down to the thing I really want and need to do.

—from which, if necessary, I can come out to help others (e.g. at the Redwoods). For instance I may arrange a conference for the Esalen Institute there. They invited me to Big Sur but I replied—as I now do—that I can't do anything outside a house of our Order.

—maybe this can be a step towards the hermit colony Fr. Flavian wants. I don't know. In this I will simply try to carry out his wishes, with him—I am not keen on it myself but it may be a way to a permanent solution of the whole question.

(The noise here, especially on weekends, is considerable. People at the lake across the road. Yelling, guns, etc. I don't grudge them their fun, even on "monks property" (—a joke). But still I'd like to be away from it.)

In any case, real quiet here is impossible. And even though I have cut down on visits for July—I could not refuse Wygal yesterday—afraid to hurt his feelings—haven't seen him for a long time. He came out with a new girl friend—a sweet girl—and we wasted an afternoon driving around, drank a couple of cans of Budweiser. We ended up at the Tobacco Barn where [Fr.] Raymond was drinking Budweiser—colder and out of bottles—with friends from Louisville, a politician and a priest. We got on to Vietnam and the priest—who had an operation on his throat and talked in a hoarse undertone—growled "they ought to drop the bomb," as if a criminal negligence were being perpetrated.

And these visits are supposed to be "charity." True, I did it entirely to please Jim: but is that *charity?* Or just being sociable. There's a difference.

July 19 [20?], 1968

My right arm is sore with a cholera vaccination. My left arm is not sore though it bears a smallpox vaccination. Next week: yellow fever. Today too I had passport pictures taken—at a sort of clip joint where the nice lady suddenly had me going for portraits—no obligation, of course, just see if you like them. We'll give you a good discount, etc. Probably end up with my portrait in their front window.

Running back and forth between Tom Jerry Smith's in St. Matthews and the Health Department Office downtown.

I bought a little book on Nepal in the Readmore, when I was getting a book of Japanese phrases. Nepal is breathtaking! Could I even get there?

A letter came from Mother Myriam. Jones, owner of Needle Rock, etc., has been chasing hippies, etc., off his property. Evidently he's going to sell in September. (But if Fr. Flavian bought it we'd have to chase people off too??)

Back in St. Matthews—a sandwich and a couple bottles of Heineken's at the Canary Cottage—and inane TV over the bar. Ludicrous crap! The all-pervading stupidity of a universal day dream: people can be their own uninteresting image without trouble or cost! The mystery is why anybody bothers.

O the Mountains of Nepal!

Stopped at Tommie's to cadge a hamburger and a ride downtown. She was "rushed"—exaggeratedly this time. Great play of woman in a rush. And she did have to get more kids on a train to Grayson—and then get up a dinner for 8 people. I realize that. (But she was taking the kids downtown anyhow.)

In the Mountains of Nepal, no trains.

Got home and scrambled some eggs—supper of scrambled eggs and rye bread and cold beer (very hot evening) and I read an article in the *New Yorker* about what the senior class at Dartmouth thinks of the Vietnam War. They are not in favor.

Downtown I got a handful of McCarthy buttons at his Campaign Headquarters on Chestnut, before taking a bus to St. Matthews.

I mailed the ms. of *Vow of Conversation* to Naomi today.

A very hot night. I sit up drinking sherry on ice and listening to jazz ("Things ain't what they used to be"). No point in trying to sleep!

O the Mountains of Nepal.

And the tigers and the fevers. And the escaped bandits from all the world. And the escaped Trappists, lost, forgotten . . .

July 21, 1968

Singapore vaccination itched a lot today. Very hot and stuffy again. A storm in the NE but it did not come near. I went to concelebration but fell asleep. Fr. Anastasius preached against false prophets—known by pride and rebellion. False prophets rock the boat. I thought that's what the true ones did.

In the evening I gave a talk on Joyce. I hope to discuss some of the stories in *Dubliners*, *Portrait of the Artist*, and read parts of *Ulysses*.

Fine poems of William Agudelo in the latest *El Corno [Emplumado]*. He is with Cardenal at Solentiname. I wrote a letter to Cardenal this evening saying that if I do not go to Nepal or Burma after Indonesia, I'll come there. It is the best idea (avoid New Zealand). And above all I don't want to be around for that stupid seminar of Basil Pennington's at Spencer (Early February).

No use being romantic about the Mountains of Nepal. It costs money to get there—and will I have contacts? Nevertheless I wrote to Lionel Landry of the Asia Society about all that. I have a strange feeling something unexpected will pan out.

I have just discovered a place called the Kingdom of Swat.

Maybe *that's* the answer.

What's the hotel? Why, of course the Hotel Swat.

O the Mountains of Swat!!

July 22, 1968

With all my joking about the Mountains of Nepal it was rather a jolt to find in the mail today an invitation to a rather important religious meeting in *Darjeeling*—nearer to the border of Nepal than the monastery is to Bardstown! I went immediately to discuss it with Fr. Flavian and he approved of my going. It is in October, hence I have to move up my plans—and change them around. Instead of spending November in Japan I can—logically—spend it in *Nepal*.

Of course—much depends on who I meet in Darjeeling and what comes out of it. I might get invited to places more interesting and important from a religious point of view. But I do hope to get a retreat in the mountains and perhaps see some monasteries. Chakravarty—who arranged the invitation—will be there and I will follow his advice.

Once again—I have a feeling that a new path is opening up.

A letter today from Leslie at the Redwoods. June Yungblut, etc.

July 23, 1968

I have been leafing through the *N.Y. Times Book Review*—as usual, a depressing experience—except there was an article on Ferlinghetti and City Lights which I read and enjoyed—and a negative review of him by Jonathan Williams—which I can't say I liked. Is he right? I don't know.

This morning Sister Luke and 4 others from Loretto came over and we had Mass—celebrated most informally outdoors at the lake, early, in the cool of the morning. It was very nice indeed. Coffee afterwards and good conversation. When the sun got high and hot they left.

Then I wrote a few letters, mostly arrangements and so on for the Asian trip. It is only nine weeks away. My smallpox vaccination is angry and red and itches a lot.

It was hot again this afternoon. Because of noise of kids at the lake (¼ mile from hermitage) I decided to go over to the Linton Farm—and it was good. Quiet, isolated, hot, but with a good breeze by the big soybean field where I have had some good hours of meditation this year. A small book on Vedanta which I don't entirely understand, but it has good insights and seems pretty hardheaded.

Also—I thought of Nepal: and of the stupidity of being romantic about it. To get to those mountains one has to pass through the poverty of Calcutta: and when in the presence of those mountains one is also in the presence of the poverty of Nepal. And typhus, and yellow fever, and malaria, and VD, and tantrism, and opium. As for Nepalese Buddhism, if it is like that of Tibet it is not exactly the kind I myself am most interested in, ferocity, ritualism, superstition, magic. No doubt many deep and mysterious things, but maybe it *needs* to disappear.

However, I'd better suspend judgment on that. I hope to meet the Dalai Lama[4] or someone like that at Darjeeling and find out more about it.

Theoria and Theory—had a piece on the Beas Community—Sikhist—active—lay—contemplatives in Punjab.

When I was coming back from my walk I saw a couple of retreatants going up to the hermitage. Avoided them. But I cannot always avoid them. Others bothering the brothers at the Gate who called. I said "No."

Real solitude is not possible here. Nor is it where Dom James is over in Edelin's woods. People come and visit him there too. (Sunday before Mass he was more talkative than I have ever seen him—got me in the sacristy and was asking if I heard about the Jesuit Provincial (Baltimore) who ran away and got married—My! My! Tsk! Tsk! Tsk!) And I was laughing like crazy, though I suppose it is really not funny and one should not laugh.

July 27, 1968

Heavy rain in the morning and then, after a hot steamy afternoon a violent thunderstorm at supper time—it blew out the bulb of my desk lamp. After the storm and supper—around bedtime—I went out and there were five small, bedraggled wet quail, picking around in the path by my doorstep and very tame. Must be from the nursery the brothers had at the Steel Building. They don't seem very well prepared for life in the woods: preferred the path to the grass that would hide them; no mistrust of a human being—did not run away, only got out of the way of my feet or skipped away if I reached for them. They are now out on the wet lawn somewhere. This place is full of foxes—not to mention the kids who shoot anything that moves, in or out of season! I feel very sorry for these quail! But there is also the wild covey of a dozen or so trained by a zealous mother who often lured me along the rose hedge away from where the little ones were hiding in the deep weeds by the gate.

Yesterday I had to go in for my second cholera shot. Rain in the afternoon pouring down on St. Matthews and on the road from the Turnpike to New Haven.

4 The Dalai Lama, presently in exile in India, is now only the spiritual head of the Tibetan Buddhist church, but prior to the Communist Chinese takeover of his country, he was also its temporal ruler, with his seat in the Potala, a great palace in Lhasa.

(I hear a mature quail whistling in the field. Perhaps it's that mother gathering in her five "civilized" ones. Hope she tells them a thing or two about *people!*)

Bro. Benedict showed me a newspaper photo of Dom Gregorio Lemercier—just married! So that's that! All the old Cardinals in Rome will be nodding wisely: they knew all along what this psychoanalysis would lead to!

For Dom G. personally—I can't judge. But it is a shame for monasticism. Whatever way you look at it, it does mean *giving up* a monastic experiment. Maybe he'll go on to something else. As for me, I'm interested in the *monastic* life and its values. In doing something with it, not just abandoning it.

I said Mass today for Beatrice Olmstead's husband—they all went to Ireland on vacation and he died of a heart attack in a Dublin boarding house.

July 29, 1968

I am working on my Joyce review article for the *Sewanee*. Some of the things said in two of the books (Darcy O'Brien and Virginia Moseley) are simply incredible. It was a nice afternoon and I would have liked to spend it over at Linton's reading the *Dhammapada*. But the work was good too and the house was not too hot. There are some nice things in *Giacomo Joyce*. But I see the idiocy of the mystique of spiritual seduction. And all the mental nonsense that goes along with such imaginings.

The inserts for *Monks Pond III*—at least the concrete poems—are ready and I have put them together. They look good, and I am happy with the various ideas—(the toucan, the fly, the German primitive children trained for war, etc.)—that I pasted in. It is not hard to do good-looking and interesting pages—if you have someone like Bro. Cassian around to process them for you! I'd be tempted to do more issues of *MP* (after IV) if I were not going to Asia.

This evening—cool and bright—I walked out on the brow of the hill after supper. Looked down at the bottom where pipe is strung out for the new sewage plant. Crisp green line of the hills across the valley. Dark green of the oak tops—for there has been lots of rain this summer. In eight weeks I am to leave here. And who knows—I may not come back. Not that I expect anything to go wrong—though it might—but I might conceivably settle in

California to start the hermit thing Fr. Flavian spoke of: it depends. Someone may give him a good piece of property, for instance . . . In any case I don't expect to be back here for a few months.

Really I don't care one way or another if I never come back. On an evening like this the place is certainly beautiful—but you can seldom count on it really being quiet (though it is at the moment). Traffic on the road. Kids at the lake. Guns. Machines, and Boone's dog yelling in the wood at night. And people coming all the time. All this is to be expected and I don't complain of it. But if I can find somewhere to *disappear* to, I will. And if I am to begin a relatively wandering life with no fixed abode, that's all right too.

I really expect little or nothing from the future. Certainly not great "experiences" or a lot of interesting new things. Maybe. But so what? What really intrigues me is the idea of starting out into something unknown, demanding and expecting nothing very special, and hoping only to do what God asks of me, whatever it may be.

July 30, 1968

I finished the Joyce review. Happy to be done with it. One less job to do between now and October—the important ones left are—review of Barthes for the *Sewanee*, and editing *Monks Pond IV.* Apart from that—only a couple of monastic chores.

In a review of Harold Nicholson's Diaries—"he hated racial injustice even more than he hated Negroes." On the whole this review—highly favorable—made the man look fatuous. But his *times* were fatuous. Our times, however, are crazy in a much more sinister and destructive way. In the same *N.Y. Times Book Review*—a picture of Robert Graves looking totally obnoxious. A most unpleasant man!

I will have to see certain people before leaving. If I don't want to be having three or four visits a week, it had better begin soon! Some will just have to be overlooked.

August 1, 1968

Rain. I had to go to town for my yellow fever shot at the Health Dept. Heavy downpour on the way in, but not much real rain after I got to Louisville. A good day —I enjoyed it. Had lunch with John Ford and Fred [Klapheke] to talk legal business (re: the *Freedom Songs* mixup).

I tried to get some travel information at American Express in Stewart's but they were very curt with me as soon as I told them all the flights were being arranged through Pan Am (Friends of monastery). However I did get a plan of Bangkok and a little tourist booklet on Thailand. I've decided to stop over at Bangkok on the way out to Calcutta. I did find out what I wanted from a nice obliging girl in Tilford's Travel Agency: I don't have to fly PAA Bangkok to Calcutta. There are good early evening flights on Air India, Swiss Air and Lufthansa.

I am expected to give a talk at the Darjeeling meeting and will talk on monasticism—on inter-monastic communication—on the importance of the level of depth and "enlightenment" sought by such groups in all the main religions.

Hoping to see P. Lal in Calcutta. Chances of meeting the Dalai Lama seem good. More anxious than ever to get into Nepal and visit monasteries.

Fighting kites in Thailand! Must see them! And dancing, etc.

Dom Leclercq (who of course is deeply involved in the Bangkok meeting) writes:

"Since I saw a Swami at St. Andre and saw all the silly western questions they all asked him which didn't exist for him and his monks, I decided, next trip, to see more non-Christian ashrams than Christian. Our first duty is to constate them (*sic*).

"The Secretariat for Non-Christians, in Rome, where the boss (a Cardinal) and the manager have both been in Japan, insisted that we try to get the Trappist monasteries out of their ghetto. But they never acknowledged the invitation, answered the questionnaire; the four abbesses were in Cîteaux and other French monasteries recently; we arranged that they come to AIM in Paris, they promised but flew away in clandestinity (*sic*). Better to despair—*Sinite mortuos sepelire mortuos* [Let the dead bury the dead, Matt. 8:22] and work with the Zen. Strange but my best hope lies with the Jesuits free from 'our traditions.'"

A very amusing and accurate summary. But I think he will find "the Zen" pretty full of conservatism and [indicipherable] too.

Talking of conservatives—stopped in at the hospital to talk to Fr. Raymond who was operated on last week. Cancer was feared but the growth turned out non-malignant. He was full of truculent opinions and satisfaction about the new birth control encyclical ("There will be a schism"). A curious thing, that encyclical! I wonder what will come of it!

August 5, 1968. Our Lady of the Snows

Surely the hottest day of this year—or the stuffiest. Phil Stark came up to cut wood before sunrise. Says he will soon be finished typing the stencils for *Monks Pond IV.*

I am working on Roland Barthes. Small books but they require close reading. Very suggestive. But I have not yet made up my mind about him.

Ping writes suggesting we go all the way up the coast into Oregon in October. All right with me. He says John Cogley in protest against Pope Paul's birth control encyclical, has given up his column in 25 diocesan papers. Who'd want to read a diocesan paper anyway? We have *The Record* and the *St. Louis* one now and I never touch either—(except an article on Dan Berrigan in the last one. He is a bit theatrical these days, now he's a malefactor—with a quasi-episcopal disarmament emblem strung around his neck like a pectoral cross. He wants me in N.Y. agitating for and with him in October or November, whenever the trial is. I definitely want to keep out of anything that savors of a public "appearance" or semi-public or *anything*, especially in America).

At supper I read a tear-sheet from the *N.Y. Daily News*, a full page, on the Vermont Carthusians. The old thing: pictures of monks with hoods up, backs to the camera. "This is the most exclusive club in the country," so the article begins. And one of them is pictured reading from an atrociously printed Latin antiphonary. Yet there is something admirable about their hanging on to their customs and authorities—even though it may mean the end of them. They refuse *all* aggiornamento. *Cartusia numquam reformata* . . . [Carthusians were never reformed . . .] Yet in the end, I think they are a bit ridiculous. Building "for the next thousand years" in huge slabs of granite. Paid for by "several philanthropic benefactors." "We are the happiest of people. You have to have a good sense of humor along with the other prerequisites. . . ."

I can see something good in their absolute, unchanging dedication to rule. And yet . . . How glad I am I never joined them.

Maybe I am no true solitary, and God knows I have certainly missed opportunities, made mistakes—and big ones too! Yet the road I am on is the right one for me and I hope I stay on it wisely—or that my luck holds.

> And the forests and every fragrant tree will provide shade
> For Israel at the command of God:
> for God will guide Israel in joy by the light of his glory,
> with his mercy and integrity for escort.
>
> *(Baruch 5:8–9)*

August 7, 1968

Very hot nights—and two nights ago a lot of noise as well. Loud, rackety beat-up cars of kids marauding up and down the highway and then Boones' dogs loose in the wood, harassing the deer, crying with almost human passion after rabbits and foxes—and the whole night alive and tense with the barbarity of Kentucky. The place is full of Wallace-voters, racists, roving about looking for trouble. All the worse since a few weeks ago some Negro racists deliberately ambushed and killed some cops in Cleveland. Then a riot. Ten killed altogether. Three cops, two of the snipers—and the rest just "people" who had the misfortune to get in the way of the bullets.

Useless to put down "what people think" of the presidency. Nixon will doubtless be nominated by the Republicans in Miami—maybe already is, who knows? Still a strong possibility of Johnson being "drafted" because Humphrey could not beat anyone—even Nixon. Small hope of McCarthy being nominated.

Conclusion: prospect of one of these for President—Nixon, Humphrey, Johnson. Three zeros, and the worst is Johnson—who might die or get shot and then we'd have Humphrey. Or God knows—Reagan as survivor of Nixon!

The next four years do not look good for America or for the world.

Very hot yesterday. Jim Holloway and Will Campbell here. We sat in the woods—too hot even to drink beer. I was able to raise some money to help with the trip, thanks to Will's generosity. Supper at Hawk's [restaurant]—took along Frère Yves from La Tourette (O.P. [Dominicans] near Lyons). The night was hot but quiet, and I slept fairly well—tired after sitting up til midnight the night before.

August 9, 1968

Yesterday I got a typhoid-paratyphoid shot and it made me very sick. At night, feverish, nightmarish sleep. When I got up I felt as if I were falling apart. Could do little except lie in bed, and when I had to go down to the monastery I was exhausted. I came back and went to bed, dazed, and sweated for a couple of hours and then felt a little better. I went out into the woods and tried to read, but nothing registered.

Now at least, in the evening, I feel better. Today the grass was cut and the place looks a little more civilized. I am hot and thirsty—and very tired.

August 10, 1968

The effects of the shot wore off. A good night. In my morning reading got side-tracked at breakfast by an article on Joyce in the summer *Sewanee Review* and so went on to re-read the *Circe* section—Nighttown, which, when I was "in the world" at first perplexed, then disturbed me. Now I find it moving and in a way "beautiful"—in its context as a bizarre, macabre, eschatalogical dance of death. In which there is, nevertheless, a kind of compassion for sin and an ultimate wisdom about it. Perhaps because of the saving grace of irony. Anyway the whole section struck me as extremely "actual"—in fact right up to the minute. What we are living at the present latest up-to-date moment is a kind of "Nighttown Christianity." Or is that too strong? Anyway his vision of the end of the world is plausible—with of course Ithaca beyond, and the big all enveloping life force of Molly's rather absurd and meaningless "yes" (to which everyone of course attaches a supreme meaning).

August 13, 1968

A fine rainy evening. There was heavy rain around dinnertime and in the early afternoon. Then it stopped and I went to the monastery to mail letters—Aelred Graham, Elsie Mitchell, and the Archbishop of Alaska (strange combination, but quite relevant in my own life right now!). Went for a walk in steamy, hot mist. The lake at St. Bernard's field is thick with green slime. I came back, got some tomatoes, lettuce, eggs. At suppertime it started raining heavily again and has been pouring ever since.

The curious thing that rather dazes me: I may not be coming back to Gethsemani. This is not my own idea—or not entirely. Fr. Flavian is very definite now about my seeking out and settling in some solitary place in the West. He came back from California Saturday evening and I saw him today.

The California situation is not entirely satisfactory.

Problem of having to rent a whole *ranch* on the Needle Rock shore. And he was turned off by Bear Harbor which he found to be full of snakes. (Amazing description of Fr. Roger kicking snakes aside right and left saying "Oh! they're all harmless!")

Incidentally Al Groth's house burned down—possibly arson to cover burglary. Winifred is living up at Ettersburg, on the mountain. A possibility.

Certainly the shore at Needle Rock etc. offers no really permanent solitude. Already full of hippies. The Indian caretaker trying unsuccessfully to run them off etc.

So what happened 10 days or so ago—I did not write it down—the Archbishop of Anchorage visits asking me to come up and give a retreat to his contemplative nuns. I replied saying I *would* and also mentioning the hermitage project. Yesterday I got an enthusiastic reply. I don't know how good the climate is—but I may end up six or eight months from now incardinated in his diocese. That is probably where I'll go if and when I get back from Asia. But before that, in September, I hope to make Anchorage my first stop on the long journey!! Fr. Flavian approves the idea.

It is so utterly new to have an abbot here who is completely open to new possibilities! And it is certainly much more stimulating for the spiritual life! Here I am suddenly on the edge of something totally new, completely unplanned and unforeseen, something that has simply dropped out of the sky. The sense that one can *move with* this new swing and explore it is very inspiring and does much to lift the burden of depression, suspicion, doubt that has become almost second nature with me after years of the other kind of policy! Now I find I have to shake myself, wake up, pray, think for myself, estimate risks and possibilities, make halfway wise decisions. But this is what we have all been needing. I have no special urge to be a hermit in Alaska, but it is an obvious place for solitude and here is a bishop who likes the idea very much! So let's look into it and see what happens.

August 15, 1968

Guns blasting off in the woods to the east. Is it squirrel season already? Seasons mean nothing here. But it sounds like intense and official hunting.

The tame quail raised by Bro. Alban, refusing to be wild, running about under the soybean plants in the monastery garden.

Yesterday, heavy rain alternating with hours of damp, hot, fog. Maybe all this has something to do with the French H-Bomb tests last week (or so) in the South Seas. Certainly we are getting some of their fallout.

When it is quiet here, it is as lovely and perfect as it was in the beginning (early hours of this morning when I got up). But when can you count on quiet? More and more visitors. Yesterday Fr. Gilbert Torpey, Fr. August Thompson. Sunday, Roger Robin. Ed Rice coming in September. Dom Leclercq. All fine. But. . . .

I tend to find myself thinking a lot about how to live in Alaska. The problem of my bad driving, etc. The thing is that I can't make sense out of a purely private endeavor to be completely alone, un-bothered, etc. This is nonsense. The only way to make sense of it is in the frank context of the Alaskan Church. This "call" has come really through the Bishop—my solitude and contemplation are to be worked out *with him*, not just on my own. Obviously it will mean some connections, some duties, some service, therefore some people. So the same thing starts all over again! Not necessarily. But I have to look carefully, use my head, and think not only in terms of personal preference and convenience but of charity, of love, for those who seek Christ as I do (the nuns with whom this all started, his priests, etc.). If I give what I can give, the rest will be taken care of. They'll fly me in and out in a helicopter if they want me that badly!

August 17, 1968

One of the hottest, stuffiest days of the summer. No breeze. Someone is firing a rifle over at the lake. It is past sundown. In the SE—huge thunderheads, lighted by the last of the sun—only thin tops—no sound of thunder. No indication of a storm approaching. Stillness. Enormous rumor of crickets, locusts, bull frogs. And the steadily repeated crack of the rifle. Probably some kid shooting at a beer can.

All evening I have been reading travel folders on India. It is probably not much better there!

Monks Pond IV all edited—except for a couple of poems still expected from Ron Punnett, the West Indian at Fort Benning.

The other evening there was an abortive riot in Louisville—after a Negro Church was bombed. Possibly white racists were trying to *provoke* a riot. Negro leaders did everything they could to calm things down.

August 18, 1968

Next week the Democratic Convention opens in Chicago. Huge crowds expected—including crowds of protesters, anti-war people, "yippies" etc.

National guardsmen have been in special training and will be stationed in two small parks near the amphitheater as well as in an armory and underground parking lot near the Loop. Police will be stationed in and around the amphitheater and an untold number of agents will be . . . everywhere including the ranks of the demonstrators. . . . A mile square area will be fenced off around the amphitheater. . . . Dignitaries will be brought to the convention by helicopter. . . . Special jails are being prepared.

What with this and with McGovern's candidacy (to get the Kennedy votes) I'd say McCarthy's chances of nomination are almost nil. The one hope for a democratic peace effort—ruined by division and confusion. Still, this is not so much the fault of the "demonstrators" as it is of the pig-headed and doctrinaire people both of right and left. Nobody really wants "peace"—what they all want is for their own interests to "prevail."

Evening.

It is as hot and stuffy a night as I can remember in Kentucky. Going to bed has no attractions. I have been walking in the field barefoot with shirt off. There it was comfortable. Not here in the hermitage.

Eating supper I finished Cesare Pavese's *The House on the Hill.* Marvelous writing! A beautiful book! Then I went out and read a French translation of Al Ghazali's *Error and Deliverance* which is also a magnificent book, one of the greatest!

I am beginning, in spite of myself, Pavese's *Among Women Only.* Fantastic stuff! What a writer!

Today in the afternoon I walked by the lake that used to belong to the Brother Novices. For a while there was a breeze there, but not for long. One of the other hermit types, Fr. Richard from Mepkin, came out and sat on the other side of this lake (pond). I thought of the old days before there was a lake, and the trees I cherished there, and the small pine Fr. Francis de Sales stole and hung upside down above the altar for Christmas Midnight Mass (maybe in 1951, or 52). What changes since those days!

I talked in Chapter on Joyce's "Araby" and other things.

August 19, 1968

Tired of heat, yet I don't want to lie and sweat in bed though dark has fallen. The steamy night is alive with frog and insect noises. Before sunset I walked in the field and looked at the sea of bluish steam about 1000 feet deep that hangs over everything, with a few pink cloud-bergs standing up high out of it in the cleaner blue. This afternoon—signs of a storm but it went away with hardly a growl.

The great pages on Al Ghazali's conversion to Sufism moved me.

A letter from Fr. Denis, the hermit, who has left Christ of the Desert and gone to a semi-deserted village parish south of Albuquerque and urges me to come to visit him there. He says that Dom Aelred will now be after me to occupy that hermitage, but I don't think so.

August 20, 1968. Feast of St. Bernard

I have been three years officially in this hermitage. I spent some of the morning cleaning out papers from the bedroom—where most of my work is stored or filed.

Files too full. Shelves too full. Boxes.

It is really clear that I have written too much useless trivial stuff whether on politics or on monastic problems. I don't take account of earlier books which perhaps had their place.

I regret less some of the recent poetry, and especially *Cables* and *Lograire*. I wish I had done more creative work and less of this trivial, sanctimonious editorializing. Easy enough to see that Fr. Raymond's new book [*Relax and Rejoice*] is a sick joke. (Half the community is laughing at it—he could not even sell it to Bruce and Co., and had to print it privately—but now claims this was due to a "liberal plot" to suppress the "truth" which he alone reveals!) But is my stuff any less ridiculous? I wonder. Of course one has a duty to speak out. But as soon as you attach yourself to a "cause" your perspective gets distorted.

Nevertheless—I am constantly appalled by the growing barbarism of this country.

Says George Wallace, racist presidential candidate from Alabama:

When I get to be president, if any anarchist lays down in front of my car that would be the last thing he would ever lay down in front of on this earth!

And when Johnson visited Australia in 1966, as he drove with the Prime Minister and some people lay down in front of the car in protest, the PM said to the driver, "Ride over the bastards." Johnson said, "You're a man after my own heart." And most Americans would approve them as "defending law and order"—and civilization.

In three days (Friday) I am to go to Washington—lunch on Saturday with [Giacomo] Soedjatmoko, the Indonesian Ambassador. I am very eager to talk to him! In four weeks—I am supposed to go to Alaska—it is hardly credible.

Today, among other things, I burned M.'s letters. Incredible stupidity in 1966! I did not even glance at any one of them. High hot flames of the pine branches in the sun!

I have prayed much more in these days. More and more sense of being lost without it.

August 22, 1968

Again—very hot and stuffy. A storm after dinner only made things steamier. I was lying down after my third typhoid shot. But the second and third did not upset me. At least the 3rd has not so far.

Cleaned up the bookshelves a bit. Fr. Flavian says that when I am away the hermitage will be used by others. Some of my modern literature had better be elsewhere, if that is the case.

Monks Pond III is about ready for sorting. It will be much bigger than the others. Phil Stark is typing IV now—bigger still than III.

When I was in the print shop Bro. Charles was hinting at all sorts of sinister events. The power had gone off. This was due to flying saucers "hovering over the power plant." Culligan, Fr. Raymond's new (private) publisher, declares that the fliers of saucers are the airmen of hell and that indeed the Devil is behind it. *All* of it. (All of what? All of *it!*) Bro. Charles is also very exercised over the great "liberal plot" at Bruce Publishing Co. to prevent Fr. Raymond's (ultra-conservative) truth from reaching the public. Bro. Charles, and indeed also Fr. Raymond, don't like Eugene McCarthy as a presidential candidate—but do think that Wallace has some good points now!—I'm afraid a lot of people around here (the neighborhood rather than the monastery itself) would agree.

Tomorrow afternoon Ron Seitz is supposed to come and pick me up and take me to the airport to go to Washington. A picture of Mount McKinley in front of me under the lamp—(came today as a feast day greeting for Sunday [Feast of St. Louis]—I cannot believe that I may see it. Or even find myself one day living near it. Is Alaska a real option? One would think not. And yet there's that Bishop. Certainly it is not the place I myself would spontaneously choose (full of military).

For myself—Bhutan! Or that tea-plantation I heard about yesterday near Darjeeling!

August 26, 1968. Monday

The short trip to Washington—a tiring but good experience, a great deal crowded into a day. Will I be able to handle such crowding for a long period? I'll have to learn to stretch things longer than the world wants them. To live at my own tempo which is slow, and yet fruitful. Rather than at this huge speed in which really nothing happens—except of course that you do get to Washington and back in a hurry!

Friday, in dark, steamy heat (a storm threatened but didn't break), Ron Seitz picked me up and drove me in to the airport. I had a long wait—ate in the Luau Room, sat around in the bar, read some of Ferlinghetti's routines, said Office.

The plane to Washington was a fast jet, about an hour, and I had the two seats to myself. Nothing to see but the window (steam, blackness, a few clean clouds standing out of it). Quiet. Read and thought. Pleasant.

Flew down into Washington at nightfall. Fantastic traffic around the National Airport. I was met by Dr. Camara Peron, who drove me to Georgetown and I liked Georgetown (remembered it vaguely from 30 years ago). Very hot.

Most of the patients appear to be nuns, priests, etc., and I get the impression that he is in the middle of a great religious mess, communities going to pieces. Nuns ready for suicide. Old authoritarian systems and new immaturities.

The Liturgical Conference (at Washington—just ended) seems to have been quite ridiculous. (My "Freedom Songs" were sung by the Ebenezer

Baptist Choir—haven't heard any reactions except a wire from June [Yungblut] and a letter from [Alexander] Peloquin.)

Late supper at the "Old Europe." Bedded down Japanese style in an air-conditioned room at Camara's. Got up about 7 and went hunting for a church on Massachusetts Avenue in which to say Mass. Spaciousness of everything. Slow, quiet Mass in Latin all alone in a big church—only one old lady.

Lunch at the Indonesian Embassy Residence with Soedjatmoko was fine. I had five hours in which we talked about Java, mysticism, everything. I now think I have a fair idea of what lies ahead and it is exciting. A whole gamut of possibilities—much of which will not get on paper. The literary people, seeing the country. Boroboden. Soto. The Dutch Jesuits who understand and the Indonesian Trappists who may or may not understand. Then the Javanese mystics. Some more esoteric, some less—and Bali. I will, at any rate, have the best possible contacts and introductions. He just became Ambassador three months ago!

I really am very interested in Soedjatmoko—a fine person and one of the few with whom I can communicate *fully* and *freely* on a deep level. There was no need for any triviality or double-talk in those five hours. We had a great deal to say. Real [indecipherable]—a person I have been waiting to meet for a lifetime. It seems we are companions on the same strange way—whatever it may be.

This makes the Asian trip all the more exciting, for it seems I am summoned to meet Asia on the *deepest* level—and it may mean a hard business of breaking through a lamentable crust of ruins, decadence and misery.

Soedjatmoko's wife—a most beautiful person in batik! And the children.

I rode away from the big house, in a huge, black, shiny, chauffeur-driven-Cadillac—and half the way to the airport was through Rock Creek Park—woods and glens—as if no city existed. The roads were very quiet. Then the big parkway, the airport traffic, the crowded halls of the airport full of sailors, soldiers, children, mothers, an occasional nun—with a new wise look (maybe saying "I got laid at the Liturgical Conference"?).

And there does seem to be a sudden aura of erotic interest about nuns, priests, etc., for in the airport I saw this rather attractive girl smiling at me. I was puzzled—didn't know if she was someone I was supposed to recognize. When I found myself a window seat and sat down hoping to have another quiet trip, she came along, sat down next to me and started a conversation. She was just a rather sweet Kentucky girl from a small town, a junior in college, who had been on a trip east having fun in Philadelphia—where she had dated a kid who had just left the seminary. She was a Catholic girl, really quite attractive and sweet, and with no ulterior motives I could detect. The plane was slow—prop flight with a stop at Charleston—twice as long a flight as the one before—I bought her a couple of drinks which made all the small talk easier.

When the plane practically emptied in Charleston, I was a bit irked to miss the peace and quiet of being alone. On the other hand it was rather touching that she just enjoyed a simple conversation and picked a middle-aged priest to talk to!

I am certainly glad it was *she* that decided she wanted me for a companion and not some stupid idiot talking about real estate or something. On the other hand I'd be smarter to travel without the Roman collar—maybe I'd have more time to pray. A priest on a plane seems to be fair game for anyone.

Got into Louisville. Ron and Sally met me at the plane and we all went for another late supper with Fr. John Loftus at the Embassy Club, which (though the food was O.K.) struck me as the epitome of all that is stupid and expensive about suburbia. All the organ playing, the dull wives, the smell of money, the aura of boredom and phoniness, the expensive, unattractive clothes. The general plush ugliness of everything. Giving me some inkling of how utterly horrible things must now be back "home" in Douglaston or Great Neck! (Or, my God, Alaska!)

Finally, a crowning American ritual, sitting dead tired with a glass of bourbon in the lounge of the Franciscan Friary watching pro football on TV—at midnight!!

The Packers beat the Dallas Cowboys—and it was, I must say, damn good football because it was pre-season and many contracts depended on it.

Football is one of the really valid and deep American rituals. It has a religious seriousness which American religion can never achieve. A comic, contemplative dynamism, a gratuity, a movement from play to play, a definitiveness that responds to some deep need, a religious need, a sense of meaning that is at once final and provisional: a substratum of dependable regularity, continuity, and an ever renewed variety, openness to new possibilities, new chances. It happens. It is done. It is possible again. It happens. Another play is decided, played out, "done" (replay for the good ones so you can really see *how* it happened) and that's enough, on to the next one—until the final gun blows them out of a huddle and the last play never happens. They disperse. Cosmic breakup. Final score 31–27 is now football history. This will last forever. It is *secure* [underscored twice] in its having happened. And we saw it happen. We existed.

Now comes the other, more stupid, yet also more dangerous ritual: the Democratic Convention. I might have met Eugene McCarthy's wife in Washington but she was at the hairdresser's getting a hairdo for the convention.

August 27, 1968. Tuesday

Fine bright day. Reading the German book by Schumann on Indonesian Mysticism—lent me by Soedjatmoko. It is very fine.

A bit of Barthes on Voltaire. "The last happy writer."

This afternoon there was a Council Meeting—Fr. Eudes will be Novice Master, Fr. Matthew, Master of Juniors, Fr. Timothy, Prefect of Studies.

I have heard nothing about the Democratic Convention—and will be surprised by nothing, except the nomination of McCarthy.

I had a typhus shot today. My arm is slightly sore—but I did not get sick as I did with the one for typhoid.

In a couple of days I must go to Louisville to get some clothes—and a back x-ray, and have Dr. Mitchell check what appears to be bursitis in my jaw! (It hurts when I eat.)

Letter from the Archbishop of Anchorage—the Vicar General will meet me at the plane—Northwestern Flight 3 from Chicago is the best—several pieces of property in mind. I can live in a trailer at the (contemplative) Precious Blood Nuns.

September 1, 1968. 13th Sunday after Pentecost

The Democratic Convention was celebrated with lusty police beatings of unarmed demonstrators and the general sentiment out is that the police were right because people should not protest. To protest is to threaten and indeed no distinction is made between the innocent protester and the assassin. They are all one. In the end Humphrey of course was nominated. So now the nation has three complete zeros to vote for—and does not seem aware that the "party system" no longer exists or means anything except as a pure empty ritual.

The day after Humphrey's nomination I went in to Louisville to buy luggage and clothes, with the help and advice of Frank O'Callaghan.

Gene Meatyard with Madeline and Chris and Melissa came over today. We ate curry and drank daiquiris and listened to calypso music. Yesterday Bob and Hanna Shepherd came over. Everyone says: "Be sure to come back," as if I might not. And really there is no reason to do so—if I can find another place, which is perfectly O.K. with Fr. Flavian. Today—for instance—constant rifle shooting to the north of my place—not exactly on monastery property. It seems may be a sort of rifle range has been set up beyond Boone's?? A right-wing group? I don't know or care. It is simply another indication of the way the wind blows here.

After the Meatyards had left I walked over to the big empty field beyond the soybeans on the Linton Farm—looked at the distant white farmhouse to the east, the high clouds.

Now I am back listening to the still mind in the dark, under the new moon.

I am too restless to do much reading. Only some things stick—a few pages on Hindu philosophy, on Java, etc. Can't get any writing done. Yet, there are a couple of things to be finished.

What (very slowly) sinks into my mind is that soon I will really leave this place, to live for a long time out of a suitcase—everything I "have" will be within the 44 lbs. a plane will take for you. Leaving my books, cottage, security, time to write, time to be alone, and going on where I don't know, with only a few plans ahead that can all be changed. And that this may not be easy at all—in fact it might be very difficult. Certainly difficult to do well. It leaves me confused, and the only way to make sense of it is prayer.

I now have a flight booked out of Louisville on September 11. Nine days to get everything in order. Am supposed first to go to New Mexico, Christ in the Desert. I had them on the end of my itinerary, assuming I would come back here in February or March. Now I don't know if I will come back at all. New Mexico is one of the places where I might eventually settle. Dom Aelred has invited me to his place any time I want to come. I can live there as a hermit if I want to.

First I'll look elsewhere!

But certainly the nights are silent there in that empty canyon.

September 3, 1968

Moon covered with mist (9 p.m.) and a yelling dog which I just upbraided. I can cry "Get out bastard" in the night, as I am leaving in a week.

Yesterday was a clear, beautiful, fall day—with not much shooting until evening.

Today they were at school. Only a few bona fide hunters were firing in the distance. It was relatively quiet.

And when it is quiet I see the beauty of the place again. But it is so seldom quiet that I must leave it.

I went over to Linton's but I have blisters because of the yellow shoes. So I guess I don't take the yellow shoes with me when I go.

Yesterday I finished the preface to [Amadee] Hallier's *Aelred* [of Rievaulx]. Today I finished the first draft of the revised of Barthes for the *Sewanee*.

I sat up late reading Indonesian poets. Torn up by Chairil Auwas, W[illibrordus] S. Rendra, Sitor Situmorang. I hope I can meet Rendra—if he is still living in Jogjakarta. All that they say demonstrates Barthes' stuff on "writing degree zero" and yet I suppose Indonesia too will come to that—and will have to.

Want to talk to Soedjatmoko and his family. I like them. It is hard to be without them. I had a day dream of him calling and my saying—"I am going to New Mexico—come there—we will watch the Apache fiesta together."

I have a flight booked to Albuquerque a week from tomorrow.

I struggle in myself with my own future—and with the fear I will be discovered before I can get away (irrational)—or even that I may die or be shot. (If I am discovered—what difference does it make? It will all be announced next Wednesday anyhow!)

I see the absurdity of attachment to these fields. As if leaving them I would somehow be in jeopardy—what an attitude to cultivate!

But it is true, I am nervous, insecure, have blisters, and my allergy rages.

I wrote today to Ron Seitz to pick me up next Tuesday. I'll sleep in the Friary at Bellarmine. Then to the plane. God be with me!

It is late. I must go to bed. I call to mind Dominique and her alleluias, and the shore. They sustain me.

September 5, 1968

Rainy, and therefore quiet—except that the guns were firing again (apart from hunters), from 3 to 6. Not at the lake—up the road—a little further away. Kids can't afford to waste ammunition in such quantities—someone is giving it to them. An eerie business!

Strange that there was so little shooting on Labor Day.

Obviously, though, I'm through here. Why live on a rifle range?

A letter came, by surprise, from Mrs. Jones—wife of the owner of Needle Rock, Bear Harbor, etc. They have made their September arrangement, whatever it was, and I can have Bear Harbor if I want it. They all agree to fix the place up, etc. I hate to disappoint them. The way things are shaping up in India are too good to be true. Harold Talbott[5] has been living near the Ashram of the Dalai Lama, in close contact with his secretary, etc. And thinks the D. will provide me with cottage and guru with no trouble at all. In any case I am to see him—and now my plan is to return to India after Indonesia and take my time—maybe also go to Bhutan etc. Maybe a long retreat in the Himalaya.

I am trying to finish reading of important books I can't take with me. Absorbed by Chogyam Trungpa's *Born in Tibet.*[6] I question Zaehner's *At Sundry Times*. I think he is off target.

5 Harold Talbott is an American student of Buddhism who became a Catholic in his first year at Harvard (1959). He was baptized while making a retreat at the Abbey of Gethsemani, where he went to receive Merton's blessing. He was later a friend and student of Dom Aelred Graham, who urged Merton to look up Talbott on his Asian journey. Talbott in turn arranged for Merton's meetings with the Dalai Lama.

6 Chogyam Trungpa Rinpoche was the eleventh Trungpa tulku. The story of his youth and escape from Tibet after the Chinese Communist incursion "as told to" Esme Cramer Roberts, *Born in Tibet*, was published by Harcourt Brace in 1968.

A fine lineup of names and addresses in Java from Soedjatmoko. Java too will be fine. One month will never be enough for that!

I have my tickets to Albuquerque, then to Anchorage. Passport still not back with Indian and Indonesian visas.

September 6, 1968

Ed Rice drove in this afternoon in a battered blue Volkswagen. He had been as far west as Salt Lake City, back through Denver, Christ of the Desert, St. Louis, Southern Illinois, New Harmony, Indiana—and for the last two days he was doing a story on a blind seminarian in Louisville.

Fine pictures of India (people, beautiful people, though starving!), Cuba, everywhere. Much talk about India and above all Katmandu.

We had supper together in the hermitage, and after that his Volkswagen wouldn't start though we rolled it until it went all the way down the steep hill. We left it at the bottom.

On the way back I said Office as the full moon rose.

For a moment, the first tip of the rising moon in the trees across the bottoms looked like a lighted palace. I thought some fabulous new building had suddenly been erected in the woods.

September 7, 1968

Dom Leclercq arrived today. He and I and Fr. Flavian had dinner and supper together and some good talks. We drove out in Ed Rice's Volkswagen to the lake where the fish hatchery is, where it was quiet and cool. Talked of the Orient, of the student troubles in France, which will begin again in the fall—and all the rest.

After supper Ed and I walked out the front avenue, and ran into Andrew Boone. I inquired why his dogs were making so much noise at night around my house, and he said he was having them chase the deer because the bucks were raping his cows (sic) and causing them to miscarry! "The only thing to do is to chase them out of the country!" Maybe Andrew's head has been a little addled by Southern racism. However, he gave me some information about all the shooting. "Eighteen men" (?) surrounded one of his cornfields and blasted at doves all afternoon—it was a real slaughter, he said. (Last Sunday.) As for the kids at the lake—they "have a mattress in the back of a station wagon for service." Well, maybe!

I observed that no one likes to live next to a whorehouse and he felt my reaction was fair enough.

I have been reading a long report on a preparatory questionnaire for the Bangkok meeting. The usual—with some special slants. In my opinion, I don't think Christian monasticism, as we now know it, has much future in Asia. Merely wearing saffron robes won't do much good.

Tonight I wrote to Mother Myriam about the meeting at Redwoods.

September 9, 1968

Rainy and warm, a misty night of bells and insects.

It is hard to believe this is my last night at Gethsemani for some time—at least for several months.

Lest I regret going, the shooters were out again this afternoon, blasting off in the rain, and evidently in Boone's cornfield. I can't figure it out! Can't be *that* many doves. But whereas you saw doves fly over in fives and sixes two weeks ago, now you see—and rarely—one alone. And it flies like mad from you into the far distance!

I have had several good talks with Fr. Flavian, especially when taking meals with him and Dom Leclercq in the Guesthouse. Certainly I am grateful to have such an Abbot. He marks a real progress.

He came up in the afternoon, left in my big yellow rain coat with a hesychast anthology on the Art of Prayer.

Bros. Maurice [Flood] and Patrick [Hart] with Phil Stark came up for Mass at the hermitage this morning and we had a good session at breakfast afterwards.

I go with a completely open mind, I hope without special illusions. My hope is simply to enjoy the long journey, profit by it, learn, change, and perhaps find something or someone who will help me advance in my own spiritual quest.

I am not starting out with a firm plan never to return or with an absolute determination to return at all costs. I do feel there is not much for me here at the moment and that I need to be open to lots of new possibilities. I hope I shall be! But I remain a monk of Gethsemani. Whether or not I will end my days here, I don't know—and perhaps it is not so important. The great thing is to respond perfectly to God's Will in this providential opportunity, whatever it may bring.

Best of all—from a letter from Bess Brigham (it came today). This was a sign in "a deep mountain town in Mexico"—on a flowered arch for some festival.

> Welcome to those who come
> In the name of glory
> The Sons of the King
> Greet you with consideration.

So I go wherever it is in the name of glory. That is enough!

And then (10:15) for some unknown reason I sit up late reading Robinson Jeffers, that Pacific Blake, and he is O.K. I am deeply moved by him, I abide by him!

> We have climbed at length to a height, to an end, this end:
> shall we go down again to Mother Asia?
> Some of us will go down, some will abide, but we sought
> More than to return to a mother. This huge, inhuman,
> remote, unruled, this ocean will show us
> The inhuman road, the unruled attempt, the remote lodestar. . . .

"And the old symbols forgotten in the glory of that your hawk's dream."[7] So—title!

Sent *Geography of Lograire* [to J. Laughlin] today.

7 Robinson Jeffers, *Selected Poems* (New York: Vintage Books), 40–41. This is an excerpt from "The Torch-Bearer's Race," written in 1928, which several times refers to the "hawk's dream," after which Merton titled this part of the journals.

PART IV New Mexico, Alaska, California

September 1968–October 1968

September 11, 1968. Chicago Airport

Quiet in O'Hare. Gate G5. Waiting TWA to Albuquerque. Not in clericals.

Peace. Over the dirty cotton quilt that covered Indiana and Illinois.

When we left Louisville: talking to a nice Negro hostess who had approached me saying "Are you a philosopher?"

I did not see Louisville fall away—into its own semi-darkness.

The tensions of the night before. The noises. The shouts in the red den full of organ music. Finished, thank God. Was any of it my fault? Perhaps. Tommie O'C. and I tongue-lashed each other sadistically, all in "fun," and I won. She ended up crying. It was no good.

So now that lies under the dirty [indecipherable] sludge of clouds, the blue sea full of drifting snow, cloud-floes. And the big brown-green river makes south.

Best exit: through the Brahanarandra—or Foramen of Monro.

Importance of *Tibetan Book of Dead*—the "clean passage," direct, into a new space or area of existence—even in one's "this present" life—clean unclogged steps into more maturity.

I stepped through a big mudhole. Like escaping through the window of a toilet.

It lifts. It talks. Meditation of the motors. Mantra. *Om. Om Om Om* over and over like a sea-cow. And sun sits on the page.

Great grey-green Limpopo. *Om.* Miles of olive prairie vanishing in smoke.

Very long *Om.* Lost in rushings, washings of air; drops, bumps. Long *Om. Om.*

Right over the land of the political pig: (Say *OM!*). Right over the grease of the death erasers: Nom de Dom.

Dominic had a coat. His heart was written on it. He gave it away to a friend. He was loved by a child and loved the child in return. He was not wrong. He loved in the wrong country—as did everybody else. The country gradually showed him a million-dollar pig. It had revealed to him the art of non-dying. It comes of wanting to live in Pork Barrel country. Out of it. Out of it is a good plane ride [to] a thundering death.

Four streaks of rat-colored smoke five miles long over the prairie. (Missouri?)

Thinking we can crack death with rollers.
Rivers, sweet sisters of earth-life, ignore the smoke.
Right up over the country of bad death
Grease fries all sky over
The numb
We too the numb we are up, up
Thinking we will cheat death
With cokes and coffee
And vodka martinis.
Right over the Snake river
Where the others once flew
In a correct sitting posture
And let the mind float free
And grabbed with all their might
(The grabbing was itself release and light.)

"The humming, rolling and crackling noises before and up to fifteen hours after death . . . recognized by Grünewald in 1618 and referred to by other writers."

(Govinda—in Evans-Wentz—TBD[1]*)*

1 *Bardo Thödöl: The Tibetan Book of the Dead; or, the After-Death Experiences on the Bardo Plane, According to Lama Kazi Dawa-Sandup's English Rendering*, compiled and edited by Walter Yeeling Evans-Wentz (Oxford: Oxford University Press, 1960). *The Tibetan Book of the Dead* describes the assistance of guiding the departed toward a higher rebirth.

Roaring of the six *lokas*: around the mind, body (in it)

pride	anger	(as it reaches out
jealousy	greed	with tickets
sloth (ignorance)	lust.	in hand)

The man who smokes and drinks and does not know he is dead. Thinks he is still alive, smoking and drinking, 12 hours after death—or 12 days.

"The deceased expressed a desire for a dream cigar."

The haunted natives hastened to provide a smoke and some drinks.

"The Sahib's grave was found carefully fenced in and covered with empty whiskey and beer bottles. . . . The dead Sahib's ghost had caused much trouble. . . . The ghost craved whiskey and beer to which it had been long habituated in the flesh. . . . The people purchased the same brands which the Sahib was known to have used . . . and poured them out regularly upon the grave. Finding this kept the ghost quiet they continued the practice in self-defense."

(Evans-Wentz, lxxvi)

Send G[eorgia] O'K[eeffe] *Conjectures [of a Guilty Bystander]*
[The Way of] Chuang Tzu
Monks Pond

[Send to Christ of the Desert] monastery *Monks Pond III. IV.*

Now
Now
Now
OM
Over country
Of good death
Indian
Country
Now—canyons.
A lake signaled to me, (Blue lake perhaps?)
Flashed in my
(Mind's) eye.
"Do battle
With the mind
Conquer
The mind.
Let the spirit

Go free."
But who?

September 12, 1968

Back in a clear mind. Chama Canyon. The river is low. I was in the cold water. Feel clean. Awake. Sitting in soft sand. Where has that big red dog gone? He fought a wasp and scattered sand and mud all over my clothes.

Georgia O'Keeffe—a woman of extraordinary quality, [a]live, full of resiliency, awareness, quietness. One of the few people one ever finds (in this country at least) who quietly does everything right. Perfection of her house and patio on ghost ranch, low, hidden in desert rocks and vegetation, but with an extraordinary view of the mountains—especially the great majestic mesa of Pedernal.

"The mystery of the self's nature remains ever unsolved to those who are in the empirical plane."

"The conditions of empirical knowledge all disappear and then the self requires its proper nature."

(H. Brattacharyya)

I.e., the self is not known *within nature*.

(Prakriti)

The true self is "supernatural" (but they don't use that term).

"The realm of the knowable begins to shrink without affecting the sense of the known."

The self (Purusa)—a spiritual essence which is experience itself without the attributes and limitations of empirical personality. Language was not devised to indicate this spiritual condition!

HB.

September 13, 1968

A journey is a bad death if you ingeniously grasp or remove all that you had and were before you started, so that in the end you do not change in the least. The stimulation enables you to grasp more raffishly at the same, familiar, distorted illusions.

You come home only confirmed in greater greed—with new skills (real or imaginary) for satisfying it.

I am not going "home."

The purpose of this death is to become truly homeless.

Bardo of small bad hermitage, empty smell, quiet musty, a cobweb, some cardboard boxes.

Very quiet. Good river. Good cliffs.

Blue clouds arising after noon. Silence!

The big red dog, wet ears full of burrs, his stomach roaring with some grass he had eaten while I was swimming.

Go on! Go on!

There is no place left.

The Yoga of Patanjali is *not* introspective, because introspection finds a self as object and finds only *Buddhi*, *Ahamkara*. These are illusory self, reflection of true self perhaps, distorted reflection. The subject is unknowable. (For Buddhism—there *is* no subject. Better?)

Prepare new dreams. Be liberated from the old ones. Then at last—NO dreams!

When asked what you see from the top of Pedernal, Georgia O'Keeffe said, "You see the whole world."

Looking out at the red cliffs, and the hillsides covered with ponderosa pine and cedar, framed in the cell window. A sense of convalescence, of inner health returning. Glad to be here at Christ of the Desert!

"Insight and detachment are synonymous as far as objects of sense are concerned."

(Brattacharyya)

Yoga: to develop the power of the mind so as to see that their use is futile and that they cannot grasp or experience the Known.

To free the knower from his "knowing"—not just from his error.

For the "Known"—to know is not to know but to *be*.

Plato: vision of Er: a soul comes forward to choose its destiny. The choice is American: "He who had first choice came forward and in a moment chose the greatest tyranny; his mind having been darkened by folly and sensuality, he had not thought out the whole matter before he chose and did not at first perceive that he was fated, among other evils, to devour his own children. . . . Now he was one of those who came from heaven and in a former life had dwelt in a well-ordered state, but his virtue was a matter of habit only and he had no philosophy. . . ."

Two Hell's Angels on the highway out of Santa Fe, their motorcycles by the road, and they heading off together into the bushes, looking fairly jovial, with vast blond beards and naked chests.

Tom Carlyle halted the rattling Volkswagen with a stove inside and a plaster-mixer in tow, to speak to a friend in a pickup coming down from the other direction. They decided together that the mixer would make good adobe.

Today I am in a quiet, cool spot, in the shade of cottonwoods, short green grass, the red mesa to the right, forest in front, big vast mesa (Mesa del Viejo) behind. A profusion of yellow: flowering shrubs; sweet smell of sagebrush; the gentle contemplative song of crickets. A beautiful autumn!

It is the yearning after sangsaric [samsaric] existence that is the cause of both gods and demons "appearing"—gives them existence.

Enlightenment = realizing unreality, facticity, of sangsaric [samsaric] existence.

Yoga—necessary for enlightenment.

"There is, disciples, a realm devoid of earth and water, fire and air. It is not endless space, nor infinite thought, nor nothingness, neither ideas nor non-ideas. Not this world nor that is it. I call it neither a coming nor a departing, nor a standing still, nor death nor birth; it is without a basis, progress or stay; it is the ending of sorrow."

"For that which clingeth to another there is a fall; but unto that which clingeth not no fall can come."

(Buddha)

Enlightenment at death = recognition of one's own formless intellect as "The Clear Light" and reality itself. The naked consciousness = the liberated self: but attachment to existence makes us refuse it.

Except for a sonic boom monstrous enough to bring down half a cliff—though what I heard roaring up the canyon was not falling rocks but only the echo (at least I suppose so).

The soft, guttural exclamations of a crow emphasize the silence—and the peace of knowing that, but for the four or five at the monastery a mile or two away, there's nobody else for miles around.

I crossed the swinging plank—and cable bridge over the Chama and looked at the ruined farm house on the other side. Came back here where the shade is better. The crickets sing. The breeze is sweet in the cottonwood.

September 16, 1968

Plane over Colorado, Kansas or somewhere.

This morning I stood on the roof of Don Devereux's small adobe house, among all the other small houses, in Acequia Madre at S[anta]F[e]. The lucid green mountains, the clear dawn behind them . . .

Below, the small but comfortable bed—the four sleeping persons—Virginia, the Armenian girl, interested in Jung and astrology—Don, Eileen, their little blond child Erik.

Two days on the Jicarilla Apache reservation, for their September fiesta—a Feast of Tabernacles—leafy booths to eat under, tents to sleep in, scattered all over the wide valley by Stone Lake—campfires and their smoke mixing with the dust of hundreds of cars and pickups, blowing across the empty danceground.

The "shade" of the family where Nelson Martinez (a Catholic Apache, slightly drunk) took us: Pearl Montoya and others cooking chili on the wood stove. Brisk wind blowing all the fires—and cool in the dusk. Lovely little Indian children everywhere.

September 16, 1968

Very bumpy flying. Passengers with blue tubes in their ears listen to Muzak—or some recorded music.

"The Great Deliverance by hearing while on the after-death plane. . . ."

If the dying man should attend consciously to the symptoms of death in himself, the living man should attend to the symptoms both of life and death in himself. For instance—hyperactivity of my gut, which is trying to be too alive is ultimately destructive.

Good fortune. Two Entero-Vioforms [tablets]—administered by Eileen—and advice on diet. She thought I got dysentery eating chili, stew and hamburgers with the Jicarilla.

Better to eat less from now on, more carefully, less obsessively. And be more indifferent about food.

Over Kansas (?) (the factories)—clouds tinted with nickels—precious chemistry—magenta from some industry.

Over Missouri (?) the clouds are packed like snow.

To the Jicarilla Reservation:

First a stop at Park View at the house of G. Abeyta, the accountant for the Indians. A lavish breakfast. Small churches, deserted houses, ghost villages, in a wide valley.

The pink dilapidated courthouse of Tierra Amarilla—the scene of Tijerina's raid—(the district attorney escaped, hiding in the attic rafters).

Distant noble cliffs of Brazos Peak. Someone in the back seat tells something of the waterfall where the snows melt in May.

Distant peaks in Colorado.

Narrow gauge railway almost abandoned.

An abandoned coal mine.

A brown, dilapidated wooden *morada* where the penitents meet to scourge themselves.

Abeyta's blind grandmother, speaking cheerful, clear, carefully pronounced Spanish.

Dulce—reservation town—neat houses. The Indians prosper (they have oil and gas wells). Abeyta lives across from the Dutch Reformed Church. (Catholic Church—spanking new—up the road, nearer the rock of which pieces fell in "the earthquake" of two years ago.) (Fr. Gregory [Christ of the Desert monk] and I concelebrate there early Sunday.)

Kozlowski, the Superintendent of the Indian Agency, has been in Alaska. Talks not so much of Alaskan Indians as of Fr. Llorente of Cordova Ala (Spanish Jesuit) who knows the Indians pretty well. K. has adopted two eskimo children and they are utterly lovely, especially the little girl, Veronica.

Out to Stone Lake—interesting wooded *cuesta* [hill] south of Dulce—peaks of shelved and eroded and inclined sandstone standing in line over the valley. Broad sweep of pasture and forest. Cars on dusty road.

September 17, 1968. [En route to Alaska]

Chicago was rainy. Celebrated the F[east] of the Stigmatization of St. Francis at the new Poor Clare convent—after talking to them the evening before. Wind. View of woods on one side. Distant city on the other.

First—went down to see the old empty convent on S. Loftus Street. High brick walls, empty corridors, brick courtyard. Church with no more adoration.

We took off an hour late, big plane full of children, heading for Anchorage, Tokyo and Seoul. Flew up slowly out of the dark into the brilliant light, this Bardo of pure sky. (Clouds full of planes seeking Chicago in the dark.)

Bardo Thodol—your own true nature confronts you as Pure Truth, "subtle, sparkling, bright, dazzling, glorious, and radiantly awesome like a mirage moving across a landscape in springtime. . . . Be not terrified. . . . From the midst of that radiance the natural sound of Reality, reverberating like a thousand thunders simultaneously sounding, will come. That is the natural sound of thine own real self. Be not daunted thereby nor terrified."[2]

Hot towels. Man (Peace Corps) talking about Bangkok, Singapore, learning awareness, State Department, to one of the mothers—his wife Japanese? A beautiful little baby which she keeps lifting up over her head (and now feeding from bottle).

"Hermit cells" in Poor Clare monastery. The Red Barn nearby. The man in the grey shirt crouching in the wood (Cleveland—a bar owner, bartender, whore and another, kidnapped, shot in the park, found by joggers). The old Poor Clare convent. Sister with the ulcered leg feared that if the convent were left unguarded teen-agers would break in the graveyard and dig up the dead.

2 This passage is excerpted and paraphrased from p. 104 of Evans-Wentz's *Bardo Thodol* and the quotes that appear on the following pages of the journal are from the same source.

Bardo Thodol "The experiencing of reality"

After missing the clear light: 4 days, 4 Buddhas, 4 nights.

water—white light of Akshobhya

anger—makes one fly to "dull smoke colored light of hell"

earth—yellow light of Ratna-Sambhava

egotism—"preference for dull bluish light from human world"

fire—red light of Amitabha

attachment—dull red light of Preta-loka

air—green light of Amogha-Siddhi

jealousy—dull green—Asura-loka (quarreling and warfare)

But—"The forty-two perfectly endowed deities issuing from within thy heart, being the product of thine own pure love, will come to shine. Know them!"

"If thou art frightened by the pure radiance of Wisdom and attracted by the impure lights of the six Lokas . . . thou wilt be whirled round and round (in Sangsara [Samsara]) and made to taste the suffering thereof."

Meanwhile, however, there was something impressive about the old empty rooms and corridors, with here and there an ancient statue lamenting the emptiness, the dark. One felt that it was a place where prayer had "been valid." Even the old brick walls of the outside were impressive.

And this morning old Sr. Margaret was starting out in the rain to go begging (for food, in stores).

A while ago we were over miles of Canadian lakes, blue, blue-green, and brown, with woods between, an occasional road. Still three hours from Anchorage. Two—probably from Alaska. Clouds again, packed thick, quilted, beneath us.

I borrowed the letters of Miller and Durrell[3] from Ron S[eitz] and don't feel like reading them. The first one, with Durrell putting down *Ulysses* (saying *Tropic of Cancer* was better) turned me off.

3 Lawrence Durrell and Henry Miller, *A Private Correspondence*, ed. George Wilkes (New York: Dutton, 1963).

(More lakes down below, between clouds. Olive green, wild stretches of watery land.)

The young Apaches were racing to give back energy to the sun. The clan that was fastest was the best painted and their first [runner] was like an African antelope with long yellow streamers flying from his head and a mirror in the center of his forehead.

From Knowledge-Holders each "holding a crescent knife and skull filled with blood, dancing and making the *mudra* of fascination."

Glad to be not in Kentucky. But here over this blanket of cold cloud hiding lakes.

The bands of the Mothers, the Dakinis, sliding upon solid cloud.

Ecce dabit voci suae vocem virtutis, date gloriam Deo super Israel, magnificentia ejus, et virtus ejus in nubibus. [Listen, he sends out his voice, his mighty voice; ascribe power to God, whose majesty is over Israel, and whose power is in the skies.]

—*Psalm 67[68]:33–34*

(The wrathful deities are peaceful deities returning in menacing form, blood drinkers, emerging from the excitements of the dead brain. "Recognition—of one's own self in such forms!—becometh more difficult!")

The high plane over the north is a dinning *orchestra* of conch shells, thigh-bone trumpets, drums, cymbals—a lama orchestra such as one hears when pressing shut the ears. Also a cosmic hissing—not to mention the crying of babies and the gabble of human conversation (and afternoon perfumes).

Shades close out the Canada sun, the afternoon and the brute big shining masses of the jet engines stand out fiercely blue-black above the cloud.

"At the same time a dull blue light from the brute world will come to shine along with the Radiance of Wisdom . . ."

Flight yoga. Training in cosmic colors.

Dull, concise bronze of ginger ale.

Last night, choosing the scotch Fr. Xavier [Carroll] offered was as silly as a choice of smoke, and I had smoke in my head when I awoke.

Ginger ale has in it perfume of stewardess.

In the war-plane's music, the natural sound of truth thunders—but very differently. Equivocally.

Cries of "Slay, slay and awe-inspiring mantras . . . [but] flee not." I close my eyes and see the colors of Indian blankets.

The little Japanese baby cries with a fine clear shining cry, prolonged, unchoking, a curving repeated descant, well punctuated with good breaths.

The black falsely jeweled souvenir aprons of the Indian runners.

Fine snow-covered mountains lift their snowledges into a gap of clouds and I am exhilarated with them. Salute the spirit dwellings. Spirit-liftings come up out of the invisible land. The little boy also is playing his telephone.

First sight of mountains of Alaska, strongly ribbed, through cloud. Superb blue of the gulf, indescribable ice patterns. Bird wings, vast, mottled, long black streamers, curves, scimitars, lyre bird tails.

I am here in answer to someone's prayer.

September 18, 1968. Eagle River

ALASKA—the Convent of the Precious Blood—surrounded by woods, with a highway (too) near. The woods of Alaska—marvelous—deep in wet grass, fern, rotten fallen trees, big-leaved thorn scrub, yellowing birch, stunted fir, aspens. Thick. Humid. Lush. Smelling of life and of rot. Rich undergrowth, full of mosses, berries—and probably (in other seasons) flowers. The air is now here cool and sharp as late November in the "outside" (i.e. "the States," "lower 48").

The convent chapel looks out through big windows at birch, a purple and green mountainside. Quiet.

Sense of belonging here. The spirit of the community is good. They will move to a better site. This is a nice house but has "a water problem."

I turn a page. The eagle feather dropped by one of the Apache runners, slides, volatile, across the slick desk.

Priests of Alaska, friendly, generous. After the workshop will look for places.

Cordova and Fr. Llorente[4]
Valdez.
Islands.
A place looking at "The Big One" (McKinley).
A place called what—Hutchinson? Cunningham?
    No. Dillingham. Now in the
    same time zone as Anchorage.

Mosaic: Alaska Paper and Funnies

Burning bon fires review by Assembly
A borough ordinance will face junkheap or major overhaul
Split assembly into snarling rural and urban
Camps writes Stephen Brent of our News
Staff. And in Dallas
Wallace[5] had a big day Tuesday
Dramatic increase "He's moving up
Fast" said a strategist and
"Garbage burned further away
Would be prohibited if
It created a nuisance"—
"When I was Governor of Alabama I met
Nelson Rockefeller and George Romney and some
Of those others and they didn't impress me."
Then four died in
Alaska planes
(Skwentna River
Kenai Penin.
Sula)
"He passed over the smoke in an attempt
To see where it was coming from."
And it was from Curtis LeMay
Speaking in the Anchorage Westward Hotel.

4 Rev. Segundo Llorente, S.J., a priest of Cordova, Alaska, was one of Merton's hosts.

5 George Corley Wallace was governor of Alabama from 1963 to 1966 and 1971 to 1979 and was a candidate for president in 1968 on the American Independent Party ticket. His running mate, General Curtis LeMay (mentioned later in this poem), was Chief of Staff, U.S. Air Force, from 1961 to 1964. He opposed the bombing halt and urged maintenance of military strength and position in Vietnam. He was in Alaska on his way to Vietnam at this time.

Also in Kenai
Many are now
Wearing Wallace buttons.

Gavora 37 owns the Market Basket Supermarket in Fairbanks.
And ferry service between Alaska and Seattle
Will be doubled.
A post is filled.
A Time Zone is changed.
Next Sunday
A Fall Dance is held
With music furnished by
Fantastic Zoot and Bros. Gundy Rose.
The public is invited
To hear Sen. Nick Begich[6]
(And of course Gen. Curtis LeMay
On Vietnam)
(Funnies)
"Come I will take you to my Uncle who was fired."
"Good."
"Uncle Salvador
Señor Sawyer is not
What we thought."
"Something is wrong at the mine."
Uncle Salvador remains proud
And turns away (Thinks): "You'll get
No help from me!"
Says: "Why are they flooding
The exploratory channel
At the 3700 foot level?"

Tigers win pennant
Drenched in champagne while

6 Nicholas Joseph Begich (1932–1972) was Superintendent of Schools, Fort Richardson, Alaska, from 1963 to 1968, a member of the Alaska Senate from 1963 to 1971, and U.S. Congressman from Alaska from 1971 until his death in 1972.

Crowds in darkness chant
"We want Tigers."
On this day (Wednesday Sept. 18)
Aries shall "utilize showmanship
Dress up product" and Taurus should
"Strive to be specific—no beating
Around the bush." Gemini "be complete
Not fragmentary." LIBRA
(Well frankly it's a good day for Libra with "a Virgo individual
Tonight")
"Romantic interests are spurred . . ."
All is glamor today for lucky
Libra. And Scorpio should stop grumbling
"About overtime."
And final word
To Aries "Compile facts."
As to Aquarius (my own
Self in workshop) "Necessity of public
Relations. Some around you are ultra-
Sensitive. Older person
Wants to be heard!" (I pray that's Mother Rita Mary!)
Russian space ship returns from moon.
Helicopter shot down in Vietnam.
Students rioting in Mexico City (for days).
Fair today, high in fifties (again).
Turned it off before the football news came on.

First Ecstasy of Rama Krishna[7]

One day in June or July when he was six years old he was walking along a narrow path between ricefields, eating puffed rice from a basket. He looked up at the sky and saw a beautiful storm cloud, and a flight of snow white cranes passing in front of it, above him. He lost consciousness and fell into a faint at the beauty of it. A peasant found him with rice scattered all about and carried him home.

7 Rama Krishna, or Ramakrishna Parahamsa (1834–1886), a Hindu ascetic and mystic, was open to other forms of religious expression. He meditated for a time as a Christian and as a Muslim, reaching the conclusion that "all religions are one." His disciples introduced a new element of social service into Hinduism.

September 19, 1968. Alaska

Louisville—Christ of the Desert—Jicarilla Apache Reservation—Santa Fe—Chicago—Anchorage—Eagle River Convent.

I am now here on a bright cold morning and the first thin dusty snow is on the lower hills. Mt. McKinley is visible in the distance from the Precious Blood Convent. Next to which I live in a trailer (very comfortable).

On the morning of the 10th I went down to the monastery for the last time to get some money, pick up mail, say goodbye to Fr. Flavian, Bros. Maurice and Patrick. No one else much knew anything about my departure. Ron Seitz came about ten. A grey cool, fall morning. We drove into Louisville. I got travelers checks, medicine in St. Matthews. An AWOL bag for camera, second pair of shoes, etc. Afternoon—a shower and short rest at O'Callaghans and in the evening a supper send-off party that probably could have been better done without. But no matter. Dan Walsh was there and I hadn't seen him for a long time. I slept at St. Bonaventure's Friary and got out early in the morning. Flew to Chicago, then Albuquerque.

I was met at the airport in Albuquerque by Tom Carlyle, a very likable hippie type who is staying at Christ of the Desert and working for them. A really good, sincere, spiritual person. One of the best. We drove up in his Volkswagen—dragging a plaster mixer with which he plans to make adobe brick for the monks.

Two days' retreat in the canyon. Swam in the cold Chama.

Then to the Jicarilla Apache encampment feast on the reservation near Dulce. A feast of Tabernacles. Booths of boughs, tents and campfires everywhere. Then the race the next day. Back to Santa Fe. Slept at the Devereuxs' in Reyena Madre. Low adobe house. Supper at the Pink Adobe—good curry but too much of it.

Flew from Albuquerque to Chicago (last sight of distant Pedernal quite clear!). Rain in Chicago. Went to the new Poor Clare convent and gave them a talk; liked the architecture. Ed Noonan, the architect, came for Mass next day—I concelebrated with Fr. Xavier Carroll who took me to the plane—with one of the Sisters who was leaving.

The Northwest plane for Anchorage, Tokyo and Seoul was late getting started. Crowded with families, American and Japanese, returning to Asia. I felt for the first time that Asia was getting close!

The flight to Alaska was mostly over clouds. Quiet. A soldier on the outside seat; the middle seat of the three empty. We didn't talk except for a little bit just before landing. (He said Anchorage wasn't any colder in winter than Syracuse, N.Y., but that there was a lot of snow.)

The clouds opened over Mt. St. Elias and after that I was overwhelmed by the vastness, the patterns of glaciers, the burnished copper sheen of the sun on the bright blue sea. The shore line. The bare purple hills. The high mountains full of snow, the dark islands stark in the sun—burnish on the water.

We swung slowly down into Anchorage and got out into cold, clear, autumn air. Everywhere the leaves have turned. Gold of the aspens and birches everywhere.

Without going actually into Anchorage we (Msgr. [John] Lunney met me) drove out on Route 1 to the convent, at Eagle River.

It is a nice house among the birches, at the foot of low mountains, looking out through the trees toward Cook Inlet and Mount McKinley—the nuns may move in a few months as the place is not quite suitable.

I have a sense of great warmth and generosity in the clergy here. The Archbishop is away at Juneau but will be back next week—all are very eager to help and I feel they are eager to have me settle here. Meanwhile I'm busy on a workshop with the nuns. They are a good community, and like all, they have their troubles.

This afternoon—in the sun at the foot of a birch, in the bushes near the monastery at a point where you can see Mt. McKinley and Mt. Foraker—great, silent and beautiful presence in the afternoon sun.

September 21, 1968. Eagle River

"One will understand the extent to which the anthropological realities of our everyday experiences are deformed by sin and correspond little to the pure norms of the new creation which is being realized in the Church. Actually, the individual who possesses a part of nature and reserves it for himself, the subject who defines himself by opposition to all that which is not 'I,' is not the person or hypostasis who shares nature in common with others and who exists as person in a positive relationship to other persons. Self-will . . . is not identical to the will of the new creation—to the will which one finds in renouncing oneself, in the unity of the Body of Christ, wherein the canons of the Church make us recognize a common and individual will. Not the properties of an individual nature, but the unique relationship of each being with God—a relationship by the Holy Spirit and realized in grace—is what constitutes the uniqueness of a human person."[8]

September 22, 1968. Sunday

6 a.m. on KHAR Anchorage; Alaskan Golden Nugget Potatoes respectfully suggest that we worship God since we are a nation under God and want to build a stronger America. Nugget Potatoes are glad of this opportunity to "voice this thinking." A good thought from a respectful potato.

Yesterday—end of worship—visit of Precious Blood priests—not without a song and Ole Man River. Evening—to the army base at Ft. Richardson—like city of shiny apartments—bourbon on the rocks—tarpon fishing on TV—wild ducks in slow motion flight—memories of Brooklyn. And supper at the Air Force base at Elmendorf (like city of shiny apartments). Heated argument between conservative and progressive clergy and laity: which is better: to kneel for communion or to stand?

September 23, 1968

Anchorage Daily News advises Aquarius to read travel folders. I thumb through my tickets to Los Angeles, Honolulu, Bangkok, Calcutta, Katmandu . . . and am eager to get going.

Climbed a mountain behind the convent, and looked out over the vast valley—Mt. McKinley—the Alaska Range—far off Redoubt Volcano and Iliamna.

Today I go to Cordova.

Graffiti in toilet—Anchorage Airport.

On the whole much more tame than usual.

For instance: "Vote for Nixon"—(spelled NIXION)

"Peace and good will to your fellow men!"

Someone declares he is on his way to Vietnam.

Another states: "Missouri is best."

Which draws the only dirty comment: "For assholes."

On the whole a very genteel set of announcements and no pictorial matter.

Another graffiti "Hickel has crabs" (Hickel is the governor).

8 Merton was reading and quoting from Vladimir Lossky (1903–1958), *À l'Image et à la Ressemblance de Dieu* (Paris: Aubion-Montaigne, 1967). Cf. p. 83.

September 23, 1968. Cordova

Landed at the cool, lovely airfield shortly after dawn. Still freezing. I rode into town on the airport bus—a school bus—with a bunch of duck hunters, very voluble about their luck and about the good weather which is bad for them as the ducks and geese have not begun to move south.

Ducks in the water of the Copper River Delta.

I find St. Joseph's Church, no one around. I walk in the rectory and after a while Fr. Llorente arrives—a remarkable person, a Spanish Jesuit who got himself sent to the Yukon 30 years ago and has been in Alaska ever since—has become a sort of legend in the region. He was going to leave to work with Mexican migrants in California, but was needed for Cordova . . . He stayed.

A small fishing town between steep mountains and blue water—a highway on one side, and Eyak Lake around at the back.

I have no hesitation in saying Eyak Lake seemed perfect in many ways—for a place to live. The quiet end of it is several miles back in the mountains, completely isolated, silent. Wild geese were feeding there. Great silver salmon were turning red and dying in shallows where they had spawned (some had been half eaten by bears). Bears would be the only problem but Fr. Llorente said they were not grizzlies. A few cabins nearer town were attractive. Also the way was impressive.

Other ideas of Fr. Llorente: Yakutat and a shrine (abandoned) of the Little Flower outside Juneau (many sea lions there).

Plans had been for me to go to Kenai Peninsula and Kodiak tomorrow but I am going to Matanuska Valley instead.

September 24, 1968. Valdez (Valdeez)

At the far end of a long blue arm of water, full of islands. The bush pilot flies low over the post office thinking it to be the Catholic Church—to alert the priest we are arriving.

The old town of Valdez, wrecked by earthquake, tidal wave. Still some buildings leaning into shallow salt water. Others, with windows smashed by a local drunkard. I think I have lost the roll of film I took in Valdez and the mountains (from the plane).

Most impressive mountains I have seen in Alaska: Drum and Wrangell and the third great massive one whose name I forget, rising out of the vast birchy plain of Copper Valley. They are sacred and majestic mountains, ominous, enormous, noble, stirring. You want to attend to them. I could not keep my eyes off them. Beauty and terror of the Chugach. Dangerous valleys. Points. Saws. Snowy nails.

September 26, 1968. Anchorage

Noises as the bishop's house awakes—noise of heat tapping in the walls, of water running, of plates being set, of the feet of domestic prelates on carpeted floors, creaking of floorboards where there is movement overhead to left and to right. Feet on stairs. Cutlery. Crockery. Planes coming down to FAA airport beyond the birches outside.

Today I fly to Juneau with Archbishop Ryan. Then to Ketchikan tomorrow and back to Anchorage Saturday.

Sound of chapel door closing as Bishop comes down to say his office before breakfast (Mass tonight—concelebration in Juneau).

The bishop's house is warm and quiet. It smells of bacon.

Plane grounded. We cannot go to Juneau where the Archbishop had planned a clergy conference and concelebration this evening. Flight tomorrow perhaps to Yakutat.

Haircut in Anchorage Westward Hotel. Manuel, an artist in hairstyles, found little to do on me, but spoke of what he had learned about wigs in Heidelberg. "Inexpensive!" He emphasized this. A nasty hint!

The Bishop is tired and will go to rest—which is only right. I write postcards and letters. Letter to Fr. Flavian on an electric typewriter in the Chancery Office (second one. A better report than yesterday's).

I walk briefly through the streets of Anchorage, viewing the huge lift of land after the 1964 earthquake, looking out at the barges drilling for oil in Cook Inlet. The mountains to the west are hidden in fog and snow clouds. Behind the city, the tops are powdered with clean snow.

I have a reservation for San Francisco on the 2nd. Plan to sleep there. A letter came from Suzanne B.,[9] so maybe I'll have supper with her. She said

9 Suzanne Butorovich was one of Merton's young correspondents; in their letters they discussed Bob Dylan, the Beatles, and the hippie movement. For Merton's letters to her, see the second volume of the letters, *The Road to Joy: Thomas Merton's Letters to New and Old Friends* (New York: Farrar, Straus & Giroux, 1989), 308–14.

she had read in Ralph Gleason's column that I had left the monastery and was going to Tibet. October 3rd I am supposed to go to Santa Barbara, and have a conference at the Center [for Democratic Institutions] on the 4th (no—3rd).

Behind Palmer: Pioneer Peak, badly named, tall and black and white in the snow—mist, rugged armatures, indestructible, great. It vanishes into snow cloud as we retreat up the valley into birch flats. McKinley hidden.

The log house of Mr. and Mrs. Peck by the windy lake. Clouds of blowing aspen and birch leaves fly across the lawn. Mr. Peck with an army field jacket and a good Dutch cigar—brought by the big silent boy from KLM who sits with a bottle of bourbon in the shadows of the kitchen.

Mrs. Peck's sister has half finished an enormous jigsaw puzzle which occupies a whole table. Mrs. Peck, a lovely, ageless Eskimo woman, plump, broad Asian smile, like the faces of Nepalese tribes in the book I saw today (Anchorage Public Library).

September 27, 1968. Yakutat

Bay with small islands. Driving rain on the docks. A few fishing boats. Beat-up motorboats, very poor. An old battered green rowboat called *The Jolly Green Giant.*

It is a village of Indians, with an FAA station nearby. Battered houses. A small Indian girl opens the door of the general store. Looks back at us as we pass. Cannery buildings falling down. Old tracks are buried in mud and grass. A dilapidated building was once a "roundhouse" though it is a large rectangle. After that, all there is is a long straight gravel road pointing in the mist between tall hemlocks out into the nowhere where more of the same will be extended to a lumber operation. The woods are full of moose, and black bear, and brown bear, and even a special bear found only at Yakutat—the glacier bear (or blue bear).

Frank Ryman had in his lodge the skin of a wolf—as big as a small bear.

Yakutat has plenty of wolves and coyotes, besides bears.

And in the village are many murders.

Tlingit Indians.

Here there was once a Russian penal colony. It was wiped out by the Indians.

Yakutat—one of the only—perhaps *the* only place that is on Yukon time. All the other places have adopted one of the other timebelts, Anchorage or Pacific.

September 27, 1968. Juneau

Alone in the empty bishop's house at Juneau (he has retired[10]—the see is vacant) after concelebration, dinner, and conference at the Cathedral. Driving rain, and a long spectacular thin waterfall down the side of the mountain becomes, in a concrete channel outside the house, the fastest torrent I have ever seen. It must be running fifty miles an hour into the choppy bay.

This morning—we flew in bad weather to Yakutat, came down out of thick clouds on to a shore full of surf and hemlock and muskeg. Desolate airstrip.

Frank Ryman drove us into the village to show me the village. Broken down houses, mostly inhabited by Tlingit Indians, an old fish cannery, and a small dock with a few fishing boats on a lovely broad bay with islands. Everything seemed covered with hemlock. Driving rain, mountains invisible. Frank Ryman has a quarter acre of land he offered me—and it is enough to put a trailer on. But it is right at the edge of the village. If I lived there I would become very involved in the life of the village and would probably become a sort of pastor.

We left Yakutat after dinner (at Ryman's "lodge" out at the airstrip), flew in rain to Juneau which turns out to be a fascinating place clinging to the feet of several mountains at the edge of a sort of fjord. I never saw such torrential rain as met us when we got out of the plane!

Earlier in the week; visit Cordova on Monday. The road that goes around to the back of Eyak Lake is one of the most beautiful places in Alaska—silent, peaceful, among high mountains, wild geese and ducks on the flats. Perhaps in many ways the best place I have seen so far. The bay there, too, is magnificent.

Tuesday we flew with a bush pilot—over the mountains and glaciers to Valdez. Then up through the pass in the Chugach to Copper Valley and Copper Center school, with the Wrangell Mountains beyond it. And down again through the Matanuska Valley to Anchorage.

10 Most Rev. Dermot O'Flanagan (1887–1973) was Bishop of Juneau from 1951 to 1968. Apparently he had just retired, and the bishop's house was vacant at the time.

Generous hospitality of Archbishop Ryan in Anchorage. I have been staying at his house since Tuesday night. A comfortable bed in the basement where he also has his bar. He is from New York and has a New York humor and urbanity.

Whatever else I may say—it is clear I like Alaska much better than Kentucky and it seems to me that if I am to be a hermit in the U.S., Alaska is probably the place for it. The SE is good—rain and all. I have still to go out to Western Alaska—and missed Kodiak where there is, I hear, an old Russian hermit. (Last week I saw the Russian church in the Indian village of Eklutna, up the road from the convent.)

Last Sunday I climbed a mountain behind the convent, guided by a boy who knew the trail. Very tired after it!

Wednesday and Thursday—wrote letters in the Chancery Office at Anchorage, two of them to Fr. Flavian, trying to describe Alaska.

September 28, 1968. Juneau

Green walls of mountains in the rain. Lights of the Federal building in rainy dusk. Narrow streets ending up against a mountain. A towering waterfall snaking down out of the clouds. Green.

Blue-green Juneau. The old cathedral. The deserted hospital. The deserted hotel. The deserted dock. The deserted school. We met Senator Gruening[11] in the airport and shook his hand. Famous people are never as tall as you expect.

Night in the comfortable bishop's house. Torrent in the channel outside. Sound of water racing smooth and even at fifty miles an hour into the bay. I oversleep. Get up just in time to put a few clothes on—but not to shower—before Fr. Manske[12] arrives (7:30) with the car to take me out along the shore. The clouds lift a little and beyond the green islands are vague, snow-covered peaks. A beautiful channel full of islands.

11 Ernest Gruening (1887–1974) was governor of Alaska Territory from 1939 to 1953 and then senator from Alaska from 1959 to 1969.

12 Monsignor James I. Manske was at this time vicar general of the diocese of Juneau in Alaska.

September 29, 1968. [Feast of] St. Michael

Quiet Sunday morning in the (empty) bishop's house. Anchorage. Rain. Wet carpet of fallen birch leaves. Wind. Gulls. Long road going off past a gravelpit toward Providence Hospital where I preached a day of recollection today. More and more leaves fall. Everyone's at Palmer, celebrating St. Michael and the Parish.

Talking of the changing of nun's names (at Mother House) Sister Charity said: "*Those who have mysteries have to change.*" Others were interested in the rigors of Trappist life, sleeping in underwear. A Kodiak grey nun knew Abbot Obrecht. There's always someone, somewhere who knows a Trappist.

Noise of heat walking around in the walls. I am hungry.

The empty house of bishops. Quiet. False flowers and false autumn weeds in a bunch on the table. Empty coke can. Two Sundays ago I was driving down from the Jicarilla reservation to Santa Fe. One Sunday ago tired from climbing the mountain at Eagle River.

"All the Sisters who have mysteries have to be changed?" And they are delighted at my monastic nickname "Uncle Louie." But the Bishop would prefer more reverence, more decorum. However, he says nothing. At Mass today I did not give the nuns the kiss of peace for fear of the Bishop. Several of the Precious Blood Sisters came with bangs—a slightly different hairdo.

There were three or four copies of *Ave Maria* on the table but I did not get to look at them to see if my statement on draft record burning was there.[13] Nor have I had any repercussions. A letter from Phil Berrigan (Allentown Prison, Pa.) was forwarded from Gethsemani. He does not mind prison life. But demonstrations and draft card burnings are not understood: they help Wallace. Is it possible he may be President? Yes, possible.

13 The article referred to was titled "Non-violence Does Not—Cannot—Mean Passivity," which first appeared in *Ave Maria* (Notre Dame) on September 7, 1968. It was later included as "Note for *Ave Maria*" in *Thomas Merton on Peace*, edited by Gordon Zahn (New York: Doubleday, 1971), 231–33.

September 29, 1968. Anchorage. 17th Sunday after Pentecost

Late afternoon. Rain. Cold. I got home from preaching the Day of Recollection to (most of) the Sisters of the Dioceses at Providence Hospital. It was good and I was less tired than I expected. The grey nuns of Kodiak (mostly old—one little young one looking slightly lost and *very* young). The ones at Marian house (various groups—Bishop and I and Frs. [Thomas] Connery and Lunney concelebrated and had dinner there last night). The Precious Blood nuns from Eagle River—my old friends—two Episcopalians with blue veils, two from Copper Center, the Good Shepherd nun from Philadelphia who, it seems, came up on the same plane with me—(Could it have been the same one?) and the Providence nuns at the hospital.

Came home. Bishop's house empty (he is at Palmer, at the parish feast of St. Michael's). I stood in the wet, empty, leaf-covered driveway and watched the seagulls flying by in the rain. I probably won't be able to go to Dillingham tomorrow. Tuesday—day of recollection for the priests and then Wednesday I finally go to California.

All this flying around Alaska has been paid for by the Bishop.

We had a good talk last evening and he agreed that if I came to Alaska it would be simply to live as a hermit with *no* kind of parish responsibility.

Yesterday morning—driving in rain up the shore of the channel, past Mendenhall Glacier, outside Juneau. Shrine of St. Therese in rain. Lovely big trees. A good spot—but not for me (would be swamped by people). Juneau is a handsome little town. I could get quite fond of it! Mass in an old church in Douglas. (The churches here are poverty stricken!) Flight out of Juneau on a big jet from Los Angeles—back into the high and prosperous realm above the clouds.

September 30, 1968

Light snow in Anchorage on the last day of September.

Flew to Dillingham in a Piper Aztec (two engines) a fast plane that goes high. Bristol Bay area—like Siberia! Miles of tundra. Big winding rivers. At times, lakes are crowded together and shine like bits of broken glass. Or are untidy and complex like the pieces of a jigsaw puzzle.

Two volcanoes: *Iliamna*—graceful, mysterious, feminine, akin to the great Mexican volcanoes. A volcano to which one speaks with reverence, lovely in the distance, standing above the sea of clouds. Lovely near at hand with smaller attendant peaks. *Redoubt* (which surely has another name, a secret and true name) handsome and noble in the distance, but ugly, sinister as you get near it. A brute of a dirty busted mountain that has exploded too often. A bear of a mountain. A dog mountain with steam curling up out of the snow crater. As the plane drew near there was turbulence and we felt the plane might at any moment be suddenly pulled out of its course and hurled against the mountain. As if it would not pull itself away. But finally it did. *Redoubt.* A volcano to which one says nothing. Pictures from the plane.

In Dillingham some time ago (a year or two) the sister of the Orthodox priest went berserk and tore through the Catholic mission with an axe, breaking down one door after another as the Catholic Father retired before her from room to room, calling the State Troopers on various telephones.

Dillingham—grey sky, smelling of snow. Cold wind. Freezing. Brown tundra. Low hemlocks. In the distance, interesting mountains. We flew to them, between them. Brown vacant slopes. A distance somewhat like New Mexico (flat, dark blue line). Another distance with snow-covered mountains vanishing into low clouds. Lake Aleknagik speaks to me. A chain of lakes far from everything. Is this it?

Aleknagik.
Nunavaugaluk (a very impressive deserted lake—separated mountains).
Akuluktok Peak.
Nuyakuk River (the big river at Dillingham—from Nuyakuk Lake).

October 2, 1968

Big black mouths of the jet engines open in silver fog. We bounce high over the Chugach lifting out of Anchorage.

We come up into the sunlight, possibly over Cordova.

"My own journey and life-goal which had colored my dreams since late boyhood was to see the beautiful Princess Fatima and if possible to win her love."

(*H. Hesse*, Journey to the East)

"I met and loved Ninnon, known as 'the foreigner'"—she was jealous of Fatima— "the princess of my dreams and yet she was probably Fatima herself without knowing it."[14]

Yesterday—Day of Recollection for some 50 priests at P[recious] B[lood] convent. Almost half of them chaplains, many of these in from "the sites" (missile launching sites, etc., in the Aleutians and Far North).

Sister Mary wrote me a very sweet note on the back of a card showing an "Alaskan Sunset." I have not been able to throw it away. Mother Rita Mary gave me a good clock. The incredible generosity of Archbishop Ryan. Tom Connery waited with me for the plane (an hour late). Msgr. [Francis A.] Murphy ended up by cooking a fine steak dinner (we flew to Dillingham together Monday). Tom Connery goes to Dillingham Friday (for two weeks).

"Among the tram ways and banks of Zurich we came upon Noah's Ark guarded by several dogs which all had the same name."

Perpetual mist grant unto them O Lord. The seatbelt sign is on "Please Fasten Your Seatbelts Thankyo!" What is this "Thankyo!"? Is it west? Is it only Alaska?

Suddenly I hear a steel band I had on tape in the hermitage.

Nine Rules for Air Travel

1. Get the last window seat in the back, next to the kitchen.
2. Get Bloody Mary when the girls start off with their wagon.
3. Read Hermann Hesse, *Journey to the East.*
4. No use looking out the window. Fog all the way up to 36,000 feet.
5. Get second Bloody Mary when girls come back down aisle.
6. Expect small dinner, racket of which is right beside you (slamming of ice box doors, etc.).
7. Sympathy and admiration for hardworking stewardesses.

14 This is taken from Hermann Hesse's *The Journey to the East,* translated from the German by Hilda Rosner (New York: Farrar, Straus & Giroux, 1961), 24.

8. Cocktail almonds in pocket for Suzanne [Butorovich], who is supposed to be at airport in San Francisco—assuming we make some kind of connection in Seattle!
9. "We had brought the magic wave with us. It cleansed everything." (Hesse)

The sky finally opened when we were over British Columbia and all its islands and on the way down into Seattle we flew over at least six big forest fires and a lot of small ones that were nearly out. But the big ones were by no means out and now south of Seattle the whole lower sky is red-brown with the smoke of big distant fires. Volcanoes stand up out of it. Mt. Hood, etc.

No connection at Seattle so we stay on this plane, and it will stop at S[an] F[rancisco].

Title for a possible book *The Fun Diary of My Uncle*—anti-salacious.

October 3, 1968

Then there was Portland (where we were not supposed to be) and the plane filled up and I finished Hermann Hesse and Paul Bowles[15] and looked out at the scarred red flanks of Lassen Peak and as we landed in SF a carton of Pepsi cans broke open and the cans rolled around all over the floor in the back galley and even a little bit forward, under the feet of some sailors.

Embraced wildly by Suzanne in airport. Her little sister Linda was so quiet. And she talked of her music and her ballet and her French (good accent). Then they went home and I slept nine hours in the (expensive) motel.

Stewardess 1—"When her eyelashes began to fall out I . . ." (inaudible).
Stewardess 2—"Real ones?"
Stewardess 1—"Yes!"

This morning the big American Freight went up ahead of us black-smoking in the fog and a big Japanese passenger came down blinking gladly from Asia and then we tugged at ourselves a little with our propellers and then came up here where we are now high over a lake of dirty cotton, in the baby blue sky of California.

15 Paul Frederick Bowles (1910–) is an American writer, poet, novelist, translator, and composer living in Tangier, Morocco. It is not certain which book of Bowles's Merton was reading at the time, since it was not returned to Gethsemani with the rest of Merton's personal effects at the time of his death.

I can't remember the last sign I saw down there in that world, but something beautiful like

XAMN RNWY BFR XING

October 8, 1968

More than a week since I last wrote in this thing. I am now at the Redwoods monastery. Dawn. Cold, hard frost, and a quiet crow softly cawing outside. It is good to be here.

Last Monday—flew to Dillingham (Alaska) over the volcanoes. A fine wild spot—desolate as Siberia. I like the lakes that are to the north of it. Tuesday—a day of recollection for priests there. Many chaplains. I spoke most of prayer. The Bishop was pleased. Wednesday I flew south to San Francisco. Met by Suzanne B. and her family. I had supper with them and slept at the International Inn which was expensive. Then on Thursday morning I flew to Santa Barbara. Spoke informally at the Center and in the evening met some people at Ferrys'—John Cogley and his wife, the Kellys, the Laucks, Mae Karam who typed *[The Geography of] Lograire* for me, and so on.

A feeling of oversaturation with talk, food, drink, movement, sensations. The Madonna Inn on the road (U.S. 101) outside San Luis Obispo exemplifies the madness of it. A totally extravagant creation, a disneyland motel, impossible fairy caves, a waterfall that starts in the urinal when you piss on the beam of an electric eye, a hostess with a skirt so short her behind was almost showing.

With the Ferrys—drove up 101 to San Francisco, arrived fairly tired, had dinner with Paul Jacobs and his wife and Czeslaw Milosz and his wife at the Yen Ching—excellent North Chinese food—sweet-sour soup, pot chicken, duck, twice-fried pork, fish, etc. A great dinner—but too much. That was October 4th.

The morning of the 4th I said Mass—with Hugh McKiernan[16]—at Casa de Marca, the IHM's place in Santa Barbara.

16 Abbot Hugh McKiernan had been superior of the Trappist Monastery of Holy Cross, Berryville, Virginia, prior to this meeting. He was currently chaplain to the IHM Sisters in Santa Barbara.

The 5th—since I am to see the Dalai Lama early in November, I went down to the Pan American Office on Union Square to change my flights. Found Dharamsala in an atlas and decided Amritsar was the place to fly to.

Then we drove off around the Embarcadero, over the Golden Gate Bridge, stopped a little at Muir Woods, then on up Route 1. Pleasant little towns, winding road, eucalyptus trees, hills, shore. We came fairly late in the afternoon to Mendocino and all the motels were full. I found a bed in the Ames Lodge, two miles out in the woods—from which I had a good walk in the morning, through young redwoods, down to the river. Very quiet and lovely.

I decided the best thing would be to come to the monastery and say Mass in the evening (as I could not contact the pastor in Mendocino about saying Mass in his church). We spent most of the morning on the country road that goes along the ridge above Bear Harbor. Finally found Bear Harbor—and was shocked to see it was being torn up by bulldozers—roads are being cut and Jones seems to be trying to open up the same sort of development as is taking place at Shelter Cove. Everything on this coast is in movement. Land is being sold at enormous prices. Little houses are going up everywhere. There is little or no hope of the real kind of solitude I look for.

October 11, 1968. Friday

Today begins a three-day conference—on contemplative life, houses of prayer, etc. "Organized" (or non-organized) at request of Mother Benedicta of the IHMs of Monroe, Michigan. Last evening Mother Myriam and I casually wondered what to do. Decided I was after all to give some talks about something and start the usual discussions. After midnight, in the rain, they all arrived from the plane at Eureka—headlights, muffled voices, doors opening and closing. A Passionist shares my bathroom and is in there now showering, shaving, etc. but I haven't yet seen him. Most of the others are nuns. Two from Alaska—Mother Rita Mary and Sr. Mary, with reports of another (minor) earthquake.

Yesterday the Ferrys left for the Oregon coast. I went to Garberville with Joe (former Brother Giacomo of Gethsemani and Vina) and got a tetanus shot at the Medical Center. I also mailed to India the first draft of my talk to be given at Darjeeling—which I hastily typed out on Wednesday—the F[east] of St. Denis.

Yesterday too, I was able to take my lunch to Needle Rock and spend the afternoon there. Quiet, empty, even the sheep ranch is now vacated. Why? For the bulldozers to come? I ate a cheese sandwich which made me sick, but not enough to spoil the afternoon. When I arrived there was a layer of mist hanging about half way down the mountain—casting metallic blue shadows on the sea far out. And near shore the water was green and ultramarine—long quiet rollers furling themselves in orderly succession and crashing on the beach. Hundreds of birds—pelicans—cormorants patrolling the water. Scores of young brown gulls. And then sea lions rising for air and swimming under the rollers just before they'd break. (The rain falling on the house sounds like the sea.)

Very quiet and peaceful on the shore. Gradually the mist descended and veiled everything so that you could barely see the waves breaking at the foot of the cliff. I can still think of nowhere I would rather settle than at that ranch—if it could stay more or less as it is.

The other day we (the Ferrys and I) drove to Patrick's Point beyond Eureka. Nothing very interesting—except that I sat in the sunny haze over the sea and listened to sea lions barking on a rock.

October 13, 1968. San Francisco

Up late in the Clift Hotel. Drove down from the Redwoods with Portia Webster and Sr. Marie, RSHM, who are both postulants there. We made good time, had supper in Ukiah and stopped for a drink in Sausalito (where I went into a bookstore for Sylvia Plath et al). Got into the hotel, big room—not as quiet as might be with traffic on Geary—turned on the radio and there was Ella Fitzgerald singing

> If you don't want my peaches
> Why do you shake my tree?

The three-day (2-½ day) workshop at Redwoods seems to have gone well—and was quickly over. On the first day (Friday) torrents of rain all day. The next day dark and misty; today bright again. The conference this morning was in the old chapel (library) and then after Mass we had a fine lunch in the community room, a short talk finally and then I went and threw things pell-mell into my bags and we left. Tomorrow I hope to get my Indonesian visa—have supper with Portia somewhere down by Fisherman's Wharf and on Tuesday fly to Bangkok.

PART V

The Far East: The Last Days

October 1968–December 1968

October 15, 1968

The Pacific is very blue. Many small white clouds are floating over it, several thousand feet below us. It is seven o'clock in Honolulu toward which we are flying. We—the planeload of people on Pan American: the silent Hawaiian soldier, the talking secretaries, the Australians, the others who like myself had to pay for excess baggage. Lesson: not to travel with so many books. I bought more yesterday, unable to resist the bookstores in San Francisco.

Yesterday I got my Indonesian visa in the World Trade Center, on the Embarcadero, and said Tierce standing on a fire escape looking out over the Bay, the Bay Bridge, the island, the ships. Then I realized I had apparently lost the letter with addresses of the people I was to meet. However, I did jot down an address in Djakarta.

There was a delay getting off the ground at San Francisco: the slow ballet of big tailfins in the sun. Now here. Now there. A quadrille of planes jockeying for place on the runway.

The moment of take-off was ecstatic. The dewy wing was suddenly covered with rivers of cold sweat running backward. The window wept jagged shining courses of tears. Joy. We left the ground—I with Christian mantras and a great sense of destiny, of being at last on my true way after years of waiting and wondering and fooling around.

May I not come back without having settled the great affair. And found also the great compassion, ***mahakaruna***. We tilted east over the shining city. There was no mist this morning. All the big buildings went by. The green parks. The big red bridge over the Golden Gate. Muir Woods, Bodega Bay, Point Reyes, and then two tiny rock islands. And then nothing. Only blue sea.

I am going home, to the home where I have never been in this body, where I have never been in this washable suit (washed by Sister Gerarda the other day at the Redwoods), where I have never been with these suitcases (in Bangkok there must be a katharsis of the suitcases!), where I have never been with these particular books, Evans-Wentz's *Tibetan Yoga and Secret Doctrines* and the others.

The smell of one of the Australians' cheroot. And, in the diffuse din of the plane, bird cries, waterfalls, announcements, and the pretty stewardess comes along handing out green mimeographed sheets of paper, or small blue cards, invitations to parties with the King of the Islands, perhaps. Someone holds high the San Francisco *Chronicle* with a big gray picture of a tiger skin.

Last week I had a dream about planes. It was at Yakutat, one of the small airstrips to which I had been flown in Alaska. There is a low ceiling and we are waiting to take off in a small plane. But a large plane, a commercial prop plane, is about to land. It comes down, and then I hear it leave again. The way is clear. Why don't we take off now? The other plane is never seen, though it lands and takes off nearby.

Not long ago I was thinking about the level of communication—as a problem to be studied on this trip—with its many aspects. And the level of communion—problems resolved beforehand by the acceptance of "words," which cannot be understood until after they have been accepted and their power experienced.

> Hrishikesa, destroyer of Titans, ogres and *canailles* [scoundrels],[1]
> Slaves flee the old group, embracing the feet of Hrishikesa, flying from Wallace,
> Free champagne is distributed to certain air passengers
> "*Ad multos annos* [For many years]," sings the airline destroyer of ogres and *canailles*
> In the sanctuary of the lucky wheel
> Blazing red circle in the fire
> We are signed between the eyes with this noble crim-
> Son element this Asia,

1 It appears that Merton was reading *Ramanuja et la mystique vishnouite* by Anne-Marie Esnoul (Paris: Editions du Seuil, 1964) on the airplane between San Francisco and Hawaii. In this volume he found quoted some unpublished French translations by J. Filliozat of devotional hymns written by the ninth-century Tamil poet Periyalvar. Using the parodistic technique he had developed several years earlier for his last major poetic work, *The Geography of Lograire*, he composed this and the following poem, which are partly Merton's translation of Periyalvar's text and partly his own interjections of images drawn from his immediate experience.

The lucky wheel spins over the macadam forts
Showering them with blood and spirits
The thousand bleeding arms of Bana
Whirl in the alcohol sky
Magic war! Many armies of fiery stars!
Smash the great rock fort in the Mathura forest
Baby Krishna plays on his pan-flute
And dances on the five heads
Of the registered brass cobra
Provided free by a loving line of governments.

Berceuse [lullaby]: to end the sorrow of mortals: *talelo* [lullaby refrain], riding the bull. *Talelo.* Riding the great blue buffalo. *Talelo!* They kill swine. They break the bone, eat the marrow of sorrow. The Tamil[2] page cures in the dry wind, the inner aviation. You striding baby, you three-step world surveyor.

Weep not. *Talelo.*
Love has lotus feet
Like the new blossoms
Bells are on her ankles.
Talelo.
You who came to drink on earth
Poisoned milk
Weep no more. *Talelo?*
The carp is leaping
In the red-rice. *Talelo.*
And in the open lotus
Stays the blackgold bee
The slow cows come
Heavy with milk
(Come, doll. *Talelo.*)
Kiss kiss one sandy sparrow
And coins tinkle on the wrist
Bells on the ankles of girls at the churns.
Talelo.

2 The Tamils are now the predominant branch of the Dravidian race of South India. Many of them also migrated to Ceylon and other countries of Southeast Asia. Their literature is the richest among those of the Dravidian languages.

You little thundercloud
With red eyes
Lotus buds
Lion cub of yasoda
The girls go
To wash in the river
But for you
They do not pencil
Their eyes.

The Lion Baby. He got rid of all the athletes.

After Honolulu.

The very loud tour got out and Honolulu was hot. The airport was at times like Whitestone, Long Island, in 1929, and at times heavenly with the scent of flowers. Hawaii could be so beautiful—the dark green mountains rising up into the clouds! And I thought: "O Wise Gauguin!" But there is no longer any place for a Gauguin!

In the airport bar I met some people heading for New York via Las Vegas—no harm to be done. Then back in my waiting room, to get on Flight 7 to Tokyo, Hong Kong and Bangkok, and there was a whole new set. They were Asians, small anonymous types of no calculable age, and the sweet little Japanese girl—or Chinese?—poor, with a lei of colored plastic. When the stewardess began the routine announcement in Chinese I thought I was hearing the language of Heaven. Seven hours to Tokyo!

Ramanuja[3] was anointing the head of his guru when the latter asserted that the eyes of the Lord were red as the ass of a mandrill. A red hot tear fell from the eyes of the disciple on the face of the master. When requested to explain his grief, Ramanuja said the eyes of the Lord were in reality as red as a delicately red lotus. The master then gathered the other disciples in secret and intimated that Ramanuja was an enemy of the true faith. They all decided to

3 Ramanuja, an eleventh-century Tamil religious leader, was instrumental in putting the Vaishnavite school of Hinduism on a solid philosophical basis as a qualified monism based on the *Upanishads* and the *Brahma Sutra;* it considers the individual soul an attribute of the supreme soul, but separate from it.

take him on pilgrimage and drown him in the river Ganges. Ramanuja took a side road and wandered off into the jungle. He met Vishnu[4] and his spouse disguised as birdcatchers. They led him to a more reliable master.

"Mr. Feresko wants to see you, Captain."

"You mean he's conscious!" (Dr. Kildare in the comic strip)

"You born today are an ambitious leader, efficient promoter and a reasoner. You are a powerful friend and with your active disposition can be an equally potent enemy." That's for today in the astrology column, syndicated in the Hong Kong *Standard*. And the ocean is empty and deep, deep, blue. A Nixon victory will be bullish for the market, they think. They think. They think. They think too that Mr. Feresko is conscious.

I am over a wing and see only a lovely distant garden of delicate Pacific clouds, like coral, like rich and delicately formed full white and pink flowers, small enough for plenty of gaps over an ocean that has to be forever sunny.

It is 8 a.m. tomorrow in Tokyo, toward which we are flying. It is 1:15 Honolulu time and we are about to have supper. In San Francisco it is nearly 5.

Hong Kong beats Singapore to retain the Ho Ho Soccer Cup.

Offerings of flowers, water and fire: they please Vishnu. A soldier heading for Vietnam studies his Bible. But in the airport he was chuckling at a joke in the *Reader's Digest*. God protect him!

On this flight—no complimentary champagne.

The utter happiness of life in a plane—quiet, time to read. But long, long. Endless noon. Tuesday afternoon turns into Wednesday afternoon, and no matter how hard we try we won't get much past 3 o'clock until after Tokyo, when we swing south, and the night will finally fall on us.

A Japanese (*nisei*) stewardess comes over and looks at this notebook and asks, "What is *that?*" I explain.

Long, long noon. Endless noon. Like Alaska in midsummer. In San Francisco it has long been dark. It is nearly 10 at night there. Here, endless sun. I have done everything. Sleep. Prayers. And I finished Hesse's *Siddhartha*.[5] Nothing changes the endless sunlight. And in this light the stewardesses come with questionnaires that we must all fill in. Why do we travel? etc.

4 Vishnu is one of the major triad (Vishnu—Shiva—Brahma) of gods in Hinduism. His devotees are Vaishnavites.

5 Siddhartha Gautama (Sanskrit) is the personal given name of the Buddha. Hermann Hesse's novel *Siddhartha*, however, relates the life of one of the Buddha's earliest disciples.

October 17, 1968. Bangkok

Last evening, the plane was late taking off and we did not leave Tokyo until after dark. I unknowingly broke the rules of the airline at Hong Kong where I walked up and down in the dark warm sea wind under the plane's huge tail, looking at the lights of Kowloon. This merited an implied reproof, a special announcement at Bangkok that passengers were under no circumstances to do this! Finally, after we passed over South Vietnam—where there were three big, silent, distant fires—we came down over the vast dim lights of Bangkok. We got out of the plane into tropical heat, a clammy night no worse than Louisville in July. Fascist faces of the passport men, a line of six officials in uniform to stamp a passport once, faces like the officers in Batista's Cuba, and the same pale uniforms. Tired, crafty, venal faces, without compassion, full, in some cases, of self-hate. Men worn out by a dirty system. A conniving one made no move to look at any bag of mine in the customs. He waved me on when I declared fifteen rolls of pan-x film—as if I were a good child. And I was grateful. Why not? He showed sense. I am only in Bangkok for two days this time.

The soldier who was reading the Bible on the plane got out here, too. The nice mother in the white suit, with whom I had a whisky in the Tokyo airport, got off with her baby at Hong Kong—a stopover before Vietnam. There was a list of dangerous places on a blackboard at Tokyo—plague at Saigon and three other Vietnamese airports.

At nearly 1 a.m., Bangkok time, after about twenty-four hours in the plane, I ride through the hot, swamp-smelling night in an "airport limousine" that is more accurately a fast and wildly rattling piece of old bus. There are three others in it: a Chinese and his wife, and a Hindu. They both go to the big fancy Siam Intercontinental. I go to the Oriental, which is thoroughly quiet. The road from the airport could be the road from any airport—from Louisville to Gethsemani in summer. The same smell of hot night and burning garbage, the same Pepsi billboards. But the shops are grated up with accordion grilles, the stucco is falling off everything, and the signs in Thai are to me unintelligible.

Bangkok.

This morning I made a partial purification of the luggage. What will I do with all those books that have to be thrown out? Leave them with Phra Khantipalo, the English *Bhikkhu* at Wat Bovoranives.[6]

6 Wat Bovoranives is one of the traditional Buddhist temples of Bangkok.

I had breakfast on the hotel terrace by the river. A hot wind. Choppy water, and great activity of boats: motorboats waiting to take tourists on a tour of the *klong*[7] markets, and rowboats as ferries to and fro across the river—one sculled by a strong woman who fought the current bravely and effectively, though I thought she and her passengers would be carried away!

Then about 10 I took a taxi to Wat Bovoranives. We drove through Chinatown with its clutter of shops and wild, dirty streets. Crowds. Motorbikes. Taxis. Buses. Trucks fixed up to look like dragons, glittering with red and chrome. Dirt. Camp. Madness. Enormous nightmare movie ads. And lovely people. Beautiful, gentle people—except those who are learning too fast from the Americans. A long ride to the *wat* but we finally get there. I pass through a gate into a quiet maze of shady lanes and alleys, large houses, canals, temples, school buildings. I ask a *bhikkhu* for directions and arrive at the domicile of Phra Khantipalo. He is extremely thin, bones sticking out in all directions. He has the look of a strict observer. But sensible. ("These people here are very tolerant and uncritical.") Khantipalo is the author of two books on Buddhism. He says he is going to a forest monastery in the northeast part of Siam in four or five days. He will have a quasi-hermit life there, with a good meditation teacher, in the jungle. We talked of *satipatthana* meditation.

In the evening I met the abbot, Venerable Chao Khun Sasana Sobhana, who was very impressive. He was tired—he had just returned from the cremation of some *bhikkhu*—but he got talking on the purpose of Theravada. He spoke of *sila*, *samadhi*, *panna (prajna)*, *mukti*, and the awareness of *mukti* (freedom), with emphasis on following one step after another, ascending by degrees. I enjoyed the conversation—there were occasional translations of difficult parts by Khantipalo—and felt it was fruitful.

The abbot told this story of Buddha and Sariputra.[8] Buddha asked Sariputra: "Do you believe in me?" Sariputra answered: "No." But Buddha commended him for this. He was the favorite disciple because he did *not* believe in Buddha, only respected him as another, but enlightened, man.

What is the "knowledge of freedom"? I asked. "When you are in Bangkok you know that you're there. Before that you only knew about Bangkok. And," he said, "one must ascend all the steps, but then when there are no

7 *Klong* means "canal." The chief market of Bangkok is an area of canals running into the Chao Phya River; the shops, which are also the owners' homes, are built on stilts to keep them above the daily tides and yearly floods.

8 Sariputra was a wandering, mendicant ascetic of the brahmanical tradition who encountered the Buddha at Rajagaha and became one of his first converts and most important disciples.

more steps one must make the leap. Knowledge of freedom is the knowledge, the experience, of this leap."

The abbot's table was piled high with presentation books for temporary *bhikkhus* who were disrobing and leaving the *wat* at the end of the rains. A boy student, on his knees, presented hot tea, but behind me. Khantipalo motioned for him to kneel where he could be seen and the tea reached.

The noise of a big motorboat on the river. I am falling asleep. I had better drop this and go to bed. (10:30)

The Thai Buddhist concept of *sila*, the "control of outgoing exuberance," is basic, somewhat like the Javanese *rasa*. There is a good pamphlet on the "Forest Wat," the idea of wisdom, beginning with *sila*. This small book, really only an extended article, "Wisdom Develops Samadhi" by the Venerable Acarya Maha Boowa Nanasampanno, a translation from the Thai published in Bangkok, is a spiritual masterpiece.[9] The author is apparently, or was, one of the masters in the Ghai forest *wats*, abbot of Wat Pa-barn-tard in the jungle of north central Thailand.

Kammatthana: "Bases of action," practical application and experiential knowledge, *dharma* teaching. This controls the "heart with outgoing exuberance." "The heart which does not have *dharma* as its guardian." Such a heart, when it finds happiness as a result of "outgoing exuberance," is a happiness which plays a part, increases the "outgoing exuberance," and makes the heart "go increasingly in the wrong direction." *Samadhi* is calm—tranquillity of heart. "Outgoing exuberance is the enemy of all beings."

Anapanasati: awareness of breathing in and out.

Khanika samadhi: momentary, changing.

Upacara samadhi: "getting close to the object."

Apana samadhi: absorption.

The method should suit one's character. After correct practice one feels "cool, bright and calm."

Inside is "the one who knows"—a function of *citta*. Preparatory incantations in kammatthana aim at uniting the one who speaks and the one who knows. Attention to breathing: in order to unite breathing and *citta:* "it becomes apparent that the most subtle breath and the heart (*citta*) have converged and become one." This leads to "finding that which is wondrous in the heart."

9 While the Venerable Nanasampanno's essay may exist as a separate pamphlet in the Thai language, it appears almost certain that the text Merton read was the English translation by Bhikkhu Pannavaddho of Wat Pa-barn-tard, which appeared in the May 1967 issue of the magazine *Visakha Puja*.

Problem of *nivritti* (vision) in *upacara samadhi.* Danger of madness.

October 18, 1968. Bangkok

Mass of St. Luke in a big church. A cathedral? Has it a bishop? It's just around the corner from the hotel. Little girls were singing in choir behind the old high altar while a priest said Mass in the center. Only a few people were present, some Americans or Europeans. A somewhat dilapidated side altar. The altar cards were old, stained with damp. The linens old, too, and the Sacred Heart statue more toneless, dowdy, dusty than many a Buddha. (Many of the Buddhas here seem too golden, too smug, too hollow.)

Yesterday afternoon I was driven out into the country to see Phra Pathom Chedi, one of the oldest and largest stupas. Rice fields. Coronet palms. Blue, shiny buffaloes. Endless lines of buses and trucks traveling like mad. A small *wat* in the fields. Many of the Buddhas were flaked with small bits of gold leaf stuck on by the faithful. At another tiny country *wat*, a side Buddha had had his face masked and buried in gold by some benefactor—as though he were being smothered by it. Behind the entrance and around the stupa was a cloister with desks, books, little *bhikkhus* studying Pali. A master was correcting a *bhikkhu* who had written something wrong on a blackboard. Khantipalo and I circumambulate the stupa with incense and flowers, he in bare feet and all bony and I sweating with my camera around my neck. The gold-roofed temples against the clouds made me think of pictures of Borobudnur.[10] There were men high up on the side of the stupa replacing old tiles and a boy up there pulling out weeds that had grown in between the tiles. Then I wandered interminably around under the trees (mostly frangipani), looking at small, good and bad Buddhas, stupas, reproductions, imitations, a run-down meditation garden confided to the Chinese. Buddhas smothered with gold, one enormous, lying down with chicken wire at his back, a protection against graffiti.

There is an Oedipus-like legend about the first builder of Phra Pathom. He killed his father without knowing it and was told to build a stupa as high as the wild pigeon flies. Phra Pathom was the retreat of King Rama VI, where he retired for the rainy seasons, trained the "Wild Tiger Volunteers," and erected a statue of his favorite dog, with an epitaph.

Phra Pathom is called the "first *chedi* [pagoda, temple]," the oldest one.

10 Borobudnur, near Jogjakarta in Java, was built about A.D. 850 under the dynasty of the Saliendra kings and is said to be the largest Buddhist temple in the world. It was partially destroyed by the Muslims but later restored by the Dutch.

The interior parts, inside the present structure, were built in the second century B.C. (about the time of Ashoka in India), and it was restored in 1853. There are old dharma wheels and "Buddha footprints," earlier than any statue and in many ways more handsome.

"The realizer does not stand outside the reality, but may be said to be at least a part of that reality. So I said that he is a self-manifestation of reality as such. This realization—that one is the self-manifestation of ultimate reality as such—is *his* realization."[11]

"The Self is not attainable by the recitation of *Veda*, nor by an effort of intellectual penetration, nor by many Vedic studies. He whom the Self chooses (selects), he can attain it. The Self makes known to him its intimacy."[12]

October 19, 1968. Calcutta

Last night I had to rush to the Bangkok airport in a taxi to catch my Lufthansa plane. Along the road were kids and kids and kids, thousands, millions of schoolchildren, mostly in neat uniforms. (Bangkok is relatively prosperous, relatively well fed, with lots of cars, trucks, jeeps, and crazy three-wheeled jeep taxis.) Finally my taxi burst out of the traffic onto a highway across the marsh near the airport. Wind. Black clouds. Distant storms. More rushing through the usual idiot process, the stamping of passports and boarding passes. When I had paid the exit tax, I was nearly down to my last baht, with only three or four left to under-over tip the porter who had done noble work getting me through—and then an announcement that the Lufthansa plane is late!

I sit in the waiting room, sweating, with all the Germans and Swedes and Indians, the Air France crews and the SAS crews, the pretty Swedish girl, the crippled German lady, the Americans, the children, and outside the glass door, jeeps, airport buses, planes, the distant black storm, lightning, porters milling around, people rushing madly to the wrong gate and returning to the benches, people wandering around with soft drinks in paper

11 Masao Abe on the concept of reality in Zen, as quoted in Aelred Graham's *Conversations: Christian and Buddhist* (New York: Harcourt, Brace, 1968), 129. Masao Abe specializes in Buddhist philosophy and comparative religion and has several times been visiting lecturer at Columbia University.

12 Taken from Ramanuja's commentary on the *Brahma Sutra*, this is Merton's translation of Olivier Lacombe's French translation of that work.

cups—and I with a paper envelope of Buddhist novitiate instructions and incense presented by the abbot of Wat Bovoranives.

There is TV in the Bangkok airport. The announcements are made by a conventionally pretty Thai girl who makes all languages sound alike—incomprehensible. Her English might be her German, if any, and all of it might be Malayan. Then in between there is a movie, or rather a series of stills, extolling Thai boxing. *FISTS*. "M.S. flight for Kuala Lumpur delayed one hour." *KNEES*. "Passengers on Air France Flight 205 please report for passport check." *FEET*. Still picture of a Thai boxer getting his head kicked off. Picture of American woman tourist screaming as boxer's head is kicked. *EVERY PART OF THE BODY IS USED*. Same American woman tourist seen from a different angle but in the same scream. *EVERY PART OF THE BODY*—Picture of a mix-up, maybe someone is getting a knee in the belly. *FISTS*. American lady tourist screams. Pnom-Penh with tourists for Angkor. *FISTS*. Flight now very late. *KNEES*. Air Vietnam lands late and will take off soon. Air Vietnam from Saigon just as if there were no war in the world. *EVERY PART OF THE BODY IS USED*. American tourist lady grabs husband's arm with both hands and screams.

When we landed in Calcutta the customs gave two utterly lovely—and haughty—Indian girls in saris a rough time. I got through quite fast though with no rupees yet, and Susan Hyde, a secretary of Peter Dunne,[13] was there to meet me with a garland of flowers: "Welcome to India." V.I.P. treatment. I felt confused, trying to talk sense to Susan about religious affairs. The Indian darkness was full of people and cows. Rough roads on which cars sped toward each other head-on. It takes some time here to discover which side anyone is driving on—he may take either side, right or left. Then into the big, beat-up, hot, teeming, incredible city. People! People! People! campfires in the streets and squares. Movie posters—those Asian movie posters with the strange, enormous faces of violent or demented Western gods, the enormous gunners, surrounded by impossible writings. They are a crass, camp deification of the more obvious emotions: love, hate, desire, greed, revenge. Why not John Wayne with eight arms? Well, he has enough guns already. Or the Dance of Shiva[14]—with Sinatra?

13 Finley Peter Dunne, Jr., was executive director of the Temple of Understanding in Washington, which sponsored the Spiritual Summit Conference in Calcutta in October 1968, at which Merton spoke on "Monastic Experience and East-West Dialogue."

14 The "Dance of Shiva" is perhaps the best-known iconographic figure in Hindu religious art. Showing the four-armed god dancing in a circle or arch of flames, it symbolizes the perpetual dualistic creation-destruction rhythm of the universe.

The situation of the tourist becomes ludicrous and impossible in a place like Calcutta. How does one take pictures of these streets with the faces, the eyes, of such people, and the cows roaming among them on the sidewalks and buzzards by the score circling over the main streets in the "best" section? Yet the people are beautiful. But the routine of the beggars is heartrending. The little girl who suddenly appeared at the window of my taxi, the utterly lovely smile with which she stretched out her hand, and then the extinguishing of the light when she drew it back empty. I had no Indian money yet. She fell away from the taxi as if she were sinking in water and drowning, and I wanted to die. I couldn't get her out of my mind. Yet when you give money to one, a dozen half kill themselves running after your cab. This morning one little kid hung on to the door and ran whining beside the cab in the traffic while the driver turned around and made gestures as if to beat him away. Sure, there is a well-practiced routine, an art, a theatre, but a starkly necessary art of dramatizing one's despair and awful emptiness. Then there was the woman who followed me three blocks sweetly murmuring something like "Daddy, Daddy, I am very poor" until I finally gave her a rupee. OK, a contest, too. But she *is* very poor. And I have come from the West, a Rich Daddy.

Meditation on the body (*satipatthana*): "investigating the parts of the body with wisdom." This must be seen and experienced in terms of *anicca, dukkha, anatta.*

Vipassana: the insight arising out of *samadhi.*

"The negation of desires of all beings . . . is the nature of this body," says my *bhikkhu*, Acarya Maha Boowa Nanasampanno, in a cryptic, condensed explanation of *anatta*. And so: purification; defilements cannot arise when this "wise investigation" is done. "Wisdom is proclaiming the truth and making the heart listen, and when it is doing this all the time where can the heart go to oppose the truth that comes from wisdom?"

Clearly seeing the "Body City" makes one a *lokavidu:* "one who knows the worlds." One who has investigated all the realms of existence. So, too, the antitourism of the external city—the true city, the city out of control, whether it be Los Angeles or Calcutta. Whether it be the trace of new cars on superhighways or of old cars on bad highways, or of blood, mucus, fecal matter in the passages of the body. Calcutta, smiling, fecal, detached, tired, inexhaustible, young-old, full of young people who seem old, is the *unmasked* city. It is the subculture of poverty and overpopulation.

Calcutta is shocking because it is all of a sudden a totally different kind of madness, the reverse of that other madness, the mad rationality of affluence and overpopulation. America seems to make sense, and is hung up in its madness, now really exploding. Calcutta has the lucidity of despair, of absolute confusion, of vitality helpless to cope with itself. Yet undefeatable, expanding without and beyond reason but with nowhere to go. An infinite crowd of men and women camping everywhere as if waiting for someone to lead them in an ultimate exodus into reasonableness, into a world that works, yet knowing already beyond contradiction that in the end *nothing* really works, and that life is all *anicca, dukkha, anatta,* that each self is the denial of the desires of all the others—and yet somehow a sign to others of some inscrutable hope. And the thing that haunts me: Gandhiji led all these people, exemplified the sense they might make out of their life, for a moment, and then, with him, that sense was extinguished again.

A sign in Calcutta: "Are you worried? Refresh yourself with cigars."

"Masters of the 7th arm, unless you destroy Mandrake at once, you will be destroyed."

(Mandrake the Magician)

Literature on Theravada available from the Buddhist Publication Society, Box 61, Kandy, Ceylon.

October 20, 1968

I have been reading the poetry of Milarepa, the great Tibetan yogi, who was born in 1052. "*Repa*"—"clad in one piece of cotton." (Because of his heat meditations?) He stands at the head of the Kagyudpa tradition. The "whispered transmission,"[15] i.e., esoteric. But he was not a *bhikkhu,* and his master, Marpa, was a layman.

"In order to perfect any practice, seemingly useless experience must be undergone. Any disciple who has entered any kind of practice must begin with seemingly unnecessary, futile things. But of course these things are a

15 The term "whispered transmission" refers to the most vital aspect of oral tradition, the handing down of certain elements of doctrine from master to pupil. Every school of Tibetan Buddhism inherited it in varying degrees.

part of the discipline. Without such seemingly trifling things there can be no perfecting of the practice."[16]

"Apart from the daily experience, there is no religious life, so satori is an occurrence of daily life with its joys and sorrows. . . . The reason why the lowest can be at once the highest is difficult to say, but it is the ultimate reality of religious experience. And only from that awareness can the religious sense of blessedness—*arigatai* in Japanese—be explained."

Yesterday I visited the Indian Museum, a bewildering big building, now yellow and shabby, with the universal dilapidation of all Calcutta. It has nice things in it if you can find them. And a lot of dull stuff, too. You look for Gupta[17] statues and end in geology or bows and arrows. I found a lot of it tedious, but there were a few sudden joys: Buddha footprints with lovely symbols lightly engraved in them; a room full of musical instruments, string and percussion, of marvelous sophisticated shapes; some Burmese pots, excellent even though 19th century.

This morning, Sunday, I went to the Jesuit Sacred Heart Church to say the Mass of the XXth Sunday after Pentecost. A bewildered sacristan set me up on a dowdy side altar—no problem!—with a very ancient missal. He filled the water cruet from an old tap at the washbasin, and sure enough I got diarrhea from the bad water. (Later, I took an Entero-Vioform pill and stopped it.) A brisk young German Jesuit shook hands with me in the sacristy.

Last night I was invited to dinner at Lois Flanagan's, a pleasant house on Ballygunge Circular Road. Among the guests were P. Lal and his wife.[18] Lal, who is charming and articulate, is working on an English translation of the *Mahabharata*.[19]

16 This quotation and the next are from Reverend Kaneko, as quoted in Aelred Graham's *Conversations*. Reverend Kaneko is a priest and scholar associated with the Higashi Hongan-ji temple in Kyoto, Japan, headquarters of the Jodo-Shin-Shu, or (True) Pure Land school of Buddhism, an offshoot of Mahayana Buddhism.

17 Gupta was a powerful dynasty, the dominant force in North India from about A.D. 320 to 480, when the Guptas were defeated by the invading White Huns, though there were Gupta kings ruling in eastern India until the early eighth century.

18 Mrs. Lois Flanagan was Information Center Director of the U.S. Consulate in Calcutta in 1968. Poet, translator, and teacher, P. Lal was professor of English at St. Xavier's College in Calcutta in 1968. He was also Special Professor of Indian Literature, History and Religion at Hofstra University in 1962 and in 1970.

19 The *Mahabharata* is one of the two great Sanskrit epics of India (the other being the *Ramayana*), which dates probably from the centuries just preceding the Christian era. Although there is a fictitious attribution to Vyasa as the author, the poem is surely anonymous or, rather, the cumulative accretion of the work of many bards in the oral tradition over a considerable period of time.

I am tired of late hours, like 11:30. Tonight I want to get to bed at 8 or 8:30, hoping I can get away with it and not be hauled out for something. But things seem quiet.

Yesterday, quite by chance, I met Chogyam Trungpa Rinpoche and his secretary, a nice young Englishman whose Tibetan name is Kunga. Today I had lunch with them and talked about going to Bhutan. But the important thing is that we are people who have been waiting to meet for a long time. Chogyam Trungpa is a completely marvelous person. Young, natural, without front or artifice, deep, awake, wise. I am sure we will be seeing a lot more of each other, whether around northern India and Sikkim or in Scotland, where I am now determined to go to see his Tibetan monastery if I can. He is a promising poet. His stuff in Tibetan is probably excellent; in English it is a little flat, but full of substance. He is also a genuine spiritual master. His place in Scotland seems to have become an instant success and I think he has something very good under way. I am certainly interested in it. The newsletter he puts out is good. His own meditations and talks, from what I have seen, are extraordinary. He has the same problems we have with "progressive" monks whose idea of modernization is to go noncontemplative, to be "productive" and academic. These are the types I will evidently find around the Dalai Lama. They showed me a small photo of a lovely shrine on a cliff in Bhutan (Tagtsang) and recommended it as a place for retreat.

Later in the afternoon I piled into a jeep with Trungpa and his secretary, Kunga, and two Australian girls and a driver. The jeep belongs to the Bhutan government. We went roaring off to a market full of things for Divali, the feast of lights, which is tomorrow. Millions of little shapeless statues of Kali, Lakshmi, Parvati, and other beings—soldiers, God knows what, sahibs, foods, sugars, paper garlands, lights, light-holders, incense. Trungpa bought a firecracker from a small, very black, bright-eyed crouching little boy.

I wrote to Dom Flavian, Dom James, Lawrence Ferlinghetti, and the Queen of Bhutan.

Octavio Paz has resigned as Mexican Ambassador to India over the treatment of Mexican students by the police. Jackie Kennedy remarried today on a Greek island.

October 22, 1968

I've had the idea of editing a collection of pieces by various Buddhists on meditation, etc., with an introduction of my own. Perhaps two collections, one entirely by Tibetans (I must talk to Chogyam Trungpa about this today) or with representatives from Tibetan Buddhism—from Theravada in Ceylon, Burma, Thailand (Khantipalo). And one from Mahayana in China and Japan. Two very interesting possibilities.

Yesterday, I drove with Amiya Chakravarty and his friend, Naresh Guha, to the home of the painter Jamini Roy.[20] Walking barefoot on the cool tiles, through low quiet rooms filled with canvasses of unutterable beauty: simple, formalized little icons with a marvelous sort of folk and Coptic quality, absolutely alive and full of charm, many Christian themes, the most lovely modern treatment of Christian subjects I have ever seen—and also of course Hindu subjects from the *Ramayana*[21] and the *Mahabharata*. Amiya bought a Christ which he will take to the nuns at Redwoods. I wish I could afford to buy a dozen canvasses; they are very cheap, $35 or $40. But money gets away from me like water on all sides and I have to watch it. Some things in the hotel are extremely expensive, others not.

Jamini Roy himself, a warm, saintly old man, saying: "Everyone who comes to my house brings God into it." The warmth and reality of his hand as you shake it or hold it. The luminous handsomeness of his bearded son, who is, I suppose, about my age. Marvelous features. All the faces glowing with humanity and peace. Great religious artists. It was a great experience.

October 24, 1968

A visit to the Narendrapur-Ramakrishna Mission Ashram. College, agricultural school, poultry farm, school for the blind, and orphanage. Ponds, palms, a water tower in a curious style, a monastic building, and guesthouse. Small tomato and cucumber sandwiches, flowers, tea. We drove around in a dark green Scout. Villages. Three big, blue buffaloes lying in a patch of purple, eating the flowers. Communists arguing under a shelter. Bengali inscriptions on every wall; they have an extraordinary visual quality. Large and small cows. Goats, calves, millions of children.

The Temple of Understanding Conference has been well organized con-

20 Jamini Roy (1887–1972) was introduced to Thomas Merton by Amiya Chakravarty. One of Roy's paintings of the crucifixion was purchased and delivered to Our Lady of the Redwoods Abbey in northern California by Chakravarty following Merton's death.

21 The *Ramayana* is an ancient Sanskrit epic consisting of twenty-four thousand couplets that recounts the adventures of Rama, a human incarnation of the god Vishnu; his winning of Sita, paragon of womanly virtue, as his wife; her abduction by the demon king of Ceylon, Ravana; her rescue by Rama, aided by the monkey hordes of the god Hanuman; and the final arrival of Rama and Sita in heaven.

sidering the problems which developed. It could not be held in Darjeeling, as planned, because of the floods. Instead it has been put on at the Birla Academy in South Calcutta. It is more than half finished now. I spoke yesterday morning, but did not actually follow my prepared text. There were good papers by two rabbis, one from New York and one from Jerusalem, and by Dr. Wei Tat,[22] a Chinese scholar from Taiwan, on the *I Ching*. Also by Sufis, Jains, and others.

The warmth of the Ramakrishna monks, alert and quiet. Especially Swami Lokesvarananda whom I like very much. They invited me back. And I was invited to Israel by Dr. Ezra Spicehandler.[23] And invited tonight to supper at the house of the Birlas, supporters of the Temple of Understanding. In the jeep I had a fine conversation with Judith Hollister,[24] warm, lovely, simple, sincere.

I did not go to a committee meeting today; went back to Narendrapur instead. Much talking yesterday. Tomorrow *Life* magazine is to take our pictures "worshipping" under the banyan tree in the botanical gardens.

Vatsala Amin, the young Jain laywoman from Bombay who presented the Jain message at the Temple of Understanding Conference, is an extremely beautiful and spiritual person. I was very impressed by her talk, and this evening had a long and good conversation with her at the Birla party. We talked about meditation, and her master, Munishri Chitrabhanu,[25] whom I would like to see if I can get to Bombay. And about her desire to live in solitude in the Himalayas, and her project of doing so. Sitting on the floor listening to sitar music was a lovely experience.

Vatsala Amin: great, soft, intelligent, dark eyes. A white sari. Vivacity and seriousness, warmth, spiritual fervor. She meditates on a picture of her

22 Dr. Wei Tat is a member of the Yuen Yuen Institute and vice president both of the Tao Teh Benevolent Association and the Dharmalaksana Buddhist Institute in Hong Kong. He is an academician of the China Academy in Taiwan.

23 Dr. Ezra Spicehandler was professor of Hebrew literature at the Cincinnati School of the Hebrew Union College–Jewish Institute of Religion and director of Jewish studies at the Hebrew Union College Biblical and Archaeological School in Jerusalem.

24 Mrs. Dickerman Hollister of Greenwich, Connecticut, founded in 1960 the Temple of Understanding, Inc., in Washington, an international organization devoted to better understanding and cooperation among the religions and religious people of the world. She was president of the organization at the time of the 1968 First Spiritual Summit Conference in Calcutta.

25 Munishri Chitrabhanu is one of the great contemporary leaders of Jainism, the heterodox Hindu religion founded by Mahavira Jnatiputra in about the sixth century B.C. Respect for the life of every living thing, even insects, is one of the central tenets of the Jain faith.

guru, preferring the one in which his skull and chin are shaved. Jain gurus shave once a year. "If he can be so perfect, so can I," she reflects. Today she left for Bombay. I on my part am impressed by her purity and perfection. She gave me a garland, like a lei, made of sandalwood, because I was her special friend. She gave another to Sister Barbara Mitchell from Manhattanville.

A telegram from Tenzin Geshe, the Dalai Lama's secretary. My interview is tentatively arranged for 10 a.m. on November 4th. I am supposed to fly to Delhi at 6 a.m., Monday, October 28th. Probably the best thing would be to go to Dharamsala November 1st or 2nd, by night train and then bus.

October 26, 1968

Rain. A cyclone is moving up from South India, threatening once again all the places in North Bengal that were ruined by floods two weeks ago. Tall coconut palms against the stormy sky. Men and women on the balconies of the apartment houses in the cool wind. Cows wandering amid the traffic. We drive with the Birlas to see the schools, the hospital, the very elegant theater they have built. And the Birla Planetarium. They were friends and patrons of Gandhiji.

In the museum at the Birla Academy there are fine Indian and Mogul paintings, folk art of the Calcutta Kalighat school and Nepalese and Tibetan *tankas*. In Huston Smith's[26] Tibetan movie the slow dance of a monk in a devil-like mask of fearsome divinity with great red sleeves. The booming, solemn, voice-splitting chant of the monks, each singing a chord by himself.

Mass today at Loreto House. I gave a short homily[27] to the Irish nuns in a big, cool academy, quiet, clean, tranquil. After Mass I am surrounded on all sides, praised, questioned, admired, revered—so much so that I can hardly eat breakfast.

At the Temple of Understanding Conference, which ended today, there were two little girls in miniskirts, Schotzy and Pattie, very sweet and naked, touchingly convinced of their own particularity, calling everything so beautiful—except when it was obviously too square—but all Calcutta beautiful,

26 Huston Smith is a former professor at Massachusetts Institute of Technology and the University of California at Berkeley. He is the author of *The World's Religions*, originally published as *The Religions of Man* (New York: Harper & Row, 1965). His documentary film on Tibetan Buddhism, *Requiem for a Faith*, may be rented from Hartley Productions, Cat Rock Road, Cos Cob, CT 06807.

27 This homily was published in the April 1970 issue of the magazine *Sisters Today* (Collegeville, MN), vol. 41, no. 8.

beautiful and the people beautiful. Last night they wandered off with some hippies into a village and smoked pot somewhere and almost got themselves killed and came back laughing about how it was all so beautiful, beautiful.

I had dinner at a Chinese restaurant in Park Street with Wei Tat, who returns to Hong Kong tomorrow.

I miss my dear Miss Vatsala Amin and her dark eyes and white sari and wonder what to do with that sandalwood garland. And for God's sake I hope I can get to the Himalayas and into a quiet cabin somewhere and get back to normal!

Sankaracharya[28] on the mind and the atman (from *The Crest-Jewel of Discrimination*):

"The Atman dwells within, free from attachment and beyond all action. A man must separate this Atman from every object of experience, as a stalk of grass is separated from its enveloping sheath. Then he must dissolve into the Atman all those appearances which make up the world of name and form. He is indeed a free soul who can remain thus absorbed in the Atman alone. . . .

"The wind collects the clouds, and the wind drives them away again. Mind creates bondage, and mind also removes bondage.

"The mind creates attachment to the body and the things of this world. Thus it binds a man, as a beast is tied by a rope. But it is also the mind which creates in a man an utter distaste for sense-objects, as if for poison. Thus it frees him from his bondage.

"The mind, therefore, is the cause of man's bondage and also of his liberation. It causes bondage when it is darkened by *rajas*. It causes liberation when it is freed from *rajas* and *tamas*, and made pure. . . .

"Therefore, the seeker after liberation must work carefully to purify the mind. When the mind has been made pure, liberation is as easy to grasp as the fruit which lies in the palm of your hand."

October 27, 1968. Feast of Christ the King. Calcutta

In ipso omnia constant . . . All is in Him, from Him, for Him (for the Father through Him).

28 Sankaracharya, one of the most important Hindu theologians, lived in India in the eighth century A.D. He wrote commentaries on the *Upanishads* and the *Bhagavad Gita* and was the founder of the Advaita Vedanta doctrine of nondualism. His best-known work is *The Crest-Jewel of Discrimination*, available in several translations, including the version translated by Swami Prabhavananda and Christopher Isherwood (Hollywood, CA: Vedanta Press, 1947), from which the following quotes are taken.

This morning Sister Barbara Mitchell and I went to say Mass in the home of Lois Flanagan. It was quiet and simple. The three little Chinese girls Lois has adopted were there, and Bob Boylan,[29] and a priest from St. Lawrence High School who had brought all the necessary things. The cyclone has not hit here yet. Everyone is now being overwarned. As we drove back to the hotel the air-raid sirens were being tested —for the imaginary war with Pakistan. There is firing at Suez and Tito says there will be a Third World War if the Russians try to take over Yugoslavia, etc., etc. Everyone has long ceased to listen to any of it.

SCIENTIFIC LIFE DIVINE MISSION,[30] A Purely Scientific Nonsectarian All Faiths Fellowship International Movement for the Perfect Development of Body, Mind and Soul . . .

Eminent Supporters of the Views . . ."

Eminent Wellwishers . . .

"Creation is the Kingdom of God composed of matters and spirits for a set scientific course to go particular functions to do and gone to reach according to His wishes manifested in the properties of ingredients . . .

"Follow the God-prescribed scientific life . . ."

Ingredients of eminent wellwishers . . . changing assemblies . . . with choral voice . . . agreeing . . . wishing well according to ingredients . . . coalitions perfect in all respects. . . . With one accord we declare, "Man is a pure scientific being . . ." Carrying on with nebulas, wind, heat, light, and sound. "All are carrying on accordingly! Scientific way of handling the situation is the best." Ashram. "Please communicate only with the headquarters."

HOW TO MAKE LIFE BLISSFUL AND WORTH DIAMONDS

"To a large majority of people the present state of affairs causes disappointment."

AUSPICIOUS ANNOUNCEMENT

"The Almighty Father has been at work now for some time and in the near future man's desire for peace and prosperity is going to be fulfilled. You may be surprised to have this news . . .

29 Robert J. Boylan was at this time Cultural Affairs Officer with the U.S. Information Service in Calcutta.

30 This and the following paragraphs appear to be drawn from either billboards or religious cult pamphlets that Merton saw in Calcutta.

"*God has declared state of emergency. BE HOLY NOW!*

"All India has become a whorehouse! Do you not love me enough to abandon this dirty habit?"

AN EYE OPENER FOR BLIND FOLLOWERS, DEVOTEES AND WORSHIPPERS

"Religio-political World History Geography and Philosophy being taught by Most Beloved World God Father Shiva like Kalpa (5000 years) ago.

"Look! The science proud European Yadavas will destroy one another in this international atomic war (Mahabharata) like 5000 years ago.

"GREAT BLUNDERS

"By preaching that a human soul in Shiva or that God is omnipresent the preachers have led mankind astray from Me. I get the golden-aged Jiwan Mukt Deity Sovereignty reestablished through Human Brahma by impartation of Godly Knowledge and Yoga to the Iron-Aged People. For further explanation contact Brahma Kumari.

"GOD'S ACTS

"At the confluence of the Iron Age and Golden Age when complete irreligiousness and unrighteousness prevails, I Knowledgeful Shiva, the God-Sermonizer of Gita descend from My Param Dham (Brahmlok) in an old man who comes to be known as Brahma or Adam."

In 1863 Baha'u'llah[31] announced to the few remaining followers of Bab that He was the chosen Manifestation of God for this age—but he was not greeted with enthusiasm by the religious leaders of Islam.

One of the swamis has flashing eyes, a black beard, rapid speech and sweeping gestures. At times he gives an irresistible impression of Groucho Marx. He has great white teeth and contempt for all competitors. Even his Kleenex is saffron!

---

31 Mirza Husayn Ali Nuri, known as Baha'u'llah ("the Spendor of God"), was the founder of the Baha'i religion. He became leader of the sect in 1863 by absorbing what remained of the Babist movement (a religious sect founded in Persia in 1844 by Mirza Ali Mohammed ibn-Radhik, who took the name Bab-ud-Din, or "Gate of Faith"). The Baha'i faith teaches the spiritual unity of all persons, is dedicated to universal peace, and contains certain elements of Oriental mysticism.

COMPLAIN NOT, BUT CREATE

"Shake off your sloth my sluggard and tunnel your way to truth, make a footpath to fortune, build bridges to business and new highroads to heaven."

[The Minister of the Silent Spirit (d. 1925)]

And amid all this, a pure gem: the little book on King Rama IV Mongkut, Bhikkhu, Abbot of Wat Bovoranives, then King of Thailand (d. 1868).[32] A really beautiful account of a holy life, simple and clear with some Franciscan signs and miracles.

"There is nothing in this world which may be clung to blamelessly, or which a man clinging thereto could be without blame."

[H. M. King Maha Mongkut (Rama IV)]

October 28, 1968. New Delhi

The flight this morning from Calcutta to New Delhi turned out beautiful. At first it was very stormy and cloudy. Then all of a sudden I looked out and there were the Himalayas—several hundred miles away, but an awesome, great white wall of the highest mountains I have ever seen. I recognized the ones like Annapurna that are behind Pokhara, and could pick out the highest ones in the group, though not individually. Everest and Kanchenjunga were in the distance. Later a big, massive one stood out but I did not know what it was. And the river Ganges. And below, the enormous plain cut up with tiny patches of farms and villages, roads and canals. A lovely pattern. Then the dry plain around Delhi. Rock outcrops. Burnt villages. As soon as I got out of the plane I decided that the air of Delhi was much better than that of Calcutta and that I was happy to be here. Harold Talbott was at the airport and a Birla man also to meet Huston Smith who hopes to show his movie of Tibetan monks to the Dalai Lama. We are to go up by train to Dharamsala next Thursday.

Real India. I haven't seen much of New Delhi yet, except a long avenue leading to a squat, huge, red dome. And the hotel, which is cleaner, newer, less crumbling than the Oberoi in Calcutta.

Soon I will discover what I am going to remember about the hotel in Calcutta. The Grand Hotel Oberoi Karma, with cows on the front doorstep, and turbaned Janissaries, and girl students in saris raising money for food

32 The book Merton was reading about him is *His Majesty King Rama the Fourth Mongkut*, edited by Phra Sasanasobhon, published in Bangkok in 1968 in commemoration of the hundredth anniversary of the holy monarch's death.

relief. The endless corridors. The endless salaams. The garden cafe where they overcharge you in the dark and give you back unrecognizable bills. The beggar with the armstump. The beggar with the humpback. The beggar woman with the baby who ran after me saying "Daddy, Daddy." And men sleeping on the steps of shops. The tall palms, the ugly white courtyard, the kites circling over the tables. Memories of the Raj.[33] Old bathtubs. Old johns of the Raj. The long mirror in which the colonel ruefully sees himself naked, too fat. The red chairs. The incense from Bangkok in the ashtray. The salaams of the elevator men. Long life to the old johns of the Raj!

And the taxis of Calcutta lowing mournfully in the wild streets like walruses or sea cows. And now in New Delhi—more bicycles, motorcycles, trees. A Moslem leaning in the dust toward a tree. The great death house of Humayun.[34] Smoke in the evening. The moon rising in the first quarter over gray domes. There are more guns in the movie posters here. More military bases. More soldiers.

"Therefore have no fears, have no terror of that deep blue light of dazzling, terrible and awful splendour, since it is the light of the Supreme Way."
[Tibetan Book of the Dead]

October 29, 1968

Early morning in New Delhi. A soft rose light, vast gentleness of sky. Many birds. Kites hopping around on the fly roofs of very modern houses. The domes in the smoky distance. The distant throbbing of a drum. I have much to read: [Giuseppe] Tucci's *The Theory and Practice of the Mandala* [London, 1969], [Armand] Desjardins' *Message des Tibetains* [*Message of the Tibetans*, London, 1969], the Dalai Lama's pamphlet on Buddhism, essays by Marco Pallis, Trungpa, and things I picked up yesterday from Dr. Lokesh Chandra of the Academy of Indian Culture.

"Man seeks to reconstruct that unity which the predominance of one or other of the features of his character has broken or threatens to demolish.

". . . to help the primeval consciousness, which is fundamentally one, to recover its integrity.

33 *Raj*, in Hindi, means "reign," "rule," or "kingdom." It is used here to refer to the "British Raj," the period of British imperial rule in India.

34 Humayun (1508–56) was one of the great Mogul emperors of India. He reigned from 1530 and made his capital at Delhi.

"... the same desire of achieving liberation of catching that instant, which once lived, redeems the Truth with us."

[Tucci, pp. vii–viii]

"*Maya—avidya*—duality develops *within* cosmic consciousness." "A magic liberty" (good!) which causes samsara. The centrifugal force by which original consciousness flies from itself, negates itself by unconsciousness and arbitrary position of images. *Shakti*: the power creating phantasms. *Shakti* is *feminine*.

Knowledge to which action (and experience) do not conform is not *indifferent*. It is an evil, a disruptive force: because it does not transform. It corrupts. The idea of initiatory knowledge is to unite knowledge, practice, and experience of revulsion and reintegration.

"Over 100 Kuki and Mizo hostiles with arms and ammunition have surrendered to the Manipur police. . . ."

(Times of India)

The mandala concept accepts the fact that cosmic processes (*maya*) express themselves in symbols of masculine and feminine deities, beatific and terrifying. It organizes them in certain schemas, representing the drama of disintegration and reintegration. Correctly read by the initiate, they "will induce the liberating psychological experience."

"First and foremost, a mandala delineates a consecrated superficies and protects it from invasion by disintegrating forces symbolized in demoniacal cycles. . . . It is a map of the cosmos" which rotates round "a central axis, Mount Sumeru," the *axis mundi* [axis of the world] uniting the inferior, underground world, the atmospheric and the celestial. Here is the "palace of the *cakravartin*, the 'Universal Monarch' of Indian tradition." The initiate identifies himself with this center—his own center is the *axis mundi*—and is transformed by it.

[Tucci, pp. 23–25]

"So the mandala is no longer a cosmogram but a psychocosmogram, the scheme of disintegration of the One to the many and the reintegration from the many to the One, to that Absolute Consciousness, entire and luminous, which Yoga causes to shine once more in the depths of our being."

[Tucci, pp. 21–25]

And yet I have a sense that all this mandala business is, for me, at least, useless. It has considerable interest, but there is no point in my seeking anything there for my own enlightenment. Why complicate what is simple? I am reading on the balcony outside my room. Five green parrots, then eight more fly shrieking over my head.

Desjardins on the choice of a guru:

"For the 'seeker after Truth' only meetings with very great masters and very great sages can be really interesting. It is better to seek, seek, and seek again a real sage, a truly liberated sage, and spend perhaps no more than a single day with him, than to dissipate one's efforts in encounters and conversations with less representative persons, or persons who are in any case further from true Realisation. It is no longer a matter of talking to Tibetans who have the title lama; it is a matter of meeting masters."

"The master's consciousness is enhanced to the point at which it contains the disciple within himself, and is one with the source of the disciple's vital energy. For the master nothing remains to be achieved in any sphere; there is nothing above or beyond what he is. Evolution has reached its end for him. He wants nothing. He rejects nothing."

[Desjardins, pp. 29–31]

Bodhicitta: the seed-thought of illumination.

(See Tucci, p. 15)

"He has pity on those who delight in serenity, how much more than upon other people who delight in existence."

[Tucci, p. 17]

"When knowledge perceives no object, it remains as pure knowledge since, as there is no one perceivable, it perceives nothing."

[Tucci, p. 17]

Harold Talbott gave me an extraordinarily interesting account of his September audience with the Dalai Lama. He is in a way under close personal care of the Dalai Lama, who is interested in him and in his studies, and has been very kind to him. Harold is impatient for initiation. The Dalai Lama seems to be very wise in his handling of the situation.

I saw some very clean and handsome *tankas* in Tibet House. There were three rooms full of them. Impressive design, and perfect colors: blue and green from minerals in Lhasa[35]; yellow from minerals of Kham or from Utpal lotus found near Lhasa; red from oxide of mercury; gold from Nepal; blue from lapis lazuli; indigo from the Indian plant nili; black from the soot of pine wood. The brushes are made of pine twigs with goat or rabbit hair inserted. Circles are described with a compass made of split bamboo. Could there be a technical connection between the painters of Russian icons and the *tanka* painters of Tibet?

The axial, vertical Brahma line of the *tanka*. The axis of life—Mt. Sumeru—the human backbone. At the summit of the head above the backbone is the hole of Brahma through which one escapes to *nirvana*. The face of Buddha in *tankas* is drawn on a full-moon day, colored on a new-moon day.

The need to combine mantra and *mudra*.

"The artist is a *sadhaka*. He must ascend, on to the spiritual plane which he intends to paint. He must transform himself into the illustrious beings whom he must adore. 'He who is not God may not adore God.'"

[Dr. Raghu Vira]

"*Shoe-lifter Arrested*. New Delhi, October 29—The police today claimed to have arrested a notorious shoe-lifter from Jama Masjid.[36] The alleged accused, Nazir, operated throughout the city, lifting shoes from shrines while devotees were at prayers. Nazir was arrested while striking a deal of stolen fancy shoes and a cycle in the Jama Masjid junk market."

(Hindustan Times Correspondent)

October 30, 1968. New Delhi

It would be interesting to see what lamas might think of the visions of the Heavenly City and Temple in Ezekiel and the Apocalypse.

Early this morning in the hotel a man next door was coughing and vomiting violently. Next he was doing his *puja*, chanting loudly in Hindi with an occasional cough. It got louder and louder. Maybe a Sikh.

There is nothing of a mandala about the Red Fort, the only sight I have sightseen in Delhi so far. It has a splendid high red wall toward the city and

35 Lhasa is the chief city of Tibet and a sacred Buddhist site because the Potala palace, located there, was the residence of the Dalai Lamas. It is near the Tsangpo (Brahmaputra) River at an altitude of 11,800 feet.

36 Jama (sometimes Jami) Masjid, begun in 1644 and completed in 1658, is one of the most important Mogul mosques of Delhi. Built of red sandstone and white marble, it is architecturally notable for its two tall minarets.

a lower wall with many pleasances toward the meadow where the river Jumna once flowed (now it is further away). There is an interesting high tunnel full of shops and raucous music as one enters. Then the gardens, the porches, the place where there were pools, the place of dancing, the little pearl mosque, most lovely. I obeyed the sign and took no pictures. Refused the importunities of a guide. There were soldiers on motorcycles and an ugly barracks with arched porches, built by the British.

I had a late lunch with Anthony Quainton and his wife from the American Embassy.[37] They are surprisingly young. I learned nothing special about Bhutan. He gave me advice about seeing an Indian official. The meals are too heavy. I wanted to sleep. But it was already past three and time had come to go to tea with Dr. Syed Vahiduddin, one of the speakers at the Temple of Understanding Conference in Calcutta. He is a Moslem and head of the Department of Philosophy at the University of Delhi. A long expensive taxi ride to the other side of Old Delhi, past Raj Ghat, the Gandhi memorial, and some difficulty finding his house at Cavalry Line on the university campus. We had a good conversation. He started by talking of the technical problems of Sufism and Hinduism in his courses at the university. Then we discussed the Temple of Understanding Conference. He told me some good Sufi stories, one about a Sufi at a reception where a courtesan had hastily been concealed behind a curtain so as not to give scandal when he arrives. She finally gets tired, comes out and recites a pretty verse to the effect, "I am what I appear to be. I hope you are the same." There was a picture of Rudolf Otto on the table. Vahiduddin had studied at Marburg. He lamented the absence of genuine Sufi masters, though there are some, hidden. And the great number of fakes who are very much in the public eye. He praised a classic Sufi who said that, "To say I am God is not pride, it is perfect modesty." Vahiduddin also said that a religion that ignores or evades the fact of death cannot make sense. (This I myself said in my talk at the Temple of Understanding Conference.)

After my visit Vahiduddin walked out with me to get a taxi. Three men, one with an instrument, another with a bag of cobras, passed us with shrill music and an offer to make the snakes dance for us right there in the dust. No thank you!

37 Anthony Quainton, at the time of Merton's visit, was a specialist in the affairs of the kingdom of Bhutan, which is bounded by Sikkim, Tibet, Assam, and East Pakistan (now Bangladesh), at the American Consulate in Calcutta.

After sunset we came to the Ladakh Buddhi Vihara. The taxi drove into the midst of a group of Tibetans playing soccer. It is a school-monastery-residence for Tibetan refugees, with a nice shiny new temple and Buddhas somewhat more convincing than the usual. Nothing is more jejune than a Buddha whose smile is stupid rather than nirvanic.

Tibetans wandered about in the dusk, some looking exactly like Eskimos. Some of the men wore high boots. One carried a rosary. One was wandering about with a big transistor giving out Tibetan music from a local station. One woman was carrying a white baby with blue eyes and red hair.

Lobsang Phuntsok Lhalungpa, a Tibetan layman, runs a radio station which broadcasts a Tibetan program in Delhi, where Harold Talbott is taking Tibetan lessons. He came to the Ladakh Vihara with his wife Deki. We went up to one of the cells and talked with Lama Geshe Tenpa Gyaltsan, a teacher who is a Gelugpa monk, and another Nyingmapa monk, a man with a shiny, fresh-shaven head. The latter, I learned, was in fact the Nechung *rinpoche*, formerly abbot of the great Tibetan monastery of Nechung, and a *tulku*. Both these monks were impressive people—so different from the Hindu swamis I've seen so far, though these too can be impressive in a different way. The Tibetans seem to have a peculiar intentness, energy, silence, and also humor. Their laughter is wonderful. Lhalungpa translated, but long stretches of talk got lost.

The two laughed when I asked the difference between their orders—Gelugpa and Nyingmapa—and said there was "really no difference." They stressed, perhaps overstressed, their unity. Someone later remarked that it was not unusual to find a Gelugpa and a Nyingmapa getting on so easily as good friends.

We talked about the goal of the monastic life. They emphasized the ideas of discipline and detachment from a life of pleasure and materialism. Nothing too clear was said about meditation, except that it has degrees and must be preceded by study. "Anyone" can do the simpler kind but a master is needed for the "more advanced." Boys begin meditation around fifteen or sixteen. They got into an involved question with Lhalungpa, a "problem" of Gelugpa meditation, which he did not translate.

We agreed on the importance of contact and understanding. They urged me to "help Westerners understand meditation," and the need for a more spiritual life. They laughed when I explained that the contemplative life was not exactly viewed with favor in the West and that monks are often considered useless. There was another lama in the next cell who is related to Lama

Deshing Rinpoche at Seattle University who sent me the writings of Gampopa. In the cell there were Tibetan manuscripts wrapped in saffron cloth, bowls of water, an offering of rice in a chalice, and dice for divination.

While we were talking about monastic affairs the King of Gyalrong came in, a quiet, sad man in a gray open-necked shirt. He sat down on the bed and said nothing. After a while, bored by the talk of meditation, he yawned and withdrew.

In the next room of the hotel, having finished his *puja* my neighbor now talks loudly on the telephone: "Hallo! Hallo! Hallo! I am going to Agra!"

Dr. Lokesh Chandra offered me a mandala, one of his reprints. I picked one, the general pattern of which attracted me as being very lively. On close inspection I find it to be full of copulation, which is all right, but I don't quite know how one meditates on it. It might be a paradoxical way to greater purity.

In his discussion of the symbolism of the mandala, Tucci explains that the Shaivite schools "divide men into three classes: first the common people, those who live a herd-like life, for whom precise laws and prohibitions are suited, since such men do not yet possess a consciousness which can, by itself, govern itself. Then comes 'heroes' who have a tendency to emerge from such a night. But their capacity wearies them. They follow their own consciousness and make their own laws, different from and contrary to those of the herd. They are lonely men who swim against the current; courageously they put themselves into contact with God and free themselves from the uniform life of association. Then come the *divya*, the holy souls, who are fully realized and so beyond the plane of *samsara*."

[Tucci, p. 51]

Five breaths pray in me: sun moon
Rain wind and fire
Five seated Buddhas reign in the breaths
Five illusions
One universe:
The white breath, yellow breath,
Green breath, blue breath,
Red fire breath, Amitabha

[Tucci, pp. 50–53]

Knowledge and Desire
And the quiescence
Of Knowledge and Desire.

Everything I think or do enters into the construction of a mandala. It is the balancing of experience over the void, not the censorship of experience. And no duality of experience—void. Experience is full because it is inexhaustible void. It is not mine. It is "uninterrupted exchange." It is dance. Five *mudras*. The dancing god embraces and penetrates the Mother. They are one motion, one silence. They are Word. Utterance and return. "Myself." No-self. The self is merely a locus in which the dance of the universe is aware of itself as complete from beginning to end—and returning to the void. Gladly. Praising, giving thanks, with all beings. Christ light—spirit—grace—gift.

(*Bodhicitta*)

"Twofold is the aspect of Divinity, one subtle, represented by the *mantra* and the other coarse, represented by an image."

[Tucci, p. 60]

Air-condition mantra. Tibetan bass of the machines.

For the Tibetans, every conceivable sound is both music and mantra. Great brasses. Trumpets snoring into the earth. They wake the mountain spirits, inviting canyon populations to a solemn rite of life and death. The clear outcry of gyelings, (shawms), the throb of drums, bells and cymbals. The "sonorous icon" with its unending trance of atonal sound repels evil. But a huge mask of evil is pressing down close. The deep sounds renew life, repel the death-grin (i.e., ignorance). The sound is the sound of emptiness. It is profound and clean. We are washed in the millennial silent roar of a rock-eating glacier.

Dance is essential for initiates.

The dance of the Supremely Wrathful One, with his long-sleeved retinue and his bride of wrath.

The dance of *dorje phurpa*, the eternal dagger, which is done in Sikkim by lamas issuing from a long period of retreat.

Padma Sambhava,[38] masked as a stag, smiles, wags his great horns, puts the evil away in a little box.

An oracle with an enormous helmet draped in a score of flags runs in a wild trance along the highest parapet of the temple.

I have a view of some of the Delhi embassies from my hotel. Over there, with the tall flagpole and red flag, is the big Chinese Embassy compound. What do they know in there? What do they do? Of what do they accuse one another, and what do they say of those they believe to be in places like this? Or is one of them secretly writing a poem?

October 31, 1968. Vigil of All Saints. Delhi

I read the Vespers of All Saints in my hotel room. Tonight I'll go by train to the Himalayas. Monsieur Daridan at the French Embassy gave me the two addresses of Dom Henri Le Saux's hermitages—in the foothills of the Himalayas, one near Madras—but I don't know which one he is at.[39] Probably the Himalaya one is too far from Dharamsala in any case.

Today I spent a long time in the Pan American office getting my ticket rewritten. In the end I *don't* go to Katmandu, at least not this time. Maybe I can do it if I come back in January. On returning from Dharamsala, Harold Talbott and I plan to go to Darjeeling and perhaps Sikkim. Then I go to Madras, Ceylon, Singapore, and Bangkok for the meeting. Last night Commissioner and Mrs. [James] George had me to dinner at the Canadian Embassy with Lhalungpa, his wife, Harold Talbott, and Gene Smith.[40] George showed a longish movie he had taken of Tibetan dances at Dalhousie, an extraordinary ceremony presided over by Khamtul Rinpoche. A couple of Tibetan hermits appeared fleetingly in the film—I may perhaps

38 Padma Sambhava, known as the "Great Guru," was invited to Tibet about A.D. 747 by King Thi-Strong-Detsan and is considered the founder of the Tibetan school of Nyingmapa Buddhism.

39 Dom Henri Le Saux was known also by his Hindu name, Swami Abhishiktananda. Merton had hoped to visit him while in India, but was unable to make connections. Le Saux has since that time died. Merton had in his library a copy of *Ermites du Succidananda* [*Hermits of Succidananda*] by Henri Le Saux and Jules Monchanin.

40 E. Gene Smith, one of the leading Tibetanists among Western scholars, is an American who studied at Leiden University in Holland and under Lama Deshung Rinpoche at Seattle University. He had first corresponded with Merton when Smith was living in Seattle.

meet them. We compared illustrations from books on Romanesque art with Tibetan mandalas, etc. Gelugpa equals like Cluny!

I was invited to another Birla party in Delhi but I did not go. Not much sightseeing either. Only the Red Fort and the big tomb. Some lovely Mogul paintings in the National Museum! Tea with Vahiduddin at the university on Tuesday—lots of good Sufi stories. Supper at the Moti Mahal restaurant where there was unfortunately no Urdu music (only on Saturdays). I am tired of too much food—and too much curry. Back to European food part of the time. The French cooking at the French Embassy was excellent, and the two very nice wines. I must say I rather like embassy parties, and Madame Daridan was particularly charming and interesting. We had a good talk sitting in the garden. She likes Shaivism and in a way seems to have some of the grace and maturity that true Shaivism must imply. But I confess I am not very open to Hindu religion, as distinct from philosophy. But I can't judge yet. Will suspend judgment until I get to Madras. I am much more impressed by the Tibetan lamas I have met.

All official modern religious art is to me forbidding, whether Christian, or Buddhist, or Hindu or whatever. Only the very unusual means anything to me—Jamini Roy, and then, perhaps, not for any connection with prayer.

November 1, 1968. Dharamsala

I came up by train from Delhi to Pathankot with Harold Talbott last night. Then by jeep with a Tibetan driver to Dharamsala. Slept well enough in a wide lower berth. It was my first overnight train trip since I went to Gethsemani to enter the monastery twenty-seven years ago. When light dawned, I looked out on fields, scattered trees, tall reeds and bamboo, brick and mud villages, a road swept by rain in the night and now by a cold wind from the mountains, men wrapped in blankets walking in the wind. Teams of oxen ploughing. Pools by the track filled with tall purple flowering weeds. A white crane starts up out of the green rushes. Long before Pathankot I was seeing the high snow-covered peaks behind Dalhousie.

On our arrival at Pathankot there was a madhouse of noise, bearers balancing several suitcases and packages on their heads and all trying to get through one small exit at once with a hundred passengers. We were met by a jeep from the Dalai Lama's headquarters.

It was a beautiful drive to Dharamsala—mountains, small villages, canyons, shrines, ruined forts, good, well cared for forest preserves. Then the climb to Dharamsala itself and the vast view over the plains from the village. It rained when we arrived and thunder talked to itself all over and around the cloud-hidden peaks. We came to the cottage Talbott lives in—everything very primitive.

In the afternoon I got my first real taste of the Himalayas. I climbed a road out of the village up into the mountains, winding through pines, past places where Tibetans live and work, including a small center for publication and a central office. Many Tibetans on the road, and some were at work on a house, singing their building song. Finally I was out alone in the pines, watching the clouds clear from the medium peaks—but not the high snowy ones—and the place was filled with a special majestic kind of mountain silence. At one point the sound of a goatherd's flute drifted up from a pasture below. An unforgettable valley with a river winding at the bottom, a couple of thousand feet below, and the rugged peaks above me, and pines twisted as in Chinese paintings. I got on a little path where I met at least five Tibetans silently praying with rosaries in their hands—and building little piles of stones. An Indian goatherd knocked over one of the piles for no reason. Great silence of the mountain, except for two men with axes higher up in the pines. Gradually the clouds thinned before one of the higher peaks, but it never fully appeared.

On the way down I met a man on the road, a man in European clothes walking with a lama. He introduced himself as Sonam Kazi,[41] the man who translated for Desjardins. He sent the lama on his way, and we went to the Tourist Hotel to drink tea and talk.

"The milk of the lioness is so precious and so powerful that if you put it in an ordinary cup, the cup breaks."

(Tibetan saying)

November 2, 1968. Dharamsala

Yesterday as I came down the path from the mountain I heard a strange humming behind me. A Tibetan came by quietly droning a monotonous sound, a prolonged "*om.*" It was something that harmonized with the mountain—an ancient syllable he had found long ago in the rocks—or perhaps it had been born with him.

41 Sonam T. Kazi, born into one of Sikkim's leading feudal families, had lived in Tibet for many years prior to the Chinese takeover. As a young man, he attended the Scottish Mission College in Kalimpong and St. Stephen's College in Delhi, but his most extended study was under several of the Nyingmapa Buddhist masters in Tibet, from whom he received advanced meditational and spiritual instruction qualifying him to become himself a teacher of Tantric Buddhism.

The Tibetan who cooks for us was formerly a monk in Tibet who got released from his vows to fight in the resistance against the Chinese.

The guru is he who "must produce the revulsion of the adept."

(Tucci, p. 76)

"The aim of all the Tantras is to teach the ways whereby we may set free the divine light which is mysteriously present and shining in each one of us, although it is enveloped in an insidious web of the psyche's weaving."

(Tucci, p. 78)

Tucci explains that there are four different Tantras to suit four categories of men (and gods):

". . . the *Kriyatantras*, particularly devoted to liturgical complications. It is a homeopathic treatment by which it is sought, gradually, to open the eyes of the officiant and to show him what a complex instrument of psychological revulsion he has at his disposal, provided that he knows how to understand its meaning. The gesture (*mudra*) of the Gods is here a smile.

"The *Caryatantras* are suited for the *rje rigs*, the nobleman, in whom a respect for ceremonial is accompanied by a capacity for spiritual meditation. These Tantras are addressed to persons who may experience the dawn of spiritual anxiety and in whom there may be present the intellectual and spiritual prerequisites for the Return. The gesture here is a look. The *Yogatantras* are addressed to the *rgyal rigs*, of royal family, powerful men, who cannot manage to renounce the goods of this world. For their meditation is offered the *mandala* with a lavish display of Gods, Goddesses and acolytes—like the court of a king in his palace. For one must begin by speaking to such men a language which they can understand, if one does not wish to drive them away for ever. What would be the use of renunciation and sacrifice to those who love the joy of living, if they are, to begin with, ignorant of the fact that real beatitude is an overcoming of that which they most desire? The gesture here is an embrace.

"The *Anuttarantantras* are reserved for the creatures who sin most, who do not distinguish good from evil, who lead impure lives. It is on the very fault itself by which they are sullied that is built up slowly the work of redemption. The gesture here is union."

Tucci points out that it would be wrong to imagine that a meditation type should be urged to follow *anuttarantantra*.

(Tucci, pp. 79–80)

"The symbolism of the ritual act is clear. A *mandala* . . . is an ideal Bodhgaya, an 'adamantine plane,' that is an incorruptible surface, the representation of the very instant in which is accomplished the revulsion to the other plane, in which one becomes Buddha."

(Tucci, p. 86)

"One is to attain enlightenment and become a Buddha only for the sake of others; it has therefore been said, '*Bodhicitta* is perfect enlightenment (attained) for the sake of others . . .'"

[S. B. Dasgupta, An Introduction to Tantric Buddhism *(Calcutta, 1958), pp. 280–83]*

Mandalas can incorporate non-Buddhist deities and even Christian symbols. "Every shape and form that arises in the soul, every link which, in a mysterious way, joins us to the Universal Life and unites us, maybe without our being aware of it, to Man's most ancient experience, the voices which reach us from the depths of the abyss, all are welcomed with almost affectionate solicitude."

(Tucci, p. 83)

Sonam Kazi is a Sikkimese who went to Tibet to consult doctors about an illness, then rode all over Tibet and took to meditation, studying under various lamas, including a woman lama in Lhasa. His daughter is supposed to be a reincarnation of this woman. She entranced Aelred Graham by reading comic books while he argued with her father. There is a sweet photo of her in the Desjardins book.

Sonam Kazi is a lay Nyingmapa monk. He has had several good gurus and seems far advanced in meditation. He is of course full of information but also of insight. He thinks I ought to find a Tibetan guru and go in for Nyingmapa Tantrism initiation along the line of "direct realization and *dzogchen* (final resolution)." At least he asked me if I were willing to risk it and I said, "Why not?" The question is finding the right man. I am not exactly dizzy with the idea of looking for a magic master but I would certainly like to learn something by experience and it does seem that the Tibetan Buddhists are the only ones who, at present, have a really large number of people who have attained to extraordinary heights in meditation and contemplation. This does not exclude Zen. But I do feel very much at home with the Tibetans, even though much that appears in books about them seems bizarre if not sinister.

What is the purpose of the mandala? Sonam Kazi said one meditates on the mandala in order to be in control of what goes on within one instead of "being controlled by it." In meditation on the mandala one is able to construct and dissolve the interior configurations at will. One meditates not to "learn" a presumed objective cosmological structure, or a religious doctrine, but to become the Buddha enthroned in one's own center.

Elements of the mandala for Tucci: it is man's psychic heritage, to be accepted, not repressed. "It is better, then, to assume possession of them at the first and then by degrees to transfigure them, just as one passes from the outer enclosure of the mandala successively through the others until one reaches the central point, the primordial equipoise regained after the experience of life."

(Tucci, p. 83)

I talked to Sonam Kazi about the "child mind," which is recovered *after* experience. Innocence—to experience—to innocence. Milarepa, angry, guilty of revenge, murder and black arts, was purified by his master Marpa, the translator, who several times made him build a house many stories high and then tear it down again. After which he was "no longer the slave of his own psyche but its lord." So too, a Desert Father came to freedom by weaving baskets and then, at the end of each year, burning all the baskets he had woven.

(Tucci, pp. 83–84)

Outside the dirty window I have just opened there is pure morning light on the lower rampart of the Himalayas. Near me are the steep green sinews of a bastion tufted with vegetation. A hut or shrine is visible, outlined on the summit. Beyond, in sunlit, back-lighted mist, the higher pointed peak. Further to the left a still higher snowy peak that was hidden in cloud last evening and is misty now. Song of birds in the bushes. Incessant soft guttural mantras of the crows. Below, in another cottage, an argument of women.

Sonam Kazi is against the mixing of traditions, even Tibetan ones. Let the Kagyudpa keep to itself. He suggests that if I edit a book of Tibetan texts, let them all be *one* tradition. *A fortiori*, we should not try to set up a pseudocommunity of people from different traditions, Asian and Western. I agree with this. Brother David Steindl-Rast's idea perplexed me a little—as being first of all too academic. But I had wondered about some different approach: a mere dream. And certainly no good in my own life. Now, since seeing the books the other night in Canada House, I am curious about re-exploring the Romanesque artistic tradition and the 12th-century writers in Christian monasticism in relation to the Eastern traditions, i.e., in the light thrown on them by the East.

Sonam Kazi spoke of acting with no desire for gain, even spiritual—whether merit or attainment. A white butterfly appears in the sun, then vanishes again. Another passes in the distance. No gain for them—or for me.

Down in the valley a bird sings, a boy whistles. The white butterfly zigzags across the top left corner of the view.

Man as body—word—spirit. Three ways of handling anger, lust, etc. Hinayana—Mahayana—Tantric.

Tucci on the liturgy and rites of the mandala:

"The disciple, blindfolded, is led to the eastern gate of the mandala and there receives from the master a short stick of wood (such as is used in India for cleaning the teeth) or a flower which he must throw on to the mandala. The section on to which these fall (which is protected by one of the five Buddhas—or their symbols) will indicate the way that is suited to the disciple."

". . . the initiate should honour this God (in the aspect of *jnanasattva*) with exoteric and esoteric ritual of various sorts: flowers, incense, lamps, vestments, umbrellas, flags, bells and standards, all of celestial quality." [But a Hinayana master from Burma went to Ceylon and was scandalized to find there monks with umbrellas—this of course was quite different.] [Merton's brackets]

(Tucci, pp. 90 and 95)

The disciple, blindfolded, is led to the east gate of the prepared mandala. Blindfolded, he casts a flower on the mandala. The flower will find his way for him into the palace. Follow your flower!

I must ask Sonam Kazi about dreams. Tucci placed under his pillow a blessed leaf given him by the Grand Lama of Sakya. He dreamed of mountains and glaciers. (See Tucci, p. 92.) A yellow butterfly goes by just over the heads of the small purple flowers outside the windows. Firecrackers explode, perhaps in the yard of the school. Hammering in the village.

Sonam Kazi criticized the facility with which some monks say *nirvana* and *samsara* are one, without knowing what they are talking about. Also, though it is true that "there is no *karma*," this cannot be rightly understood by many, for in fact there is *karma*, but on another level. He also liked the idea of Trappist silence at meals, at work, everywhere. He said the name Trappist was interesting since in Tibetan "*trapa*" means "schoolman" or monk. He likes Krishnamurti.

The *bhikkhus* at the conference all had umbrellas. They all sat in a saffron row at the banquet, eating and drinking nothing and saying almost nothing except, "You should have had this affair before noon."[42] They smiled and were content.

This cottage has a washroom with two stools. Concrete floor. A hole in the corner leading out. You empty the washbasin on the floor and the water runs out the hole. Through this hole a cobra or krait could easily come. Fortunately the nights are cold. There are banana trees everywhere—the nights are not cold enough to harm them. Two wrenlike birds bicker together in a bush outside the window.

Sonam Kazi condemned "world-evasion," which he thinks ruined Buddhism in India. He would be against an eremitism entirely cut off from all contact, at least for me. But in another context he admired the recluses who severed all contacts, seeing only a few people or perhaps none at all, reserving special contacts only for a restricted list. Harold asked whether others would respect this arrangement. Sonam Kazi thought they would. When a hermit goes on full retreat he places a mantra, an image, and a seal on the outside of his cell, and the mantra reads: "All gods, men, and demons keep out of this retreat."

Cocks crow in the valley. The tall illuminated grasses bend in the wind. One white butterfly hovers and settles. Another passes in a hurry. How glad I am not to be in any city.

Tucci in explaining the liturgy of the mandala speaks of palingenesis, "the revulsion which has taken place and by which consciousness that was refracted, lost and dissipated in time and space, has become, once again, one and luminous."

(Tucci, p. 97)

Whatever may be of value of all the details of mandala meditation—and all the emergences of all the Buddhas from all the diamond wombs—this passage remains exact and important: ". . . the mystic knows that the principle of salvation is within him. He knows also that this principle will remain inert if he does not, with all his strength, *seek it, find it and make it active.* On the way of redemption, to which he has devoted himself, he has need of all

42 Theravada monks do not eat after noon.

his will-power and vigilance in order to put in motion the forces of his own psyche so that it, which keeps him bound, may furnish him, nonetheless with the means of salvation provided that he knows how to penetrate into his psyche and subdue it."

(Tucci, p. 110)

November 3, 1968

Quiet after sunrise. In the silent, cool, misty air of morning a sound of someone chanting *puja* floats up from the village. The report of a gun far down in the valley echoes along the walls of the mountain. Now too they are shooting. Yesterday, near the army post at Palampur, there was machine-gun fire back in the mountains while we sat by the road in the tea plantation talking with Khamtul Rinpoche.

We had some trouble locating Khamtul Rinpoche. We went to the place where he is setting up a new monastery and lay colony, also on a tea plantation near Palampur (he is moving away from Dalhousie), but he wasn't there. A monk served us some tea. We waited a while but Khamtul did not come. Later we met him on the road at a lovely place with many pines and a fine view of the mountains. (Khamtul Rinpoche is the one who was in Commissioner George's film.) He is an impressive, heavily built Tibetan with a brown woolen cap on his head. We sat on the ground amid young tea plants and pines and talked, again with Sonam Kazi translating. Khamtul Rinpoche spoke about the need for a guru and direct experience rather than book knowledge; about the union of study and meditation. We discussed the "direct realization" method, including some curious stuff about working the soul of a dead man out of its body with complete liberation after death—through small holes in the skull or a place where the skin is blown off—weird! And about the need of a guru. "And," he asked, "have you come to write a strange book about us? What are your motives?" After quite a few questions, he said I would be helped by talking to "some of the Tibetan tulkus who are in India" and added that Gyalwa Karmapa, the important guru who has a monastery in Sikkim, was coming to Delhi on the 15th. Afterward someone said no, it was Calcutta on the 15th. In any case I do hope to meet Karmapa somewhere.

It was a long drive back to Dharamsala. The mountains were lovely in the evening light. We arrived after dark, went to a (rather crumby) restaurant in town for some food, and Harold Talbott bought a paper with a banner headline, LBJ ORDERS COMPLETE BOMBING HALT and WAIT FULL SCALE

PEACE TALKS CLEARED—a dramatic announcement. It is long overdue, but I am glad of it, even though it may be only a matter of last-minute expediency for the election—I hope it can mean peace.

What is important is not liberation from the body but liberation from the mind. We are not entangled in our own body but entangled in our own mind.

Spiritual sterility can be due to the fact that fertilization by the union of *prajna* and *upaya* (wisdom and discipline) has not taken place. Wisdom as sperm, discipline as ovum give us the "new creature," the living reintegrated and growing "personality" (in a special spiritual sense: not "individual"). Hence comes new consciousness. "Pollution" is the spilling of the seed without union, without fertilization of discipline, without "return" to the summit of consciousness. A mere spilling out of passion with no realization. "The end of passion is the cause of sorrow, the precipitation of the *bodhicitta*."

(Tucci, pp. 108–33)

Bhikkhu Khantipalo in Bangkok has spoken of peaceful coexistence with insects, etc. One tries to catch poisonous ones, tactfully, and throw them out of one's hut. Matchboxes, he said, are good for catching scorpions. In the forest *wats*, a noisy large lizard sometimes gets in the straw of the roof and disturbs the meditation of the *bhikkhus* by loud guttural cries.

Gandhiji's broken glasses—Johnson has stopped the bombing. Two magpies are fighting in a tree.

Are Tantrism, and meditation on the mandala, the evocations of minute visual detail like the Ignatian method in some respects? And as useless for me? A white butterfly goes by in the sun.

One difference is the sixth point above the mandala's five points. The mandala is constructed only to be dissolved. One must see clearly the five points—or there is no sixth, which also includes them all. No six without five. The six make "eternal life." Note that when the body is regarded as a mandala, the five *chakras* (sex, navel, heart, throat, head) are completed by the sixth "above the head."

For the dissolution of a mandala the dusts and colors are taken in ceremony with the solemn snoring of trumpets and thrown into a mountain stream.

The highest of vows, Sonam Kazi said, is that in which there is no longer anything to be accomplished. Nothing is vowed. No one vows it. Tibetans sacrifice their own gods and destroy spirits. They also mock, solemnly and liturgically, the sacrifice itself—a spirit in butter, an image of a god to be burned in a straw temple.

Reverend Sirs, I am not here to write a manual of Christian Mantras!

I must see John Driver if I get to Wales. He wrote a dissertation at Oxford on Nyingmapa, but his professor would not accept it. He is connected with Trungpa Rinpoche and his place in Scotland. The dissertation is apparently brilliant.

I met a woman and child walking silently, and woman slowly spinning a prayer wheel—with great reverence and it was not at all absurd or routine—the child with a lovely smile.

Harold Talbott says the Dalai Lama has to see a lot of blue-haired ladies in pants—losers. And people looking for a freak religion. And rich people who have nothing better to do than come up here out of curiosity. His Western visitors are not well screened. He has very few real advisers who know anything about the world as it is. The Dalai Lama is still studying under his tutor and also is going on with Tantric studies, and I was told by Tenzin Geshe, his secretary, that he enjoys his new house, where he has quieter quarters, is less disturbed, and has a garden to walk in now, without being followed around by cops.

The Dalai Lama is loved by his people—and they are a beautiful, loving people. They surround his house with love and prayer, they have a new *soongkhor* [barbed-wire fence] for protection along the fence. Probably no leader in the world is so much loved by his followers and means so much to them. He means everything to them. For that reason it would be especially terrible and cruel if any evil should strike him. I pray for his safety and fear for him. May God protect and preserve him.

7 P.M. Tenzin Geshe, the very young secretary of the Dalai Lama, has just left. He came down to tell us of plans for my audience tomorrow at 10 A.M. A young, intelligent, eager guy. He seems to be only in his twenties, and the

Dalai Lama himself only thirty-three. He brought me the first copy of a mimeographed newspaper that is being put out here for Tibetans. There are great problems for the Tibetan refugees like those I saw today in Upper Dharamsala living in many tents under the trees on the steep mountainside, clinging precariously to a world in which they have no place and only waiting to be moved somewhere else—to "camps."

We had walked up, Harold and I, to Upper Dharamsala by the back road to McLeod Ganj, which is where the Dalai Lama lives. It is really the top of the mountain we are on now. Suddenly we were in a Tibetan village with a new, spanking white *chorten* in the middle of it. There we met Sonam Kazi, who was expecting us to come by bus. We climbed higher to the empty buildings of Swarg Ashram which the Dalai Lama has just vacated to move to his new quarters. A lovely site, but cramped. The buildings are old and ramshackle, and as Sonam said, "the roof leaks like hell." Then further on up to the top—an empty house surrounded by prayer flags.

Tibetans are established all over the mountain in huts, houses, tents, anything. Prayer flags flutter among the trees. Rock mandalas are along all the pathways. OM MANI PADME HUM ("Hail to the jewel in the lotus") is carved on every boulder. It is moving to see so many Tibetans going about silently praying—almost all of them are constantly carrying rosaries. We visited a small monastic community of lamas under the Dalai Lama's private chaplain, the Khempo of Namgyal Tra-Tsang, whom I met. We were ushered into his room where he sat studying Tibetan block-print texts in narrow oblong sheets. He was wearing tinted glasses. The usual rows of little bowls of water. A *tanka*. Marigolds growing in old tin cans. Artificial flowers in a Coke bottle. A little butter lamp burning. A jar with a plentiful supply of Entero-Vioform tablets. Shelves of Tibetan texts carefully wrapped in bright yellow and orange cloth. A beautiful room—the Coke bottle was not immediately obvious—it did not look like a junk yard, but like a shrine, as a lama's room should. A quiet, scholarly man, eloquent and articulate, with a lot to say.

The Khempo of Namgyal deflected a question of mine about metaphysics—he returned to it later—by saying that the real ground of his Gelugpa study and practice was the knowledge of suffering, and that only when a person was fully convinced of the immensity of suffering and its complete universality and saw the need of deliverance from it, and sought deliverance for *all* beings, could he begin to understand *sunyata*.

Thus when European authors such as Tucci seem to talk of *bodhicitta* as an intellectual or metaphysical seed of enlightenment, the *khempo* showed it clearly to be a right view of suffering and a deep sense of compassion for everything and everyone that suffers. Then he went on to talk of *Prajnaparamita* and the teachings of Nagarjuna[43] as the intellectual basis of his own tradition, and of the need to study these and to practice them, to reduce them to experience. He also—like all the others—stressed the need of a master for progress in meditation. He spoke of Santi Deva[44] and I replied that I liked Santi Deva very much, had reread him this summer. He said the compassion of Santi Deva was so great that his teaching touched the heart very deeply and awakened a spiritual response. When one read the *Prajnaparamita* on suffering and was thoroughly moved, "so that all the hairs of the body stood on end," one was ready for meditation—called to it—and indeed to further study. He was very reserved about mandalas—"I would not even pronounce the name mandala except that you have come from such a great distance"—and insisted on the esoteric secrecy of Tantric disciplines and symbols. This refusal to speak directly of symbols was very interesting.

He insisted on the "ax of true doctrine" which must be used to cut the root of ignorance—and that one must know how to use the ax, otherwise he harms himself. So a man who is skilled in catching snakes can safely catch them, but one who is not skilled gets bitten. Meditation: laying the ax to the root. (The coming of Christ in the desert.)

"It is the tradition of the fortunate seekers never to be content with partial practice."

(Milarepa)

Sankaracharya on the ego (from *The Crest-Jewel of Discrimination*):

"When we say: 'This man is that same Devadatta whom I have previously met,' we establish a person's identity by disregarding those attributes superimposed upon him by the circumstances of our former meeting. In just the same way, when we consider the scriptural teaching 'That art Thou,' we must disregard those attributes which have been superimposed upon 'That' and 'Thou. . . .'

43 Nagarjuna, a South Indian who lived probably in the second or third century A.D., was converted to Buddhism and became one of the founders of the Madhyamika, or "Middle Path," sect of Buddhism.

44 Santi Deva (691–743), the son of a king, renounced his inheritance to become a Buddhist monk. After Nagarjuna, he was probably the most important philosopher of the Madhyamika school of Mahayana Buddhism.

"Cease to follow the way of the world, cease to follow the way of the flesh, cease to follow the way of tradition. Get rid of this false identification and know the true Atman. . . .

"Cease to identify yourself with race, clan, name, form and walk of life. These belong to the body, the garment of decay. Abandon, also, the idea that you are the doer of actions or the thinker of thoughts. These belong to the ego, the subtle covering. Realize that you are that Being which is eternal happiness.

"Man's life of bondage to the world of birth and death has many causes. The root of them all is the ego, the first-begotten child of ignorance.

"As long as a man identifies himself with this wicked ego, there can be no possibility of liberation. For liberation is its very opposite.

"Once freed from this eclipsing demon of an ego, man regains his true nature, just as the moon shines forth when freed from the darkness of an eclipse. He becomes pure, infinite, eternally blissful and self-luminous."

(Sankaracharya, pp. 86, 91, 96)

I promised Tenzin Geshe I would have people send him information and subscriptions to good magazines. Apparently they are not very well informed here in Dharamsala; they have to depend on *Life*, *Time*, *Reader's Digest*, and so on. I said I thought the weekly edition of *Le Monde* was essential and that I would get "Ping" Ferry to put them on the mailing list of the Center for the Study of Democratic Institutions.

An Indian security policeman was here in this room, at this desk, this morning looking at my passport, studying the Indian visa, taking down notes about where I had been and where I intended to go. He got me to write out in block letters the titles of two books I had written on Zen. And he said, "I suppose we can now expect a book from you on Tibetan Buddhism." I said I thought not.

When we went on up the mountain from Swarg Ashram I heard a great commotion in the tall trees and looked up to see marvelous gray apes with black faces crashing and swinging through the branches. They were huge, almost as big as people. Six or seven beautiful, funny Hanumans.[45] It would be wonderful to live in a hermitage with apes in the trees around it. They

45 In Hindu mythology Hanuman is a monkey god, the son of the wind and a monkey nymph. In the *Ramayana* he leads the monkey hosts that assist Rama, the hero.

would be fantastic company, better than squirrels, endlessly amusing, seemingly clumsy yet infinitely agile and smart. So much bigger than monkeys, and making much more commotion in the branches. A storm of heavy apes!

Yesterday Sonam Kazi, Harold, and I drove to Palampur to meet some lamas at the Tibetan camps there. It was a fine drive on a bad road, with great views of the mountains. We went beyond Palampur to the camp, on a tea plantation, where the Tibetans are newly established, some in tents among the tea gardens, with prayer flags flying, some in the buildings of the village. We had a talk with a Nyingmapa lama, Chhokling Rinpoche, who wanted to know if I believed in reincarnation before answering questions concerning enlightenment. Like everyone else, he spoke of masters, and the need of finding one, and how one finds one—of being drawn to him supernaturally, sometimes with instant recognition. He asked me a koanlike question about the origin of the mind. I could not answer it directly but apparently my nonanswer was "right," and he said I would profit by "meeting some of the *tulkus* that are in India." Sonam Kazi said, "You have passed the first test," and he seemed pleased.

One of the "*tulkus* that are in India" and whom I met today is a ten-year-old boy, a lively and intelligent kid living up on the mountain here in a rather poor cottage with an older lama, another boy lama, and a Tibetan family with a huge black dog that was all ready to bite a few chunks out of Harold and me. The boy was charming and I took some pictures of him as he was petulantly rolling down his sleeves to be more ceremonious. He went into his cell and sat cross-legged on his seat and received us with poise and formality. I took his picture there too but it was probably too dark to come out. Then we went down to the drama school where a girl was playing a lovely instrument, the name of which I forgot to ask—a string instrument laid out flat and played with two sticks. It had a charming sound—while around the corner was a radio playing popular Indian music—which I find pretty good! Here there was a young Canadian who is teaching the little tulku English and says he does not learn his lessons. "He is intelligent but too lazy to think."

November 4, 1968

Today I am to see the Dalai Lama—but meanwhile the world goes on, and finance booms (zooms). We have run out of toilet paper and are using

Saturday's newspaper. I became absorbed in the news of business—too good to pass over.

MUSTARD OIL SUBDUED ON POOR ENQUIRIES

Groundnut oil eased by Rs.5 to Rs.388 for want of support. Sesame and cottonseed oil also came down by Rs.5 in sympathy. (Happy to report, however, that later groundnut oils rose again Rs.5 "owing to fall in arrivals from Uttar Pradesh.")

PULSES DEPRESSED, WHEAT LOOKS UP

Pulses, especially dal moong, dal masoor, etc. I like dal. I hate to see it depressed. (Dal = lentils.)

BOMBING HALT IMPARTS FIRMNESS TO SHARES

A smart rally was witnessed on the Bombay stock exchange—transactions were mostly squarish and of jobbing in nature (*sic*). Reports about the bombing halt order over VietNam (*sic*) given by President Johnson imparted firmness to the market.

A Christ mandala, in St. Paul's "to understand the length and the breadth, the height and the depth . . ."

"The human body is better than a wishing gem."

(Milarepa)

The three poisons: craving,
hatred,
ignorance.

"A virtue for one engaged on any esoteric path is primarily a mode of knowing, or, to be more accurate, a factor dispositive for enlightenment."[46]

November 4, 1968. Afternoon

I had my audience with the Dalai Lama this morning in his new quarters. It was a bright, sunny day—blue sky, the mountains absolutely clear. Tenzin

46 From Marco Pallis, "Considerations on Tantric Spirituality," in *The Bulletin of Tibetology* (Gangtok, Sikkim: Namgyal Institute of Tibetology), vol. 2, no. 2 (August 1965).

Geshe sent a jeep down. We went up the long way round through the army post and past the old deserted Anglican Church of St. John in the Wilderness. Everything at McLeod Ganj is admirably situated, high over the valley, with snow-covered mountains behind, all pine trees, with apes in them, and a vast view over the plains to the south. Our passports were inspected by an Indian official at the gate of the Dalai Lama's place. There were several monks standing around—like monks standing around anywhere—perhaps waiting to go somewhere. A brief wait in a sitting room, all spanking new, a lively, bright Tibetan carpet, bookshelves full of *Kangyur* and *Tangyur* scriptures presented to the Dalai Lama by Suzuki.[47]

The Dalai Lama is most impressive as a person. He is strong and alert, bigger than I expected (for some reason I thought he would be small). A very solid, energetic, generous, and warm person, very capably trying to handle enormous problems—none of which he mentioned directly. There was not a word of politics. The whole conversation was about religion and philosophy and especially ways of meditation. He said he was glad to see me, had heard a lot about me. I talked mostly of my own personal concerns, my interest in Tibetan mysticism. Some of what he replied was confidential and frank. In general he advised me to get a good base in Madhyamika philosophy (Nagarjuna and other authentic *Indian* sources) and to consult qualified Tibetan scholars, uniting study and practice. *Dzogchen* was good, he said, provided one had a sufficient grounding in metaphysics—or anyway Madhyamika, which is beyond metaphysics. One gets the impression that he is very sensitive about partial and distorted Western views of Tibetan mysticism and especially about popular myths. He himself offered to give me another audience the day after tomorrow and said he had some questions he wanted to ask me.

The Dalai Lama is also sensitive about the views of other Buddhists concerning Tibetan Buddhism, especially some Theravada Buddhists who accuse Tibetan Buddhism of corruption by non-Buddhist elements.

The Dalai Lama told me that Sonam Kazi knew all about *dzogchen* and could help me, which of course he already has. It is important, the Dalai Lama said, not to misunderstand the simplicity of *dzogchen*, or to imagine it is "easy," or that one can evade the difficulties of the ascent by taking this "direct path." He recommended Geshe Sopa of the New Jersey monastery

47 Daisetz Teitaro Suzuki (1870–1966) was one of the great intercultural scholars of our time who, in his many books and lectures, interpreted Zen Buddhism to the West and Christianity to the East. Merton went to New York to meet Suzuki when he was at Columbia in 1964, and they corresponded frequently before and after.

who has been teaching at the University of Wisconsin, and Geshe Ugyen Tseten of Rikon, Switzerland.

Murti on Madhyamika: "Its dialectic is of crucial importance. This dialectic is the consciousness of the total and interminable conflict in reason and the consequent attempt to resolve the conflict by rising to a higher standpoint."
[T. R. V. Murti, The Central Philosophy of Buddhism *(London, 1960), p. 126]*

In the afternoon I got a little reading done and then had quite a good meditation. Talking with various *rinpoches* has certainly been helpful, and above all the Dalai Lama himself. I have great confidence in him as a really charismatic person. The Tibetans are all quite impressive and their solidity does a great deal to counteract the bizarre reports about some of their practices. It is all very good experience.

Thinking about my own life and future, it is still a very open question. I am beginning to appreciate the hermitage at Gethsemani more than I did last summer when things seemed so noisy and crowded. Even here in the mountains there are few places where one does not run into someone. Roads and paths and trails are all full of people. To have real solitude one would have to get very high up and far back!

For solitude, Alaska really seems the very best place. But everyone I have talked to says I must also consider others and keep open to them to some extent. The *rinpoches* all advise against absolute solitude and stress "compassion." They seem to agree that being in solitude much of the year and coming "out" for a while would be a good solution.

The idea of being in Alaska and then going out to Japan or the U.S. strikes me as a rather good solution. And, in some small way, helping in Alaska itself. On the way back from this trip I think I will need to go to Europe to see Trungpa Rinpoche's place in Scotland and the Tibetan monastery in Switzerland. Also to see Marco Pallis and then John Driver in Wales. I must write to "Donald" Allchin about Wales.

The way in which I have been suddenly brought here constantly surprises me. The few days so far in Dharamsala have all been extremely fruitful in every way: the beauty and quiet of the mountains, my own reading and meditation, encounters with lamas, everything.

In a way it is wonderful to be without letters. No one now knows where to reach me. Undoubtedly there is some mail accumulating for me at the USIS office in Calcutta. But it will be ten days or more before I see any of it. And Brother Patrick is sending on only what is most essential.

Trying to get a better perspective on the earlier part of this year, there is a lot I cannot quite understand. And perhaps do not need to understand. The last months have been demanding and fruitful. I have needed the experience of this journey. Much as the hermitage has meant, I have been needing to get away from Gethsemani and it was long overdue.

This evening the lights in the cottage went dead for a while. I stood out in the moonlight, listening to drums down in the village and looking up at the stars. The same constellations as over the hermitage and the porch opening in about the same direction, southeast toward Aquila and the Dolphin. Aquarius out over the plain, the Swan up above. Cassiopeia over the mountains.

November 5, 1968

The metaphysician as wounded man. A wounded man is not an agnostic—he just has different questions, arising out of his wound. Recognition of the wound as a substitute for real identity, when one can "think of nothing else."

Buddha rejected the dogmatism of idealism and materialism and substituted a critical dialectic, "long before anything approximating to it was found in the West." "Criticism is deliverance of the human mind from all entanglements and passions. It is freedom itself. This is the true Madhyamika standpoint."

(Murti, p. 41)

Note that Buddha neither said "there is a self" nor "there is not a self." But among many Buddhists there appears to be a kind of dogmatism that says "there is not a self" instead of taking the true middle. Also Buddha replied by silence because he considered the *condition of the questioner* and the effect of a dogmatic reply on him. Buddha did not say "there is no self" to prevent the bewilderment of Vacchagotta.[48] "For he would have said: 'Formerly indeed I had a self but now I have not one any more.'"

It was Buddha's aim not to give a "final" speculative answer but *to be free from all theories* and to know, by experience, "the nature of form and how form arises and how form perishes." He wanted "not a third position lying between two extremes but a no-position that supersedes them both." This is the Middle Way.

(Murti, pp. 45–47)

48 Vaccha(gotta) was a wandering ascetic who recognized the uniqueness of the Buddha and whose discussions with him, as recorded in several of the earliest texts, present some of the most important points of the Buddha's doctrine.

Buddhist dialectic and "alienation" might be a good theme for my Bangkok conference. Like Marxism, Buddhism considers that a fundamental egocentrism, "providing for the self" (with possible economic implications in a more modern context) leads to dogmatism about the self—either that it is eternal or that it does not exist at all. A truly critical attitude implies a certain freedom from predetermination by economic and sociological factors. The notion of "I" implies the notion of "mind." I am "my property"—I am constituted by what separates me from "not I"—i.e., by what is mine "and not anybody else's."

As long as "I" assert the "I" dogmatically there is lacking a critical awareness that experiences the "I" dynamically in a continuum of cause and effect—a chain of economic or other causations and coordinated interrelationships.

Hence, the implicit alienation in Samkhya-prakriti exists but has no value except in relation to *purusha*. It is for *purusha*.

(Murti, pp. 61 ff.)

November 5, 1968

The "mandala awareness" of space. For instance, this mountain, where a provisional Tibetan pattern of dwellings and relationships has been, very sketchily, set up. You get oriented by visiting various *rinpoches*, each one a reincarnation of a spiritual figure, each one seated in his shrinelike cell, among *tankas*, flowers, bowls, rugs, lamps, and images. Each *rinpoche* figures henceforth as one who "is seated" in a particular plane, near or far: the Khempo of Namgyal Tra-Tsang high up on the mountain with his little community. Ratod Rinpoche just up the hill, a quarter of a mile from here, near the official headquarters of the Dalai Lama's administration. The little *tulku*, who can hardly be imagined as sitting still for very long, higher up, just below the *khempo*. And the Dalai Lama himself in a sort of center, where he is certainly very "seated" and guarded and fenced in. Thus what was for me on Friday a rugged, nondescript mountain with a lot of miscellaneous dwellings, rocks, woods, farms, flocks, gulfs, falls, and heights, is now spiritually ordered by permanent seated presences, burning with a lamplike continuity and significance, centers of awareness and reminders of *dharma*. One instinctively sees the mountain as a mandala, slightly askew no doubt, with a central presence and surrounding presences more or less amiable. The *rinpoches* were all very amiable. The central presence is a fully awake, energetic, alert, nondusty, nondim, nonwhispering Buddha.

Shooting down in the valley: not firecrackers, army rifles. Maneuvers or shooting range. Mock warfare. Outside and below the mandala. I open the window for fresh sunlit air.

A second earthquake: one came about an hour ago—now this one. The first lasted several seconds, shaking the house more violently. This lasted a little longer, long enough for the "when will it stop?" anxiety to surface. But this was less violent. After the silence and rumbling, then the burst of voices, the outcry of birds, the barking of many dogs. And life resumes its quiet course once again. Nothing has fallen. At this moment the elections are perhaps ending, the polls closing in America.

Last night I dreamed that I was, temporarily, back at Gethsemani. I was dressed in a Buddhist monk's habit, but with more black and red and gold, a "Zen habit," in color more Tibetan than Zen. I was going to tell Brother Donald [Kane], the cook in the diet kitchen, that I would be there for supper. I met some women in the corridor, visitors and students of Asian religion, to whom I was explaining I was a kind of Zen monk and Gelugpa together, when I woke up. It was 6 A.M. Time to get up.

Other recent dreams, dimly remembered. Strange towns. Towns in the south of France. Working my way along the Riviera. How to get to the "next place"? I forget what the problem is, or if it is solved. Another: I'm in some town and have a small, silvery toy balloon, but it has a dangerous explosive gas in it. I throw it in the air and hope it will float completely away before anything happens. It rises too slowly, departs too slowly—but nothing happens. The dream changes.

Two white butterflies alight on separate flowers. They rise, play together briefly, accidentally, in the air, then depart in different directions.

E. C. Dimock, Jr., on Vaishnava poetry:

Vaishnava (Bengali) poetry originated in the Vaishnava *bhakti* sects of the 16th and 17th centuries. For the most part they are love poems, of the love between the god Krishna and Radha,[49] most beautiful of the *gopis*, sung in *kirtan* ("praise") gatherings with drum and cymbals. But some are hymns to Chaitanya, a 15th-century Bengali Vaishnava saint considered to be an incarnation of Krishna. Krishna has many aspects, but for the Vaishnavas,

49 Radha, in Hindu mythology, was leader of the *gopis*, cowherdesses of Vrindavana, and was the god Krishna's favorite love. As such, over the centuries she and their relationship became the subject of countless songs, poems, and paintings.

"Krishna was the lover and beloved, whose foremost characteristic is the giving and receiving of joy, who is approachable only by *bhakti*, by devotion and selfless dedication."

The *sardaya*, "the man of sensibility," who is aware of certain associations in Bengali, can appreciate in Vaishnava lyrics their interplay of the erotic and the mystical. The mood of the poems is called *madhurya-bhava*, a mood of identification in which poet or reader enters into the love-longing of Radha or another of the *gopis*. One of the formalities is the *bhanita*, or signature line, usually at the end of the poem, in which the poet identifies himself by name.

Here are some examples I like from the *In Praise of Krishna* anthology. The translations are by Professor Dimock in collaboration with the poet Denise Levertov.[50]

I would set fire to my house
for him. I would bear
The scorn of the world.
He thinks his sorrow is joy
When I weep, he weeps.

When the sound of your flute reaches my ears
it compels me to leave my home, my friends,
it draws me into the dark towards you.

I no longer count the pain of coming here
Says Govinda-dasa (*Bhanita*)

His life cuts into my life
as the stain of the moon's rabbit
engraves the moon.

Others have many loves, I have
Only you, dearer to me than life.

50 Edward C. Dimock, Jr., and Denise Levertov, *In Praise of Krishna: Songs from the Bengali* (London: Cape, 1968).

You are the kohl on my eyes, the ornaments
on my body,
you, dark moon.

As wing to bird,
water to fish,
life to the living—
so you to me.
But tell me
Madhava, beloved,
who are you?
Who are you really?
Vidyapati says, they are one another.

Cruel Kama pierces me with his arrows:
the lightning flashes, the peacocks dance,
frogs and waterbirds, drunk with delight,
call incessantly—and my heart is heavy.
Darkness on earth,
the sky intermittently lit with a sullen glare . . .
Vidyapati says,
How will you pass this night without your lord?

Sankaracharya on *brahman*, the real *samadhi*, etc. (from *The Crest-Jewel of Discrimination*):

"The knowledge that we are Brahman is like a fire which altogether consumes the thick forest of ignorance. When a man has realized his oneness with Brahman, how can he harbor any seed of death and rebirth? . . .

"Thus the wise man discriminates between the real and the unreal. His unsealed vision perceives the Real. He knows his own Atman to be pure indivisible consciousness. He is set free from ignorance, misery and the power of distraction. He enters directly into peace. . . .

"Those who echo borrowed teachings are not free from the world. But those who have attained *samadhi* by emerging the external universe, the sense-organs, the mind and the ego in the pure consciousness of the Atman—they alone are free from the world, with its bonds and snares. . . .

"If a man loves Brahman with an exclusive and steadfast devotion, he becomes Brahman. By thinking of nothing but the wasp, the cockroach is changed into a wasp."

(Sankaracharya, pp. 105–8)

November 6, 1968. Second audience with the Dalai Lama

We drove up earlier, at 8:30, a bright, clear morning. More people and more trucks on the road: army trucks roaring around the corners, ambling buffaloes, students on their way to school, and the Jubilee Bus Company's silver dragons. At the entry to the Dalai Lama's residence there were pilgrims, maybe *sadhakas*, with marigolds on their hats or in their hair.

Most of the audience was taken up with a discussion of epistemology, then of *samadhi*. In other words, "the mind." A lot of it, at first, was rather scholastic, starting with *sunyata* and the empirical existence of things known—the practical empirical existence of things grounded in *sunyata*—enhanced rather than lessened in a way. I tried to bring in something about *sila*, freedom, grace, gift, but Tenzin Geshe had some difficulty translating what I meant. Then we discussed various theories of knowledge, Tibetan and Western-Thomist. There is a controversy among Tibetans as to whether in order to know something one must know the *word for it* as well [as] apprehend the concept.

We got back to the question of meditation and *samadhi*. I said it was important for monks in the world to be living examples of the freedom and transformation of consciousness which meditation can give. The Dalai Lama then talked about *samadhi* in the sense of controlled concentration.

He demonstrated the sitting position for meditation which he said was essential. In the Tibetan meditation posture the right hand (discipline) is above the left (wisdom). In Zen it is the other way round. Then we got on to "concentrating on the mind." Other objects of concentration may be an object, an image, a name. But how does one concentrate on the mind itself? There is division: the I who concentrates . . . the mind as object of concentration . . . observing the concentration . . . all three one mind. He was very existential, I think, about the mind as "what is concentrated on."

It was a very lively conversation and I think we all enjoyed it. He certainly seemed to. I like the solidity of the Dalai Lama's ideas. He is a very consecutive thinker and moves from step to step. His ideas of the interior life are built on very solid foundations and on a real awareness of practical problems. He insists on detachment, on an "unworldly life," yet sees it as a way to complete understanding of, and participation in, the problems of life and the world. But renunciation and detachment must come first. Evidently he misses the full monastic life and wishes he had more time to meditate and study himself. At the end he invited us back again Friday to talk about Western monasticism. "And meanwhile think more about the mind," he said as we left him.

T. R. V. Murti on Tantra:

"Tantra is the unique combination of mantra, ritual, worship and yoga on an absolutistic basis. It is both philosophy and religion, and aims at the transmutation of human personality, by Tantric practices suited to the spiritual temperament and needs of the individual, into the absolute. . . . It is *sunyata* that provided the metaphysical basis for the rise of Tantra. With its phenomenalising aspect, *karuna* (corresponding to the Hindu concept of *sat*), the formless absolute (*sunya*) manifests itself as the concrete world. But the forms neither exhaust nor do they bring down the absolute. It is through these forms again that man ascends and finds his consummation with the universal principle."

(Murti, p. 109)

With a clear and sensible exposition like the above I am left musing on St. Irenaeus, St. Gregory of Nyssa, the catechesis of St. Cyril of Jerusalem, early Christian liturgy, baptism, and Eucharist as initiation into the *Pascha Christi* [the Passover of Christ]. And, of course, the influence of the mystery religions is important here.

For Marco Pallis, the Buddha icon "touching the earth" means Buddha's reply to Mara,[51] who disputes his right to the "throne" of enlightenment. Sitting on the earth under the bodhi tree, Mara asserts that the earth is "his," as does Satan in the temptation of Christ. Buddha "touched the Earth, mother of all creatures, calling on her to witness that the throne was his by right and the Earth testified that this was so."

Imagine [the Buddha seated on] a lotus on the waters—"existence with its teeming possibilities." (Cf. the baptism of Christ in the liturgy of January 13.) Buddha overcomes *samsara*, "not by mere denial but by showing forth its true nature." The Buddha's right hand points downward to touch the earth; the other hand supports a begging bowl—symbolizing acceptance of

51 Mara is the tempter, a spirit of evil who tried to divert the Buddha from his meditation on the path of truth.

the gift—grace. Pallis says, "In the two gestures displayed by the Buddha-image the whole programme of man's spiritual exigencies is summed up." An *active* attitude toward the world and a *passive* attitude toward heaven. The ignorant man does the opposite: he passively accepts the world and resists grace, gift, and heaven.[52]

Marco Pallis on grace in Buddhism:

"The word 'grace' corresponds to a whole dimension of spiritual experience; it is unthinkable that this should be absent from one of the great religions of the world.

"The function of grace . . . to condition man's homecoming to the center itself . . . which provides the incentive to start on the Way and the energy to face and overcome its many and various obstacles. Likewise grace is the welcoming hand into the center when man finds himself at long last on the brink of the great divide where all familiar human landmarks have disappeared."

(Pallis, p. 5)

Murti on Madhyamika:

Madhyamika does not oppose one thesis with another. It seeks the flaw both in thesis and in antithesis. It investigates the beginningless illusion that holds "views" to be true in so far as they appeal to us and when they appeal to us we argue that they are not "views" but absolute truth. All views are rejected for this reason. "The Madhyamika dialectic, unlike the Hegelian, is purely analytic in character. Criticism is Sunyata—the utter negation of thought as revelatory of the real."

"The death of thought is the birth of Prajna, knowledge devoid of distinction," i.e., intuition of the unconditioned. Absolute reality is not set over against empirical reality. The empirical, liberated from conventional thought forms, is identical with the absolute. "Transcendent to thought, the absolute is thoroughly immanent in experience." This is Madhyamika.

Madhyamika is critical of thought, open to experience. It accepts the phenomenalization of the absolute and knows this as twofold.

1) Avidya: through ignorance and defilements.

2) Prajna: "the free conscious assumption of phenomenal forms activated by *prajna* and *karuna*."

52 For this and the following quotes see Marco Pallis, "Is There Room for 'Grace' in Buddhism?" in *Studies in Comparative Religion*, August 1968, Pates Manor, Bedfont, Middlesex, England.

"The former is the unconscious activity of the ignorant, and the latter is that of the Enlightened Buddhas and Bodhisattvas."

Hence, not escape from the world into idealism, but the transformation of consciousness by a detached and compassionate acceptance of the empirical world in its interrelatedness. *To be part of this interrelatedness.*

(Murti, pp. 140–43)

After reading Murti on Madhyamika, a reflection on the unconscious content and inner contradiction of my own drama. There I was riding through Lower Dharamsala, up the mountain, through McLeod Ganj, in the Dalai Lama's jeep, wearing a snow-white Cistercian robe and black scapular. Smiles of all the Tibetans recognizing the jeep. *Namaste* gestures (palms raised together before the nose), stares of Indians. Am I part of it? Trying to fit into an interrelation, but on my own terms? Trying to find a dogmatic solution to this contradiction? Learning to accept the contradiction? One must, provisionally at least, experience all roles as slightly strange, ridiculous, contrived. Wearing my monastic habit because Marco Pallis strongly urged me to—and it is right, I guess, thoroughly expected. Yet recognizing that it is at odds with my own policy of *not* appearing as a monk, a priest, a cleric, in "the world." The role of "tourist" is less offensive. However, I have the feeling that everybody here knows all about everything and that as an "American lama" I am a joyful and acceptable portent to all the Tibetans. Smiles everywhere. Every Tibetan lights up, even when I am in no jeep, no habit, and only in corduroy pants and turtleneck jersey.

A drum in the village, with an erratic beat; and before, shrill, enthusiastic brass getting nowhere. Cries of children nearer the house. Light of setting sun on the brown mountainside. A long, quiet meditation.

Sankaracharya on the *atman*, *brahman*, and *maya* (*The Crest-Jewel of Discrimination*):

"Hold fast to the truth that you are the Atman. Give up identifying yourself with the ego, or any of the coverings. Remain completely indifferent to them, as though they were broken jars of clay. . . .

"This entire universe of which we speak and think is nothing but Brahman. Brahman dwells beyond the range of Maya. There is nothing else. Are jars, pots and vessels distinct from the clay of which they are made? Man drinks the wine of Maya, becomes deluded and begins to see things as separate from each other, so that he talks of 'you' and 'I.'"

(Sankaracharya, pp. 112–14)

November 7, 1968

The contemplative life must provide an area, a space of liberty, of silence, in which possibilities are allowed to surface and new choices—beyond routine choice—become manifest. It should create a new experience of time, not as stopgap, stillness, but as "*temps vierge*"[53]—not a blank to be filled or an untouched space to be conquered and violated, but a space which can enjoy its own potentialities and hopes—and its own presence to itself. One's *own* time. But not dominated by one's own ego and its demands. Hence open to others—*compassionate* time, rooted in the sense of common illusion and in criticism of it.

Marcuse has shown how mass culture tends to be anticulture—to stifle creative work by the sheer volume of what is "produced," or reproduced. In which case, poetry, for example, must start with an awareness of its contradiction and *use* it—as antipoetry—which freely draws on the material of superabundant nonsense at its disposal. One no longer has to parody, it is enough to quote—and feed back quotations into the mass consumption of pseudoculture.

The static created by the feedback of arguments or of cultural declarations—or of "art" into their own system—is enough to show the inner contradictions of the system. So Madhyamika shows the opponent the absurdity of his position "on principles and arguments accepted by him." However, when his supposed values are returned to him in irony, as static, he will not accept the implications. That is *his* problem.

Madhyamika does not propound "another truth." It is content to reduce "the opponent's position to absurdity on principles and consequences which the opponent himself would accept." If he does not in fact accept them in this form the logic of his position demands their acceptance. But then, argument is at an end. The purpose of Madhyamika is not to convince, but to explode the argument itself. Is this sadism? No, it is compassion! It exorcises the devil of dogmatism.

(Murti, pp. 145–46)

53 "*Temps vierge,*" French, literally, "virginal time." See Merton's *Conjectures of a Guilty Bystander* (p. 17 of the original Doubleday edition) for his use of the phrase *point vierge* to describe "the first chirps of the waking birds" at dawn.

Quoting from the *Kasyapaparivarta*, Murti points out that "*Sunyata* is the antidote for all dogmatic views, but him I call the incurable who takes *sunyata* itself as a theory."

(Murti, p. 164)

I asked Sonam Kazi about Marxism and monasticism, in view of my Bangkok talk. He said that as long as one is not attached to wealth and power, Communism can do him no harm. Sonam Kazi has often been the official interpreter in important meetings for the Dalai Lama, for instance at a dinner with Nehru and Chou En-lai. He probably knows as much as any one person about the whole Tibetan question, and he is by no means a reactionary about it. He has a definitely broad view, realizes to what extent the Tibetan landlords and abbots were wrong or shortsighted, and discounts stories about the Chinese poisoning lamas at banquets and so on. He was in Tibet in 1957 and spoke to various abbots of the big monasteries, asking what they expected to do. They had no idea, although the Chinese Communists were by that time right on their doorstep. The monasteries were too big and too rich. And too many monks who did not belong there were intent on holding onto their property until it was taken from them by force. The 13th Dalai Lama had foreseen this many years before and warned them, but his warning was not understood.

I had a fine visit with Chobgye Thicchen Rinpoche, a lama, mystic, and poet of the Sakyapa school, one of the best so far. Sonam says Chobgye Thicchen is very advanced in Tantrism and a great mystic. He even knows how to impart the technique of severing one's soul from the body. He taught this to another lama who was later captured by Communists. The lama, when he was being led off to prison camp, simply severed soul from body—pfft!—and that was the end of it. Liberation!

We talked first about *samadhi*, beginning with concentration on an object, then going beyond that to meditation without object and without concept. I asked a lot of questions about *bodhicitta*, Maitreya[54] and *karuna*. *Bodhicitta*, Thicchen said, is the most fundamental of these three concepts, which all center on love and compassion. He spoke of three kinds of *bodhicitta*: (1) "kingly"—in which one seeks spiritual power to save oneself and

54 Credited with the authorship of a number of treatises that form the basis for the Yogacara school of Mahayana Buddhism, Maitreya, whose name comes from the Sanskrit word for "friendly," is the *bodhisattva* expected to appear as another Buddha five thousand years after the death of Gautama, the historical Buddha.

then save others; (2) "that of boatman"—in which one ferries oneself together with others to salvation; (3) "that of shepherd"—in which one goes behind all the others and enters salvation last—and this is the most perfect.

Chobgye Thicchen quoted something from the founder of the Sakyapa school that went more or less like this:

If you are attached to worldly things, you are not a religious man.

If you are attached to appearances, you cannot meditate.

If you are attached to your own soul, you cannot have *bodhicitta*.

If you are attached to doctrines, you cannot reach the highest attainment.

He asked me to give an outline of Christian meditation and mysticism, which I did. He seemed very pleased and wrote a poem for me, and I wrote one for him. He also spoke of the need for good interpreters, Sonam Kazi being the best. He told of his experiences with a Polish lady he was instructing: with a good interpreter they went on famously; with a bad one she ended up asking things like, "How many little bowls of water are up there?" and he pointed to the shelf with his water offerings.

On the way down we met the Gadong oracle,[55] an old lama, and a former member of the Tibetan cabinet, an old man with a big brown beard, who had also formed part of a delegation that went to look for and identify the present Dalai Lama as a child.

The Dalai Lama's proper name is Gejong Tenzin Gyatso.

Sonam and I were looking at the stars. He said for Tibetans the Dolphin and Eagle go together as "the sling."

"Know the sufferings although there is nothing to know; relinquish the causes of misery although there is nothing to relinquish; be earnest in cessation although there is nothing to cease; practise the means of cessation though there is nothing to practise."[56]

The flower endeavoring
Of excess good will
Regards him the Sunshine
Making command of many learned.
To that beautiful one

55 Before the Chinese takeover of Tibet and his flight to India, this lama had been the medium for a spirit in a temple at Gadong, a small town west of Lhasa, and was frequently consulted by the leaders of the theocratic government of Tibet.

56 The Buddha, as quoted in the Dalai Lama's pamphlet *An Introduction to Buddhism* (New Delhi: Tibet House, 1965), 8.

Adored by all the Occident,
This bee wishes all the best
With its heartfelt delight.[57]

"People who make no mental effort, even if they remain in mountain retreats, are like animals hibernating in their holes, only accumulating causes for a descent into hell."

(Tibetan saying quoted by the Dalai Lama, pp. 15–16)

"Let us embrace the day which assigns each of us to his dwelling, which on our being rescued from here, and released from the snares of the world, restores us to paradise and the kingdom of heaven. . . ."[58]

I have to pack early. My last interview with the Dalai Lama will be in the morning, with the jeep coming for me at 8:15. Then right after dinner we leave by jeep for Pathankot to take the evening train for Delhi.

The sky is reddening behind the big spur of mountains to the east. The days here have been good ones. Plenty of time for reading and meditation, and some extraordinary encounters. So far my talks with Buddhists have been open and frank and there has been full communication on a really deep level. We seem to recognize in one another a certain depth of spiritual experience, and it is unquestionable. On this level I find in the Buddhists a deeper attainment and certitude than in Catholic contemplatives. On the other hand, in Catholics, such as the nuns at Loretto Motherhouse [Kentucky] and *a fortiori* the Redwoods [California], the *desire* is deep and genuine and so too is a certain attainment, even though it is much less articulate.

Nixon of course has won the presidential election. But Humphrey was closer than I expected. Wallace was nowhere, and I am glad to hear he did *not* take Kentucky (Nixon did). Our new president is depressing. What can one expect of him?

57 A free translation by Sonam Kazi of the poem by Chobgye Thicchen Rinpoche dedicated to Thomas Merton during his visit in Dharamsala.

58 St. Cyprian, *De Mortalitate*, Reading V, Second Nocturne, Octave of All Saints (November 8) in the Autumn Cistercian Breviary, which Merton had with him on his Asian journey; he stopped at various times during the day and night to pray the (canonical) Office.

November 8, 1968

My third interview with the Dalai Lama was in some ways the best. He asked a lot of questions about Western monastic life, particularly the vows, the rule of silence, the ascetic way, etc. But what concerned him most was:

1) Did the "vows" have any connection with a spiritual transmission or initiation?

2) Having made vows, did the monks continue to progress along a spiritual way, toward an eventual illumination, and what were the degrees of that progress? And supposing a monk died without having attained to perfect illumination? What ascetic methods were used to help purify the mind of passions? He is interested in the "mystical life," rather than in external observances.

And some incidental questions: What were the motives for the monks not eating meat? Did they drink alcoholic beverages? Did they have movies? And so on.

I asked him about the question of Marxism and monasticism, which is to be the topic of my Bangkok lecture. He said that from a certain point of view it was impossible for monks and Communists to get along, but that perhaps it should not be entirely impossible *if* Marxism meant *only* the establishment of an equitable economic and social structure. Also there was perhaps some truth in Marx's critique of religion in view of the fact that religious leaders had so consistently been hand in glove with secular power. Still, on the other hand, militant atheism did in fact strive to suppress all forms of religion, good or bad.

Finally, we got into a rather technical discussion of mind, whether as consciousness, *prajna* or *dhyana*, and the relation of *prajna* to *sunyata*. In the abstract, *prajna* and *sunyata* can be considered from a dialectic viewpoint, but not when *prajna* is seen as realization. The greatest error is to become attached to *sunyata* as if it were an object, an "absolute truth."

It was a very warm and cordial discussion and at the end I felt we had become very good friends and were somehow quite close to one another. I feel a great respect and fondness for him as a person and believe, too, that there is a real spiritual bond between us. He remarked that I was a "Catholic *geshe*," which, Harold said, was the highest possible praise from a Gelugpa, like an honorary doctorate!

November 11, 1968. Calcutta

Before coming to Calcutta, I spent the weekend in Delhi, arriving there before dawn from Pathankot. The afternoon before, a good jeep ride through the Kangra Valley to Pathankot. The mountains were covered with a pile of high clouds, blue under them. Trees. A river. Nurpur and a Mogul castle. Winding roads. Shady villages. Many buses. Flocks of sheep and goats.

In Delhi there were empty streets for the taxi. Wide avenues. Here and there campfires. People living in tents in front of government buildings.

I went to the Imperial Hotel, older, less expensive, and quieter than the Ashoka. A bath and tea and the newspaper; there are student riots in Benares, Rawalpindi, Amritsar, and a dozen other places.

The first thing I did after tea was to go to the 18th-century observatory, Jantar Mantar, with its endless abstract shapes and patterns. In a few minutes I had run out of film. In the afternoon, after too expensive a dinner at the Oberoi Intercontinental, which is shiny and American and depresses me, I drove out into the country with the Lhalungpas to see the Cambodian monk at the Ashoka Vihara. The temple there is an old mosque, small and tranquil. We sat on the floor and talked. The monk spoke of his visit to the U.S., where he had been impressed with Hollywood movies and the RCA building in New York. Then came out again into the sunlight, marigolds, garden, dog, dust, gate, road. Gutb Minar, the tall Moslem tower, rose nearby out of trees and half-ruined domes. The Moslem aspect of Delhi is arresting—but the tombs perplex one. Except the tomb of Sufi Nizamuddin—and the other burial places of poets around it, where poems are sung on the proper anniversary in September. I would have liked to wander quietly among them.

We heard some Urdu singing in the evening at the Moti Mahal Restaurant. We were tearing red chickens with teeth and fingers to the sound of drums and accordion and the civilized gestures, dialogue, complaints, and witticisms of the singers. The singing was accomplished, intelligent, sophisticated, and very human. It belonged to a better civilization; contrast that with the rock music in the Laguna where we stopped first on the way, and the live Muzak at the Oberoi Intercontinental—appalling! The place quickly became crowded. We had to leave so that others could get to the table. Then a wild taxi ride—the Sikh driver nearly killed three people and then got lost, couldn't find our hotel. We found it for him.

Sunday morning Lobsang Lhalungpa and Deki came and we drove out to a Moslem college, meeting the principal, et al. It seemed to be an alert and sound place. The principal spoke of the Islamic Institute at McGill and other places where he had studied.

There were snake charmers outside the Moslem college, but they had disappeared by the time we left.

After the visit to the Moslem college I said Mass in Holy Family Hospital, not in the chapel, as I at first expected, but in the room of James George, the Canadian High Commissioner, who had had a minor operation the day before. He sat cross-legged on the bed with his wife, their son and daughter on either side. Also there were the Lhalungpas, Kunga, the companion of Trungpa Rinpoche, who is staying at the High Commissioner's, and Harold Talbott, who served the Mass. Afterward we went to the Georges' and had lunch in their garden. Trungpa Rinpoche was there; he is hoping to meet the Karmapa Lama in Delhi.

Sunday morning I finished the notes for my Bangkok talk and sent them off and wrote to Fr. Flavian, asking if I might return through Europe. The cost of many stamps is breaking me! I had borrowed a typewriter from Commissioner George, and today Mrs. George and her son drove us at 5 to the Palam airport in the dark—and there drank coffee, asking questions about reincarnation.

Yesterday I also decided to write a newsletter, mostly about the Dalai Lama, Dharamsala, and all that. I sent it to Brother Patrick for mimeographing. Also sent my films to John Howard Griffin for processing, including a roll on Jantar Mantar—a fascinating place!

SONGS OF EXPERIENCE: INDIA, ONE
POEM AND PRAYER TO GOLDEN EXPENSIVE MOTHER OBEROI

O thou Mother Oberoi
Cross-eyed goddess of death
Showing your blue tongue
Dancing upon Shiva or someone
With sharks in front gas—
Tanks empty the ambassadors
Coming tonight they
Shine you up
You Intercon-
Tinental Mam-
Moth Mother Kali Con-
Crete Oberoi not yet
Stained with the greygreen
Aftermoss of the monsoons

And a big clean pool
(Shacks out front and kids
In the red flowers and
Goats) a big clean pool I say
With one American
General Motors type
Doing a slow breast-
Stroke in the chlorinated
Indigo water where no
Slate-blue buffalo has ever
Got wet
O thou merciful naked
Jumping millionaire
Rich in skeletons and buffets
You have taken
All our money away
Wearing a precious collar
Of men's heads
(Those blacks love you at night
In a trance of drums
Sitting with red headlights
Between their eyebrows)
With shacks out front
When kids are playing
With dusty asses
In scarlet flowers
While on your immaculate
Carpets all the am-
Bassadors from General Electric
Slowly chase their blue-haired wives
In high-heeled sneakers.

November 12, 1968

Returning to Calcutta, I have a completely new impression: greater respect for this vast, crumby city. There is a kind of nobility in its sordidness: the sheer *quantity* of everything. And in some ways the absence of all that the rich world regards as quality, except in the banks, the Governor's mansion, and the high prices in the Oberoi Grand. First, as we came in from the airport, I saw how many ponds there are along the roads, among the fields, and new, but already shabby, apartments. How many purple flowers in the ponds. How many lotuses. How many long brick walls painted with Communist slogans in Bengali, with powerful decorative effect. And again, all the cows and slate-blue buffaloes, twice as many as in Delhi. Then as we got into town, the sidewalk markets, the rickshaws, the fantastic and dowdy buildings, the tattered posters advertising Bengali movies. On Maniktala Main Road I saw no sign of Bramachari's Ashram,[59] which I am told has moved—no one seems to know where—and I can't find out.

Further and further into town. Buildings. Crowds. Rags. Dirt, laughter, torpor, movement. Calcutta is overwhelming: the elemental city, with no room left for masks. Only the naked truth of overpopulation, underemployment, hunger, disease, a mixture of great vitality and permanent exhaustion—but an exhaustion in which the vitality renews itself. How does it happen that the skinny men in bare feet trotting with rickshaws don't all drop dead? And maybe many do!

Before, when I was here first, I was too shocked; the trauma made me see the city as a big blur. Now I see detail, contrast, the infinite variety of light and shade. All the colors—though they are drab and obscure, they are colors. This is one of the greatest cities in the world, with a character completely its own, full of contrasts and yet *beyond* contrast. The vast noise of Calcutta seems somehow to be also a silence. There was a spectacular robbery on Sudder Street three weeks ago and it is a city of crime; somehow the crime gets lost in the sheer massive poverty and exhaustion—the innocence of despair. The place gives no impression of wickedness. For the masses of Calcutta, you dimly begin to think, there is no judgment. Only their misery. And instead of being judged, they are a judgment on the rest of the world. Yet curiously nonprophetic—nonaccusatory. Passive. Not exactly resentful. Not yet . . .

How long before it explodes? What will the explosion mean?

One imagines an enormous, elemental, thoughtless, confused violence like that of a sweeping storm of rain after a sultry summer day. Will it cleanse anything? Clear the air? Will the city simply go on stifling in its

59 A follower of the "messiah" Jagad-Bondhu, M. B. Bramachari was a monk from Calcutta whom Merton's Columbia classmate Seymour Freedgood had befriended when Bramachari came to the United States in the early 1930s. Merton wrote a personal tribute to Bramachari for a festschrift honoring him in October 1964, which was probably published in India. A typescript of the tribute is in the Merton archives at Bellarmine College, Louisville, Kentucky.

own steam? It breathes, sprawls, broods, sweats, moves, lies down, and gets up again.

"Exemploque pari furit omnis turba, suoque
Marte cadunt subiti per mutua vulnera fratres."
"The same madness raged through them all, and those
who had been brothers an hour before perished by wounds they gave each other."

(Ovid, *Metamorphoses III*)

[Edward] Conze deplores the "dragon's brood,"—the alphabet seed—the armed machinery rising out of the earth. It disturbs his meditation. I argue with Harold Talbott that the world is crazy, but he thinks this an extreme opinion.

November 12, 1968. Darjeeling

This is a much finer place than I expected—a king of places, full of Tibetans, prayer flags, high in mists, wonderful mountains, all hidden as we came up the wretched road along which there have been some seventy very bad landslides. We were held up an hour in Kurseong waiting for the worst stretch to open up again.

But from the plane which we took from Calcutta to Bagdogra, all the high mountains were visible above the clouds: Kanchenjunga nearest, and Everest several hundred miles away, tall with a black side, a stately mountain. And the lovely pointed one next to it. Directly below, it might have been Indiana as well as India. But we went over the Ganges. The ride from Bagdogra was long, through thick woods, then higher and higher into the clouds. Finally we came to the Windamere Hotel, the most pleasant place I have been to in India. We arrived, up a long flight of steps, out of breath, in the dark. Had tea. It is cold.

In the plane I read a good article on Michel Foucault—or fairly good, I did not agree with all the judgments—in *Encounter* and also began one by Raymond Aron[60] on de Gaulle and the Jews. In the morning, before the flight, I had several hours to read in the Oberoi Grand—and then was glad to get out of it.

60 Raymond Claude Ferdinand Aron is a French university professor and influential political journalist.

There was a white-robed, bearded, European Jesuit in the pharmacy at Kurseong. I said nothing. Bought some apple juice. Then some beer further up the road in a clean little Tibetan-run liquor store. I will probably go down again to the scholasticate at Kurseong, but much later. And to St. Joseph's College here also.

November 13, 1968. Darjeeling

The "Windermere"[61] is really named Windamere. And since "the disaster" the town has been short of electric power, so last night in the middle of dinner all the lights went out and we groped our way to the sitting room where there was firelight, then candlelight, then the too bright light of a Coleman lantern. The Windamere is too cenobitic. Everyone gets together and talks, or participates in a kind of common gathering, as do the three silent Englishmen who just drink beer and listen. A German family from East Pakistan are, I guess, the nicest. They have two pretty little children. Then there are the two girls from N'Orleans, one who works for a travel agency and the other for an airline, so they planned themselves a trip which included a stay on a houseboat in Kashmir and of course all the temples of Katmandu. They had shared the same ride with us up the mountain from Bagdogra, which took four hours with the delay at Kurseong.

Will we be able to get into Sikkim? I don't know. There was talk of this last night. The Sikh army major assured us the only way was to drive three hours to Siliguri and then ten hours roundabout to Gangtok. Another said there was a footbridge nearby and if a jeep would meet us at the other side . . . Harold has failed to contact Gangtok by phone and has sent a telegram.

I remained in bed until dawn rather than light a candle. No use trying to read by candlelight, and as I have a slight cold I thought I'd stay under the good blankets. As soon as it was a little light outside the window I got into my clothes and went out, up the hill to the temple on top with all its prayer flags and incense. The children meanwhile were chanting down at the Tibetan school—joyous, lusty chanting that fitted in with the mountains. And there was Kanchenjunga, dim in the dawn and in haze, not colored by the sun but dovelike in its blue-gray—a lovely sight but hard to photograph. I went back after breakfast when the light was better. The view of this mountain is incomparable. I need to go back for more.

61 Merton is playing here on Windermere, largest of the lakes in the Lake District of England, where Wordsworth spent nearly sixty years of his life and which so many other notable English poets celebrated in their poetry.

Seeing the Loreto College next to the hotel, I went to inquire about saying Mass. Mother Damian nearly swooned, then pulled herself together and sent me down to the Loreto Convent. There is no chapel at the college, it's a government school. I said Mass in the big, 19th-century English-type convent-school chapel: a few nuns on one side, a few little girls in uniform, hastily rounded up, on the other. It was about 10:15. Then coffee and talk with the sisters, who are mostly old, all in the regular habit. No experimenting with other clothes here! Two daughters of the Queen of Bhutan are in the convent school here and one of them has information about an interesting back-scratching fire demon that is in Bhutan. I have not met any of the students yet. I'm waiting to hear from the people at the Tibetan Center.

November 14, 1968

A friend took us to the Tibetan Refugee Center today and it seemed, relatively, a happy and busy place. This afternoon, Jimpa, a Tibetan monk who is teaching with the Jesuits, will come to talk about interpreting. Fr. Sherburne,[62] also.

"The self is not different from the states nor identical with them; there is no self without the states nor is it to be considered nonexistent."

[Nagarjuna]

CONVERSATIONS

Madam my action
Thankyo.
A little to one side
(Be my traum)

I am your Enrico
Don' you remembram?
Thankyo!
M-m-m-a-m.
Should we wait?

Madam it is my turn
I am your Enro.

(M-m-u-m-rico.)

62 Fr. Richard Sherburne, S.J., was at this time preparing a doctoral dissertation on an eleventh-century Indian source of later Gelugpa (Yellow Hat) meditational practice at Seattle University. When he met Merton in Darjeeling, he was studying Sanskrit and Tibetan in preparation for his work in Buddhist studies.

Do you forgat? Is Muttons?

I am your Traum

A little to one side

Thankyo.

"*Not too diplomatic!*"

Madam Mein Traum
Ready in a moment.

A little to one side

Thankyo
(M-action!)
You are my lifetime Pigeon
I am your dream of flight
Madam: my action
(To stop is a better mistake.)
Thankyo
(Sent from Enrico)
(Interception by T. Muttons)

"Reflective consciousness is necessarily the consciousness of the false."

"The essence of the Madhyamika attitude . . . consists in not allowing oneself to be entangled in views and theories, but just to observe the nature of things without standpoints."

(Murti, p. 213)

In Madhyamika, dialectical critique does not clear the way for something else such as Kant's *Practical Reason*, or the guarantee of God by faith. It is at once freedom and *tathata*—realization—not of God, in God. Negation and realization become one in the liberation from conceptual "answers about."

(Murti, p. 213)

"The Madhyamika method is to *de*conceptualize the mind and to disburden it of all notions, empirical as well as a priori. The dialectic is not an avenue for the acquisition of information, but a catharsis; it is primarily a path of purification of the intellect."

"It is the abolition of all restrictions which conceptual patterns necessarily impose. It is not nihilism, which is itself a standpoint asserting that nothing is. The dialectic is rejection of all views including the nihilistic."

(Murti, p. 112)

Our friend's jeep has pleasantly flowered covers over the seat cushions. She met us at the Loreto Convent, out in the sun on the wide terrace after Mass in the cold church. Nuns in black veils and some with shawls and mittens. A diamond jubilarian who sweetly complained that she "couldn't contemplate"; she put her head in the sacristy door to tell me this before Mass.

I said Mass in the spacious sanctuary, served by a middle-aged Nepalese called Peter. There were faint answers to the prayers from a few nuns and Indian women. I did not preach. After Mass, breakfast was plentiful. I was surrounded by nuns plying me with questions: Have the Trappists changed their rules? Their Office? Do they have recreation now? Do they have games? Do they speak? Five little girls filed in to look at me to reassure themselves that I could speak. I said I was still able to speak.

Before Mass, I had leafed through a book on Grenoble and the Alps of Dauphine in the convent parlor—curious to remember how I wanted to go there as a child. Nice mountains but a dull little city. The same points of interest, including the curious "ciborium" in the cathedral which I could never understand. Pictures of the Grand Chartreuse. That place is still able to stir me! La Salette, an ugly church. Maybe after all I shall go there: if I go to those Alps at all it will be because of La Salette.

Tibetan students who waylay you on the road above the Tibetan school and ask your address, inviting you to become their pen pal. I assure them I have more than enough pen pals already. Lusty chanting in the school after dawn when Kanchenjunga is full of light. I walked and said Lauds under the cryptomeria trees on Observatory Hill, and the chanting came up strong and clear from below. A man was doing vigorous exercises by the shelter that overlooks the valley. He had a mean white dog that pissed and scratched in the marigolds and then came over to me with the kind of electric tension and barely audible growl that a dog has when he is not afraid to bite. I continued my promenade in the direction of the hotel. The man was shimmying in the sun.

At the Tibetan Refugee Center there was a young nun with shaved head and a sweet smile who, I learned, went to work in the local carpet factory. She posed for a picture with three others who looked like old men. Also polite, bedraggled monks, in lay clothes, marked with all the signs of a hard frustrated life, working in a carpet factory. One is the dyemaker. He showed me his kettle for boiling green leaves and the weed he used.

Little kids in the crèche, some sweetly smiling and making the "*namaste*" gesture, others crying loudly. Babies bundled up in cribs, one silently lying with its arms in the shape of a cross, staring at the ceiling. In the distance a long line of little children went walking away in the warm sun, guided by teachers.

Women singing at work in the carpet factory. Spinners. Weavers. Dye mixers. In other shops: leatherworkers, carpenters, woodworkers, cooks. One cook was proudly stirring a stew of curry and potatoes in a huge black kettle. I bought a heavy, woolly, shaggy coat, something to wear while reading in the cold hotel. I have it on now. It is good and warm.

In the afternoon I visited with Fr. Stanford[63] at St. Joseph's School in North Point. Noise, kids, tea, wide grassless playgrounds, gardens, hyper-Gothic buildings, a big Victorian courtyard, crests, blazers, scarves, and all sorts of exhortations (*sursum corda* [Lift up your hearts]) to "the boys." Some were neat wide-eyed little kids, including a shy one from Bhutan, the only one I spoke to, and others with mod hairdos and perfect swaggers. Some of them looked like little bastards. Very much the Jesuit School! We got out as fast as we could. A Canadian Brother drove me back in a jeep through the cold town, the jeep loaded with students hitchhiking in to the movies.

November 15, 1968

It is the Feast of the Dedication of the Church of Gethsemani. I said Lauds of the feast on the side of Observatory Hill again, with the Tibetan kids chanting. And men came by, Tibetans, chanting softly to themselves. And a woman with a prayer wheel and a sweet little chant of her own. And an Indian jogging. And an old beggarwoman with no face left, one eye to see with, nose and mouth burned away, chanting, too, her tongue moving inside the hole in the scar tissue that served her for a mouth.

Conze comments on the fact that communication between East and West has not so far done much for philosophy. "So far European and particularly British philosophers have reacted by becoming more provincial than ever before."

(Conze [Buddhist Thought in India *(London, 1962)*], *p. 9)*

". . . the Madhyamika does not deny the real; he only denies *doctrines* about the real. For him, the real as transcendent to thought can be reached only by the denial of the determinations which systems of philosophy ascribe to it . . . His denial of the *views* of the real is not denial of the real, and he makes the denial of views—the dialectic itself—the means for realising the real."

(Murti, p. 218)

63 Fr. Maurice Stanford, S.J., a Canadian who had been an educator for many years in the Darjeeling district, at the time of Merton's visit was headmaster of St. Joseph's College in North Point.

Drove with Fr. Vincent Curmi[64] to the Mim Tea Estate—a marvelous drive. It is one of the places I had heard of indirectly long before coming to India because Gene Smith had spent some time in the little Tibetan *gompa* near there and the *gompa* to some extent is supported by the Tea Estate. I hope to make a little retreat at Mim at the beginning of next week, there is a guest cottage there. The drive was marvelous. Past Ghoom, and doubling back into the mountains, one goes down for several miles through jungle and cryptomeria trees on a very steep slope and finally comes out on the plantation, clinging to the slopes, with a magnificent view of Kanchenjunga—and of the hills gutted by landslides across the valley. Down in the bottom there is a place where a village was entirely destroyed. A thousand feet below Mim Tea Estate, a man in the valley shot a leopard. Why? Who was it harming? Goats perhaps. Or was it just going to lower and warmer places?

After we had some tea and saw the tea factory (good smell!) we climbed back into the hills to the *gompa*. A narrow path led among some cottages, then up into the trees and over to another spur. A very small, very poor little building, in a good spot, with a rusty corrugated iron roof. I don't know how they get thirty people into it, except that they are mostly kids. Drugpa Thugsey Rinpoche, the abbot, who was recommended to me by Sonam Kazi, was absent. The others spoke Nepali but did not have much to say. Most of the monks, kids, and students, are Nepalese. I went into the oratory which is dark and poor and not very heavily ornamented. But one got a sense of reality and spiritual power in there. We stopped briefly for tea in the *rinpoche*'s cell. It was very poor, with none of the usual decorations, only a picture of Nehru, an old calendar, etc. Again, a sense that something very real went on here, in spite of the poverty and squalor. There are people who come all the way from France to consult this *rinpoche*, including doctors.

November 16, 1968

We started out early on a cold morning, about 7:45, in our friend's jeep with Jimpa Rinpoche and a big picturesque Tibetan type as guide to find other *rinpoches*. Also, Fr. Sherburne and Harold Talbott. I was feeling the cold as we hurried up the road toward Ghoom. I've had a bad throat; it

64 Fr. Vincent Curmi, S.J., a French-Canadian Jesuit, pastor of Our Lady of Snows Church near North Point at the time of Merton's visit, had made a Nepali-language liturgy for his parishioners.

seems to be aggravated by the coal smoke that fills the air. We went looking first for Chatral Rinpoche at his hermitage above Ghoom. Two *chortens*, a small temple, some huts. In the temple there is a statue of Padma Sambhava which is decorated with Deki Lhalungpa's jewels. But I did not see it. Chatral Rinpoche was not there. We were told he was at an *ani gompa*, a nunnery, down the road, supervising the painting of a fresco in the oratory. So off we went toward Bagdogra and with some difficulty found the tiny nunnery—two or three cottages just down behind the parapet off the road—and there was Chatral, the greatest *rinpoche* I have met so far and a very impressive person.

Chatral looked like a vigorous old peasant in a Bhutanese jacket tied at the neck with thongs and a red woolen cap on his head. He had a week's growth of beard, bright eyes, a strong voice, and was very articulate, much more communicative than I expected. We had a fine talk and all through it Jimpa, the interpreter, laughed and said several times, "These are hermit questions. . . . This is another hermit question." We started talking about *dzogchen* and Nyingmapa meditation and "direct realization" and soon saw that we agreed very well. We must have talked for two hours or more, covering all sorts of ground, mostly around about the idea of *dzogchen*, but also taking in some points of Christian doctrine compared with Buddhist: *dharmakaya*—the Risen Christ, suffering, compassion for all creatures, motives for "helping others"—but all leading back to *dzogchen*, the ultimate emptiness, the unity of *sunyata* and *karuna*, going "beyond the *dharmakaya*" and "beyond God" to the ultimate perfect emptiness. He said he had meditated in solitude for thirty years or more and had not attained to perfect emptiness and I said I hadn't either.

The unspoken or half-spoken message of the talk was our complete understanding of each other as people who were somehow *on the edge* of great realization and knew it and were trying, somehow or other, to go out and get lost in it—and that it was a grace for us to meet one another. I wish I could see more of Chatral. He burst out and called me a *rangjung Sangay* (which apparently means a "natural Buddha") and said he had been named a *Sangay dorje*.[65] He wrote "*rangjung Sangay*" for me in Tibetan and said that when I entered the "great kingdom" and "the palace," then America and all

65 *Sangay* is Tibetan for "Buddha." *Dorje* is the Tibetan equivalent of the Sanskrit *vajra*—"adamantine" or "diamond," hence, "pure and indestructible." Thus, the term is an honorific accorded only to the most saintly or learned lamas.

that was in it would seem like nothing. He told me, seriously, that perhaps he and I would attain to complete Buddhahood in our next lives, perhaps even in this life, and the parting note was a kind of compact that we would both do our best to make it in *this* life. I was profoundly moved, because he is so obviously a great man, the true practitioner of *dzogchen*, the best of the Nyingmapa lamas, marked by complete simplicity and freedom. He was surprised at getting on so well with a Christian and at one point laughed and said, "There must be something wrong here!" If I were going to settle down with a Tibetan guru, I think Chatral would be the one I'd choose. But I don't know yet if that is what I'll be able to do—or whether I need to.

After that we drove on down to the Sakyapa monastery on the hillside right by the village of Ghoom. It has a nice, fresh painted temple. Monks were vigorously chopping wood on the terrace outside, under the flapping prayer flag, and we sat inside with the *rinpoche* whose name I forget—he is a friend of Jimpa's—a very Chinese-looking man with a long whispy beard. We talked a bit, though somewhat evasively, of mantras and *mudras*, and I told him about LSD. At this he said that realization had to come from discipline and not from pills. (He hadn't heard of psychedelic drugs.) Then we talked of meditation. Once again there was the usual reaction of pleased surprise at learning that meditation existed in the West, and he said, "You in the West have great potentiality for creation, but also for destruction." He gave us all scarves, photos were taken, and we visited the temple, which is quite beautiful inside.

When I got back to Darjeeling I had a very sore throat, so I sat in the sun on the hotel terrace most of the afternoon reading Murti. Then said Office in my room, as the chill of evening crept up the mountain. In the dusk I went out to get some throat lozenges and an inhaler and some brandy, which I have not yet opened. I kept waking up all night but the cold broke and this morning I felt better. I was plied with good American medicines by the Jesuits and their pills seemed fairly effective!

November 17, 1968

On being tired of Kanchenjunga. On the mountain being mercifully hidden by clouds. On sneaking a look at the mountain anyway before Mass. I walked the length of St. Joseph's College to sneak a look at the mountain, then turned away back to church. It was a long Mass, a concelebration with Fr. Curmi, an hour and ten minutes in Nepali, which meant of course that I just mumbled along in English during the Canon. But there was good singing—Nepalese music with drums and small bell-like cymbals. The women sitting in the pews in front were recollected and devout; the men were at the back. It was very moving. We went afterward to St. Joseph's for breakfast with the Jesuits. The librarian, an old Belgian with a neat white goatee, told me, "We have twenty-two of your books in the library." After we left the Jesuits a cold mist began blowing up out of the valleys—not comforting for my cold.

On being tired of blue domes. On objecting to pleasure domes. "Dear Mr. Khan, I take exception to that new dome. The one in Xanadu.[66] On being tired of icebergs 30,000 feet high."

The view of Natu-la-Pass, where the Chinese stand armed and ready, from the toilet of room 14 at the Windamere Hotel Private Limited. View of Tibet from a toilet. Tired of mountains and pleasure domes. On having a cold in the pleasure domes. Having to use a Vicks inhaler in Xanadu. On being overcharged by the druggist (chemist) for the Vicks inhaler. On being given Dristan Nasal Mist by a Jesuit.

By the blue dome of Raj Bhavan, outside the fences of course, I add my own small contribution of green phlegm to the gods of spit on the street. Note the bloody sputum of contemplatives and/or betel chewers.

Objection to the blue clouds of soft coal smoke rising from Darjeeling to aggravate my allergy.

On meeting the Czechs on Mall Road, near the part that is being repaired. Looking down, identifying the Tibetan Refugee Center from high above.

Little Tibetan children carrying bunches of marigolds. An Indian rides on a pony led by a boy. No reins. He holds a baby in his arms. He rides smiling past the mountain which has to be taken for granted. Today is Sunday also at Gethsemani, half around the world from here. No Sunday conference. No conferences for a long time. But I must talk to the Jesuits at St. Joseph's Friday and the Jesuits at Kurseong Sunday—to tell them that all that happens in the American Church is not exactly as presented in *Time*—such is the request.

Several times during the long silent ride in the Land Rover to the Mim Tea Estate today I wondered, "Why am I going there?" But I am glad to be here in this utterly quiet bungalow. The owners are out and won't be back until late. I have already refused dinner and asked for tea only, tea to be sent

66 See Samuel Taylor Coleridge's "Kubla Khan": "In Xanadu did Kubla Kahn / A stately pleasure-dome decree: / Where Alph, the sacred river, ran / Through caverns measureless to man / Down to a sunless sea."

to the bungalow. A fire is lit in the bungalow grate, and it is good. Hah! It is good. Fog hides the mountains. Fog gets in the sore throat. No matter. Fire and a variety of remedies and a big bed, with covers and fresh sheets turned back, awaits the tired *penseur* [thinker].

"Dear Father Merriton," said the note, "Please make yourself at home the moment you arrive and just ask the bearer for anything you may require." Without my having to ask, the generator went on, the lights began to work, tea was provided in the big comfortable drawing room. I escaped quickly to the bungalow, aside, apart, alone, silent. Fire lit. Books unpacked, including one on Japan by Ruth Benedict and also Anaïs Nin's *Under the Glass Bell*, which I hope to finish. Along with the Buddhist books I have to return to Harold Talbott, who remains in the Windamere where he reads wrapped in a blanket.

I'm glad I came here. All morning alone on the mountainside, in the warm sun, now overclouded. Plenty of time to think. Reassessment of this whole Indian experience in more critical terms. Too much movement. Too much "looking for" something: an answer, a vision, "something other." And this breeds illusion. Illusion that there *is* something else. Differentiation—the old splitting-up process that leads to mindlessness, instead of the mindfulness of seeing all-in-emptiness and not having to break it up against itself. Four legs good; two legs bad.

Hence the annoyance with Kanchenjunga, its big crude blush in the sunrise, outside my bungalow window at 5:45. What do I care for a 28,000-foot postcard when I have this bloody cold? All morning Kanchenjunga has been clouded over. Only rarely do you see the peak through the clouds, or one of the other surrounding peaks. Better that way. More modest. Really, Kanchenjunga, you are not to blame for all these Darjeeling hotels. But I think you know what I mean!

I am still not able fully to appreciate what this exposure to Asia has meant. There has been so much—and yet also so little. I have only been here a month! It seems a long time since Bangkok and even since Delhi and Dharamsala. Meeting the Dalai Lama and the various Tibetans, lamas or "enlightened" laymen, has been the most significant thing of all, especially in the way we were able to communicate with one another and share an essentially spiritual experience of "Buddhism" which is also somehow in harmony with Christianity.

On the other hand, though the Jesuits at St. Joseph's have repeatedly dropped hints about the need for contemplative Catholic foundations in

India, I do not get any impression of being called to come here and settle down. Certainly not in this "sensitive" border area where there would be constant problems with the government.

If I were to be a hermit in India it would have to mean something other than this comfortable bungalow! Something more like what Dom Le Saux (Swami Abhishiktananda) is doing.

Though I fully appreciate the many advantages of the hermitage at Gethsemani, I still have the feeling that the lack of quiet and the general turbulence there, external and internal, last summer are indications that I ought to move. And so far the best indications seem to point to Alaska or to the area around the Redwoods.

Another question: would this move be *temporary* or *permanent?* I do not think I ought to separate myself completely from Gethsemani, even while maintaining an official residence there, legally only. I suppose I ought eventually to end my days there. I do in many ways miss it. There is no problem of my wanting simply to "leave Gethsemani." It is my monastery and being away has helped me see it in perspective and love it more.

Now suppose some loon comes up to me and says, "Have you found the *real* Asia?" I am at a loss to know what one means by "the real Asia." It is *all* real as far as I can see. Though certainly a lot if it has been corrupted by the West. Neither Victorian Darjeeling nor the Kennedy-era Oberoi can be called *ideal* Asia. I remember Deki Lhalungpa laughing at the phony American minarets in the Taj dining room at the Oberoi. Still, that is Asia too.

Darjeeling is a quaintly fraudulent relic of something incredible. And the Indians, or the Nepalese, Sikkimese, and others around here, are still trying to believe in it, and maintain it. English hats, tweeds, walking sticks, old school ties (St. Joseph's)—for the rich ones at least. Shivering in the Windamere over Madhyamika dialectic—is that the "real Asia"? I have a definite feeling it is a waste of time—something I didn't need to do. However, if I have discovered I didn't need to do it, it has not been a waste of time.

This deep valley, the Mim Tea Estate, above Darjeeling: it is beautiful and quiet and it is right for Martin Hall, the manager, and his wife, who are in their own way hermits and appreciate my need for a couple of days of silence. Yet it has nothing I could not, essentially, have found at Needle Rock or Bear Harbor—nothing I did not find there last May. Or did I find an illusion of Asia that needed to be dissolved by experience? *Here*?

What *does* this valley have? Landslides. Hundreds of them. The mountains are terribly gashed, except where the forest is thick. Whole sections of tea plantations were carried away six weeks ago. And it is obviously going to be worse the next time there are really heavy rains. The place is a frightening example of *anicca*—"impermanence." A good place, therefore, to adjust one's perspectives. I find my mind rebelling against the landslides. I am distracted by reforestation projects and the other devices to *deny* them, *forbid* them. I want this all to be *permanent.* A permanent postcard for meditation, daydreams. The landslides are ironic and silent comments on the apparent permanence, the "eternal snows" of solid Kanchenjunga. And *political* instability. Over there, only a couple of hundred miles as the crow flies, is the Tibetan border where the Chinese armies are!

The sun is high, at the zenith. Clear soft sound of a temple bell far down in the valley. Voices of children near the cottages above me on the mountainside. The sun is warm. Everything falls into place. Nothing is to be decided; nor is "Asia" to be put in some category or other. There is nothing to be judged. But it must be cold for the lamas, at night, in their high, draughty little *gompas!*

". . . The roving gaze of the mariner who never attaches himself to what he sees, whose very glance is roving, floating, sailing on, who looks at every person and object with a sense of the enormous space around them, with a sense of the distance one can put between oneself and one's desires, the sense of the enormousness of the world and of the tides and currents that carry us onward."[67]

As the generator turns off and the lights go out at Mim Tea Estate the bearer brought me two candles and an ancient matchbox marked "Deer and Tiger Safety matches." A tiger is sneaking up on an unsuspecting stag as it drinks from a pool. On the back it says:

Price 6 P
Price 6 P
Price 6 P.

In it there are three ancient matches.

Mrs. Hall, solicitous about my cold, said I must have a fire in the bungalow after lunch because of the cold wind that starts punctually at 11 each morning and brings clouds of icy mist down over the plantation and valley. So I spent the afternoon in the bungalow. I finished Murti on Madhyamika, meditated, sometimes sleepily, and was entirely content. But the bungalow could have been anywhere. It could have been, just as well, my own

67 From Anaïs Nin's "The All-Seeing," in *Under a Glass Bell* (New York: Dutton, 1948).

hermitage at Gethsemani—only much quieter. Mrs. Hall saw to it that the bearer came in with "a proper tea." I only take lunch in the dining room. The rest in the bungalow, and have disconcerted them by wanting only soup for supper.

November 19, 1968. Mim Tea Estate

Last night I had a curious dream about Kanchenjunga. I was looking at the mountain and it was pure white, absolutely pure, especially the peaks that lie to the west. And I saw the pure beauty of their shape and outline, all in white. And I heard a voice saying—or got the clear idea of: "There is another side to the mountain." I realized that it was turned around and everything was lined up differently; I was seeing from the Tibetan side. This morning my quarrel with the mountain is ended. Not that it is a big love affair—but why get mad at a mountain? It is beautiful, chastely white in the morning sun—and right in view of the bungalow window.

There is another side of Kanchenjunga and of every mountain—the side that has never been photographed and turned into postcards. That is the only side worth seeing.

Out on the mountainside in the warm sun there is the sound of an ax where someone splits wood for fuel at the tea factory. Some children are playing in the same place high up on the edge of the woods. Far below, the lovely blue veil of a woman walking with children along a winding path through a tea garden. Reading the Commemorations of St. Elizabeth [Feast] in the Office made me want to read her life, study her holiness, her miracles. Will do this when I next have a chance. Thought of Sister Helen Elizabeth and St. Joseph's Infirmary in Louisville: the time I was there in 1950, already eighteen years ago! How everything has changed—*anicca!*

Later: I took three more photos of the mountain. An act of reconciliation? No, a camera cannot reconcile one with anything. Nor can it see a real mountain. The camera does not know what it takes: it captures materials with which you reconstruct not so much what you saw as what you thought you saw. Hence the best photography is aware, mindful, of illusion and uses illusion, permitting and encouraging it—especially unconscious and powerful illusions that are not normally admitted on the scene.

Nonviolent Himalayan bees: after one had lit on me quietly three times without stinging, I let it crawl on my head a while, picking up sweat for some eclectic and gentle honeycomb, or just picking up sweat for no reason. Another crawled on my hand and I studied it. Certainly a bee. I could not determine whether it was stingless, or just well behaved.

The three doors (they are one door).

1. The door of emptiness. Of no-where. Of no place for a self, which cannot be entered by a self. And therefore is of no use to someone who is going somewhere. Is it a door at all? The door of no-door.

2. The door without sign, without indicator, without information. Not particularized. Hence no one can say of it "This is *it!* This is *the door.*" It is not recognizable as a door. It is not led up to by other things pointing to it: "We are not it, but that is it—the door." No signs saying "Exit." No use looking for indications. Any door with a sign on it, any door that proclaims itself to be a door, is not the door. But do not look for a sign saying "Not-door." Or even "No Exit."

3. The door without wish. The undesired. The unplanned door. The door never expected. Never wanted. Not desirable as door. Not a joke, not a trap door. Not select. Not exclusive. Not for a few. Not for many. Not *for*. Door without aim. Door without end. Does not respond to a key—so do not imagine you have a key. Do not have your hopes on possession of the key.

There is no use asking for it. Yet you must ask. Who? For what? When you have asked for a list of all the doors, this one is not on the list. When you have asked the numbers of all the doors, this one is without a number. Do not be deceived into thinking this door is merely hard to find and difficult to open. When sought it fades. Recedes. Diminishes. Is nothing. There is no threshold. No footing. It is not empty space. It is neither this world nor another. It is not based on anything. Because it has no foundation, it is the end of sorrow. Nothing remains to be done. Therefore there is no threshold, no step, no advance, no recession, no entry, no nonentry. Such is the door that ends all doors; the unbuilt, the impossible, the undestroyed, through which all the fires go when they have "gone out."

Christ said, "I am the door." The nailed door. The cross, they nail the door shut with death. The resurrection: "You see, I am *not* a door." "Why do you look up to heaven?" *Attolite portas principes vestras.* [Lift up your gates, princes. (Psalm 23[24]:9)] For what? The King of Glory. *Ego sum ostium* [I am the door. (John 10:7)] I am the opening, the "shewing," the revelation, the door of light, the Light itself. "I am the Light," and the light is in the world from the beginning. (It seemed to be darkness.)

Lucernarium. [The time when the lamps are lighted.] The value of expecting the moment to light up the evening lamps. Here at the Tea Estate the generator goes on at 5 and off at 9. There is a period of about twenty minutes in which it is not easy to read in the bungalow, except right next to the window. But in the meantime a fire has been lighted. It flowers and speaks in the silent room. Prayer of fire! Agni [the god of fire]. Worshipful patterns of flame. Each fire is different. Each has its own particular shape. Then suddenly the porch light is on and so I switch on my own light, to write more. To write, among other things, a letter to Brother Patrick, to be mailed in Darjeeling when I return there tomorrow. I haven't heard from J. Laughlin since I got to Asia and he has three books I am wondering about. Apparently the book of poems, *Sensation Time at the Home*,[68] is being considered for publication next and I hear it has passed the censor. I must also send a card to Czeslaw Milosz. During tea I was thinking of the evening in San Francisco with him and his wife and Paul Jacobs and wife and the Ferrys. After dinner at a Chinese restaurant, when the Jacobs had left and "Ping" Ferry had got lost trying to find us after taking Mrs. Jacobs home, we sat for a couple of hours at a sidewalk cafe drinking wine, while an interminable line of Dixie tourists—Alabama, Tennessee—filed slowly by into a topless joint upstairs.

Kanchenjunga this afternoon. The clouds of the morning parted slightly and the mountain, the massif of attendant peaks, put on a great, slow, silent *dorje* dance of snow and mist, light and shadow, surface and sinew, sudden cloud towers spiraling up out of icy holes, blue expanses of half-revealed rock, peaks appearing and disappearing with the top of Kanchenjunga remaining the visible and constant president over the whole slow show. It went on for hours. Very stately and beautiful. Then toward evening the clouds cleared some more, except for a long apron of mist and shadow below the main peaks. There were a few discreet showings of whorehouse pink but most of it was shape and line and shadow and form. O Tantric Mother Mountain! Yin-yang palace of opposites in unity! Palace of *anicca*, impermanence and patience, solidity and nonbeing, existence and wisdom. A great *consent* to be and not-be, a compact to delude no one who does not first want to be deluded. The full beauty of the mountain is not seen until you too consent to the impossible paradox: it is and is not. When nothing more needs to be said, the smoke of ideas clears, the mountain is SEEN.

68 *Sensation Time at the Home* was a small collection of Merton's last shorter poems, which were not published separately, but were included as a section of *The Collected Poems* (New York: New Directions, 1977).

Testament of Kanchenjunga. Testament of fatherless old Melchizedek. Testament from before the time of oxen and sacrifice. Testament without Law. NEW Testament. Full circle! The sun sets in the East! The nuns at Loreto kept asking me, "Have you seen the snows?" Could they have been serious?

Conze says: "By atomizing society, modern civilization has thrown the mutual relations of people into a profound disorder from which it can be rescued only by conscious and sustained effort, and at the same time technical progress and the prestige of science have dimmed the immediate awareness of the spiritual world: Traditional religion saw these things quite differently. There the soul of man was regarded as essentially solitary, the true struggle took place in a condition of withdrawal from society, and the decisive victories were won in solitude, face to face with the deepest forces of reality itself. . . ."

(Conze, p. 81)

"True love requires contact with the truth, and the truth must be found in solitude. The ability to bear solitude, and to spend long stretches of time alone by oneself in quiet meditation, is therefore one of the more elementary qualifications for those who aspire towards selfless love."

(Conze, p. 85)

This is the chapter on Buddhist social virtues.[69] *Maitri*—friendly love—is not exclusive, it is rooted in truth rather than in passionate need. Compassion is proportionate to detachment; otherwise we use others for our own ends under the pretext of "love." Actually, we are dominated by illusion. Love that perpetuates the illusion does no good to others or to ourselves. Ultimately the illusion has to be destroyed by *prajna*, which is also one with perfect compassion (*karuna*).

My cold is still quite bad but I think that staying indoors with a fire this afternoon has helped it. Whatever may be the answer, or nonanswer, to my question, this is a good retreat and I appreciate the quiet more than I can say. This quiet, with time to read, study, meditate, and *not talk to anyone*, is something essential in my life.

---

69 Actually, the chapter (chap. 6) in Conze's *Buddhist Thought in India* is entitled "The Cultivation of the Social Emotions." The discussion of *maitri* ("friendliness") begins near the top of p. 82 in the Ann Arbor paperback edition.

Darjeeling.
And to dissolve the heaps. Afternoon lumber water filling can full
Taxi call kids. Sharp cries spread rev motor whisper pony feet
    Hoo! Hoo!
Motor going gone (hill)
Looking back her long hair shining pattern of crosses
    unionjacks
shadows on the walk (Hoo! Hoo! Ponyfeet)
Ponysaddle afternoon all rich god Ganesha fills his waterpot.
All to dissolve the lagers (layers) spreads of sounds—waters,
    boards, planks, plankfall fur, voice near, man holds basket of
    green leaves. Going. Gone.
Sensations neutral low degree burn (sun) warmskin. Hears a little
    water,
Again fills watercan the poor one—not rich Ganesha, he is gone in
scarf and glasses.
All come worship fun in the sun.
And to dissolve the fun. Worker basket empty and gone.
    Ganesha
gone in an
Oxblood muffler though not cold after good hot dinner
All come have fun dissolve values. Tibetan boss explains garden.
Layers of sounds hammer upon the ear spread selves away rich
roaring bark (spurs values) menaces bishop (Distances)
Image yards. Bogus is this freight!
Gate measure stransound gone taxi Water whumps in can and
fills softer, softer, gone of hearing.
Dog is crazy angry barkleap fighting any wires.
Gone basket of foliage
Bangs on an old bucket. *Inutile* [useless]!
Motorbike argues with some slops. Taxicry downhill in small
city. Outcry!
Disarms v. chords.
Image yards spread wide open
Eye tracks work their way everywhere.
Mountain winds can harm voice.
Sensation neutral low four o'clock tone is general. Must call
a nun on the telephone.

Two bad cheers for the small sun: burning a little
life sunstorm: is not yet overcloudy winter!
Send aid ideas to dissolve heaps—to spread their freight.

November 21, 1968

Anatomy of nice thought rot. No use isolating consciousness and then *feeding* it, exacerbating it. The ruse of nourishing the self with ideas of self-dissolution. The "perfectly safe" consciousness, put on a diet of select thoughts, poisons itself. The exposed consciousness is in less trouble. It relaxes. Is free in fresh air. Is perhaps a little dirtied—but normal or more normal. Less garbage. Select garbage, luxury garbage is the worst poison.

Man tortured by telephone (below thin floor). Cries louder and louder, until he screams high "hellos" that fly beyond Kanchenjunga. Gasps. Despairing cockcrows. Yelps. Hound yells. Pursues a distant fading voice. Over far wires speeds the crazed hound, pleading for help, challenging the victim to turn around and come back. Falls off the wire in despair. Telephone, chair, desk, office, whole hotel, all come crashing to the ground.

Wrote the card to Milosz this morning, sitting in hot sun. Cards to Sr. Thérèse Lentfoehr, John and Rena Niles, Tom Jerry Smith. Letter to Richard Chi. And one to Nyanaponika Thera.

Mass of the Presentation at Loreto Convent. I hoarsely uttered a homily. Voice gone. Cold still bad. Woke up several times in the night coughing. Double whiskies in the warm drawing room no help. The German Consul from Dacca had better luck with grog; we had a discussion and comparison of the respective value of Indian and German rum. His cold is better. As for me, in the long run I must conclude the Jesuit remedies have failed. As Mother Lucovina said, while I was eating breakfast after Mass, "It must run its course." The old deaf sister inquired whether my week had been consoling or if it had been "the mountain of myrrh."

My interest in Buddhism has disturbed some of the Catholics, clergy and religious. They wonder what there can be in it. I met the bishop in the dark, Gothic bishop's house last night, Eric Benjamin—he is Nepalese—very nice, a good bishop; alert, straight, concerned about his people and working hard for them, particularly since "the disaster." He hoped I would talk to the nuns, and plans are being made for this on Saturday.

There has been continuous firing all morning of an automatic rifle in the deep valley northeast of here. I looked down toward the sound. Tiny houses clinging to the slope. Further up I discern a quiet, isolated *gompa*. The shots are from some hidden lair of the army.

I finished Murti at Mim. Also all I intend to read of Conze's *Buddhist Thought in India*, and Dr. [T. Y.] Pemba's novel *Idols by the Path*. It is interesting, full of violence, but probably gives a fair idea of Tibet before and after the Chinese takeover. And of Tibetans in this part of India.

"And the ice and the upper radiance of snow are brilliant with timeless immunity from the flux and warmth of life. Overhead they transcend all life, all the soft, moist fire of the blood. So that a man must needs live under the radiance of his own negation."[70]

November 22, 1968. Darjeeling

When you begin each day by describing the look of the same mountain, you are living in the grip of delusion. Today the peak of Kanchenjunga was hidden by massive clouds, but the lower attendant peaks stood out all the more beautiful and noble in their own right. If Kanchenjunga were not there they would all be great mountains on their own. At the end of the line I noticed one that seemed to have had its top cut off, and as I had not noticed anything before I concluded that this beheading had taken place during the night.

When you begin each day by giving small Indian coins to Tibetan beggars with prayer wheels and to the old faceless lady from Lhasa, you are simply entrenching your own position in the wheel of birth and death.

We were admiring the Bhutanese swords and daggers at Dr. Pemba's house. Fr. Curmi was there, too. The beauty of a great heavy dagger. Mrs. Pemba said she had oiled it a little. I slid it back into its sheath. Pictures of Bhutan. Mrs. Pemba is Bhutanese, a wonderful person with a life and substantiality and strength such as one no longer sees in cities. Her laugh is marvelous; she explodes with delight over little things, and is full of humor. So is Pemba, who is more sophisticated. He is, I think, the first Tibetan M.D.—from Lhasa?—well, he practiced there, having trained at University College Hospital in London. He had a lot of tales about J. B. S. Haldane, whom he admires greatly.

Dr. Pemba admires Chatral Rinpoche, too. He says he is very humble. He laughs about Chatral's unconventional clothes. Chatral puts all the

70 See D. H. Lawrence's *Twilight in Italy* (New York: Viking, Compass Books, 1962), 6.

money he gets into building, improving, and ornamenting various *gompas* on the mountainsides around Ghoom.

Most interesting of all: there have been eight hermits making the three-year retreat at Chatral's place. They have just finished and eight others have started. There is a long waiting list. When we were there the other day one of the monks was laying the foundation for a new hermit cell.

Dr. Pemba was called in to attend to the ruined knee of one of the retreatants. He had gone into the long retreat with a bad knee and it had become progressively worse with a tubercular condition that by then was horrible. Yet he did not want to see a doctor because he feared he would be pulled out and sent to the hospital. He was within a few months of ending his retreat. Dr. Pemba asked him why he withdrew like this instead of going out and helping others, and he replied that everyone had a different thing to do; most people needed to help others, but some needed to seek a very rare attainment which could only be found in solitude. Such attainment was good not only for the monk himself but improved the whole world. Anyway Dr. Pemba fixed him up so he could finish his retreat. The hermits on retreat see no one but their master (who gives them something to meditate on each day) and the brother who brings them food. The life is now a "little easier" in the sense that they are allowed to leave their unheated cells and walk around in a courtyard, but without seeing anyone.

When we left Pemba's there were no lights on the pitch-dark steps and in the streets. A small Bhutanese servant boy lights our way down the long flight of steps to the road. Then we go on in the dark. Past the big old guild-hall-type place, now roaring and singing crazily with a movie going on inside. Big dark building afflicted with a disease, possessed by giant voices, amplified gunfire, and the flatulence of electronic symphony. Bam Bam Bam Ro-o-oar! A chest of pent-up Tibetan mountain demons booming in the night? No, nothing so respectable. No real thunders. Only a storm of jail-breaking Anzacs[71] running amok within the secure compass of four walls and a box office.

As we make our way through the dark, past the dimness of the Shangri-La Restaurant, through the emptiness of the big square, Fr. Curmi told of problems in his Nepalese parish: feuds, strains, and now two families ready to war with each other over a knocked-up teen-age girl.

71 Anzacs is an acronym for Australian and New Zealand Army Corps, the colloquial name for the soldiers from these countries who served in World War II.

November 24, 1968. The 24th Sunday after Pentecost

On Friday I said the Mass of St. Cecilia in the bishop's chapel. And yesterday the Mass of Our Lady, with the new Eucharistic prayer IV, in Latin, which is very fine. A quiet chapel with a Burma-teak altar. But this morning there was no one around, the bishop's house was locked up and I couldn't get in. I leave at 11:30 for Kurseong and may be able to say Mass at the Jesuit scholasticate there.

Under the entry porch at the bishop's house there are many flowers in pots and on stands. And two sets of red buffalo horns. The motorcycle is absent. The door is locked and though I press the white bell button five, six times, I never hear anything ring. I walk around to the back. The back door is locked. I start up the hill, soon meeting a young man who salutes me as if he knows me. Perhaps one of the seminarians I spoke to the other day. I ask him about somewhere to say Mass, but he doesn't seem to understand. I decide not to go down to the Loreto Convent, their chapel being also a parish church and indeed a cathedral, and arrangements made for Sunday Masses. Don't interfere. Wait till Kurseong.

Yesterday, a visit to Kalu Rinpoche at his hermit center at Sonada. He is a small, thin man with a strange concavity at the temples as if his skull had been pressed in by huge thumbs. Soft-spoken like all of them, he kept fingering his rosary, and patiently answered my many questions on the hermit retreat.

At first he was evasive about it and talked of Mahayana in general until he was apparently satisfied and said I had the "true Mahayana spirit." Then he went on in more detail. There are sixteen hermits, fifteen men and one woman, now in the three-year retreat at his place. They are not admitted to the retreat until after their fundamental monastic formation. They are examined by him on their capacity to undertake the retreat, and each case is decided on its own merits.

The three-year period is divided into various stages: first, one with a great deal of active praying, with many genuflections and prostrations and mantras counted in *lakhs* [100,000] on the rosary. Then prayers and prostrations before the Buddha image must be accompanied by meditation. They are in addition to the ordinary daily *puja* of the monks. The *puja* is done in private. The hermits do nothing in common. They see only their guru, the cook who dishes out their food, and the doctor, if they are ill. They use a Tibetan doctor for small things, a "modern" doctor for serious complaints.

During this active prayer there is much attention to taking refuge in the Buddha, the Dharma, and the Sangha. Renouncing all sin. Meditation on hell and death. An offering of unbloody sacrifice, a round silver dish (I saw one) full of barley and rice, representing the world and all good things in it, offered in praise and thanks. Emphasis on *compassion* and unselfishness. The hermit's retreat is not for his own salvation but for that of all sentient beings. Much contemplation of guardian deities, the nice ones and the terrible.

This initial period goes on for four months and is followed by another of proximate preparation for an initiation, after which the hermit spends about two years, the remainder of his retreat, in the higher *dzogchen* contemplation. The translation was not clear, but I think Karlu said that in this period there was more emphasis on contemplation of "terrifying deities." Jimpa Rinpoche, my translator, had by now become sensitive about the "terrifying deities" and tended to giggle when they were mentioned; so some things got lost in his translation.

The hermit's day begins about 2 or 3 A.M. He gets some tea about 5, a meal about 11. All go to collect their food, it is not brought secretly to their cells. At this time they see each other but don't talk probably. They can walk outside the cells. Is firewood provided?

Khempo Kalu Rinpoche invited me to come and make this hermit retreat at his place or, failing that, to write to him with my questions. That was very kind of him. With my reaction to this climate at its best and with the noise of the Indian radio in a cottage across the road from the hermitage, I guess it's still Alaska or California or Kentucky for me.

Kalu Rinpoche gave me three pictures of deities, printed in black and white outline, colored by him, quite touching.

Harold Talbott and I briefly discussed the possibility of getting Sonam Kazi or someone to set up a good Tibetan meditation center in America, perhaps in New Mexico, in some indirect connection with Christ in the Desert. Harold left this morning for Bagdogra, Calcutta, Delhi, and Dharamsala. He has been extremely helpful and generous; he paid my bill at the Windamere and shared all kinds of time, ideas, information, and help.

My cold is not yet cured. Because of it I'll be glad to get out of Darjeeling. The weather has been "perfect" these last days, but has not helped. It's one of the most stubborn colds I have ever had. I reflect that where I really caught it was Calcutta, and it was the same cold that landed Peter Dunne in the hospital after the Temple of Understanding Conference. I still have it, with a headache. I do not especially look forward to Kurseong where I am to talk to the Jesuit scholastics. I spoke at St. Joseph's, North Point, to the fathers and brothers, and at Loreto Convent to the communities of Loreto and Bethany. There were more Indians and Nepalese among the latter. I was consoled by the intent faces of the Nepalese who seemed to respond even more than all the others to what I tried to say about prayer. But they all responded and I got the impression of a great hunger for encouragement and instruction about the life of prayer and meditation. At St. Joseph's I talked about dialogue with Buddhists and many seemed interested, but I wonder if it was worthwhile, or if they were interested for the right reasons—hard to say.

After the Loreto talk I came back in the lightless streets. But there was some light from Victoria Hospital and some light from the new moon. Two women were screaming abuse at each other in the dark, in one of the "apartments." And two men on the road above listening with interest.

Harold and I had a farewell party, sitting in my room.

Have I failed in my solemn tourist duty of perpetual motion by not going to Kalimpong? Or even to the old Ghoom monastery, a "sight"? Not even getting out to take a photo of the shiny little new one just by the road to Darjeeling? To go to Kalimpong would take most of the day, now that the bridge is out, and one would have to spend the night there.

To go to Sikkim, I find, one needs a permit from Delhi—I am going to be smart and get one here in Darjeeling—and again it takes hours by roundabout roads to get there since "the disaster."

No answer from the Queen of Bhutan. ("Well you know," said our friend, "she has her family problems.")

No special interest, after all, in Katmandu. Literally everybody here seems to be either coming from Katmandu or going there. All the hippies at the Calcutta meeting were keyed up about it. The Mim Tea Estate, a couple of miles from the Nepal border, full of Nepalese, run by a Nepalese, seemed to me to be good enough as far as Nepal is concerned, at least this time. Maybe later in January?

My mind turns to Ceylon, Thailand, Indonesia. I want to see something else. I have seen the mountains and the *gompas*.

Out there this morning the Natu-la Pass stood out clear in the distance, and I have seen the road winding up to it out of Gangtok, in Sikkim. Hundreds of little children were running through the dirty main street of

Ghoom. Women were taking advantage of the sun to wash their hair. Sitting in the sun combing one another's hair. Or delousing the children.

Have I failed in my solemn duty as tourist by not taking a photo of a woman of Ghoom, sitting by the roadside, delousing the head of her eight-year-old son?

In Calcutta there has been a Marxist riot led by Maoist students. They burned [Robert] McNamara in effigy and set fire to buses. Tomorrow I will be there.

Kanchenjunga has been hidden for three days. I will probably not see it again.

Kurseong.

True, Kanchenjunga was hidden as we drove out from Darjeeling. The lower peaks were visible but the higher peak itself was lost in a great snow-cloud. Some of the blanks were visible in a dim room of shadow and snow. I looked back as we swung into Ghoom, and that was the end of it.

Outside of the window of a Jesuit scripture scholar's cell, which has been loaned to me for the night, there is a brilliant and somber fiery sunset amid low blue clouds. The scholasticate here at Kurseong is high up on the mountain and looks far out over the Ganges plain. The school has an excellent library. I wanted to dip into Fr. De Smet's thesis on the theological ideas in Sankaracharya, but did not get a chance. I read a few songs of Tukaram, the greatest Marathi poet, and some Sufis; there was no time for more.

Tukaram lived in Maharashtra (the region around Bombay) from 1598 to 1650—within two years of being an exact contemporary of Descartes. He was ordained by Chaitanya in a dream and began teaching. He was ordered by some brahmins to throw his books in the river. He did so and went into a seventeen-day fast and meditation, after which the river returned his books to him.

Said Mass in a private oratory during the afternoon of Sunday—better than Darjeeling.

Sankirtana is the Indian term for singing the names and exploits of the Lord in the company of the saints. "To join the Lord in his sports (*lilas*)."

In his preface to a book by the Abbé [Jules] Monchanin, a Frenchman who became a hermit on the banks of the sacred river Cauvery in South India, Pierre Emmanuel writes of vocation: *"Qu'est-ce qu'une vocation? Un* *appel, et une réponse. Cette définition ne nous tient pas quitte: concevoir l'appel de Dieu comme l'ordre exprès d'accomplir une tâche, certes ce n'est pas toujours faux, mais ce n'est vrai qu'après une longue élaboration intérieure où il arrive que rien de tel ne soit perçu. Il arrive aussi que l'ordre mûrisse avec l'être qui devra l'accomplir: qu'il soit en quelque sorte cet être même, parvenu à maturité. Enfin, mûrir peut être une mystérieuse façon de mourir, pour qu'avec la mort commence la tâche. . . . Il faut qu'il y ait un choix vertigineux, une déhiscence définitive par quoi se déchire la certitude qu'il a conquise d'être appelé. Ce qui—comme on dit, et le mot ici est juste—*consacre *une vocation et l'élève à la hauteur du sacrifice qu'elle devient, c'est une rupture avec l'ordre apparent de l'être, avec sa maturité formelle ou son efficacité visible.* [What is a vocation? A call and a response. This definition does not say everything: to conceive the call of God as an expressed order to carry out a task certainly is not always false, but it is only true after a long interior struggle in which it becomes obvious that no such constraint is apparent. It also happens that the order comes to maturity along with the one who must carry it out and that it becomes in some way this very being, who has now arrived at full maturity. Finally, the process of maturing can be a mysterious way of dying, provided that with death the task begins. . . . There has to be a dizzying choice, a definitive dehiscence (rupture) by which the certitude he has gained of being called is torn asunder. That which—as one says, and the word is rightly used here—*consecrates* a vocation and raises it to the height of the sacrifice which it becomes is a breaking with the apparent order of being, with its formal full development or its visible efficacy.]"[72]

I wanted to copy a few more lines from Pierre Emmanuel in the Kurseong scholasticate but some people came in to see me and I was occupied until 8:15, when I went down to the front door to get in the jeep and go down to the main road. There I was eventually picked up by the Mount Everest Taxis' car 291, which was full—only room for one man in the front seat—and moreover the driver was determined to get to Bagdogra without using gas. He coasted most of the way down the hill with the motor off, and in the end conked out fifty yards from the gate to the airport. We walked in. There are about two hours left until plane time (flight 224 to Calcutta). I sit in the relatively cool restaurant. Fans are going slowly. Army types are shouting in Bengali—or is it Hindi?

72 From Pierre Emmanuel's "*La Loi d'exode,*" preface to *De l'esthétique à la mystique* by Jules Monchanin (Paris: Casterman, 1967), 7–8.

A last sight of Kanchenjunga, bright and clear in the morning sun, appearing over the hills of Ghoom as I came out into the corridor with my bags. Good view from the front of the monastery. A surprise.

Kurseong has a big, cold, solid, Belgian-type Jesuit scholasticate. One gets the impression of a well-ordered and "fervent" community in the old style, a typically good Jesuit house in the familiar tradition. I talked about prayer and Job arguing with God, basically from notes I'd used in Alaska and California with quite a few added notions about a possible *Indian* contribution to a renewal of the Catholic theology of prayer. I also spoke of *bhakti* sacrifice, the contemplation of the Trinity and the *theological* idea of the Person. Many liked it, though some of the faculty may have misunderstood it, and a few of the questions were critical. The best of the Indian group, especially Fr. Cherian Curiyikad, the scripture man, and quite a few scholastics seemed much in favor. On the whole it was a good response.

I was in the room of Fr. Volkaert, another scripture scholar, whose Revised Standard Version of the Bible I borrowed for use in my lecture. I had a couple of talks with Fr. Louis Schillebeeckx, S.J., the brother of Fr. Edward Schillebeeckx, O.P. He has notes on prayer and on the Holy Spirit from the days when he was Magister Spiritus, and they are quite good. He is a contemplative. In his last words to me he urged me to see his brother in Nijmegen. It was a concelebration in English in a renovated chapel. "*Om*" was inscribed over the lectern.

Calcutta—"A-a-a-a-chya!"

It is a city I love. Flying out today was beautiful. I don't mean the bizarre, macabre beauty of the disintegrating slums, the old fallen splendor, but the subtle beauty of all the suburban ponds and groves, with men solemnly bathing in the early morning and white cranes standing lovely and still amid the lotuses and flying up in twos and threes against the fresh green of the coconut palms. Yet the city, too, its crumbling walls alive with Bengali inscriptions and palimpsests of old movie posters. And the occasional English spires, 18th-century domes—I do not tire of Calcutta. But perhaps it was only because I was there only a few hours; I stayed overnight in Bob Boylan's apartment and read all the mail that had piled up for me. There was one from Dom Leclercq, who is now in Delhi, at the Oberoi Intercontinental. He is going on to Tokyo. I wired him from the Calcutta airport. And contact prints had come from John Griffin of the photos I had taken at Dharamsala. The one of the Dalai Lama is especially good, also the one of

Khamtul Rinpoche, and the little *tulku* in his cell was very visible. Mother Myriam of the Redwoods writes that the commission of bishops to take care of contemplatives has been set up. Fr. Flavian says "Come home if you get sick." (This written before he received my request to prolong the trip!) Fr. Eudes is going to Rome. Fr. Chrysogonus is out on some commission. Naomi Burton is going ahead with the publication of *My Argument with the Gestapo* at Doubleday. She wants a preface by W. H. Auden or Robert Lowell, the poets. The *Time-Life* Bible with my piece in it is coming out after all,[73] so I will have some money. Dan Walsh has sent a big check for my travel fund. Most generous! Bob Lax says Emmett Williams wants some of my stuff for an anthology of concrete poetry. My talk at Bangkok is to be on December 10th; address: c/o Mission Étrangère le Pacis, 254 Silom Road.

I had a long wait in the airport talking to a man from Melbourne who had been to Rishikesh—and was disappointed—and who had been looking for lamas in Darjeeling. He had met a couple I did not know. He knows the Mouni Sadhu–Arthur Osborne set in Melbourne.

November 26, 1968. Madras

Flying into Madras is lovely. The city is all self-evident, spread out along the ocean with its vast beach, its harbor, its rivers, its broad avenues. Then the plane swings inland over the hot fields, neat, cultivated, green flat land. Many coconut palms. Many huts made of palm-leaf matting. Poor as they are, they weather much better than the somewhat pretentious "modern style" houses that are shiny and bright for a month and go black or gray-green in the first monsoon.

Madras is a bright and leisurely city. The people are less desperate than the Bengalis. It is more truly India than Delhi or Calcutta (whatever "truly India" might be—as if I were capable of knowing and defining it!).

Coming in, I spotted St. Thomas Mount—again bright, neat, self-evident. I have not yet seen the cathedral, which is probably confusing rather than evident.

"The discovery of a violently active star, the hottest known and apparently newly created, was reported by Leicester University scientists. The star is considered an important find for X-ray astronomy. . . ."

73 The *Time-Life* Bible did not materialize, but Merton's contribution to it, a long essay, was published as a book called *Opening the Bible* (Collegeville, MN: Liturgical Press, 1970).

"A snake weighing over two *maunds* [25 lbs. in Madras] and twenty-five feet long and two feet in diameter was caught by two villagers in the Buatnagar District of Nepal on Sunday. . . ."

"When the train was passing through a jungle area . . . he removed a hose pipe and brought the train to a halt. His accomplices hiding in the jungle came out and looted forty bags of peas. The guard and other crew were made to keep silent, being threatened with dire consequences. . . ."

"Ho Dons in front of us, my father on our trail behind us: what can you do now, tailless one?" (Tarzan)

"Butar—listen! If I untie you will you guide this Ben-ko while I battle your enemies on the gryf?"

Butar: "I will guide." (Tarzan)

(The Indian Express, *Madras*)

November 27, 1968. Madras

There is cholera in North Madras. And in many places in South India attacks are made on police stations or houses of merchants by gangs of Naxalites—presumably Maoist Communists.[74] Brutal killings in any case. Yet nothing can change the loveliness of this city of which I saw something last evening with Dr. Raghavan.[75] He came over from the university, where a Gandhi seminar is in progress. We had some tea and then drove around in the dusk. And then the dark of nightfall.

Today there is rain outside; it is one of the monsoon seasons here.

"Many hundreds and thousands of years ago, during an epoch, not yet definitely determined, of that period of the earth's history which geologists call the Tertiary period, most likely toward the end of it, a specially highly developed race of anthropoid apes lived somewhere in the tropical zone—probably on a great continent that has now sunk to the bottom of the Indian Ocean. Darwin has given us an approximate description of these ancestors

74 While some of the Naxalites may have been "Maoist Communists," as someone evidently characterized them to Merton, it does not appear certain that all of them were Communist organized.

75 Dr. V. Raghavan, professor emeritus of Sanskrit at the University of Madras, is one of the world's most eminent Sanskritists. Perhaps his most useful contribution for the general public was his *The Indian Heritage: An Anthology of Sanskrit Literature* (Bangalore: Indian Institute of Culture, 1956).

of ours. They are completely covered with hair, they had beards and pointed ears, and they lived in bands in the trees."

"Perfectly white cats with blue eyes are always, or almost always, deaf."[76]

Some important dates in history of the East India Company:

1639 Fort St. George, which became Madras.

1659 Fort William, a "factory," to become the city of Calcutta.

1661 The British acquire Bombay from Portugal.

1686 The Company is at war with Aurangzeb, the Mogul emperor.

We drove past Fort St. George in the shadows, with a large garden around it. Stairways and walls and windows and a steeple. The old East India Company headquarters. University of Madras—a long line of spanking new buildings on the sea front. Dr. Raghavan pointed out his office. The old law college is fantastic, a Saracenic Coney Island, but dignified.

The beach is the finest thing in Madras. There was a new moon and a strong, steady breeze off the water; people sitting in small scattered groups, cooling off in the dark. Hulls of fishing boats ("country boats") pulled up on the sand. A very wide beach. Dr. Raghavan and I watched the surf roll in and looked at the stars. He told me the names of some of the constellations in Sanskrit. The moon prevented our seeing the Southern Cross clearly.

Then we went to San Thomé. Smaller than I expected, the cathedral is in an entirely Christian quarter. Its architecture is standard 19th-century Gothic, spacious, full of the old-style statues, and over the chancel arch the words "Thomas, one of the twelve, called Didymus." I find the inscription strangely touching. I kneel for a while looking up to the shadows of the sanctuary where all is still as it was before the Council. Then we depart. An Indian Christian beggarwoman displays a dramatically spread-eagled sleeping baby on her lap. I give her a few *paise*. But Dr. Raghavan stands no nonsense from other beggars and is particularly severe with the ones in the Shaivite temple in Mylapore, not far from San Thomé. It is called Kapaleeswara, the temple of Shiva, whose goddess consort took the form of the peacock to worship him. Extraordinary life and seeming confusion of the temple, full of people milling around barefoot (I too) in the sand, children playing and yelling, dozens of shrines with different devotions going on—especially one with waving camphor torches for Ganesha, who

76 See Friedrich Engels, "The Part Played by Labour in the Transition from Ape to Men," in *Dialectics of Nature*, translated by Clemens Dutt (New York: International Publishers, 1940), 279, 282.

has a prominent well-lighted booth facing the entry. Less going on at the Shiva lingam which stands alone, half draped, black, heavy, tumescent. Other shrines and porches and halls. A group of women doing a *puja* of their own. And a group of Vedic scholars chanting the *Vedas* strongly in another place. Over it all the chant of ancient *Devaram* hymns in Tamil comes over a public address system. We trace the music to its source and find an affable temple singer, a friend of Dr. Raghavan's seated in a small cell before a microphone, accompanied by an acolyte with cymbals. Handsomeness of the Tamil chant. Then other shrines, and two dowdy peacocks in a big enclosure with iron railings. Finally out the back to the dark broad tank full of lotuses. This was my first real exposure to South Indian Hinduism. Very alive—especially the many young pilgrims dressed in black, as a sign of their vow to go to Sabarimalai, a holy place sacred to Ayyappan [Hindu deity] in the jungles of Kerala.

Mass this morning at St. Thomas Mount. I drove out there in pounding rain, the monsoon is running late here, and the car climbed the hill by a back way. Otherwise you go up a long flight of steps. I entered the little church and found the high altar prepared. It was delightful, a perfect hermitage, with a few Indian women and a couple of Italians—a priest and layman visiting their relative, the pastor. I said the Mass of St. Thomas, looking at the ancient gray carved stone that was found on the site. The altar is a sort of folk-art baroque, with a folk-type icon of the saint in a quasi-Franciscan tunic, being pierced by a spear. Then another folk-art-type Virgin and Child, garlanded by the faithful, ascribed to St. Luke, naturally, but obviously 17th or 18th century. The old pulpit was charming, too. A very lovely little church, so quiet, so isolated, so simple, so fresh. It stands on an abrupt hill overlooking an army camp and the airport. One of the nicest things I have found in India or anywhere. I felt my pilgrimage to it was a great grace. Next door there is a crèche for abandoned children, run by some Franciscan sisters. I saw the little dark-eyed babies, drank some lemonade, signed the visitors' book and escaped before the sisters could read it. More rain, and we drove on to Mahabalipuram.

I got Lawrence's *Twilight in Italy* in Darjeeling and now, here in Madras, a little way down Mount Road, a thin volume of his *Selected Poems* (edited by J. Reeves). I'm curious to read again after so many years his "Virgin Youth" when today I have seen the Shiva lingam at Mahabalipuram, standing black and alone at the edge of the ocean, washed by spray of great waves breaking on the rocks.

He stands like a lighthouse, a night churns
Round his base, his dark light rolls
Into darkness, and darkly returns.
Is he calling, the lone one? Is his deep
Silence full of summons?

There is no "problem," however, in the black lingam. It is washed by the sea, and the sea is woman: it is no void, no question. No English anguish about Mahabalipuram. How right the "lighthouse" stanza of Lawrence is, though, for this lingam on the rocky point! Night and sea are the same: so they are transferable. Lawrence's experience is convincing though his poetry is usually bad. Does *rasa* apply here? Not really. Something else perhaps. Too much mother, too many wrong words. I mean now in some of the other poems. ("But when I draw the scanty cloak of silence over my eyes . . .") Beautiful things in his prose, such as the two monks walking in a yard above Lago Maggiore, reminding me somehow of Kurseong. I forget where I read this—maybe while waiting in the room at Darjeeling, waiting to leave that Sunday morning.

Much more sophisticated than Lawrence is a love song of Vidyapati in which Radha complains that Krishna is a "country boy" and rough, and does not know the art of love. Yet she hears her ankle bells buzzing like bees.

This morning two Indian nuns gave away the secret of how to get to St. Thomas Mount. I had looked in vain in the phone book. Quite by chance I ran into them in the corridor by my room just as I was getting ready to leave. They were setting up a table of linens and purses to sell. They said they were of the same order as those at the Mount and one fished out a little address book with the phone number. When I came back late in the afternoon, they were tired and smiling, getting their things together. I asked if they had a good day and they said yes.

November 28, 1968. Madras

The trip to Mahabalipuram was fine. Especially the South Indian landscape under monsoon clouds. Dark green foliage, bright green paddy, thousands of tall palms, sheets of bright water, blue mountains in the south with fine shapes. I asked the Catholic driver if those were the mountains where Ramana Maharshi[77] had been. He said yes and smiled. Then the sea, and

77 Bhagavan Sri Ramana Maharshi (1879–1950) is one of the great Hindu saints and teachers of modern times in India. He has been accorded the title of "Bhagavan" by popular devotion, i.e., one of the supreme sages who are recognized as being "one with God."

the little thatched huts of the fishing villages. In a way all this was more charming than anything I had seen in India—more peaceful, more relaxed, better kept. Here one finally got some sense of what rural India might once have been.

Mahabalipuram is the remains of a culture such as I have not seen before. A complex of shrines carved out of, or built into, a great ancient rock formation—not cliffs but low rambling outcrops and boulders, smoothed and shaped by millions of years. Caves, porches, figures, steps, markings, lines of holes, gods and goddesses—but spread around without too much profusion.

I remember the black cat on the roof at Darjeeling, with two crazy little kittens playing and sliding on the green corrugated iron, and grabbing at her, tackling her while she stared at me fixedly, her tail slightly twitching. Cat on the kitchen roof, amid the coal smoke from the hotel chimney. The mountains and the deep valley and the big blue flowers, the view from the toilet window of room 14!

Bob Lax wants me to come to Greece. I still don't know if I can get to Europe at all. I looked today at the JAL, Air France, and Lufthansa schedules. Probably better *not* to try a direct flight—not that there is one really. But say, via Moscow? (JAL and then what?) Or come back through India. Bombay-Athens, Delhi-Athens, all reasonable. But not in May! Better perhaps Tokyo-Anchorage-Amsterdam. Then Switzerland-Athens, and then back to England for Wales, and Scotland. What about the letter from the man at Orval [Belgian abbey] about the old Grandmontine [hermit order] priory that is falling into ruins? . . . (At Puy near Chevier in the Indre.)

On personal Isvara, the only means of realization of *atman*. ". . . Steadfast devotion to a personal *isvara* who is but the highest expression of the Absolute, the crystallization of the formless. The personal *isvara*, in the fullest measure of his grace, reveals his highest nature which lies far beyond all predications and form, to that devotee who has merged his entire being in the Lord."[78]

A sense of silence and of space, at Mahabalipuram, of unpredictable views, of the palms and nearby sea. I would have liked to wander a long time

78 Source not yet identified.

among the rocks, but the kids selling postcards and trying to act as guides were a nuisance, so I moved on. To the beach, which is also admirable. Bright blue of the Bay of Bengal. A cool wind coming in strong off the sea. The shore temple, smaller than I expected, very weatherbeaten, but a real gem. It is especially interesting when seen in relation to the rest of the complex. And in relation to Sankara, a contemporary of this shrine, who lived at Kancheepuram, which I did not see.

Dr. Raghavan had had quite a bit to say about his guru, Sankaracharya of Kanchi, whom I have not met—he is traveling in the villages. I forgot I had read about him in Koestler's (bad) book *The Lotus and the Robot.* Rereading an excerpt—I find Sankaracharya saying: "Adaptations have no place in the standards of spiritual discipline."

Against shortening or changing the ancient rituals. No concessions to be made. One who cannot fulfill his obligations can somehow substitute by regret and repentance, but the obligations are not to be slackened. Koestler was bothered by this "unyielding attitude." Sankaracharya's views, he thought, "bore no relation to contemporaneity."

In the discourses of Sankaracharya of Kanchi (Raghavan gave me a book of them) I find great emphasis for instance on the *oral* tradition of the *Vedas* and the *exact* chanting of the Vedic texts—and the discipline of learning how to do so. His belief in the importance and efficacy of this. Also, his belief in strict ascetic and religious practice. "To the extent that we make sacrifices in performing acts which we sincerely believe to be good, to that extent will our soul, or *atman*, get elevated. Even acts done in ignorance, but with faith, will produce spiritual reward. The moment we begin to question why a particular religious practice should be observed . . . we are beginning to lose faith, or *bhakti*.

"When we perform with faith the prescribed *karmas* and *anushthanas* and dedicate them to God, as taught by the Vedas, we attain *jnana* which clears the way for God-realisation.

"If *sannyasins* are to take up a profession . . . they could not become *brahmanishtas,* persons with their minds fixed in the Paramatman which is their only avocation according to the Sastras [Shastras]."

Sannyasins, he adds, should not be grouped in associations (*sangha*). "Forming an association pulls down the *sannyasins* to the level of worldly men."

Sankaracharya of Kanchi interpreted the Adam and Eve story as a degradation of a Hindu philosophical idea. Atman (Adam) and Jiva (Eve). Jiva eats the fruit of the tree while Atman looks on. (Some interesting possibilities here: cf. my dialogue with Suzuki. Koestler dismisses the whole thing.)

Sankaracharya of Kanchi on the difference between hallucinations and mystic experience: hallucinations are temporary and due to lack of control. "They are caused by the wishes and fears of the ego. The mystic's mind is a blank, his experience is shapeless and without object."

By Hindu tradition, the *brahmachari* or student begs food for himself and his guru. This gives time for study, instead of work, and it instills into him "a sense of *vinaya* (discipline) without which no *vidya* (knowledge) can be received and can fructify in the mind.

Aardra darsanam: a *puja* to be performed at the conjunction of the full moon and the star Aardra in December-January. One bathes the images of Shiva in milk and sandal-[wood] paste in honor of Shiva and his dance, for everything that happens is his divine play.

A conversation last evening with Dr. Raghavan on *rasa* and Indian aesthetics. He spoke of the importance of suggestion to convey aesthetic implications which transcend ordinary speech. Poetry is not ordinary speech, nor is poetic experience ordinary experience. It is closer to religious experience. *Rasa* is above all *santa*: [tranquil] contemplative peace. We discussed the difference between aesthetic experience and religious experience: the aesthetic lasts only as long as the object is present. Religious knowledge does not require the presence of "an object." Once one has known *brahman* one's life is permanently transformed from within. I spoke of William Blake and his fourfold vision.

I visited the National Gallery and Government Museum this morning. Nice paintings of the Rajput, Mogul, and Kangra schools. What is the relation of painting to modes of music? Excellent bronzes. Some nice folk art. Musical instruments again—I seek them out especially. Such lovely shapes! A vina, sitars, temple drums, an arrangement of eighteen porcelain cups to be filled to different levels with water and lightly played with a stick of bamboo. Among the modern paintings—mostly Indian and third-rate—I spotted one which I thought was a very good imitation of Dufy. The card said Duffy. The signature said Dufy. There was also a not very good Gauguin. And a couple of standard Jamini Roys.

Surendranath Dasgupta on idealism:

The *Ahirbudhnya Samhita* is a post-Upanishadic work from the Vaishnava school of thought which deals with time and Isvara.

"Time is regarded as the element that combines the *prakriti* with the *purushas*." It is the instrument through which the spontaneous thought of Isvara acts. The power of God is not *physical* or mechanical; it is self-manifestation in thought movement that separates thought and object (mind substance) passing entirely into actuality without obstruction. It is creativity emerging in self-diremption from pure stillness, not as event but as pure consciousness. This self-diremption with power and object is *time* and all that is measured by time. The *brahman* perceived he would be many and thus he became many, in time. "Time is identified with the thought movement of God and is regarded as the first category of its inner movement, which is responsible not only for the creation of the cosmos but also of the colony of individual selves." It is without external cause.

Individuals are pure insofar as they are "in God" but involved in moral struggle insofar as they are "outside him," cut off by extraneous limits, but they must purify themselves of separative root tendencies. *Not, however, from matter.* Matter and spirit are two necessary poles in the dialectic.

November 29, 1968. Colombo

The follies of tourism. *Time* and tourism! The dissolution of one's touristic duty into incredibly long blank areas of time. Waiting in strange airports. Or in airline offices. Or in free buses from airports to hotels. The flight to Colombo was barely two hours, perhaps less. (I forgot to look.) But there were more than two hours of waiting before we started and we were almost an hour in the airport bus at Colombo. Some Poles had visa problems and eventually could not come with us. Yet it was cool in the Air Ceylon office in Madras, next to the hotel with the sea wind blowing in everywhere, and the faces at the airport were good, the chairs comfortable. I read large chunks of Lawrence's *Twilight in Italy* and found it boring, especially the bit about the amateur dramatics. It's not a good book, barely interesting, though occasionally he'll have an intuition that makes sense—such as, self and not-self. The "selfless" world of the machine. A good angle. Are we really heading for a kind of technological corruption of Buddhism? A secular *nirvana?*

The flight to Ceylon: flying smokes of hot, steamy, monsoon cloud and the flat gray-green coast of South India full of rain-ponds and lagoons.

Then India veered off blackly to the west, the sun went down, and presently the lights of Jaffna were under us. There are many flat islands along the Ceylon coast. Coming down into Colombo was lovely. We sailed in low over the harbor full of lighted ships.

"On the West the City of Columbo, so-called from a Tree the natives call Amba (which bears the mango fruit) growing in that place; but this never bare fruit but only leaves, which in their Language is Cola, and thence they call the Tree Colambo, which the Christians in honor of Columbus turned to Columbo."[79]

Driving into any Asian city at night is like driving into, say Flushing, Long Island—except for the coconut palms. Colombo, evidently, is cleaner and better ordered than any of the others I have seen so far: Bangkok, Delhi, Calcutta. (Madras is not bad.) Neat houses, open to the night air, with people sitting peacefully talking inside. Good shops. Gardens. Flowers in the dark. Flowers in lighted shops. Piles of fruit. As usual I am in Hotel Karma. My *karma*. Nineteen Twenties, British Rajkarma. The faded cream splendor of the Galle Face Hotel. Everywhere I run into it: the big empty rooms, carpeted stairs, slowly turning fans, mahogany floors, where once the Cantabs [Cambridge students] walked grandly in black tie (at night) or blazer and flannels (afternoon). And the music, too—now American—but still the same songs (names I forget) they played in the Thirties. Meaningless songs that still disturb some dark residue of sentiment somewhere in me, enough to embarrass me, but not much.

I ordered arrack [an alcoholic drink] in the Mascarella Room but the waiter told me, in horror, they could not carry it. "A wild crowd would come. There would be no respect for the hotel." My idea of the magic powers of arrack was thus confirmed. I drank some local rum, with profound sentiments of "respect for the hotel." As for the Mascarella Room, it could be any room in any college town, any bar and grill off any campus or in an Omaha hotel. The same dim lights, same tables, same people, same dancing. A local band, but straight American music, competent, brisk, minutes of quiet watching the moonlit sea, and discovered I was directly over the night club and the muffled noise of the band reached up through the pillow. I went right to sleep anyway.

79 From Robert Knox's *Historical Relation of Zeilon* (London, 1681; reissued, Colombo, 1958).

On the shore. A hot night. Warm, rubbery waves shining under the moon. It is just after the first quarter; Poya day [weekly holiday] was the day before. A new strange feeling out there—westward nothing until Africa. And out there—to the south, nothing til Antarctica. Wow! I was shocked to see Orion hanging almost upside down in the north. I still could not pick out the Southern Cross with assurance but think I saw some of it in the mist and moonlight in the south.

It is evening and again I have not done my duty as a sightseer. I went out onto Galle Face Green this morning (earlier two men were vigorously shadowboxing there), walked along the shore to "The Fort," that is to downtown Colombo, and found the place charming. I went to check my Singapore flight at Air Ceylon, then walked about the streets looking at the big old English buildings—banks, shipping offices, government offices, etc. A couple of shiny new buildings are there, too. But the clock-tower lighthouse right in the middle of town gives the place a curiously *West* Indian flavor for some reason. Big gardens around what I take to be the governor general's mansion. Everywhere there are police and military, very aggressive, with sharp fixed bayonets or machine guns even. Ed Rice had told me something of this but I had forgotten. There is a Post Office strike and I suppose they are there to prevent rioting, looking vicious and humorless as such types usually do. It's their business.

The King of Kandy, wrote Knox, has a palace like a labyrinth called "The Woodstock Bower," "with many turnings and windings and doors, he himself having contrived all these Buildings and the manner of them. . . . By means of these contrivances it is not easie [*sic*] to know in what part or place his Person is, neither doth he care they should. He has strong Watches day and night about his Court. . . . At night they all have their set places within the Court where they cannot one come to the speeche of the other. . . . There are also elephants which are appointed all night to stand and watch, lest there should be any Tumult; which if there should, could presently trample down a multitude."

I went into the old Anglican Church on the harbor front and prayed a little. It has a certain charm, built in Dutch times. Afterward I read some of the memorial tablets, curiously touching in their "eloquence," or in the simple visual quality of their lettering, especially the older ones in the back.

Then I went into the Taprobane Hotel and got a bottle of Ceylonese beer which turned out to be fairly good, better than Indian. I bought Elias Canetti's *Auto-da-Fé* at the Taprobane bookstand, anticipating future hours in airports.

There is little that is Oriental here—or little that I have seen that is so. I have not been to any Buddhist temples, but tried a couple of times, vainly, to contact Walpola Rahula at the Buddhist University. I went to the USIS office at Bob Boylan's suggestion and ended up having lunch with the director, Victor Stier,[80] at his house. Some talk with his child about the relative merits of various funnies. But the wife is the one who has seen Buz Sawyer in the international edition of the *Herald-Tribune.* Buz has been out of jail for some time. The Mexican mine problem is settled. A new adventure has begun. I am glad to hear of this evident progress.

I went back to the Taprobane in the evening only to find it hot, messy, full of drunks, and with an accordionist wandering among the tables playing "Danny Boy" and "Annie Laurie." A disaster. However, upstairs in the Harbor Room I got a (bad) dinner with a good view of the docks and lighted ships, so that I began to consider the idea of returning to India, if I return, by boat from Djakarta. Back at my own home, the Galle Face, I thought the Mascarella Room, though pretty awful, was a bit better and more decent than the Taprobane, at least the musical part of it! But here too the Ceylonese girl singer calls herself "Heather."

November 30, 1968. Kandy

Last night I did manage to contact Walpola Rahula by phone and plan to see him when I get back to Colombo on Tuesday. Today I took the early train to Kandy. Got here about 10:30. The trains in Ceylon are extraordinarily cheap. I paid only 6/55 for the three-hour journey, second class, and had a compartment ("For Clergy Only") all to myself, though expecting a bunch of *bhikkhus* to move in on me at any station. Six rupees are what a taxi might easily charge you just to get to the station. Actually, the taxi in Colombo was three, and the one in Kandy two. The latter was pure robbery; no distance at all from the hotel to the station. The views from the train were sometimes quite impressive: coconuts, rice, tea, bananas, bamboo, and mountains covered with jungle.

Now I find myself looking out the hotel window at an inexplicable English village church up against what might, but for a couple of coconut

80 Merton had had a letter of introduction to Victor Stier from their mutual friend, W. H. Ferry.

palms, be a Surrey hillside. But the breeze is cool and a letter was awaiting me from the German *bhikkhu*, Nyanaponika Thera. After dinner I went to him in his hermitage in the jungle. It is a very solid little house near a rest house for convalescing monks. One cave-dwelling monk was there convalescing; he looked seedy and harassed. But we went to see another cave hermit and his cave was reasonably tidy and comfortable, after having been suitably humanized by generations of hermits. It seemed perfectly dry. The front had been blocked off with a brick wall and a door. It was an attractive cave with slanting ceiling and floor, a ledge to sleep on, one to eat on, and a place for a small, simple shrine. It was roomy and I must say attractive. The tenant was a young German *bhikkhu* who recently completed his training at the same South Ceylon island monastery in a lake near Galle as Nyanaponika Thera. He is only temporarily there, occupying the place of another hermit who is on a trip to India.

Nyanaponika Thera is old now, in his sixties or perhaps seventies. Originally a German Jew, he became a Buddhist years ago. Now he lives as a hermit in the cottage once occupied by his master, also a German and now dead. He writes and is charged with a great deal of editorial work for the local Buddhist publishing outfit, which does some quite good things. He went to Europe last year and saw the Tibetans in Switzerland. (Rikon is near Winterthur which is near Zurich. Tossthal is the name of the locality.) His hermitage is in full jungle, in a reservation, but the jungle is right at the edge of Kandy so he is really not far from town. But it is very wild and quiet. We walked out on the brow of a hill where the jungle has been cleared a bit and there is a fine view of the peaks to the southwest and northwest. I hope my camera caught some of the enchanted beauty of this landscape! Ceylon is incomparable!

After that I saw a little temple, Gangaramaya, on the edge of the same jungle, but down below. There is a great Buddha carved out of a huge rock rising out of the earth, and a small temple built around it. Fascinating Ceylonese folk-type paintings on the walls and ceiling. And the Buddha figure, behind glass, still quite impressive, much more so than modern ones. This one must be about two hundred years old.

Later I visited Bishop Nanayakkara in the cathedral compound; built by Sylvestrines [monks], it was originally a monastery. The cathedral is fairly handsome in its 18th-century colonial sort of way. Bishop Nanayakkara is very progressive and we talked long about my idea of Buddhist dialogue and of a meditation monastery that would be open to Buddhism. He drove me up to the top of the hill looking down on Kandy—it is lighted up after nightfall—and continued to talk about the Church today and the problems of Christians. I think he sees the situation clearly—or in any event we agree.

Anything going to or coming from the King of Kandy is held sacred, says Knox, and the people move aside out of the way not only of the white flowers that he likes, when they are being brought to him, but also his dirty linens when they are taken to the lake to be laundered. "And when they are carried to washing, which is daily, all, even the greatest, rise up, as they come by, which is known by being carried on a hand heaved upwards, covered with a painted cloth." [Knox, *op. cit.*]

December 1, 1968

It is hardly like any December or Advent I have ever known! A clear, hot sky. Flowering trees. A hot day coming. I woke at the sound of many crows fighting in the air. Then the booming drum at the Temple of Buddha's Tooth. Now, the traffic of buses and a cool breeze sways the curtains. The jungle is very near, it comes right to the top of the city and is visible a bare hundred yards from this window. Yet I am on a very noisy corner as far as traffic is concerned!

December 2, 1968. Kandy

Yesterday much of my time was spent with the bishop, visiting the monastery of the Sylvestrines, a quiet place on a hillside amid tall palms, with pleasant cloister and chapel. There I met the retired bishop of Kandy, a jovial and deaf Italian with a long gray beard, Bishop Regno. He said he judged from my *Seven Storey Mountain* that I had been one of the "first hippies." "Oh! Oh! Oh!" he said with upraised hands, "All the whisky! All the cigarettes!" I reminded him that hippies had no interest in whisky and that they smoked pot, not cigarettes, but I don't think this penetrated the wall of deafness. In spite of which he urged me, since the world was going utterly mad, to write on the authority of the Pope. Then I saw the seminary, a large, roomy, shady place, where all the twelve dioceses of Ceylon send their candidates for training. A big Romanesque German-style church. When I came back in the evening for dinner and a talk to the seminarians, the *Alma [Mater] Redemptoris* [Loving Mother of the Redeemer] was sung rather faintly in Latin and Gregorian and I could not feel this was any more out of place then, say, English hymns!

The bishop then took me out to a village called Ibbagamuwa where there is an Anglican ashram on a coconut estate. It is the ashram of Brother Johan Devananda, a nice young Anglican priest. The official name of the place is Devasarana. Even the Ceylonese, as we approached the sign, had to read it out slowly the first time, syllable by syllable. The buildings are all very simple; in fact, they are nothing but the watchhouses, chicken runs, etc. that were there before. The chapel is in an open chicken house with a concrete floor. One sits on mats. The altar is a low table. The bronze lamps are Ceylonese. The Anglican bishop of Kurunegala was on retreat at the ashram and we spoke to him briefly. The atmosphere of the place is quiet, open, filled with concern for liturgical experiment and ecumenism, i.e., adaptation to a Buddhist type of spirituality. It is certainly "poor" and simple, a good example of what a monastic experiment in Asia should look like. There are no postulants at present, but an Anglican priest in the United States is waiting "enthusiastically" to come here. There were some postulants but they left. A few lay volunteers are helping and one of them brought us fresh green coconuts, of which we drank the sweet liquid before driving away.

A village on the way back: a movie house and a temple standing side by side at the foot of a huge rock, on the top of which a steel frame shows the outline of a Buddha figure. Apparently a giant statue is to be poured in concrete. I thought at first it must be an electric sign! I saw one elephant working with logs by the road on the way out, two on the way back. On the whole one sees fewer than I expected. (I saw none in India.) I hear they are slowly dying out.

A hot afternoon. I walked alone, glad to be alone, to the Kandy museum, a little up the road past the Temple of the Tooth. There are curious and delightful small things in the museum: ivories, lacquers, paintings, textiles, swords, bronzes, vessels, medical texts on strips of bark. The red-black-gold style of Kandyan painting I find very pleasing and the painted "ceremonial boards" are diverting. All essentially folk art, the paintings at least. The lacquers and ivories are very sophisticated. Fine carved ivory combs. There is a great sense of design in everything. Lovely lacquer boxes. Three especially fine lacquer jars from the Maldive Islands. The rest local. After that I walked a little by the lake in the cool breeze, thinking of my Advent sermon to be preached in the cathedral where I said the most crowded evening Mass.

December 3, 1968. Kandy

Heavy rain. A longer and louder drum continues in the Temple of the Tooth. It is pre–Poya day. My bags are packed and I am ready to leave, not sure whether or not the railroad is on strike, but everyone says it is not. (Ceylon was threatened with an almost general strike; the postal strike nearly turned into a bigger one, involving utilities, transportation and other public services. But now everyone says it is being settled.) Yesterday was spent entirely on a long trip to Dambulla and Polonnaruwa[81]—the most impressive things I have seen in Asia, and doubtless I would have liked Anuradhapura even better, but it was too far. I drove 186 miles in a car provided by the bishop. (The hired car rate of a rupee a mile would have been for me exorbitant.) On and off, since I have been here, there have been suggestions and queries about the possibility of a contemplative Christian monastery, a small foundation from Gethsemani or a hermitage. It needs some thought. I hope to write to Fr. Flavian about it. There is much to be said for the idea. Also, should I come back, after Indonesia? The only thing is that I don't want to get caught in endless talks and visits to novitiates and seminaries.

KANDY EXPRESS

Inward parcels
Outward parcels
(Chamber of Horrors?)
Lordly blue ponds.
Men standing in river pouring water over
themselves from beat-up pails.
Coconuts, bananas, everywhere.
A Baur & Co Manure Works (Kelaniya)
Grand Land Auction
Little boy in yellow suit too big hat walks
tracks with brother
Schoolgirls walk tracks
Everybody walks tracks.

81 Dambulla is one of the most important archaeological sites in Ceylon, about forty-five miles north of Kandy; it is an enormous black rock in which are five cave-temples with magnificent carvings dating to about the first century B.C. Polonnaruwa is an ancient ruined city in central Ceylon. It became a royal residence for the Sinhalese kings from the eighth to the twelfth centuries.

"Trespassers on the Railway will be prosecuted!"

2nd class on Kandy Express much more comfortable than plane—entire compartment to myself—plenty of room, air, see everything, etc.

Enderamulla

Tall girl in green—lovely walks on tracks.
Bhikkhu with umbrella walks tracks.
Please refrain from
Traveling on footboards
Keeping carriage doors open
They are dangerous practices

Ragama
Man selling papers chants like sutras
"Never drink cold water lest the souls in it be injured."

(Digha Nikaya)

Little boy in tall grass near tracks waves
back delightedly when I wave.

Straw i.e. palm-mat flags scarecrows (or scaredemons?) in paddy.

Train speeds gladly amid paddy and
coconut—saying "Mahinda, Mahindi, Mahinda!"

Buffaloes swimming, great muzzles
yawning up out of the green-brown water.

Great train monster—Buddhabuddha!
Sawing everything down to tea's smallest leaf.

High Blue mountains begin to show
their heads in distance.

Magelegoda. Buddha shrine on station platform.

"The people, pleased with one another and happy dancing
their children in their hands, dwelt with open doors!"

A white crane standing in sunny water
briefly shakes herself.
Another flies low over green paddy and alights.

Now the creeks are faster—begin to have rapids.
Hills. Irrigation tanks.

Ambepussa—slopes, tunnels, jungle.
Steep black rocks.

A lovely swift-flowing river with large sandbanks.
Jungle covered hills.

More coconut and paddy—bamboo and banana
Yellow robed bhikkhu walking away in coolgreen shadow

Far ahead—a big stone block of mountain
standing as monolithic as a fat lingam.
Polgahawela. (new station built—obviously
with endless delays)

Rambukkana.
A new side to the same mountain—it is two.
An interesting and massive shape.

White stupa in the midst of rice fields.
An enchanted dirt road winds (empty) into the hills.
Train slowly climbs.
Spear pointed peaks to the north.
Peaks everywhere—
Sweet cool smell of vegetation.
Tunnels.
Rock cluttered mountainsides.
Now we look down a hundred or two hundred feet
to paddy in the valley below.
Rock pools shaded by immense green leaves.
Longer and longer tunnels.
Deeper and deeper valleys.
Lovely pattern of terraced paddy
Waterfalls. White thatched houses far below.
Looking back—lingam from other side.
We have climbed the flank of it.
Ranges of peaks behind us. Deep valleys.
Two small boys with bundles on their heads
stand on path and watch train.
Black cliffs shine with water.
Small houses buried in masses of red flowers.
Kadugannawa.
Three pigeons sit motionless on the tile roof.
Men setting out rice seedlings.
First tea factory I've seen yet (about 1000 feet)
Others follow.
Man and dog walk quickly through paddy,
Fresh paddy set out in shallow water,
full of cloud reflections.
Women washing clothes in all the creeks.
We go faster—going down—the streams are with us,
rushing down the watershed to Kandy

(It is 10:30)
Tea set out everywhere in the shade of coconuts.
Women in a stream cover their breasts as train passes.

Graceful girl looks up at train, turns away, throws a bar of red soap in the grass, takes bucket and stands in stream, pours water suddenly over her head once—then moves out and does it again and again rapidly, vigorously. Her wet shift clings to her body. She is very beautiful—in her gestures. Little boy comes to stream with a tiny puppy and a string. Ties one end of string to puppy's neck, tethers him safely on the bank, goes to wash.

Girl is beautifully cool and wet.
Boy flings clods of earth at tethered cow.
Woman scrubs another woman's back.
Bathers and launderers everywhere.

Peradeniya Junction. Kandy soon.

New white houses
Shady gardens
Red earth
We come to Kandy.

University in valley
Stupa on mountainside
Temple on a ridge
Radio tower on the top.

On August 3, 1858, Sir Henry Ward cut the first sod for the railway line from Colombo to Kandy and forever ended a long drawn out discussion which had gone on for about 40 years

about a proposed railway connection to the hills.
Picks up spade, ends controversy

I now ride in car number 6700 (2nd class)
Amid the wet shadows of massive plantations
and cocoa trees.

Do not block corridors.
Proceed from talk to action.
"I am afraid, I am afraid of silence,"
Said the Vicar General,
"I was afraid of those Trappists."
Dark night of the soul:
"I too am disgusted:
But how avoid illusion?"

What if the mind becomes one-pointed
And the "one point" is then removed?

Return journey—heavy rains—a line of red oil barrels—a crow flies down onto the rainy station platform—dances awkwardly along the edge, investigates a very wet sheet of newspaper. He tries to pick it up. It falls apart. He flies up again into the rain.

At the place where the girls were bathing the river is now red and swollen with up-country storms. Rain falls—no human being is to be seen.

The mountains are all buried in rain-mist. The valleys are full of it. The shadows of palms rise up in it near at hand, then vanish in the clatter of a black cut full of ferns and cobras.

Sanghamitta Poya. Full moon Poya day of Unduwap (December 4) marks anniversary of establishment of bhikkhuism in Ceylon at Anuradhapura, by Arhat Theri Sanghamitta. 245 B.C.

Rattling down the mountain the Kandy Express sings
Tsongkapa, Tsongkapa, Tsongkapa . . .
Praise of Yellow Hats.
Mirigama East.
Pink orchids among coconuts.
Veyangoda.

That which grew slowly toward me Friday
Flies rapidly away from me Tuesday.
I have seen that buffalo before
I have seen that boy before.

No man twice crosses the same river.

I have seen that felled coconut trunk before.

We rush blindly
In a runaway train
Through the great estates
Headlong to the sea.
That same sea which Queen Victoria
By a miracle of steam
Changed into sodawater.

Promotion of the essentials of religion is possible in many ways. "The root is this: guarding one's speech, so that neither praising one's own sect nor blaming other sects should take place . . . or that it should be moderate. Other sects ought to be duly honored in every case.

"If one is acting thus, he is both promoting his own sect and benefiting other sects. . . .

"Therefore concord alone is meritorious, that they should both hear and obey each other's morals. . . ."

(—*12th Rock Edict of Ashoka*)

> "Here no living being must be killed or sacrificed
> And no festival meeting must be held
> For King Devanampriya Pryadarsin saw much evil in festival meetings. . . ."

(—*1st Rock Edict of Ashoka*)

December 4, 1968. Colombo

Today I fly to Singapore and the long day of sitting around has begun. I moved out of room 208, in the Galle Face, at 11:15 to pay my bill and wait for the Air Ceylon bus, promised at 11:45. At 11:55 a pretty Air Ceylon hostess tells me the bus will be at 12:30. So I open up the bag again.

Outside on Galle Face Green the kites rise and dip in the strong sea wind—wild and happy Asian kites—two like big black disheveled and long-legged birds that flap and jump in the wind. Others with long spotted tails twist in the air like freckled dragons or serpents. Others have unidentifiable shapes. Asia is a kite-loving continent; there were wrecks of small Tibetan boys' kites on all the roofs and wires of Darjeeling.

BUZ SAWYER

(A whole new scene in the Paris *Herald-Tribune* of December 2)

Mr. Sawyer, here's Mr. Price, U.S. Treasury Department.
Yes I'm interested in the kind of plants and flowers grown on the Butterfly Ranch.
Now here's an aerial survey. Did you get a good look at the flowers in the center?
No I landed on the side.
Or these tall plants growing at the upper end?
No, why, are you a botanist?
Confidentially, he's from the Bureau of Narcotics.

Do you understand? "Tall plants"?
Mr. Tallplants are you growing narcotics on your rancho?

No I landed only yesterday on the butterfly.
But confidentially: take a look at this flower. What do you sniff?
Yes, it is growing immense at the upper end!
There must be something growing here Mr. Rancho!
I agree: and I give you full control of the department.
None too soon. There are criminals everywhere;
Fortunately there are also folks like ourselves.
Viva Mister Sawyer!

(After his visit with Hunter Rockwell, Rex Morgan returns home to find Keith already there.)

De Gaulle's gold flows back—New clashes along the Jordan River—New fears grip Italy—Scientist probes riddle of night lights and babies (major breakthrough in improving the reliability of the rhythm method of birth control).

"Dr. Duvan said the idea of night lights came to him during research on the effects of moonlight . . . on the breeding habits of certain marine animals, chickens and rats. Sea urchins apparently had their sexual cycles 'entrained' by the cycles of the moon, he said. Thus at full moon the ovaries of sea urchins are unusually large in size."

Smiling boy died from poison.

Week-long *Koran* reading contest will be telecast from the Herdeka Stadium, Kuala Lumpur.

"A soldier who pleaded guilty to causing hurt to ten children by rashly discharging his shotgun was told by a magistrate today, 'This is a rash action on your part . . .' The incident occurred when Private Ho Ngen, of the crow eradication team, was on his rounds in L. Sorong 3, Geylang . . ."

I remember the Moslems' sunset gun going off in Kandy and shaking the bishop's house. And the evening I returned from Polonnaruwa the gun went off as I stepped out of the car and a thousand crows flew up into the rain by the Temple of the Tooth.

Polonnaruwa was such an experience that I could not write hastily of it and cannot write now, or not at all adequately. Perhaps I have spoiled it by trying to talk of it at a dinner party, or to casual acquaintances. Yet when I spoke about it to Walpola Rahula at the Buddhist University, I think the idea got across and he said, "Those who carved those statues were not ordinary men."

I visited Polonnaruwa on Monday. Today is Thursday. Heavy rain in Kandy, and on all the valleys and paddy land and jungle and teak and rubber as we go down to the eastern plains. ("We" is the bishop's driver and the vicar general of the Kandy diocese, a Celonese Sylvestrine with a Dutch name.) By Dambulla the rain has almost stopped. The nobility and formality of an ancient, moustachioed guide who presents himself under a bo tree. We start up the long sweep of black rock, the vicar general lagging behind, complaining that he dislikes "paganism," telling me I will get much better photos somewhere else, and saying they are all out to cheat me. ("They" being especially the *bhikkhus*.) Over to the east the black rock of Sigiriya stands up in the distant rain. We do not go there. What I want to see is Polonnaruwa. The high round rock of Dambulla is also quiet, sacred. The landscape is good: miles of scrub, distant "tanks" (artificial lakes dating back to the Middle Ages), distant mountains, abrupt, blue, heads hidden in rain clouds.

At the cave *vihara* of Dambulla, an undistinguished cloisterlike porch fronts the line of caves. The caves are dark. The dirt of the cave floors under bare feet is not quite damp, not quite dry. Dark. The old man has two small candles. He holds them up. I discover that I am right up against an enormous reclining Buddha, somewhere around the knee. Curious effect of big gold Buddha lying down in the dark. I glimpse a few frescoes but those in this first cave are not so exciting. Later, some good ones, but hard to see. The guide is not interested in the frescoes, which are good, only in the rank of Buddhas, which are not good. Lines of stone and sandalwood Buddhas sit and guard the frescoes. The Buddhas in the frescoes are lovely. Frescoes all over the walls and roof of the cave. Scenes. Histories. Myths. Monsters. "Cutting, cutting," says the guide, who consents to show a scene he regards as worthwhile: now sinners being chopped up in hell, now Tamils being chopped up in war. And suddenly I recognize an intent, gold-faced, mad-eyed, black-bearded Celonese king I had previously met on a postcard. It is a wood sculpture, painted. Some nice primitive fish were swimming on the ceiling, following a line of water in the rock.

Polonnaruwa with its vast area under trees. Fences. Few people. No beggars. A dirt road. Lost. Then we find Gal Vihara and the other monastic complex stupas. Cells. Distant mountains, like Yucatan.

The path dips down to Gal Vihara: a wide, quiet hollow, surrounded with trees. A low outcrop of rock, with a cave cut into it, and beside the cave a big seated Buddha on the left, a reclining Buddha on the right, and Ananda,[82] I guess, standing by the head of the reclining Buddha. In the cave, another seated Buddha. The vicar general, shying away from "paganism," hangs back and sits under a tree reading the guidebook. I am able to approach the Buddhas barefoot and undisturbed, my feet in wet grass, wet sand. Then the silence of the extraordinary faces. The great smiles. Huge and yet subtle. Filled with every possibility, questioning nothing, knowing everything, rejecting nothing, the peace not of emotional resignation but of Madhyamika, of *sunyata*, that has seen through every question without trying to discredit anyone or anything—*without refutation*—without establishing some other argument. For the doctrinaire, the mind that needs well-established positions, such peace, such silence, can be frightening. I was knocked over with a rush of relief and thankfulness at the *obvious* clarity of the figures, the clarity and fluidity of shape and line, the design of the monumental bodies composed into the rock shape and landscape, figure, rock and tree. And the sweep of bare rock sloping away on the other side of the hollow, where you can go back and see different aspects of the figures.

Looking at these figures I was suddenly, almost forcibly, jerked clean out of the habitual, half-tied vision of things, and an inner clearness, clarity, as if exploding from the rocks themselves, became evident and obvious. The queer *evidence* of the reclining figure, the smile, the sad smile of Ananda standing with arms folded (much more "imperative" than Da Vinci's Mona Lisa because completely simple and straightforward). The thing about all this is that there is no puzzle, no problem, and really no "mystery." All problems are resolved and everything is clear, simply because what matters is clear. The rock, all matter, all life, is charged with *dharmakaya*—everything is emptiness and everything is compassion. I don't know when in my life I have ever had such a sense of beauty and spiritual validity running together in one aesthetic illumination. Surely, with Mahabalipuram and Polonnaruwa my Asian pilgrimage has come clear and purified itself. I mean, I know and have seen what I was obscurely looking for. I don't know what else remains but I have now seen and have pierced through the surface and have got beyond the shadow and the disguise. This is Asia in its purity,

82 Ananda was the Buddha's favorite disciple. He was a cousin of the Buddha's and his personal attendant for the last twenty-five years of his life. Ananda is credited with having persuaded the Buddha to permit the admission of women into his order.

not covered over with garbage, Asian or European or American, and it is clear, pure, complete. It says everything; it needs nothing. And because it needs nothing it can afford to be silent, unnoticed, undiscovered. It does not need to be discovered. It is we, Asians included, who need to discover it.

The whole thing is very much a Zen garden, a span of bareness and openness and evidence, and the great figures, motionless, yet with the lines in full movement, waves of vesture and bodily form, a beautiful and holy vision. The rest of the "city," the old palace complex, I had no time for. We just drove around the roads and saw the ruined shapes, and started on the long drive home to Kandy.

December 5, 1968. Singapore

Lee Beng Tjie, professor of philosophy at the University of Singapore, met me at the plane with his wife. He drove me to the hotel, The Raffles, and then out to Mount Faber, where we had a view of the lights of the city and the harbor in rain. Today I said Mass in the dining room of his flat and we went to an excellent Chinese lunch at a hotel in Chinatown, the Majestic. They called for me again in the evening and we went to a place up Beach Road where they provide you with the fixings, and with a hibachi-type of stove. You put this on the table, pick out your own fragments of hard-to-identify meats with chopsticks, and drop them in the boiling water. You hope that when you fish them out again they will be more or less done. I must admit that as an experience this was highly instructive, but as a dinner it turned out to be somewhat less than impressive. The Chinese families sitting around us seemed to be busy with the enjoyment. I admit that I have much to learn before I can profitably enter into it.

Beng Tjie says that he has a hard time getting Chuang Tzu and Lao Tzu through to Asian students. The ones here have been formed by English linguistic analysis to some extent. He thought what I have done in "War and the Crisis of Language"[83] was the sort of thing that Wittgenstein was really getting at—but I am not so sure.

SULTAN LEADS RAIDS ON SEA-MINE "PIRATES."

"The Sultan of Perak led a police party on a raid yesterday that dealt a crippling blow to the million-dollar syndicates engaged in illegal mining of tin off the Duidings Coast." The whole story is good funnypaper stuff: even

83 This article by Merton was included in *Thomas Merton on Peace*, with a foreword by Gordon C. Zahn, later revised and titled *The Nonviolent Alternative* (New York: Farrar, Straus & Giroux, 1980), 234–47.

floating pumping stations, "palongs" (fishing boats) "converted at an average cost of $35,000 . . . boats seized . . . men "detained." Huts burnt! Hurray for the Sultan of Perak! He is thwarting rich evildoers!

Two more Bonn [Germany] officials commit suicide. France threatened by crisis, strikes, etc.

December 6, 1968. Singapore

I am now preparing to leave Singapore, the city of transistors, tape recorders, cameras, perfumes, silk shirts, fine liquors—carrying away only a stock of 35 mm. Plus X film. I am glad I came here. It is an interesting, "worldly" town, very different from India, a new Asian city, the cosmopolitan kind, "worldly" too in a Chinese sense. Singapore has a Chinese kind of practicality and reality along with the big Western buildings which, as it happens, are clean and well-kept. The place is not run down, and hence Calcutta is not a *necessary* pattern for all Asia! And these evidences are needed in order to give a complete picture of Asia. Out in the suburbs by the university, it is like Santa Barbara or Sacramento.

I saw the other side of Colombo going out to the Katunayake airport. There were many screwy Catholic statues exhibited in public but sometimes under glass, so that the Catholic saints come a little closer to Ganesha and Hindu camp after all. Suddenly there is a point where religion becomes laughable. Then you decide that you are nevertheless religious.

My next stop will be the Bangkok meeting to which I do not especially look forward. Then Indonesia, a whole new journey begins there. And I am still not sure where it wiil take me or what I can or should plan on. Certainly I am sick of hotels and planes. But the journey is only begun. Some of the places I really wanted to see from the beginning have not yet been touched.

"Most men will not swim before they are able to."[84]

For Nagarjuna, all things are self-contradictory. The root of the Steppenwolf sickness is Steppenwolf's conviction that he is *uniquely* self-contradictory, and that his self-contradiction is resolved into a duality of wolf and man, self-love and self-hate. But this duality arises from ignorance of the fact that all "things" are self-contradictory in their very claim to privacy. The Steppenwolf, however, creates a double illusion by the price he places on private individuality as capable of special and unique relationships.

---

84 Novalis, as quoted with approval by Hesse's Steppenwolf.

"They had run out of seashells and were using faded photographs, soiled fans, time-tables, playing cards, broken toys, imitation jewelry, junk that memory had made precious, far more precious than anything the sea might yield."[85]

December 7, 1968. Bangkok

I find that I was secretly enraged and humiliated by the fact of having overweight luggage yesterday. Today, first thing after getting up and saying Office, I went all through my baggage, ruthlessly separating out things to be somehow disposed of. For instance, all cold-country clothes can go into the zipper bag which perhaps I can get the abbot from Hong Kong to take there. Which means, however, I won't be able to go back to Sikkim, Bhutan, or Nepal. Stupid books I bought can be discarded here or somewhere. I make a desperate plan to finish several books here in Bangkok. But of course with the conference this will be impossible. I sent contact prints to John Griffin with a few marked for enlargement. Took nine rolls of Pan X to the Borneo Studio on Silom Road, hoping they will not be ruined [they weren't]. Better finally burn up that incense. Threw some useless pills in the toilet. But I find it hard to make any firm plan that *positively* excludes a return to India, South India that is, in January.

After arranging my flight for Djakarta on the evening of the 15th, I went dutifully to the palace and the Temple of the Emerald Buddha. I didn't see the palace—it wasn't open to the public today—but went through the temple. I saw some of the paintings but was distracted by a Thai soldier who had four U.S. quarters and wanted to change them for 20 baht. But 20 was all I had. The temple itself was impressive in the dark, ornate, spacious way and the small, precious, green Buddha enshrined high up in a lighted niche was somehow moving. The buildings and sculptures of the temple compound I thought precious and bizarre rather than beautiful. They are saved by a kind of proportion which is very evident as soon as you get away from them a little. The guardian deities are not frightening, only grotesque. I kept remembering a picture of one of them on a calendar in the infirm[ary] refectory at Gethsemani sometime back in 1965.

The palace temple, however, has a basic dignity, a kind of splendor that is genuine, not gross. A bit decadent, perhaps, but I hesitate to say it. There are of course Disneyland tendencies in all these Thai *wats*, and I suppose at

85 Nathanael West, *Miss Lonelyhearts* (New York: New Directions, 1969), 26.

times they go over the line. For instance, in another *wat* I passed near the palace, the "guardian deities" on two doors were British 19th-century soldiers with white uniforms, helmets, and rifles. All this makes the Tiger Balm Gardens in Singapore (which I missed) more understandable. As for the frescoes: yes, they were good too, in their way, yet so close to a comic strip. (This is not meant to imply a judgment, good or bad.) After all I think the murals are perhaps the best thing in the whole temple. Well, Hanuman has a prominent place in all this. He is at once a monkey, god, and a successful fighter. And I think this says much that illumines the whole comic-book, and pre-comic-book tradition.

One of the villains of the temple is a "bad yak" called Nonkatal. Here a "yak" is not a Tibetan animal but an inhabitant of Ceylon. "Nonkatal behaves carelessly with a girl in heaven . . . he is commanded to become a buffalo."

"Rama, the hero, arrives at the palace of the king and sees the second queen on the throne alone. She tells Rama that the king wants him to become a hermit for a period of fourteen years and after that time he is to return and take the throne as king of Ayodhya. Rama is pleased to do as the king's will commands. . . . The chief officer has set up a farewell parade for Rama. . . . The king's heart grows sad and troubled by what he has done to Rama, and, as if he can stand no more, dies suddenly in the night."

Caption of a picture in which the yaks are trying to force Hanuman into a huge black cauldron: "The Yaks try very hard to slay Hanuman by putting him in the mash. Hanuman turns and slays the Yaks instead."

"The human merry-go-round sees many changes: the illusion that cost India the efforts of thousands of years to unmask is the same illusion that the West has labored just as hard to maintain and strengthen."[86]

December 8, 1968. Bangkok

A Dutch abbot who is staying with an attaché of the Dutch Legation came around to the hotel yesterday and we went to Silom Road again, to find Dom Leclercq and others who had arrived. Most of the delegates were arriving today and I will go to the Red Cross place where we are supposed to stay and where the meeting is to be held. It is 30 kilometers out of Bangkok. The Dutch abbot was trying to talk me into participating in a TV interview but I am not sure it is such a good idea, for various reasons. And

86 Hermann Hesse, *Steppenwolf* (New York: Bantam, 1969), 69.

first of all I find the idea very distasteful. The suggestion that it would be "good for the Church" strikes me as fatuous as far as my own participation is concerned. It would be much "better for the Church" if I refrained.

It is good to have a second time round with these cities. Calcutta, Delhi, and now Bangkok. It now seems quite a different city. I did not recognize the road in from the airport, and the city which had seemed, before, somewhat squalid, now appears to be, as it is, in many ways affluent and splendid. What has happened, of course, is that the experience of places like Calcutta and Pathankot has changed everything and given a better perspective in which to view Bangkok. The shops are full of good things. There is a lot to eat. Lots of fruits, rice, bottles, medicines, shirts, shoes, machinery, and meat (for non-Buddhists). And the stores near the Oriental Hotel are really splendid. So too is the Oriental itself. I have a fine split-level dwelling high over the river, and you enter it through an open veranda on the other side, looking out over the city.

I went to Silom Road, walked into the French Foreign Missions place and found it deserted. I wandered around in the rooms looking at the titles of books on the shelves: [Sir Walter] Scott's *Marmion*, André Maurois, along with Edward Schillebeeckx, a set of Huysmans, I forget what else—lots of magazines from *Études* to *Paris-Match*. Finally Fr. Leduc appeared, and presently—he told me to wait—the superior, P. Verdier, came in with Abbot de Floris, who is running the meeting, and Fr. Gordan.[87] They said there was mail for me; it turned out to be a letter from Winifred Karp, the young girl who stayed with the nuns at the Redwoods, forwarded from Calcutta. I have a hunch some of my mail will be getting lost in this shift.

The flight over Malaysia: dark-blue land, islands fringed with fine sand, aquamarine sea. Lots of clouds. It was a Japan Air Lines plane. They made me weigh my hand luggage, which put me overweight for the economy class allowance, so instead of just paying more for nothing I paid the difference for a first-class ticket, thus covering it with the bigger baggage allowance. And had a very comfortable ride, overeating, drinking two free,

87 Fr. Leduc was a priest of the French Foreign Mission Society of Paris, bursar of the organization at the time of the Bangkok meeting, and later superior of the society's residence in Bangkok. Fr. P. Verdier, a Belgian priest, was the superior of a small, recently organized monastic community in Bangkok at the time of this meeting. Abbot de Floris was secretary general of the A.I.M. (Aide à l'Implantation Monastique) of Vanves, France, the organization that sponsored the Bangkok conference Merton attended. And Fr. Paul Gordan was a monk of the Benedictine abbey of Beuron in Germany and secretary general of the Benedictine Confederation at St. Anselm's College in Rome.

and strong, Bloody Marys, and talking to a diplomatic courier for the State Department, who by now is getting ready to fly on to Karachi in Pakistan on the night Pan Am plane.

This evening I took a walk through Bangkok, down past the Post Office and into Chinatown. A Chinese Buddhist temple was all lit up and having some kind of fair, preparing a stage for a show, food for a banquet, and booths were selling all kinds of trinkets, lights, and incense. I went in and wandered around. There were hundreds of kids playing. Older people happy and fairly busy preparing whatever it was. Perhaps something to do with the king, whose birthday was yesterday. The city is full of flags, signs saying "Long live our noble King" and huge pictures of Phumiphol Aduldet himself, now as a Thai general and now as a *bhikkhu* in the lotus posture.

Last night I had a good Hungarian dinner at Nikas No. 1 (where, however, I seem to have been grossly shortchanged) and went on to see an Italian movie about some criminals in Milan, a quasi-documentary. It was not bad, very well filmed, and worth seeing.

Today is the Feast of the Immaculate Conception. In a little while I leave the hotel. I'm going to say Mass at St. Louis Church, have lunch at the Apostolic Delegation, and then on to the Red Cross place this afternoon.

A Glossary of Asian Terms

Abhidharma: a Buddhist metaphysical system; pure, intuitive knowledge of the *dharmas*.

Advaita Vedanta (Sanskrit; Advaita, "monism"; Vedanta, literally, "end of the *Vedas*"): in Hinduism, a school of Vedanta philosophy that believes in the oneness of God, soul, and universe.

Amitabha: in Mahayana Buddhism, a Buddha who vowed to create a pure land, to be glorified as the Buddha of Boundless Light, and to save all having faith in his vows.

ananda (Sanskrit, "bliss"): bliss or pure joy; in Hinduism, an important attribute of the supreme being Brahman, and therefore also the highest state of the individual self; unconditioned union of the self with the Godhead.

anapanasati: in Buddhism and yoga, a technique for developing the ability to meditate, to free the mind from every other thought except the awareness of breathing in and out; when this concentration has been achieved, one is ready to move on to higher forms of meditation.

anatma(n) (Sanskrit), **anatta** (Pali): in Buddhism, the doctrine of non-ego, the denial of a permanent, unchanging self.

anatta: *See* anatma(n).

anicca (Pali): in Theravada Buddhism, impermanence or change; with *anatta* (no-self) and *dukkha* (suffering) it is one of the "Three Signs of Being."

arhat: one who has reached the end of the fourfold way and attained *nirvana*.

atman (Sanskrit), **atta** (Pali): in Hinduism, "breath," self, soul, universal self, Supreme Spirit; the innermost essence of each individual that is eternal and of the same nature as the supreme universal soul. Buddha taught the opposing doctrine of *anatman* (Pali, *anatta*), in which he showed that humans possessed no permanent element, nor anything comparable to the unchanging, immortal "soul" of Christianity.

avidya: in Buddhism, ignorance or nonawareness.

Bardo Thödöl: *The Tibetan Book of the Dead.*

bardo: in Tibetan Buddhism, the period following death and before rebirth.

bhakti (Sanskrit): in Hinduism, religious devotion, love directed toward a personal deity.

bhikkhu (Pali), **bhikshu** (Sanskrit): a Buddhist monk, mendicant holy man, or priest.

Bodhgaya: the place in northeast India (near Gaya in Bihar State) where the Buddha received enlightenment as he sat meditating under a bo (or bodhi, actually a pipal) tree.

bodhi (Sanskrit, Pali): perfect wisdom or enlightenment; the full perception of transcendental wisdom.

bodhicitta: in all sects of Buddhism, the thought of enlightenment, human consciousness, the Buddha-mind, the Buddha-nature, the mind of an Enlightened Being, or enlightened-mindedness.

bodhisattva: in Mahayana Buddhism, one who, having attained enlightenment *(bodhi)*, is on the way to Buddhahood but postpones this goal to keep a vow to help all life attain salvation.

brahman (Sanskrit): in Madhyamika Buddhism, the absolute; in Hinduism, the supreme being, reality, and principle of life.

brahmanishtas: in Hinduism, devotees.

chorten (Tibetan): a cenotaph in memory of Buddha or a canonized saint.

citta (Pali): in Buddhism, mind, pure consciousness.

dharma (Sanskrit), **dhamma** (Pali): in both Hinduism and Buddhism, variously according to context, the way, the law, righteousness, reality; the path that one should follow in accordance with one's nature and station in life.

dharmakaya (Sanskrit): the cosmic body of the Buddha, the essence of all beings.

dhyana (Sanskrit), **jhana** (Pali): in both Buddhism and Hinduism, concentrated contemplation, a state of mind achieved through higher meditation. *Ch'an*, the Chinese form of *dhyana*, forms the basis for the Japanese term "Zen."

dukkha (Pali): in the Abhidharma and other schools of Buddhism, suffering or pain.

dzogchen (Tibetan, "great perfection"): the simplest and most beneficial way to rediscover instantly for oneself the transcendental awareness that is within, whose all-inclusive qualities are either presently active or lying latent in human beings, thus dissolving in the process all discrimination such as ignorance and awareness.

Five Precepts: in Buddhism, not to kill, to steal, to do sexual wrong, to lie, or to use intoxicants or drugs.

Gelugpa: the "Yellow Hats," one of the four principal sects of Tibetan Buddhism and the one to which the Dalai Lama belongs. It was founded in the late fourteenth century by Tsongkapa, one of the greatest Buddhist scholars of the period.

geshe: in Tibetan Buddhism, a title of respect for a learned lama, roughly equivalent to the Western Doctor of Divinity.

gompa (Tibetan, literally, "a solitary place"): in Tibet and the neighboring Himalayan regions, a Buddhist monastery.

Hesychast (from the Greek, "hermit"): one of a sect of Eastern Christian mystics that originated among the monks of Mt. Athos in the fourteenth century.

Hinayana: *See* Theravada.

japa (Sanskrit): the repetition of a holy word as a form of prayer or devotion.

jnana (Sanskrit): in Hinduism, transcendent knowledge through which the believer is aware of identity with Brahman, the supreme being.

jnanasattva (Sanskrit; *jnana*, "knowledge"; *sattva*, "state of being"): in Tibetan Buddhism, ideal being, the projection of God into a regenerated being who has offered to God all honor and worship.

Kagyudpa: one of the four principal schools of Tibetan Buddhism, renowned for its emphasis on meditation. Sometimes called "The School of Successive Order, it was founded in the eleventh century by Marpa and Milarepa.

karma (Sanskrit), **kamma** (Pali): literally "action"; the law of cause and effect.

karuna: in Mahayana Buddhism, compassion, a trait of *bodhisattvas*.

koan: in Zen Buddhism, a problem that cannot be solved by the intellect alone.

lama: title applied in the Tibetan world to any spiritual figure of unusual eminence, notably to those dynasties of abbots (such as the Dalai Lama) through which a recognized spiritual influence has perpetuated itself by successive incarnations.

Madhyamika: the "Middle Path" school of Buddhism, based largely in the teachings of Nagarjuna, who probably lived in the second or third century A.D. Its doctrine draws heavily on the *Prajnaparamita Sutras*, and it was the forerunner of the more extensive Mahayana school of Buddhism.

Mahayana (Sanskrit; *mahat*, "great"; *yana*, "vehicle"): also called the Great Vehicle, a branch of Buddhism made up of various syncretistic sects that are found chiefly in Tibet, Nepal, China, and Japan, have scriptures based on a Sanskrit canon, believe in a god or gods, and usually teach the *bodhisattva* ideal of compassion and universal salvation.

mandala (Sanskrit): in both Buddhism and Hinduism, a diagrammatic picture used as an aid in meditation or ritual.

maya (Sanskrit): an extra-physical wonder-working power in the Vedas; the illusion-creating power of a god or demon; or the powerful force that creates the cosmic illusion that the phenomenal world is real.

Middle Path, or Middle Way: Buddhism's description of the path lying between all extremes, as, for instance, between asceticism and self-indulgence; advocated by the Buddha as the proper path for many to follow.

mudra (Sanskrit, "seal," "token"): a mystic or symbolic gesture of the hand and fingers.

nirvana (Sanskrit), **nibbana** (Pali): the attainment of final enlightenment; freedom from rebirth; the ultimate stage of realization according to the teachings of Buddha.

nivritti (Sanskrit): the negation or control of passion, as opposed to *pravritti* (passion).

Nyingmapa: the "Red Hats," the oldest of the four principal schools of Tibetan Buddhism. It traces its origins to Padma Sambhava, who came to Tibet in the eighth century, translated many Tantric works into Tibetan, and founded the first monastery.

prajna (Sanskrit): in Buddhism, supreme knowledge or wisdom; spiritual awakening; wisdom that brings liberation.

Prajnaparamita Sutras (Sanskrit): in Buddhism, one of the most important early texts of the Mahayana and Madhyamika philosophies. The core of the sutras, which describes the emptiness of all form, is called the *Prajnaparamita Hridaya*, and is recited daily in thousands of monasteries in Asia.

prakriti (Sanskrit): in Hinduism and Buddhism, primitive matter, the primordial ground of phenomena, the ultimate material cause of the universe, world substance.

puja (Sanskrit): in Hinduism, worship of or devotional service to a deity, usually at a shrine; worship may range from simple prayers and lighting incense to more elaborate rituals with a priest.

purusha (Sanskrit, "human"): in Hinduism and Buddhism, consciousness, as opposed to *prakriti* (matter).

rajas (Sanskrit): in Hinduism and Buddhism, the principle of activity or restlessness; passion.

rinpoche (Tibetan, "the precious one"): in Tibetan Buddhism, the deferential title given to the religious elite, spiritual masters, and ecclesiastical dignitaries.

roshi (Japanese): in Rinzai Zen Buddhism, one who has finished his entire training with a teacher and is considered qualified to be a teacher in turn. Of the many men who spend some years in Zen monasteries, only a few actually receive permission to teach by the koan method.

sadhaka (Sanskrit): in Hinduism, an aspirant dedicated to the practice of a spiritual discipline; a devotee.

Sakyapa: one of the four principal schools of Tibetan Buddhism. It was founded in the eleventh century as a reform movement to correct "abuses" in the Nyingmapa school and was responsible for the conversion of Kubla Khan and Mongolia to Buddhism and for the compilation of the Tibetan Buddhist scriptures, the *Kangyur* and the *Tangyur*, in the fourteenth century.

samadhi (Sanskrit, Pali): profound meditation; in Hinduism, the final stage in yoga, in which the mind is so deeply absorbed that it loses itself; in Buddhism, the final step in the Eightfold Path, which leads to liberation and the achievement of *nirvana*.

samsara (Sanskrit): transmigration of the soul, metempsychosis; the ceaseless round of birth and death; the phenomenal realm of flux; the opposite of *nirvana*.

Sangha (Sanskrit, Pali): the Buddhist monastic order. It was founded by the historic Buddha himself and still continues in the Theravada sect.

sannyasin (Sanskrit): in Hinduism, a monk, a wandering religious mendicant, or any person who has renounced the material world and entered into the fourth and final stage of human life in the Hindu worldview.

sat (Sanskrit): in Hinduism, reality or being, absolute existence.

satipatthana (Pali): the four awakenings of mindfulness, one of the fundamental meditation practices of Theravada Buddhism, which consists of mindfulness of body, feeling, mind, and mental objects, in that order.

satori (Japanese): in Zen Buddhism, awakening, illumination, enlightenment; the state of consciousness held to be comparable to that special level of insight attained by the Buddha while seated in meditation under the sacred Tree of Enlightenment in the sixth century B.C.

sila (Sanskrit): in Buddhism, the practice of moral virtues, morality.

stupa (Sanskrit): originally a mound for relics, in particular the Buddha's, but later developed into elaborate architectural forms.

sunya, sunyata (Sanskrit): in certain schools of Buddhism, particularly Madhyamika and Zen, emptiness, the Void; the nature of reality; enlightenment of the nature of essencelessness.

sutra (Sanskrit), **sutta** (Pali): Buddhist scripture, a discourse by the Buddha or a disciple that is accepted as authoritative teaching.

tamas (Sanskrit): in Hinduism, ignorance, indifference, or inertia.

tanka: in the art of Tibet, a religious painting executed on silk or brocade; it is used as an aid to meditation, for the invocation of deities, or carried in processions.

Theravada (Pali, "a doctrine or teaching of the elders"): the Southern school of Buddhism, now dominant in Burma, Thailand, and Ceylon. Earlier than the Mahayana ("Greater Vehicle"), it is often called Hinayana ("Lesser Vehicle"). Based solely on the Pali canon of scriptures, it is nontheistic and dominantly monastic.

tulku (Tibetan, "living Buddha"): in Tibetan Buddhism, a person recognized as the reincarnation of one who had advanced far on the path to enlightenment in an earlier incarnation. After being recognized, usually at a young age, a *tulku* is brought to the monastery of his previous incarnation and thoroughly trained to assume its leadership upon his maturity.

Vajrayana (Sanskrit, "thunderbolt" or "adamantine," "invincible"): the Tantric school of Tibetan Buddhism.

vinaya (Sanskrit, Pali): discipline; the rule or code that governs the life and training of the Sangha, the Buddhist monastic orders. The *Vinaya Pitaka* is one of the most important works in the Pali canon of Abhidarmika Buddhism.

vipassana (Pali): in Theravada Buddhism, the meditation that brings insight; the step of realization that follows *samatha*, the meditation that brings tranquillity.

wat (Thai, "temple"; from the Sanskrit *vata*, "enclosed space"): a Buddhist temple or monastery in Thailand.

Zen (Japanese): a Japanese school of Mahayana Buddhism that teaches self-discipline, deep meditation, and the attainment of enlightenment by direct intuitive insight into a self-validating transcendent truth beyond all intellectual conceptions and usually expresses its teaching in paradoxical and nonlogical forms.

Index

Abdesalam, Sidi, 112
Aberle, Kathleen, 61
Abeyta, G., 178
Aelred (Hallier), 163
Aesthetic experience versus religious, 305
Agnes, Mother, Abbess of Poor Clares, 21
Agudelo, William, 144
Air travel, nine rules, 197–98
Alaska, xiii, xvi, 157, 165, 182–98; Anchorage, 183, 187, 188, 190, 194 – 95; Archbishop Ryan of, 152, 153, 161, 187,193, 194, 195, 197, 199; Convent of the Precious Blood, Eagle River, 182, 186, 194, 195, 197; Cordova, 188, 189, 192; Dillingham, 183, 196, 197, 199; en route, 179–82, 186; Juneau, 191, 192, 193, 195; Merton's possible move there, 153, 154, 158, 160, 193, 195, 252, 282, 293; mosaic by Merton on, 183–85; Valdez, 183, 189–90, 192; Yakutat, 191,192
Alban, Bro., 133, 153
Allchin, Donald, 57, 77, 252
Allport, Gordon, 46
Altizer, Thomas J. J., 72, 72n.
American Friends Service Committee(AFSC), 12
Amin, Vatsala, 221–22, 223
Among Women (Pavese), 155
Anastasius, Fr., 25, 28–29, 31, 32, 35, 36, 37–38, 40, 62, 144
Anathemata (Jones), 41
Angela, Mother, of Savannah Carmel, 123
Anita, Sr., Carmelite nun, 123
Antiwar movement, 5, 12–13, 22, 47, 52, 56, 58, 62, 65, 109, 110, 112, 124, 150, 155
Antoniutti, Cardinal, 31, 36, 69
Aron, Raymond, 271, 271n.
Art and the artist, 27, 230
Ascension (Coltrane), 48
Asian Abbots meeting. *See* Bangkok
Asian journey: en route, 205–9; invitation and preparation, xiv–xv, xvi, 35, 55, 65, 66, 86, 100, 129, 133, 134, 141, 143, 145, 146, 149, 154, 159; significance for Merton, 281–82, 323–24. *See also* Bangkok, Ceylon; India; Indonesia; Singapore
Asphodel Bookshop, 125, 134
Astavakra Gita, 82, 91, 91n., 93, 94, 98, 100, 103, 104
Atkins, Fr. Anselm, 31, 134
At Sundry Times (Zaehner), 164
Attack upon Christendom (Kierkegaard), 136, 138
Augustine, Dom (of Conyers), 24, 32, 38, 41
Auto-da-Fé (Canetti), 309
Autumn, 176
Auwas, Chairil, 163

Baez, Joan, 7
Baha'i faith, 225, 225n.
Baker, James, 57, 129
Baldwin, Fr., 24–25, 26, 28, 32, 35, 38, 41, 125
Bamberger, Fr. Eudes, 25, 26, 46, 124, 161, 298
Bane, Sr. Elaine, 20, 20n., 21, 22
Bangkok, Thailand, xvi, 210–14; Asian Abbots meeting, xiv, xvii, xviii, 132, 149, 166, 268, 298, 325, 326, 327–28; death of Merton, xvii–xix; en route from America, 205–10; en route from Ceylon, 328–29; Oriental Hotel, xvii, 328; Phra Pathom Chedi, 213–14; preparation and anticipation, 35, 55,

Bangkok, Thailand (*cont.*)
65, 66, 86, 129; Red Cross headquarters, xvii–xviii, 327; Temple of the Emerald Buddha, 326–27; Wat Bovoranives, 210, 210n., 211, 215
Bardo, 172n., 175, 179
Bardo Thodol (Evans-Wentz), 172n., 179, 179n., 180
Barnard, Roger, 5
Barthes, Roland, 150, 161, 163
Basho, 18, 19, 27
Basil, Fr., 130
Battuta, Ibn, 82
Bellarmine College, xv, 8n., 68; Merton Center/Merton collection, xv, 27, 52
Bending the Bow (Duncan), 60
Benedict, Bro., 61, 147
Benedict, Ruth, 281
Benedicta, Mother, of IHM, 200
Benedictine order, xiv, 45, 86n., 328
Benjamin, Bishop Eric, 289
Berrigan, Dan, 110, 150
Berrigan, Phil, 110, 124, 194
Berry, Wendell, 22, 60
Bhagavad Gita, 103
Birkel, Paul, 27
Black Power movement, 6, 51
Black Revolution (Merton), 52
Black Skin, White Masks (Fanon), 134, 136
Blake, William, 63–64, 71, 72, 72n., 80, 120, 305
Boggs, James, 61
Bolivia, 24
Bonhoeffer, Dietrich, 37, 39, 40
Boone, Andy, 46, 47, 81, 131, 162, 165
Born in Tibet (Rinpoche), 164, 164n.
Bowles, Paul, 198, 198n.
Boyd, Malcolm, 49, 66
Boylan, Robert J., 224, 224n., 297, 309
Bramachari, M. B., 270, 270n.
Brattacharyya, H., 174, 175
Breathitt, Gov., 14
Breitenbeck, Bishop, 123, 128, 134
Brigham, Besmilr, 137, 167
Buddhism/Zen Buddhism, xiv, 18, 44, 48, 49, 57, 60, 68, 74, 83, 103, 113, 119, 132, 135, 149, 175, 176, 209n., 211–14, 214n., 217–18, 252, 253–54, 259–61, 278–79, 281, 289; Ceylon, 312, 313, 313n., 321–24; Mahayana, 263, 292; social virtures, 287, 287n.; Tantras and Tantrism, 237n., 238–39, 241, 244, 259, 263; Theravada, 242, 242n., 251; Tibetan, xiv-xv, xvii, 145, 146n., 217, 217n., 220, 222, 222n., 227, 229–30, 230n., 232–33, 234, 235, 235n., 236, 239, 245, 251, 264, 264n.; "touching the earth" icon, 259–60. *See also* Mandala
Buddhist Thought in India (Conze), 276, 290
Burma, 133
Burns, Abbot Flavian, xiv, 24, 28, 31, 32, 35, 38, 40–41, 42, 49, 55, 58, 69, 70, 75, 77, 87, 122, 128, 129, 132, 134, 139, 144, 148, 152–53, 157, 162, 165, 166, 186, 190, 193, 268, 298
Burton [Stone], Naomi 10, 11, 12, 23n., 50, 52, 99–100, 132, 133, 143, 298
Butorovich, Suzanne, 190, 190n., 191, 198, 199

California, xvi, 82, 87, 92, 95–113, 117–23, 138, 198–201; Bear Harbor, 97, 99, 100, 110, 117, 120, 121, 125, 139, 164, 200; Eureka, 95. 96–97, 112, 118; Needle Rock, 97, 98, 110, 117, 119–20, 125, 129, 130, 143, 153, 201; proposed hermitage or laura, 132, 139, 142, 147, 152–53; proposed Lenten visit, 122–23; redwoods, 96–97, 101, 118; San Francisco, 101, 102, 107, 118, 199–200, 201; Santa Barbara, 199. *See also* Our Lady of the Redwoods
Callistus, Fr., 25, 31, 33, 37
Camillus, Bro., 62
Campbell, Will, 151
Cardenal, Ernesto, 82, 144
Cargo cults, 6, 10, 55, 56, 59, 61
Carlyle, Tom, 176, 186
Carmelites, 20n., 21, 69, 123
Carole, postulant, 110, 119
Carroll, Fr. Xavier, 181, 186
Carroll, Joe, 16
Carruth, Hayden, 56
Carthusians, 22, 150
Cassian, Bro., 147

Caste War in Yucatan, The (Reed), 6
Cecilia, Sr., 110
Chakravarty, Amiya, xv, xvii, 133, 133n., 141, 145, 220
Chandra, Lokesh, 227, 233
Change of Skin (Fuentes), 60
Char, René, 79, 130, 134
Charity, Sr., 194
Charron, Marie, 27, 50, 134
Chaucer, Geoffrey, 91
Chi, Richard, 48, 49, 76, 86, 289
Chile, 12, 31, 33, 37, 39, 69, 83
Chitrabhanu, Munishri, 221, 221n.
Christianity, 16, 44, 62, 78, 138–39, 152, 278, 281, 310
Christofora, Sr., 110
Christopher, Bro., 133
Chrysostom, Bro., 133
Cistercian Studies, xvi
Cistercian (Trappistine) order, xiv, 13, 98, 104, 107, 121. *See also* Trappists
Civilization and Its Discontents (Freud), 82
Clare, Mother Francis, 21, 63, 69, 73, 123
Clement, Bro., 14, 17, 35, 46
Cleveland, 80
Cogley, John, 150, 199
Cohen, Marvin, 137
Collins, Br. Frederic, 12, 31, 33, 37
Colombam, Dom, 32, 35, 37, 41
Colteran, Ted, 5–6
Comedy, 108–9
Commemorations of Saint Elizabeth, 284
Compte, Fr. Ephrem, 63
Connery, Tom, 197
Conscience of Joyce, The (O'Brien), 140, 141, 147
Consciousness, 227, 228, 252, 260, 261, 266, 274, 289
Conze, Edward, 271, 276, 287
"Creative Silences" (Merton), 131
Crest-Jewel of Discrimination, The (Sankaracharya), 223, 223n., 247–48, 257–58, 261
"Cross Fighters, The" (Merton), 22
Culture, American, 67, 69, 140, 156, 217
Curiyikad, Fr. Cherian, 297
Curmi, Fr. Vincent, 277, 277n., 279–80, 290, 291
Ceylon, xvii, 294, 306–24; Advent sermon, Merton's, 312; ashram, 312; Colombo, 306, 307–9, 320, 325; Dambulla, 313, 313n., 322; en route, 306–7; hermits and hermitages, 310; Kandy, 308, 309–20, 321; poems/prose pastiche, Merton's, 313–19, 320–21; Polonnauwa, 313, 313n., 321–23

Dadelson, de, J. D., 83
Dalai Lama, xiii, xv, xvii, 146, 146n., 164n., 222, 227, 229, 245, 246, 254, 265, 297; first audience with Merton, 245, 249, 250–52; second audience, 258–59; third audience, 266
Dana, Doris, 4, 4n., 5, 6, 7, 23, 52
Daridan, Monsieur and Madame, 235, 236
Dasgupta, Surendranath, 306
Davenport, Guy, 3, 4
Day, Dorothy, 4n.
Death, 11, 34, 44, 51, 60, 85, 174, 177; journey as, 174; Merton's, xvii–xix,
Debray, Regis, 24
De Floris, Abbot, 328, 328n.
Delius, Betty, 27
Democratic National Convention, Chicago, 1968, 155, 161–62
Descartes, René, 92, 92n.
Desjardins, Armand, 227, 229, 237
De Smet, Fr., 295
Devereux, Don, 105–6, 121, 133, 177, 186
Devereux, Eileen, 121, 177
Diane, Sister, 110, 111, 119
Dimock, Jr., Edward C., 255, 256, 256n.
Di Prima, Diane, 23
Dominique, Sr., 98, 110, 164
Domostroy (Sylvester), 100
Doors, as metaphor, 285
Dormition Abbey, Jerusalem, 46
Downhill All the Way (Woolf), 3
Dreams: in Buddhism, 241; of Kanchenjunga, xiii, 284; Merton's, 34, 56, 110, 112, 141, 206, 255
Driver, John, 245, 252
DuBois, Cora, 10
Dumont, Fr. P. Charles, 35, 37, 43
Dunn, Finley Peter, 215, 215n.

Dunne, Peter, 293–94
Dylan, Bob, 48
Dzogchen, 251, 278, 279

Eclipse, 3
Edson, Russell, 60
Edward, Dom, of Berryville, 69
Egan, Eileen, 142
Elaine Michael, Sr., from Allegany, 123
Elizabeth, Sr., Carmelite nun, 21, 22, 123
Emmanuel, Pierre, 295–96, 296n.
Emmett, Dorothy, 18
Engels, Friedrich, 300, 300n.
Engenberger, Hans Magnus, 58, 120
Enlightenment, 176, 229, 246, 249, 250, 261
Enslin, Ted, 137
Error and Deliverance (Gharali), 155
Essential Lenny Bruce, The, 74, 82
Evans-Wentz, Walter Yeeling, 28, 172, 172n., 173, 206
"Evening" (Merton), 7
Everson, William (Bro. Antoninus), 9

Faith and Violence (Merton), 23, 23n., 49
Ferlinghetti, Lawrence, 101, 106, 120, 158
Ferry, W. H. "Ping," 83, 86, 106, 131, 138, 142, 150, 199, 201, 248, 286, 309n.
Fessard, G., 18
Final Integration (Arasteh), 45, 70
Flanagan, Fr. Raymond, 62, 66, 142–43, 149–50, 156, 157
Flanagan, Lois, 218, 224
Floating Bear magazine, 23
Flood, Bro. Maurice, 20, 166, 186
Football, xv, 160–61
Ford, Ed, 117
Ford, John, 3, 6, 11, 27, 52, 76, 135, 141, 148
Forest, James, 22, 59
Foucault, Michel, 133, 133n., 271
Fox, Abbot James, 35, 36, 43; and abbatial election, 24–25, 26, 28, 32, 38, 40, 41; conflicts with Merton, xiv, 12–13, 14, 26, 31, 52, 58; hermitage, 17, 17n., 36, 46, 77, 80, 125, 131, 146; policies, 31–32, 38, 42, 49; resignation, xiv, 8, 14, 30, 42, 46; sermon, 70
Fox, Msgr. Robert, 24
Franciscan orders, xv, 16, 20n., 21, 140
Freedgood, Anne, 44
Freedgood, Seymour, 44–45, 46, 270n.
Freedom songs, Merton's, 73, 80, 135, 148, 158

Gannon, Fr. Jim, 76
Gannon, Leo and family, 23, 31, 36
Gardiner, Margaret, 127
Geography of Lograire (Merton), 49, 50, 51, 59, 127, 129, 132, 133, 156, 167, 199, 206n.
George, James, and wife, 235, 268
Gerarda, Sr., 110, 205
Geshe, Tenzin, 222, 245–46, 248, 250–51, 258
Gethsemani: community, 28–29, 35, 37–38, 39–43, 122, 125, 131, 133, 142, 282; construction at, 68; Dom Frederic's Lake, 4; Edelin's Place, 17, 17n.; hermitages, 17, 28, 38; Merton's burial at, xviii, xix; Merton's last day at, xvi, 186; Merton's writing at, xiii; retreats at, 20, 20n.; St. Bernard's pond and field, 11, 44, 47, 59, 152; teachers at, 8n.; walks at, 3–4, 6, 11, 15, 16–17, 28, 33, 44, 47, 48, 76–77, 146, 152, 155. *See also* Merton, Thomas
Ghazali, Al, 155, 156
Ghost Dance (Mooney), 32
Giroux, Bob, 46, 50
God, 94, 102, 103, 147, 230, 231, 274, 306
Gordan, Fr. Paul, 328, 328n.
Gorman, Jim, 57
Goulet, Dennis, 48
Grace, 260, 260n.
Graham, Dom Aelred, xv, 83, 104, 106, 121, 152, 163, 164n., 214n., 218n., 239
Greece, 129
Greene, Jonathan, 60, 83, 128, 129, 130
Gregory, Fr., 104, 105, 178
Griffin, Gregory, 19, 34
Griffin, John Howard, 4n., 6, 73n., 80, 86, 106, 110, 268, 297, 326
Groth, Al, 101, 111, 119, 153

Gruening, Ernest, 193, 193n.
Guevara, Che, 24
Guha, Naresh, 220
Gyaltsan, Lama Geshe Tenpa, 232

Hackett, J. W., 4
Haldane, J. B. S., 290
Hall, Martin, and wife, 282, 283, 284
Hamilton, Al, 45
Hammer, Carolyn, 7, 14, 49, 77, 83
Harris, John, 31
Hart, Bro. Patrick, 166, 186, 252, 268, 286
Haughton, Rosemary, 4, 4n.
Havana, 118
Hegel, G. W. F., 96
Helen Elizabeth, Sr., 284
Hesse, Hermann, xvi, 91, 196, 197, 197n., 198, 325
Hicks, Freddy, 74, 75
Hilarion, Fr., 18, 25, 31, 46, 76, 125, 126
Hildelith, Dame, 22
Hill, Ken, 4–5
Hinduism, 209, 209n., 236, 255, 255n., 301, 302n.
Hines, Fr. Denis, 104, 107, 121
Hinson, Glenn, 18
Hisamatsu, 113
Hocks, Paula, 133
Hogan, Tim, 57, 66
Hollister, Judith, 221, 221n.
Hollo, Anselm, 48, 60, 86, 87, 137
Holloway, Jim, 151
Holy Spirit Monastery, GA, 13
Homer (Fitzgerald), 32
House on the Hill, The (Pavese), 155
Huntington, Pat, 54
Hyde, Susan, 215

Ian, Janis, 3
I Ching, 31
Idols by the Path (Pemba), 290
Ignatow, David, 60
IHN Sisters, Santa Barbara, 199, 199n.
Immaculate Heart of Mary Sisters, 73
India: Ashoka Vihara, monk at, 267; ashrams, 220, 246, 248, 270; Bhutan, 19, 231, 231n., 273, 290; Calcutta, xvii, 149, 214–18, 226–27, 266, 269–71, 295,297–98, 325; Darjeeling, 144, 146, 149, 158, 200, 271–76, 279, 282, 303, 320; Dharamsala, xiii, xv, xvii, 226, 235, 236–66; hermitages, 235, 242; hermit center, Sonada, 292–93; hermits, 291, 292–93, 295; Himalayas, 226, 237, 240, 271; homily, Merton's, given at Loreto Convent, 289, 294; homily, Merton's, given at Loreto House, 222, 222n; Kurseong, Merton's talk to Jesuit scholastics, 294, 297; Loreto College and Convent, 273, 274–75, 289; Madras, xvii, 298–306; Mahabalipuram, 302–4, 323; Mim Tea Plantation, xiii, 277, 280–86, 290; New Delhi, xvii, 226–36, 266–69; St. Joseph's College, 276, 276n., 279–80, 281–82, 294; St. Thomas Mount, 301, 302; San Thomé, 300–301; Temple of Understanding Conference, 220–21, 294
Indonesia, 129, 132, 137–38, 157, 163; Rawa Seneng monastery, xvii, 129
"Inner Experience, The" (Merton), xv–xvi
In Praise of Krishna (Dimock and Levertov), 256
Irenaeus, Bro., 133
Ishi Means Man (Merton), 4n., 11n.
Isidore, Bro., 14

Jackson, Melvin, 56
Jackson, Merrill, 22
Jacobs, Paul, 199, 286
Jainism, 221, 221n., 222
Jane, Mother, from Jackson Carmel, 69, 73, 123
Jeffers, Robinson, 138, 167, 167n.
Jerome, Bro., 9
Jesuits, 146, 159, 271, 273, 276, 276n., 277, 279–80, 281, 294, 295
John of the Cross, Fr., 66
Johnson, Lyndon B., 46–47, 51, 52, 55, 56, 61, 65, 69, 75, 76, 88, 151, 243, 250
Jones, Frank, 100, 117, 143, 200
Jones, Gracie, 112–13, 120, 129, 164
Journal of Ecumenical Studies (Merton article for), 14
Journal of My Escape from the Nazis (Merton), 27, 50–51, 57, 100, 132, 133, 134, 298

Journey to the East (Hesse), 196, 197, 197n.
Joyce, James, Merton on, 76, 77, 140, 142, 144, 147, 148, 152, 156

Kanchenjunga, 271, 272, 275, 277, 279, 281, 283, 286–87, 295, 297; Merton's dream of, xiii, 284
Karam, Mae, 199
Karmapa, Lama Gyalwa, 243, 268
Karp, Winifred, 328
Katallagete magazine, 33
Kathleen, Sr., 22
Katryn, Sr., 98, 101, 104, 110, 120
Kazi, Sonam T., xvii, 237, 237n., 239–43, 245, 246, 249, 251, 263, 264, 277, 293
Kelty, Fr. Matthew, 24, 25, 46, 161
Kennedy, Ethel, 126
Kennedy, Robert, 74–75, 76, 126–27, 128
Kentucky, 8. *See also* Gethsemani
Kerouac, Jack, 23
Kevin, Bro., 59
Khantipalo, Bhikku, 244
Khantipalo, Phra, 211, 212
King, Coretta, 79, 80
King, Martin Luther, 77–79, 80, 81, 128
King, Winston, 18, 57, 74
Klapheke, Fred, 148
Kolbsheim, 4n., 6
Kozlowski, Supt., 178
Kraemer-Rains, 52
Krishnamurti, 241

Lal, P., 149, 218
La Mystique et les mystiques (Ravier), 118
Landry, Lionel, 144
Language and Silence (Steiner), 32, 34, 35
Laughlin, James, 9, 52, 167, 286
Laura project, 131
Lavanoux, Maurice, 75
Lawrence, D. H., 290n., 301
Lawrence, Peter, 61
Lax, Bob, 24, 44, 126, 128, 129, 130, 298, 303
Leavis, F. R., 34
Leclercq, Dom Jean, xiv, 9, 35, 55, 66, 149, 154, 165, 166, 297, 327
Leduc, Fr., 328., 328n.
Lee Beng Tjie, 324
Leff, Gordon, 140
Lekai, Louis, 130–31
Lemercier, Dom Gregorio, 147
Lentfoehr, Sr. Thérèse, 11, 289
Le Saux, Dom Henri, 235, 235n., 282
Leslie, Sr., 110, 112, 118, 119, 145
L'Étranger (Camus), Merton's article on, 65
Levertov, Denise, 22, 256, 256n.
Lévi-Strauss, Claude, 15, 34
Lhalungpa, Lobsang Phuntsok, 232, 235, 267, 268, 282
Literary Essays of Thomas Merton, The (Hart, ed.), 72n.
Llorente, Fr., of Cordova, 178, 183, 183n., 189
Loftus, Fr. John, xv, 52, 63, 160
Lokesvarananda, Swami, 221
London, 3
Loneliness, 12
Lossky, Vladmir, 187–88, 188n.
Lotus and the Robot, The (Koestler), 304
Loughlin, John, 14
Louise, Sr., 21, 22
Lowell, Jim, 134
LSD, 279
Lucovina, Mother, 289
Lum's restaurant, Lexington, KY, 77–78
Lu Tung, 101
Lytle, Andrew, 121

M.: advocates Merton leave vocation, 11, 18; after break-up with Merton, 18, 29; letters burned, 157; phone calls from Merton to, 11
Madhyamika, 252, 253, 260, 262, 274, 276, 323
Maharshi, Ramana, 302, 302n.
Mailer, Norman, 5
Maitreya, 263, 263n.
Malinowski, Bronislaw Kasper, 59, 59n.
Maloney, Bishop, 70
Mambu (Burridge), 10
Man at Play (Rahner), 14
Mandala, 227, 228–29, 233–34, 236, 238–40, 241, 242, 244, 246, 247, 250, 254, 255

Manske, Fr. James I., 193, 193n.
Marcuse, Herbert, 125, 262
Marie, Sr., postulant, RSHM, 201
Maritain, Jacques, 4n., 6, 52
Maritain, Raïssa, 4n.
Martin, Fr. Vincent, 45–46, 57
Martinez, Nelson, 177
"Marxism and Monastic Perspectives" (Merton), xviii, 263, 266, 268, 298
Mary, Sr., Precious Blood Convent, 197, 200
Maurer, Bro. Job, 24
McCarthy, Colman, 27
McDonough, Archbishop, 70
McIntyre, Cardinal, 73
McKiernan, Hugh, 199, 199n.
Meatyard, Chris, 137, 162
Meatyard, Gene (and family), 3, 4, 22, 48, 77, 162
Meditation, 63, 68, 128, 132, 137, 145, 162, 171, 211, 216, 232–33, 238, 239–40, 242, 244, 247, 251, 258, 261, 271, 273n., 278, 279, 283–84; proposed Tibetan center, 293, 310
Meerloo, Joost, 10
Merton, Gertrude Merton (Aunt Kit), 84–85, 100, 125
Merton Legacy Trust, 3, 6, 10–11, 12, 27, 52
Merton, Thomas: and abbatial election, xiv, 6, 8, 24–25, 32, 35–36, 37–38, 39–43; on American politics, 127, 134, 138–39, 140, 143, 151, 155, 156, 157–58, 161, 194, 265; anxiety before last journeys, 164; becoming homeless, 174; birthday, 47, 58; conflicts between outer world and monastic life, 12–13, 20, 21, 25, 39, 43, 49, 50, 54, 57, 58, 63, 66, 68, 75, 82–83, 103, 113, 125, 129, 130, 131, 132, 137, 142, 146, 148, 154, 261; contemplates leaving Gethsemani, 117, 147–48, 152–53, 154, 158, 162–63, 166, 252, 253, 282; correspondence and letter writing, 14–15, 19, 22, 27, 30, 31, 47, 50, 66, 68, 126, 141, 144, 145, 152, 190n., 193, 219, 252, 268, 286, 289; and Dalai Lama, xiii, xv, xvii, 146, 149, 200, 222, 246, 265, 297; and Dalai Lama, first audience, 245, 249, 250–52; and Dalai Lama second audience, 258–59; and Dalai Lama third audience, 266; death of, xvii-xix; on death, 11, 34, 44, 51, 60, 85, 174, 177; deluded woman and problems of fame, 61, 63, 73, 82, 83, 86, 129, 142; dissatisfaction with Gethsemani, 122, 125, 131, 133, 138, 142, 146, 147–48, 153, 181, 252, 253, 282; emotionality of, 7; fasting, 15, 18–19, 25, 130; gardening, 62, 65, 74, 81–82, 137; health of, 9, 12, 13–14, 19, 34, 43–44, 62, 82, 87, 106, 133, 152, 161, 177–78, 201, 277–78, 279–80, 287, 289, 293–94; hermitage, 17, 54, 62, 74, 80, 81, 83, 85, 86, 87, 125, 128, 241, 252, 253, 282, 293; journal entry, final, xvii, 326–29; journals kept by, xiii–xiv, xvii, 9, 118, 134; and karma, 307; last night and day at Gethsemani, 166, 171, 186; M., relationship with, 11, 18, 29, 157; memories of England, 3, 11; Native Americans, interest in, 4n., 10; nickname, 194; premonition/thoughts of death, 147, 163, 205; reflections on past, 15, 26, 29, 45, 130, 155–56, 236, 275, 284; religious observances of (e.g. Mass said), 11, 13, 14, 19, 20, 21, 23, 24, 29, 30–31, 33, 34, 35, 45, 55, 60, 61, 74, 76, 84–85, 86, 98, 105, 112, 119, 121, 140, 158, 159, 186, 193, 195, 199, 213, 218, 235, 265n., 268, 273, 274–75, 276, 279–80, 291, 295, 301, 308, 324, 329; routine/mundane activities, 18, 25, 33, 49, 61, 66, 87–88, 119, 130; and search for Buddhist teacher (guru), 229, 238, 239, 243, 247, 251–52, 277, 279; social conscience, 10, 12, 24, 37, 49, 51–52, 55–56, 58, 66–67, 69, 107, 123–24, 127, 194; temps vierge, use of term, 262, 262n.; travel, see main entry of destinations; travel denied, xiv; travel, premonastic days, xiii; Vietnam War opposition, 5, 33, 51, 52, 56, 62, 65, 67, 134, 138–39, 142–43; vocation of, 9, 15, 20, 21, 29, 39, 72, 135, 136, 137, 147, 151, 162, 252, 282, 295–96; vow of poverty, xvi; and women, 75–76, 77, 160; on his writing and writing plans, 23–24, 28, 35, 49, 50–51, 52, 56,

Merton, Thomas (*cont.*)
63, 66, 73, 84, 118, 128, 129, 130, 142, 156, 219–20, 240, 298; years at Gethsemani, 156, 236; years in monastic life, xviii
Message of Contemplatives, 8
Message of the Tibetans (Desjardins), 227, 239
"Messenger, Carol, Responsory (1948)" (Merton), 7
Metamorphoses III (Ovid), 271
Methodius, Fr., 13
Milarepa, 217–18, 240, 247, 250
Milosz, Czeslaw, 199, 286, 289
Miss Lonelyhearts (West), 326
Mistral, Gabriela, 6
Mitchell, Sr. Barbara, 222, 224
Mitchell, Elsie, 152
Molière, 109
Monastery of Christ in the Desert. *See* New Mexico
Monasticism and contemplative life, 15, 16, 19, 20, 21, 25, 26, 30, 38, 45, 56, 63, 93, 96, 107, 113, 123, 128, 133, 147, 150–51, 166, 200, 232, 240, 262, 278, 281–82, 297, 298; and Dalai Lama, 259, 266; of lamas/Indian holy men, 246–49, 291, 292–93; proposed monastery for Ceylon, 313
Monchanin, Abbé Jules, 295, 296n.
Monks Pond, xvi, 28, 45, 45n., 48, 57, 60, 61, 80–81, 86, 123, 125, 134, 136, 137, 141, 147, 148, 150, 154, 157, 173
Monte Alban, 4
Montoya, Pearl, 177
Moseley, Virginia, 147
Mountains/metaphor for Merton, xiii, 96, 101, 103, 178, 182, 187, 188, 189–90, 195–96, 226, 240, 254, 284, 286; Kanchenjunga, 271, 272, 275, 277, 279, 281, 283, 284, 286–87, 295, 297
Mount Analogue (Daumal), 106–7, 120
Muggeridge, Malcolm, 55
Mulloy, Joseph, 56, 57, 65
Murphy, Fr. David, 46
Murphy, Fr. Francis A., 197
Murti, T. R. V., 252, 253, 254, 259, 260–61, 262–63, 274, 276, 279, 283, 290
Music, 44, 48, 54, 56, 58, 73, 105, 119, 128, 144, 201
Myriam, Mother, 101, 104, 110, 119, 120, 141, 143, 166, 200, 297
Mystics and Zen Masters (Merton), 27

Nabokov, Peter, 106, 107, 121
Nagarjuna, 247, 247n., 251, 273, 325
Naked Society (Packard), 134
Nanasampanno, Venerable, 212, 212n., 216
Nanayakkara, Bishop, 310–11
Nat Turner (Styron), Merton review of, 33, 34, 35, 37
Nature, Merton's entries on, 3, 5, 6, 11, 15, 16, 18, 23, 27, 32, 33, 35, 37, 48, 52, 56, 58, 63, 64, 65–66, 70–71, 74, 76–77, 79, 80, 87, 94, 97, 99, 100, 104, 107, 120, 132, 146, 147, 177, 237, 240, 241
See also Autumn; Night Sky; Spring; Summer; Winter
Nepal, 143, 144, 145, 149, 277, 294
New Apocalypse (Altizer), 72, 72n., 80
New Clairvaux Abbey, CA, 13, 41
New Directions Publishers, 18
New Mexico, xiv, xvi, 83, 103–7, 121–22, 138, 162–63, 165, 186; Albuquerque, 186; Dulce, 178; en route, 171; Jicarilla Apache reservation, 177, 178–79, 181, 186; Monastery of Christ in the Desert, Abiquiu, xiv, xvi, 83, 103–7, 121–22, 138, 162–63, 173, 174–75, 186, 293; Santa Fe, 177, 186
New York Review of Books, 65
Nhat Hanh, Thich, 79, 88
Nicholson, Harold, 148
Niedecker, Lorine, 30
Night sky, 10, 16, 46, 47, 52, 54, 264, 300, 308
Niles, John Jacob, 7, 49, 86–87, 128, 289
Niles, Rena, 49, 86–87, 289
"Non-violence Does Not-Cannot-Mean Passivity" (Merton), 194n.
Noonan, Ed, 186
Norbert, Sr., 22
"Notes on Love" (Merton), 19
Nuns. *See* Our Lady of the Redwoods; *specific orders*

Oakham, England, 11
O'Brien, Darcy, 140
O'Callaghan, Frank, 121, 129, 162
O'Callaghan, Tommie, 6, 11, 27, 48, 52, 54, 56, 80, 117, 121, 129, 141–42, 143, 171, 186
O'Flanagan, Most Rev. Dermot, 192, 192n.
O'Gorman, Ned, 24
O'Keeff, Georgia, 106, 107, 173, 175
Oliver, Pat, 27
Olmstead, Beatrice, 147
One Dimensional Man (Marcuse), 125
Origen, 15
Orthodoxy, 92, 100
Osservatore, 8
Our Lady of the Redwoods, xiv, 82, 98–99, 101, 105, 110–13, 117–20, 122, 123, 125, 131, 138, 141, 145, 199, 205, 265, 282, 293
Our Lady of the Valley, RI, xiii

Pachomius, Bro., 23
Pallis, Marco, 133, 133n., 227, 250n., 252, 259–60, 260n., 261
Pascal, Blaise, 93, 93n.
Passionists, 21
Pasternak, Boris, 15, 39; Merton on Georgian Letters of, 15, 35
Paton, Alan, 16
Paul, Fr. (Merton's former novice), 13
Paul VI, Pope, 8
Pavese, Cesare, 50, 155
Peace News, 5
Peaks and Lamas (Pallis), 133n.
"Peace and Revolution" (Merton), 142
Peck, Mr. and Mrs., 191
Peloquin, Alexander, 73, 80, 159
Pemba, T. Y., and wife, 290, 291
Penco, Gregorio, 8
Peron, Camara, 158
Philomena, Mother, 69, 71
Photography (Merton's), xvi, 4, 4n., 19, 34, 73, 73n., 86, 106, 110, 119, 129, 196, 249, 266, 272, 279, 284, 297–98, 310, 322
Pius XII, Pope, 8
Plato, 175–76
Poetry, 16, 22, 27, 30, 31, 32, 60, 71, 83, 87, 130, 134, 137, 144, 163, 217, 233–34, 301–2, 305; dedicated to Merton, 264–65, 265n.; haiku, Merton on, 4, 27; magazine (Merton's), *see Monks Pond;* Merton's, 10, 16, 24, 94, 95, 102, 144, 156, 171–74. 183–85, 206–8, 268–69, 273–74, 288–89, 313–19, 320–21; Niles setting of Merton's poems to music, 7; Vaishnava, 255–57. *See also* Geography of Lograire; Sensation Time at the Home
Pomaire (Merton's Spanish Publisher), 6
Ponge, Francis, 97
Poor Clares, xvi, 20n., 21, 63, 69, 71, 179–80, 186
Poor People's March, Albuquerque, 107–8, 121, 123
Popov, Eugene, 100
Population, 24, 71
Port Royal (Sainte-Beuve), 92, 92n.
Poulet, Georges, 92n., 93, 93n., 108
Power, 93
Prakriti, 174
Prayer (Heiler), 136, 141
Private Correspondence, A (Durrell and Miller), 180, 180n.
Psycholofia, 74
Punnett, Ron, 154

Quainton, Anthony, 231, 231n.

Rabelais, François, 140
Race War, The (Segal), 55
Racism, 50, 51, 66, 81, 108–9, 113, 151, 155
Raghavan, V., 299, 299n., 300, 304
Rahner, Hugo, 14, 72, 72n.
Rahula, Walpola, 309, 321
Rama Krishna, 185, 185n.
Ramanuja, 208, 208n.
Ramanuja et la mystique vishnouite (Esnoul), 206n.
Rambusch, Bob, 22
Randall, Margaret, 28
Reed, Nelson, 6
Regina Laudis monastery, Bethlehem, CT, 3
Regno, Bishop, 311–12
Reiter, George, 6, 27, 28, 48
Rendra, Willibrordus S., 163

Reno, Fr. Roger, 32
Requiem for a Faith (film), 222, 222n., 226
"Return to Paradise" (Penco), 8–9
Revolution, 24, 51, 81
Revolution in Anthropology, The (Jarvic), 55–56
Rice, Ed, 24, 154, 165, 308
Richard, Fr., from Mepkin, 155
Richardson, Sr. Jane Marie, 20, 20n., 21
Rinpoches: Chatral, 278–79, 290–91; Chhokling, 249; Chobgye Thicchen, 263–64, 265; Chogyam Trungpa, 164, 164n., 219, 227, 252, 268; Drugpa Thugsey, 277; Jimpa, 277, 279, 292; Khamtul, 243, 298; Khempo Kalu, 292, 293
Rita Mary, Mother, Precious Blood Convent, 197, 200
Road to Joy, The: Thomas Merton's Letters to New and Old Friends, 190n.
Roberts, Jackie, 7
Robertson, Fr. Vernon, 68
Robin, Roger, 154
Roger, Fr., 99, 104, 111, 112, 118, 119, 120, 153
Rogers, Beatrice, 76, 79
Roman Catholic Church, 21, 30, 40, 69, 72, 77, 83–84, 149, 158, 310, 328; birth control encyclical, 150; Pastoral Letter, "The Church in Our Day," 40, 40n.
Roshi, Shibuyama, 74
Roy, Jamini, xvii, 220, 220n., 236, 305
Rule of Saint Benedict, The, 86, 86n.
Run to the Mountain (Merton), xiii
Ryan, Dr., 57
Ryman, Frank, 191

Saarikoski, Pentti, 137
"Sacred City, The" (Merton), 4, 4n.
St. Bonaventure, Olean, NY, xiii
St. Cyril of Jerusalem, 259
St. Gregory of Nyssa, 259
St. Irenaeus, 259
St. Joseph's Infirmary, Louisville, 284
St. Mary's Seminary, 8n.
St. Rose's Priory, 12
Sales, de, Fr. Francis, 156
Sankaracharya, 223, 223n., 247–48, 257–58, 261, 295, 304
Santi Deva, 135, 247, 247n.
Sartre, His Philosophy and Existential Psychoanalysis (Stern), 95, 95n., 96n., 113
Savory, Teo, 22, 22n.
Schickel, William, 75
Schillebeeckz, Fr. Edward, 297
Schillebeeckz, Fr. Louis, 297
Schmidlin, Br. Richard, 11
Schumann, Martha, 27
Seabury Press, 16
"Secular Saint, The" (Novak), 84
Seeds of Contemplation (Merton), 22
Seitz, Ron and Sally, xv, 54, 117, 130, 157, 158, 160, 163, 180, 186
Selected Poems (Lawrence), 301; "lighthouse" stanza, 302
"Selections from the Dialogues of the Zen Master Shen Hui (8th century A.D.)," 45, 45n., 76
Sensation Time at the Home (Merton), 286, 286n.
Seven Storey Mountain, The (Merton), xiii, 311
Shalom, Sister, 110
Shaw, Bernard, 28
Sheep, 94–95
Shepherd, Bob, 4, 49, 86–87, 128, 162
Shepherd, Hanna, 49, 86–87, 162
Sherburne, Fr. Richard, 273, 273n., 277–78
Shine, Bro. Kevin, 8
Siddhartha (Hesse), xvi, 209, 209n.
Silence, 54
Singapore, 324–26
Sisters of Loretto, 20, 20n., 123, 145, 265
Sisto, Dick, 130
Sitting Bull/Wounded Knee, 14
Situorang, Sitor, 163
Slate, John, 11
Smith, Carleton, 19
Smith, E. Gene, 235, 235n., 277
Smith, Huston, 222, 222n., 226
Smith, Raphael, 19
Smith, T. J., 84, 289

Snakes, 107, 121, 153
Snyder, Gary, 23, 60
Sobhana, Venerable Chao Khun Sasana, 211–12
Soedjatmoko, Giacomo, 157, 159, 161, 163, 165
Solitude, 122, 127, 130, 132, 135, 137, 139, 142, 146, 153, 162, 200, 241, 252, 278, 282, 287, 290
Sopa, Geshe, 251
Spicehandler, Ezra, 221
Spring, 58–59, 62, 63, 64, 84
Springs of Contemplation, The (Richardson, ed.), 20n.
Stanford, Fr. Maurice, 276, 276n.
Stark, Phil, 125, 141, 150, 157, 166
Steindl-Rast, Bro. David, 83, 240
Steppenwolf (Hesse), 325, 325n., 327
Stier, Victor, 309, 309n.
Studies in Human Time, 92n.
"Study of Zen, The" (Merton), 60
Styron, William, 34
Sufism, 10, 119, 156, 231, 236
Summer, 126, 131, 142, 144, 151, 152, 154, 155, 156, 157
Suzuki, 251, 251n.
Syvestrines, 311

Tadié, Marie, 6, 6n., 52
Talbott, Harold, xv, xvii, 164, 164n., 226, 229, 232, 235, 236, 237, 242, 243, 246, 249, 266, 268, 271, 272, 277, 281, 293, 294
"Tenebrae" (Levertov), 22
Ten Rungs (Buber), 47
Terry, Clark, 54
Theology of Experience, The (Haughton), 4n.
Theology of Proclamation (Rahner), 72, 72n., 74
Theopane the Recluse, 98
Theory and Practice of the Mandala, The (Tucci), 227
Thera, Nyanaponika, 289, 310
Thomas, Bro., 44
Thompson, Fr. August, 154
Tibet, 28, 145, 146n.; dance, 234–35; exiled Tibetans, 219, 226, 231, 237–38, 243, 246, 264, 271, 272, 273, 275, 276, 280, 310; music, 234; saying, 237, 265. *See also* Buddhism, Tibetan; Dalai Lama
Tibetan Book of the Dead, 171, 172, 172n., 227
Tibetan Yoga and Secret Doctrines (Evans-Wentz), 206
Time-Life Bible, Merton's introduction, 26, 28, 298, 298n.
Timothy, Fr., 25, 161
Tlinglit Indians, 191, 192
Tobin, Sr. Mary Luke, 20, 20n., 145
"Torch-bearer's Race, The" (Jeffers), 167, 167n.
Torpey, Fr. Gilbert, 154
Trappist order, xiii, 46, 149, 159, 194, 199n., 241, 275
Travels in Yucatan (Stephens), 23
Tristes Tropiques (Lévi-Strauss), 15
Tseten, Geshe Ugyen, 252
Tucci, Giuseppe, xvii, 227–28, 229, 233, 234, 238, 239, 240, 241, 242–43, 244, 246
Tukaram, 295
Twilight in Italy (Lawrence), 290, 290n., 301, 306

Unamuno, de, Miguel, 95–96, 96n.
Under a Glass Bell (Nin), 281, 283, 283n.
U. S. Catholic Reporter, Merton in, 62, 66
U. S. S. Pueblo incident, 46, 47, 50, 65, 69
Utah, 94–95

Vahiduddin, Syed, 231, 236
Vatican II, 20n., 30
Verdier, Fr. P., 328, 328n.
Veronica, Sister, 110, 119
Victor, Bro., 46, 128
Vidyapati, 302
Vietnam War, 5, 12–13, 22, 35, 46–47, 51, 52, 57, 58, 61, 65, 76, 77, 88, 139, 142–43, 183n., 243–44, 250
Violence, 47, 51, 66–67, 69, 79, 86, 151, 155

Vira, Raghu, 230
Vita Monastica, 8
Volkaert, Fr., 297
"Vow of Conversation" (Merton), 35, 143

Waddell, Fr. Chrysogonus, 8, 42, 298
Wagner, Dom Eusebius, 41
Walden Two (Skinner), 75
Walsh, Fr. Daniel, xv-xvi, 8, 8n., 48, 65, 76, 101, 126, 127, 128, 186, 298
Walsh, Richard, 136
"War and the Crisis of Language" (Merton), 324, 324n.
"War and the Crisis of Meaning" (Merton), 81
Washington, DC, Merton's trip to, xv, 157, 158–61
Washington Peace Mobilization, 1967, 5
Webster, Portia, postulant, 101, 110, 201
Weisskopf, Walter, 70
Wei Tat, 221, 221n., 223
"Wild Places" (Merton), 99, 99n.
Wilfrid, Bro., 20
William, Sister, 110
Williams, Emmett, 298
Williams, Jonathan, 3, 4
Williams, Robert, 73, 135
Willett, John, 126
Willett, Thompson, 25, 75, 76
Wilson, Keith, 28, 45
Winter, 33–34, 36, 37, 44, 52, 54–55, 56, 58, 60, 61
Winzen, Dom Damasus, 83
Wolff, Helen, 35
Woods, Shore, Desert (Merton), xiv
Work, 103
Wu, John, 132, 141
Wygal, James, 6, 57, 63, 142–43

Yelchaninov, Alexander, 92, 92n., 100
Yoga, 175, 176
Yungblut, John, 31, 79
Yungblut, June, 13, 31, 79, 145, 159
Yves, Frère, 151

Zen and the Birds of Appetite (Merton), 60n., 61, 133n.
Zukofsky, Louis, 30